ORESAMA TEACHER

Wait just a second! I only made my debut one chapter ago, so why am I already on the cover?! More to the point, there aren't enough main characters! And you're the only girl!! You're trying to create a harem, aren't you, Kurosaki?! How despicable! Unfortunately, you aren't my type. Even if the floor in the Ninja Mansion tilts at an 80-degree angle, I'll never fall for you!

WOW, YOU'RE ANNOYING.

Vol. 6

Story & Art by

Izumi Tsubaki

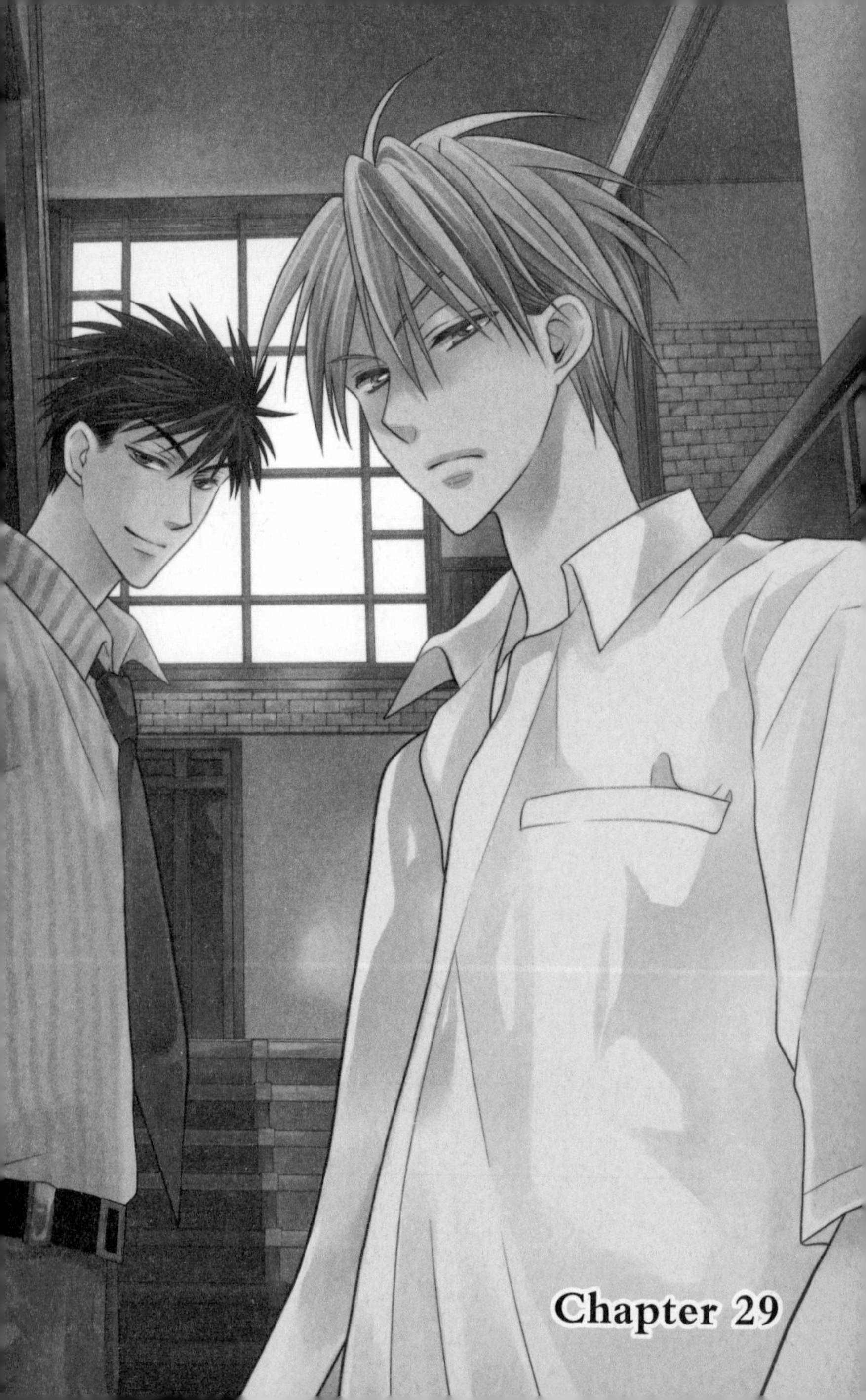
Chapter 29

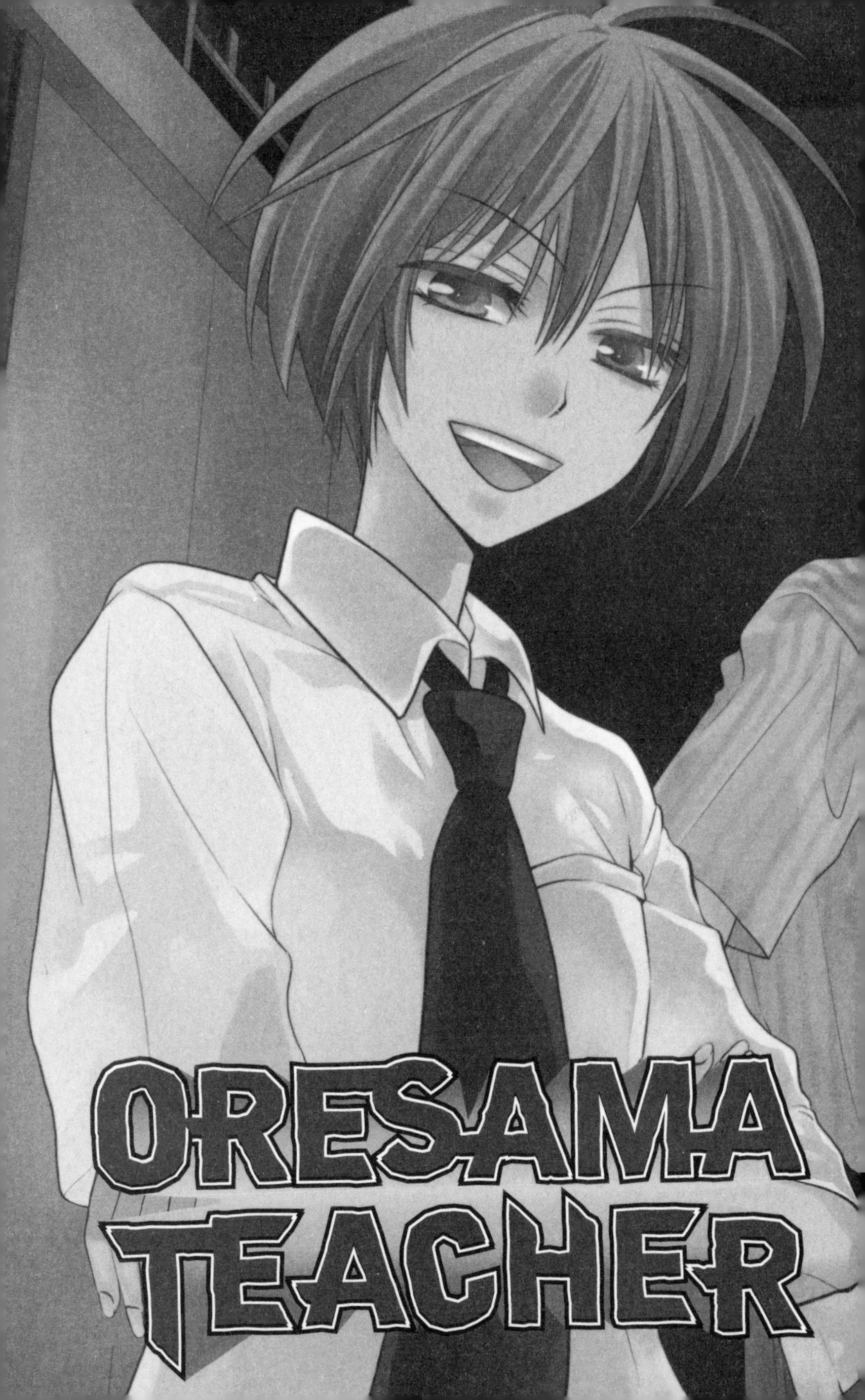
ORESAMA
TEACHER

ORESAMA TEACHER

Volume 6
CONTENTS

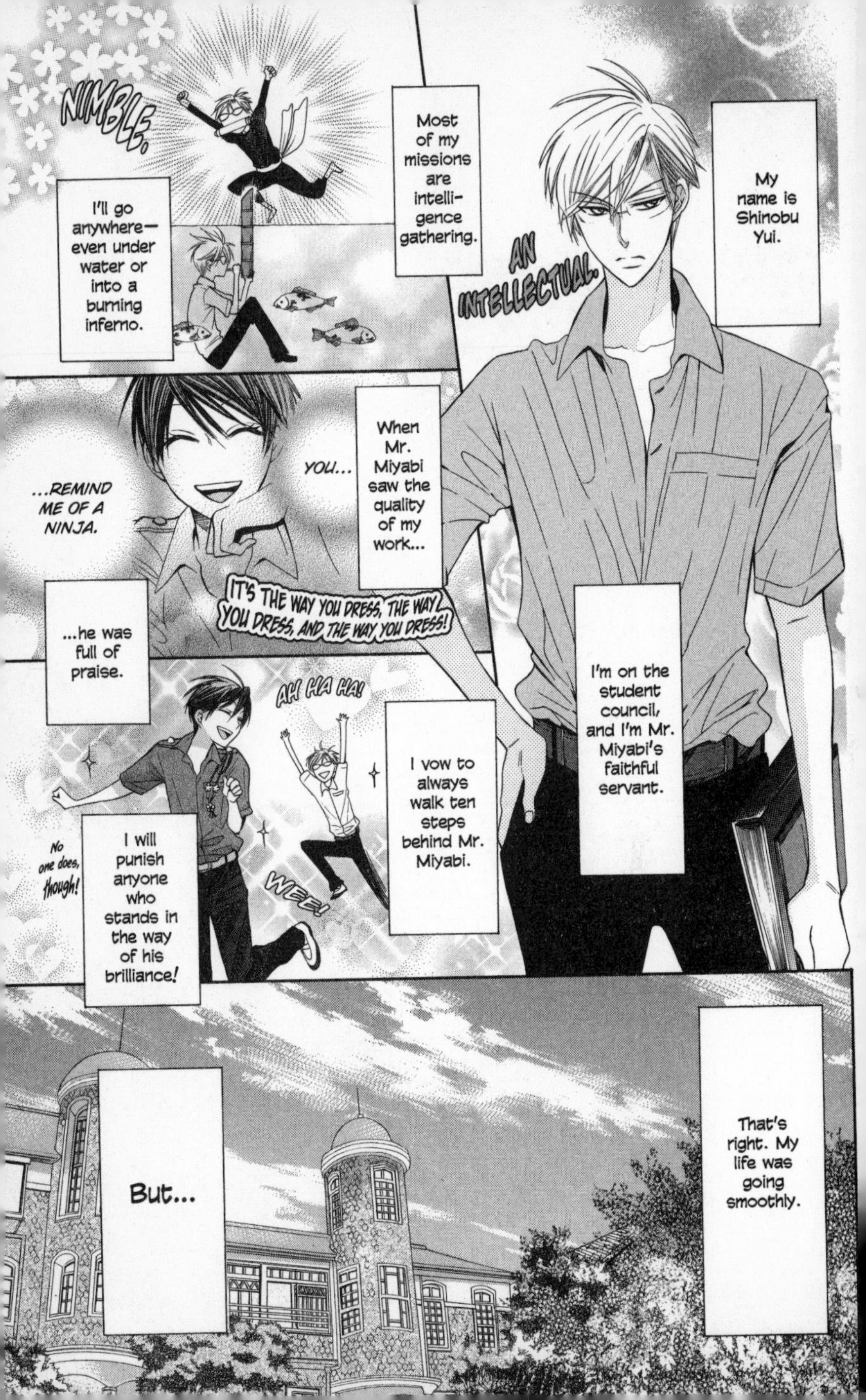
My name is Shinobu Yui.
AN INTELLECTUAL.
I'm on the student council, and I'm Mr. Miyabi's faithful servant.
Most of my missions are intelligence gathering.
NIMBLE.
I'll go anywhere—even under water or into a burning inferno.
When Mr. Miyabi saw the quality of my work...
YOU...
...REMIND ME OF A NINJA.
IT'S THE WAY YOU DRESS, THE WAY YOU DRESS, AND THE WAY YOU DRESS!
...he was full of praise.
I vow to always walk ten steps behind Mr. Miyabi.
AH HA HA!
WEE!
I will punish anyone who stands in the way of his brilliance!
No one does, though!
That's right. My life was going smoothly.
But...

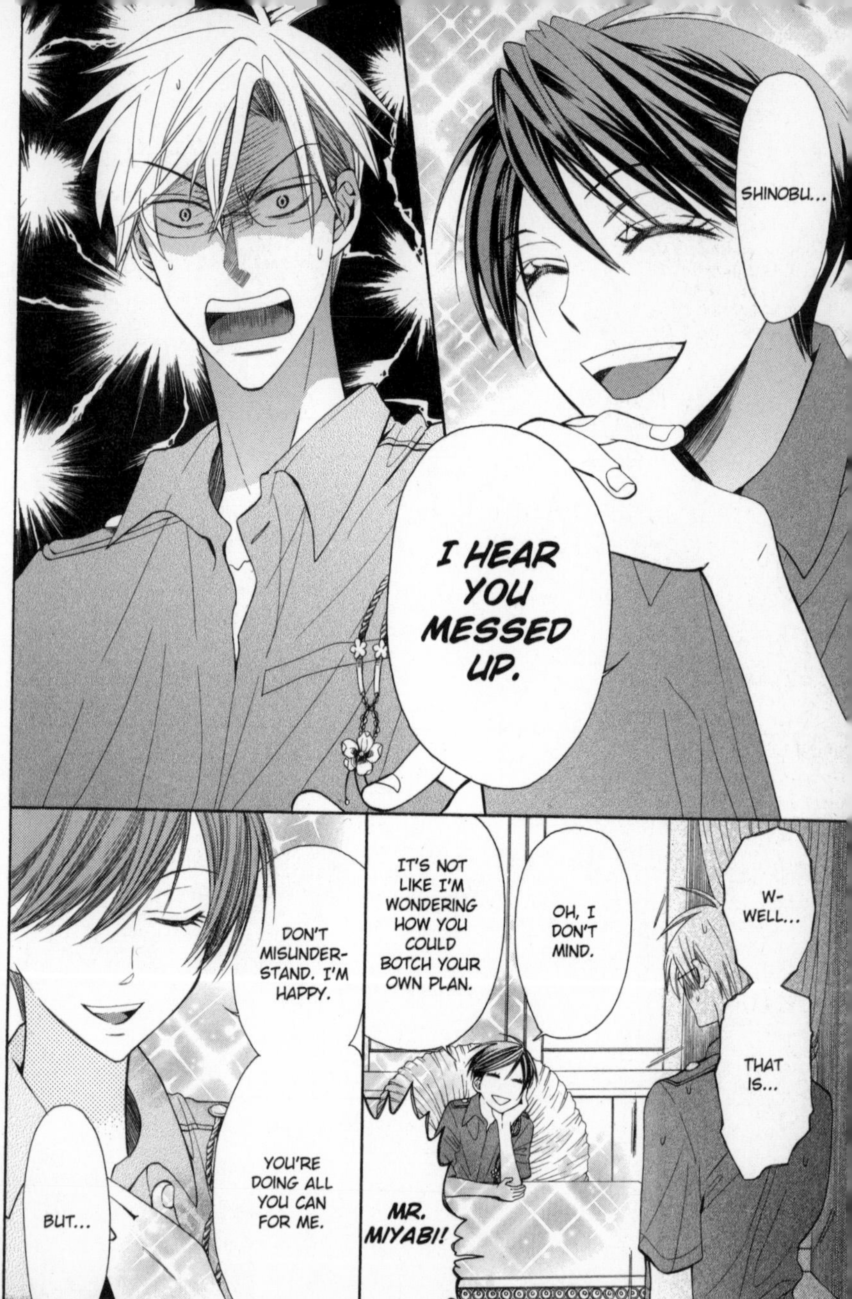
SHINOBU...
I HEAR YOU MESSED UP.
W-WELL...
THAT IS...
MR. MIYABI!
OH, I DON'T MIND.
IT'S NOT LIKE I'M WONDERING HOW YOU COULD BOTCH YOUR OWN PLAN.
DON'T MISUNDERSTAND. I'M HAPPY.
YOU'RE DOING ALL YOU CAN FOR ME.
BUT...

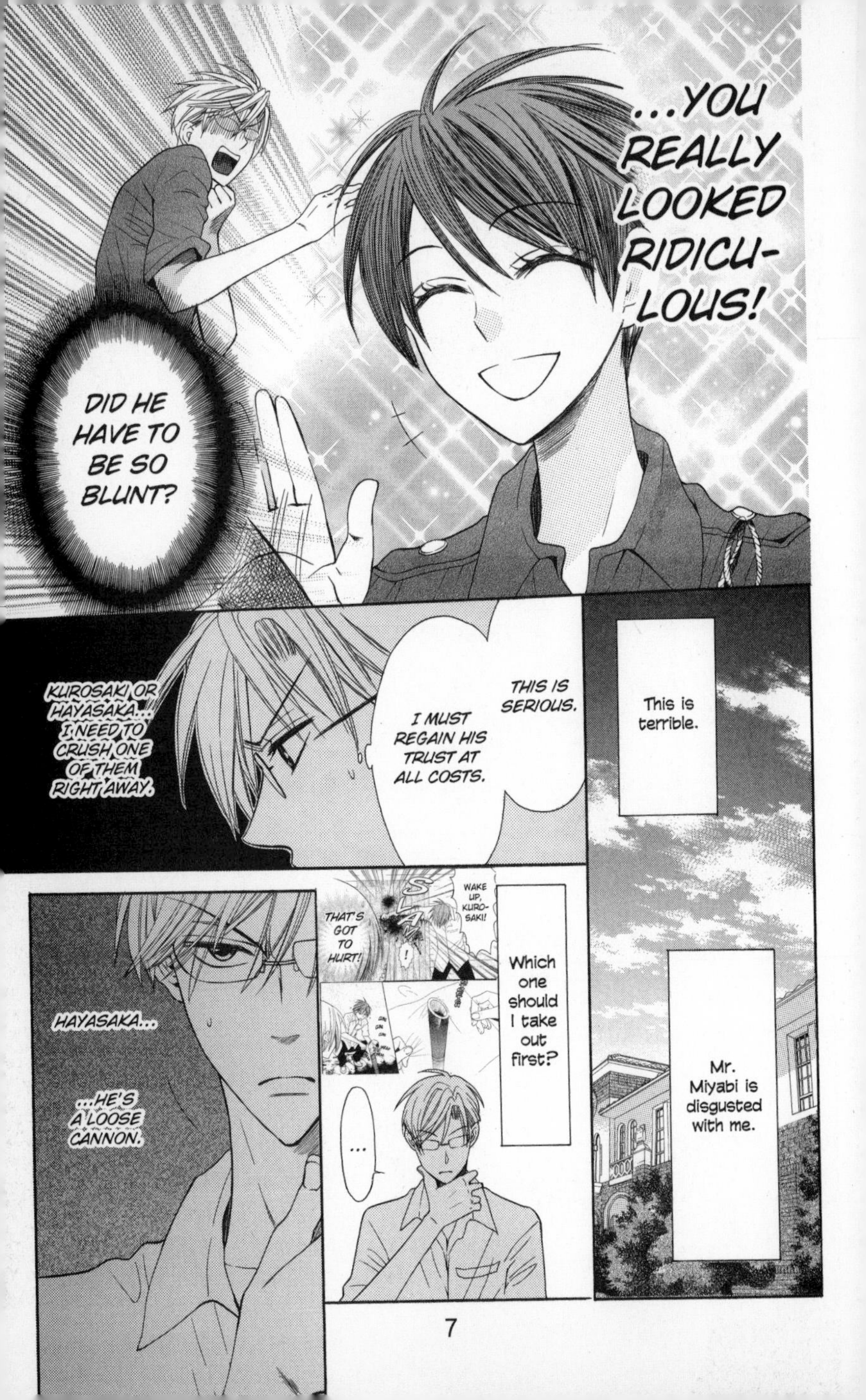
...YOU REALLY LOOKED RIDICU-LOUS!
DID HE HAVE TO BE SO BLUNT?
This is terrible.
THIS IS SERIOUS.
I MUST REGAIN HIS TRUST AT ALL COSTS.
KUROSAKI OR HAYASAKA... I NEED TO CRUSH ONE OF THEM RIGHT AWAY.
Mr. Miyabi is disgusted with me.
Which one should I take out first?
WAKE UP, KURO-SAKI!
THAT'S GOT TO HURT!
...
HAYASAKA...
...HE'S A LOOSE CANNON.

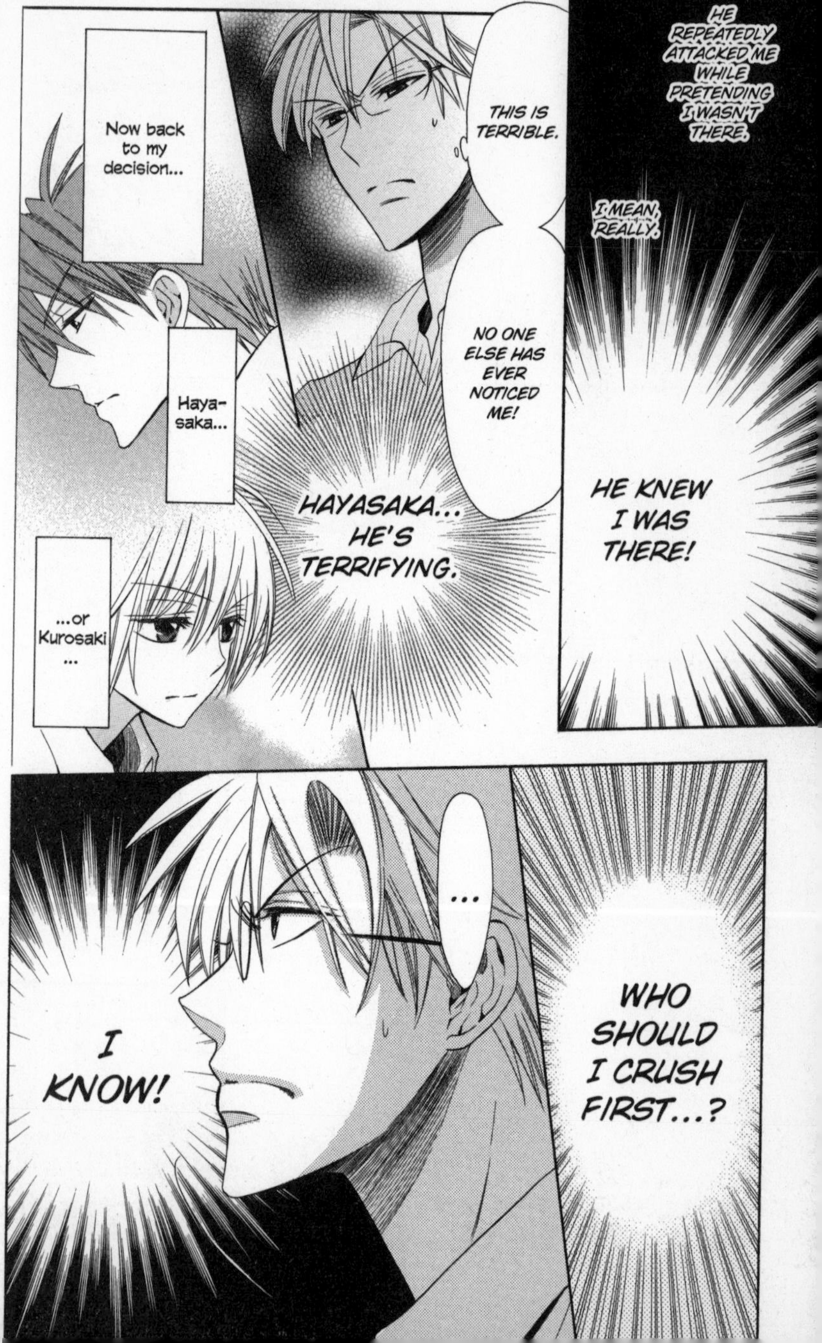
HE REPEATEDLY ATTACKED ME WHILE PRETENDING I WASN'T THERE.
I MEAN, REALLY.
HE KNEW I WAS THERE!
THIS IS TERRIBLE.
NO ONE ELSE HAS EVER NOTICED ME!
HAYASAKA... HE'S TERRIFYING.
Now back to my decision...
Haya-saka...
...or Kurosaki...
WHO SHOULD I CRUSH FIRST...?
...
I KNOW!

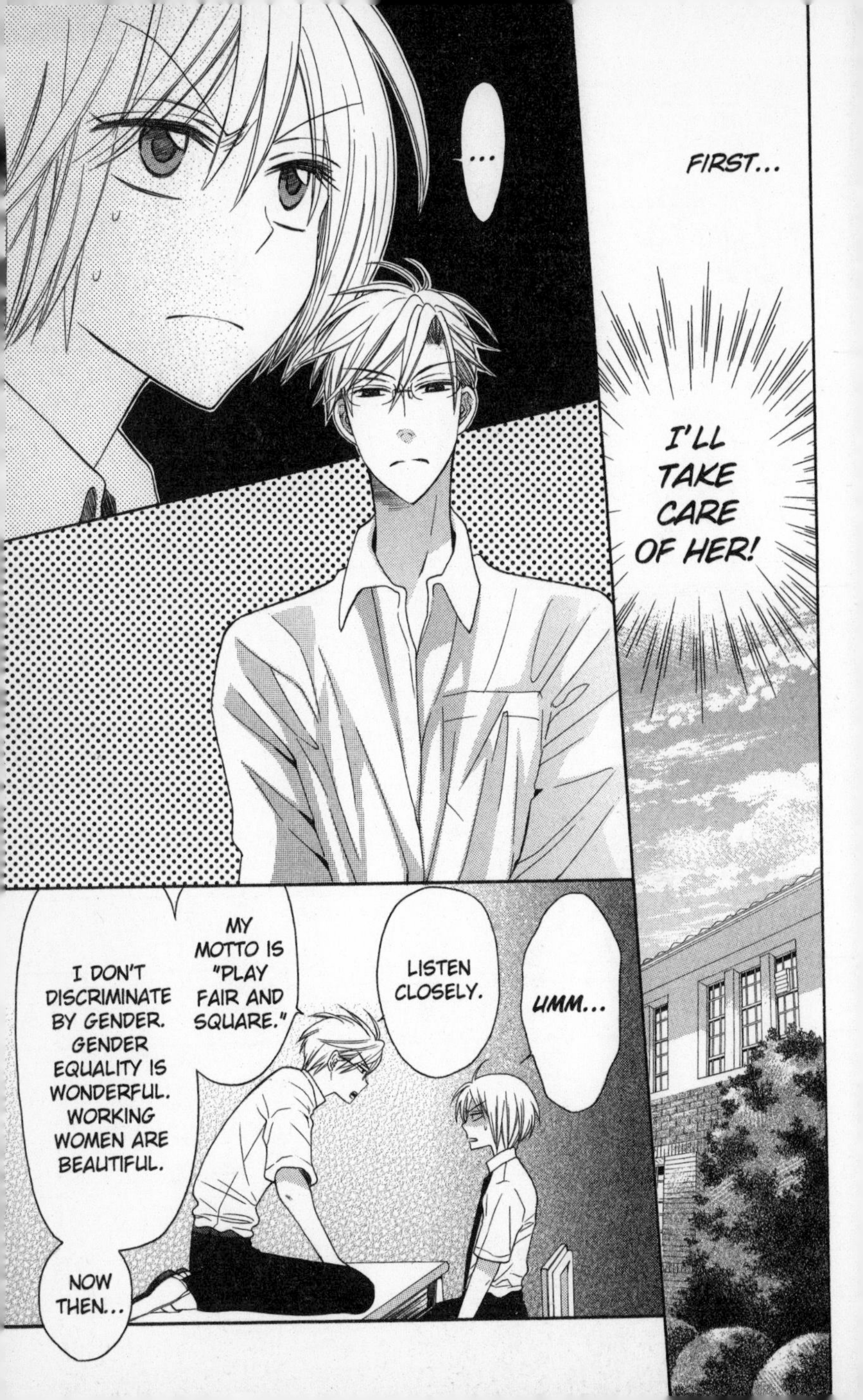
FIRST...
I'LL TAKE CARE OF HER!
...
UMM...
LISTEN CLOSELY.
MY MOTTO IS "PLAY FAIR AND SQUARE."
I DON'T DISCRIMINATE BY GENDER. GENDER EQUALITY IS WONDERFUL. WORKING WOMEN ARE BEAUTIFUL.
NOW THEN...

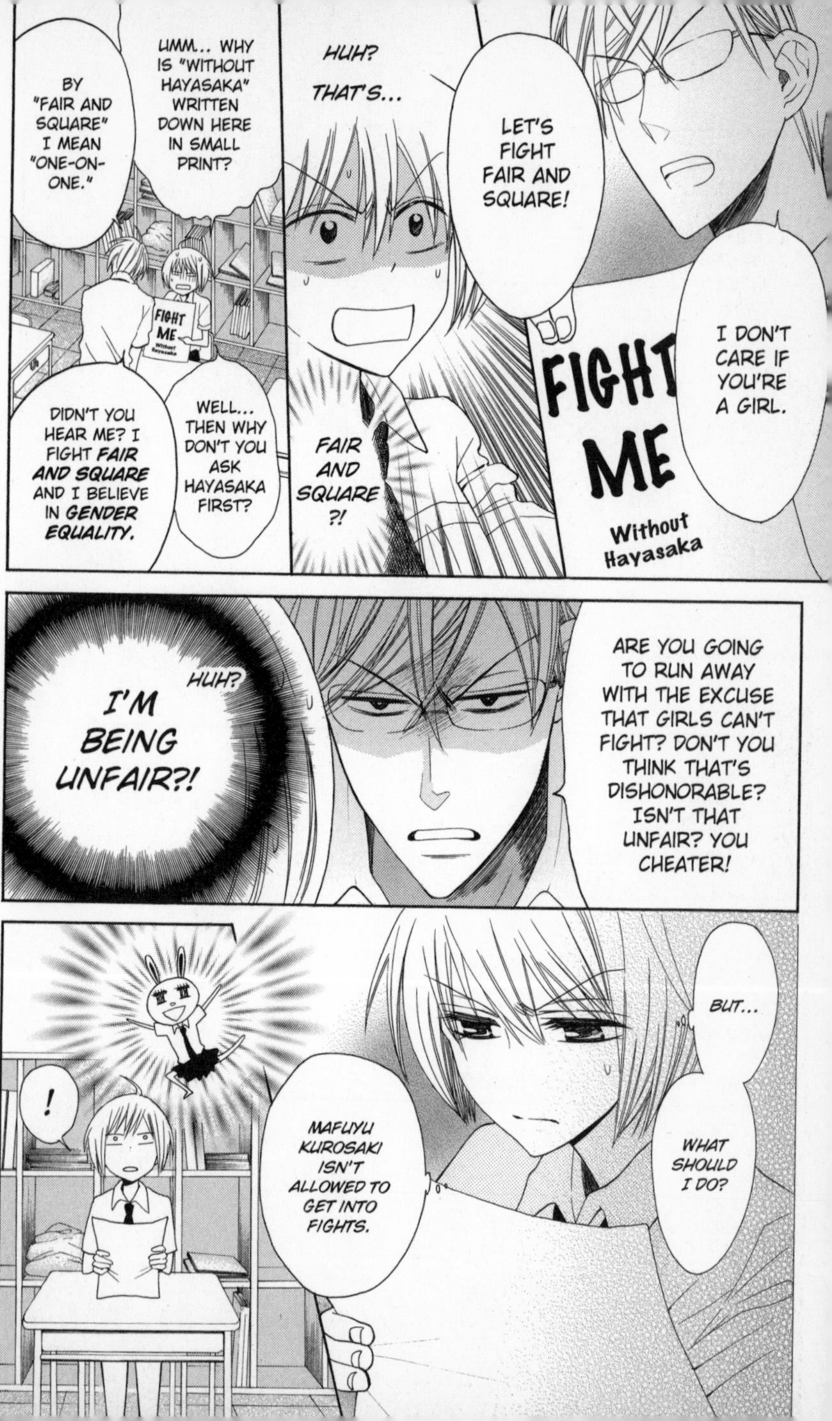
LET'S FIGHT FAIR AND SQUARE!
I DON'T CARE IF YOU'RE A GIRL.
FIGHT ME
Without Hayasaka
HUH? THAT'S...
FAIR AND SQUARE ?!
UMM... WHY IS "WITHOUT HAYASAKA" WRITTEN DOWN HERE IN SMALL PRINT?
BY "FAIR AND SQUARE" I MEAN "ONE-ON-ONE."
WELL... THEN WHY DON'T YOU ASK HAYASAKA FIRST?
DIDN'T YOU HEAR ME? I FIGHT FAIR AND SQUARE AND I BELIEVE IN GENDER EQUALITY.
ARE YOU GOING TO RUN AWAY WITH THE EXCUSE THAT GIRLS CAN'T FIGHT? DON'T YOU THINK THAT'S DISHONORABLE? ISN'T THAT UNFAIR? YOU CHEATER!
HUH?
I'M BEING UNFAIR?!
BUT...
WHAT SHOULD I DO?
MAFUYU KUROSAKI ISN'T ALLOWED TO GET INTO FIGHTS.
!

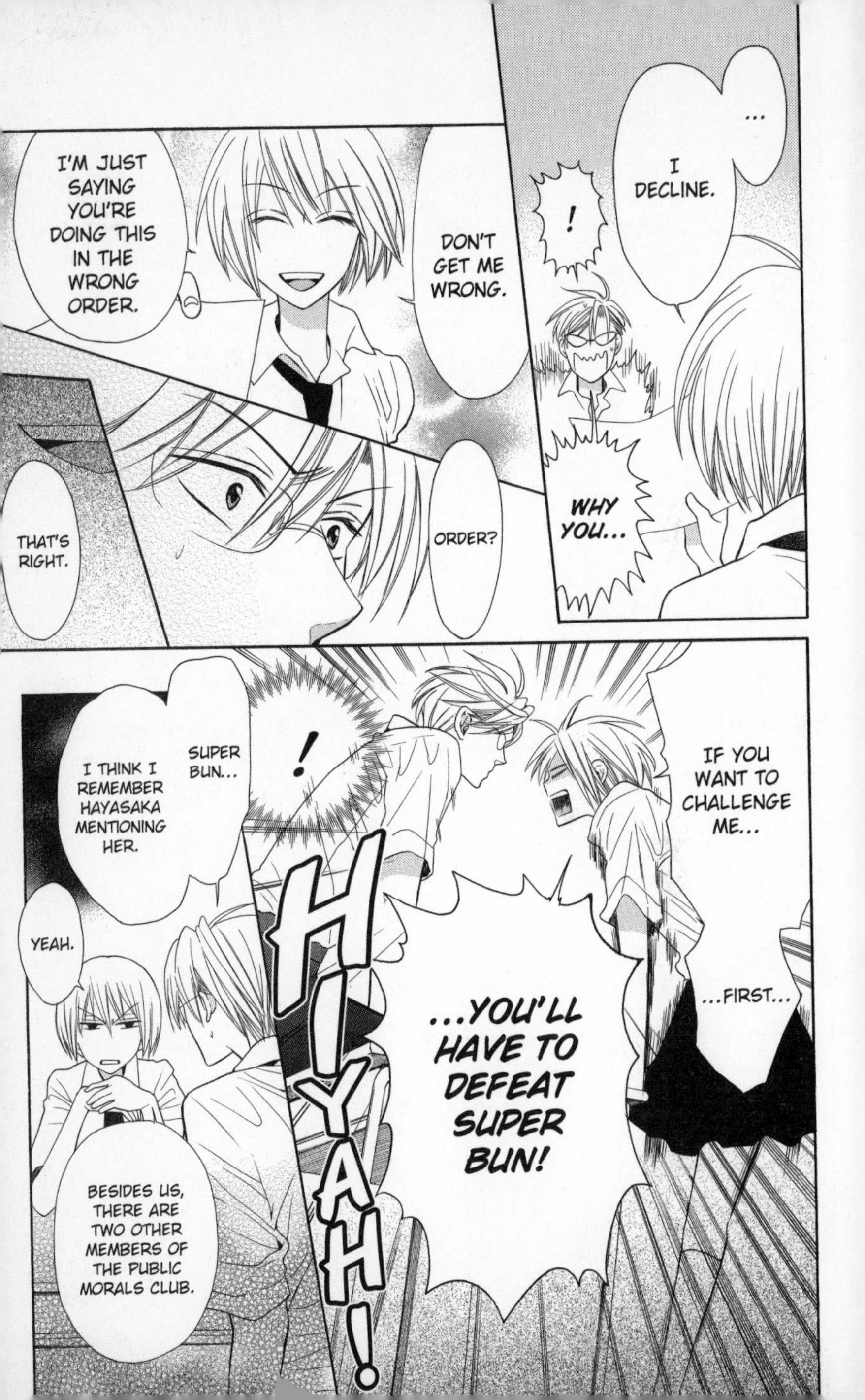
...
I DECLINE.
!
WHY YOU...
DON'T GET ME WRONG.
I'M JUST SAYING YOU'RE DOING THIS IN THE WRONG ORDER.
ORDER?
THAT'S RIGHT.
IF YOU WANT TO CHALLENGE ME...
...FIRST...
!
...YOU'LL HAVE TO DEFEAT SUPER BUN!
HI-YAH!
SUPER BUN...
I THINK I REMEMBER HAYASAKA MENTIONING HER.
YEAH.
BESIDES US, THERE ARE TWO OTHER MEMBERS OF THE PUBLIC MORALS CLUB.

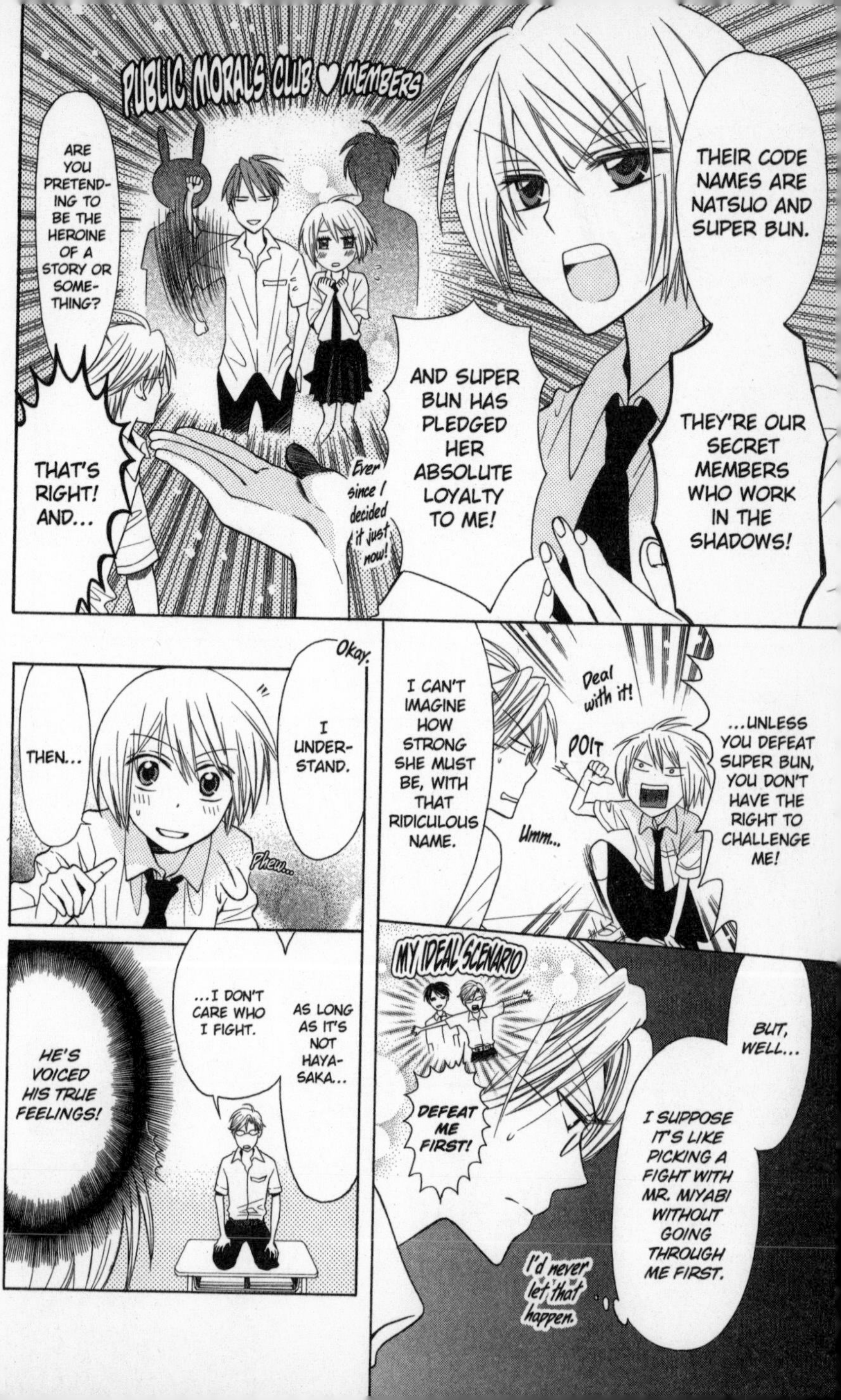
THEIR CODE NAMES ARE NATSUO AND SUPER BUN.
PUBLIC MORALS CLUB ♥ MEMBERS
THEY'RE OUR SECRET MEMBERS WHO WORK IN THE SHADOWS!
AND SUPER BUN HAS PLEDGED HER ABSOLUTE LOYALTY TO ME!
Ever since I decided it just now!
THAT'S RIGHT! AND...
ARE YOU PRETENDING TO BE THE HEROINE OF A STORY OR SOMETHING?
...UNLESS YOU DEFEAT SUPER BUN, YOU DON'T HAVE THE RIGHT TO CHALLENGE ME!
Deal with it!
POIT
I CAN'T IMAGINE HOW STRONG SHE MUST BE, WITH THAT RIDICULOUS NAME.
Umm...
Okay.
I UNDERSTAND.
THEN...
Phew...
BUT, WELL...
MY IDEAL SCENARIO
DEFEAT ME FIRST!
I SUPPOSE IT'S LIKE PICKING A FIGHT WITH MR. MIYABI WITHOUT GOING THROUGH ME FIRST.
I'd never let that happen.
AS LONG AS IT'S NOT HAYASAKA...
...I DON'T CARE WHO I FIGHT.
HE'S VOICED HIS TRUE FEELINGS!

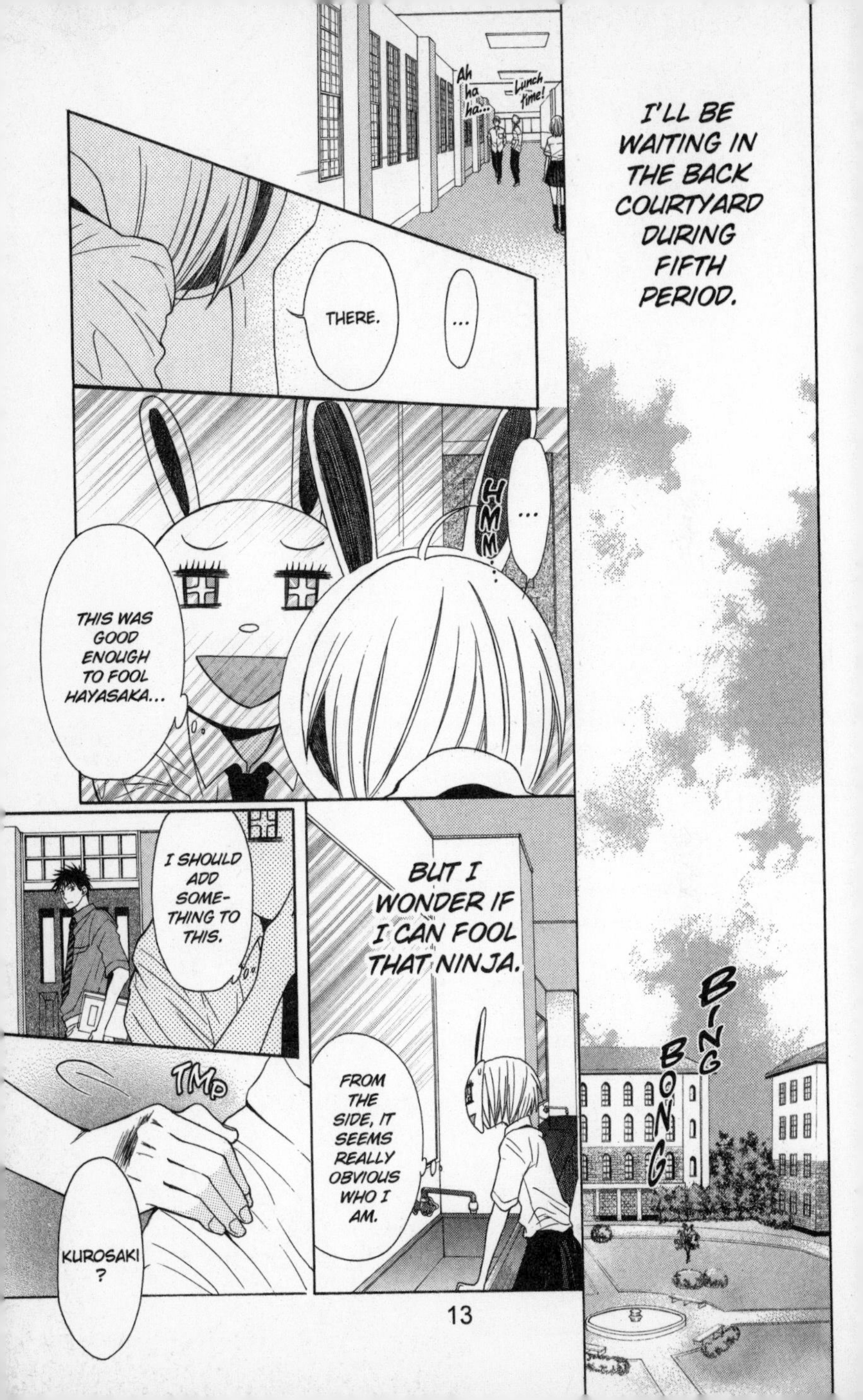
I'LL BE WAITING IN THE BACK COURTYARD DURING FIFTH PERIOD.
BING
BONG
Lunch time!
Ah ha ha...
...
THERE.
...
HMM...
THIS WAS GOOD ENOUGH TO FOOL HAYASAKA...
BUT I WONDER IF I CAN FOOL THAT NINJA.
FROM THE SIDE, IT SEEMS REALLY OBVIOUS WHO I AM.
I SHOULD ADD SOME-THING TO THIS.
TMP
KUROSAKI?

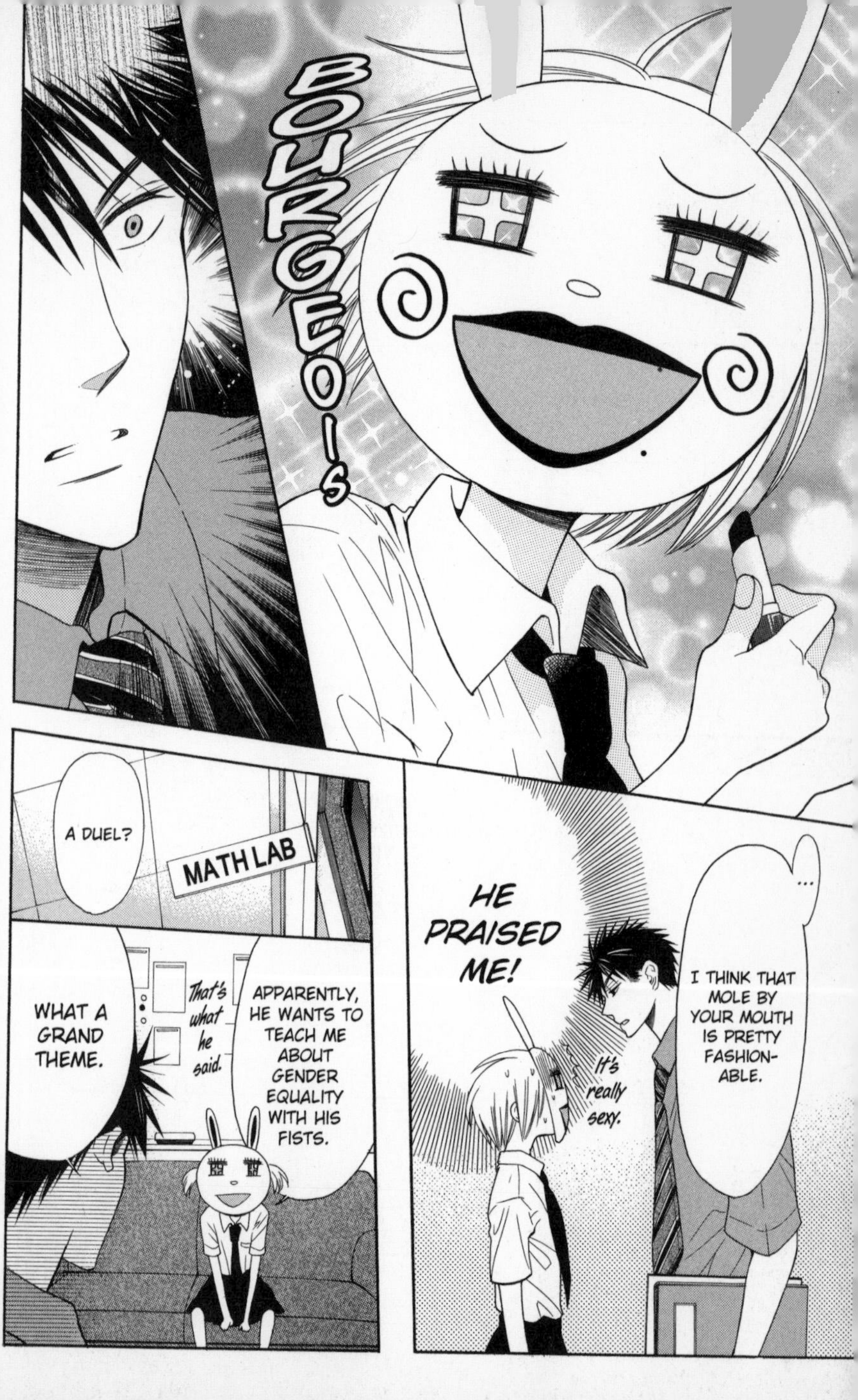
BOURGEOIS
...
I THINK THAT MOLE BY YOUR MOUTH IS PRETTY FASHION-ABLE.
It's really sexy.
HE PRAISED ME!
MATH LAB
A DUEL?
APPARENTLY, HE WANTS TO TEACH ME ABOUT GENDER EQUALITY WITH HIS FISTS.
That's what he said.
WHAT A GRAND THEME.

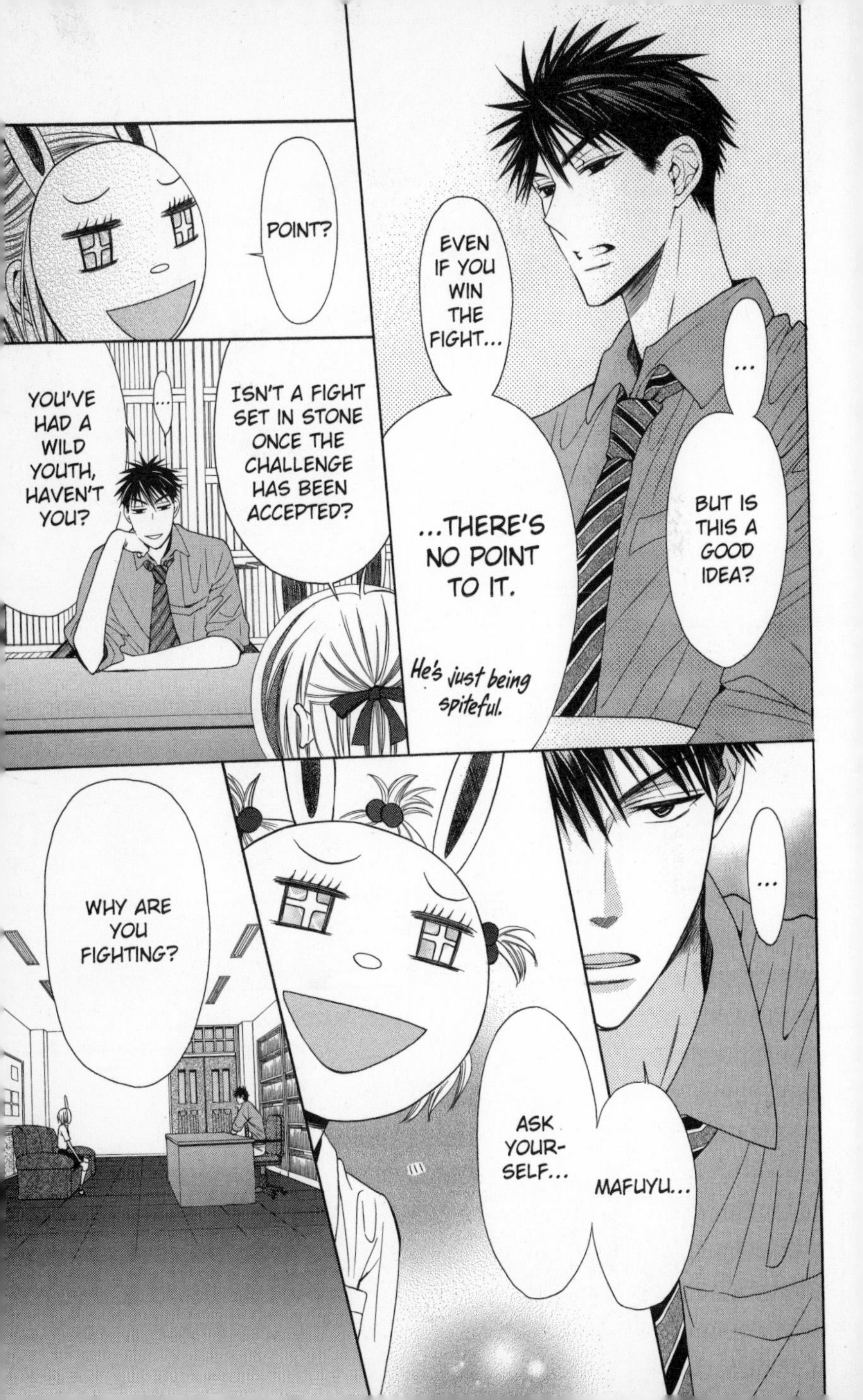
...
BUT IS THIS A GOOD IDEA?
EVEN IF YOU WIN THE FIGHT...
...THERE'S NO POINT TO IT.
He's just being spiteful.
POINT?
ISN'T A FIGHT SET IN STONE ONCE THE CHALLENGE HAS BEEN ACCEPTED?
...
YOU'VE HAD A WILD YOUTH, HAVEN'T YOU?
...
ASK YOUR-SELF...
MAFUYU...
WHY ARE YOU FIGHTING?

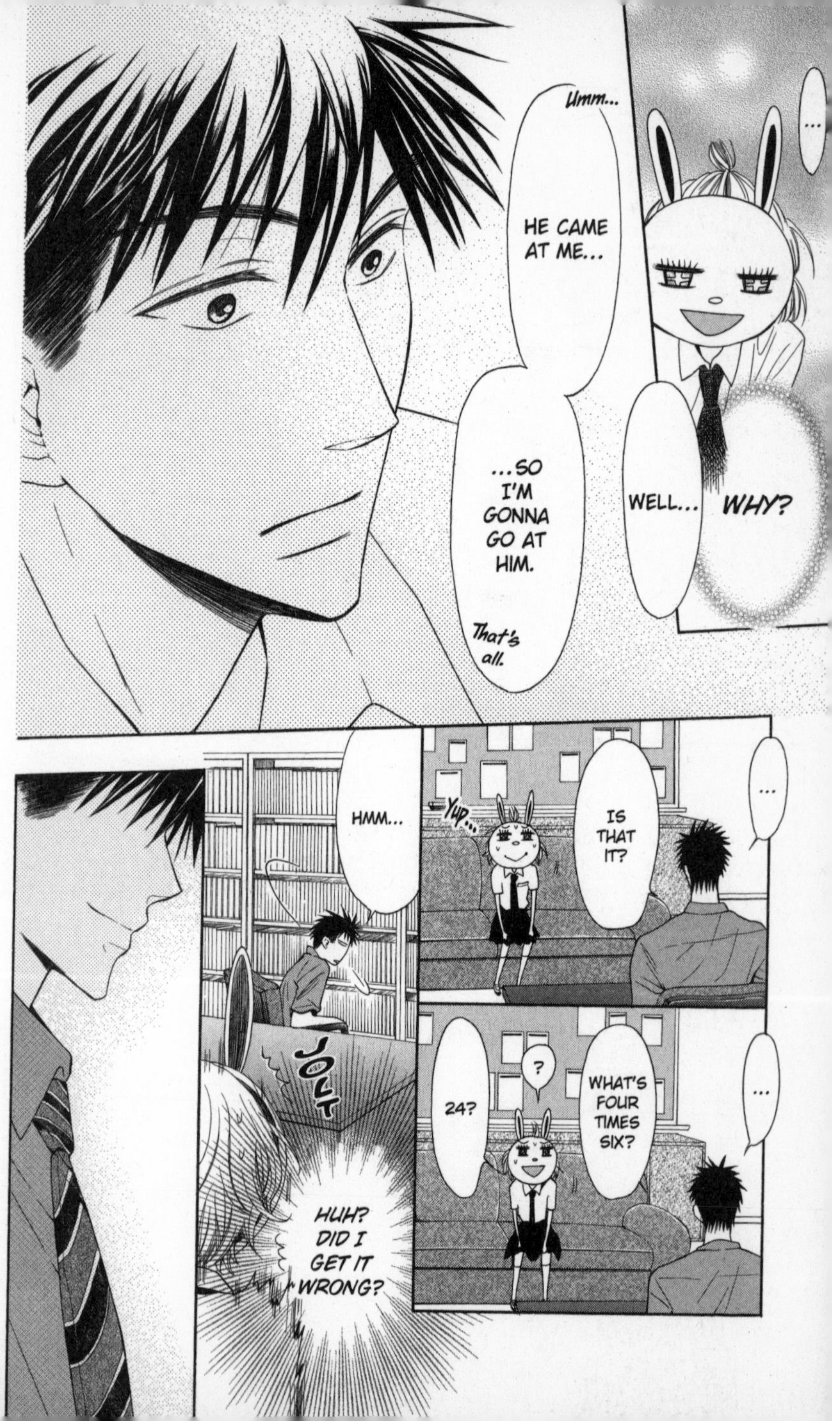
...
WHY?
WELL...
Umm...
HE CAME AT ME...
...SO I'M GONNA GO AT HIM.
That's all.
...
IS THAT IT?
Yup...
...
WHAT'S FOUR TIMES SIX?
?
24?
HMM...
JOLT
HUH? DID I GET IT WRONG?

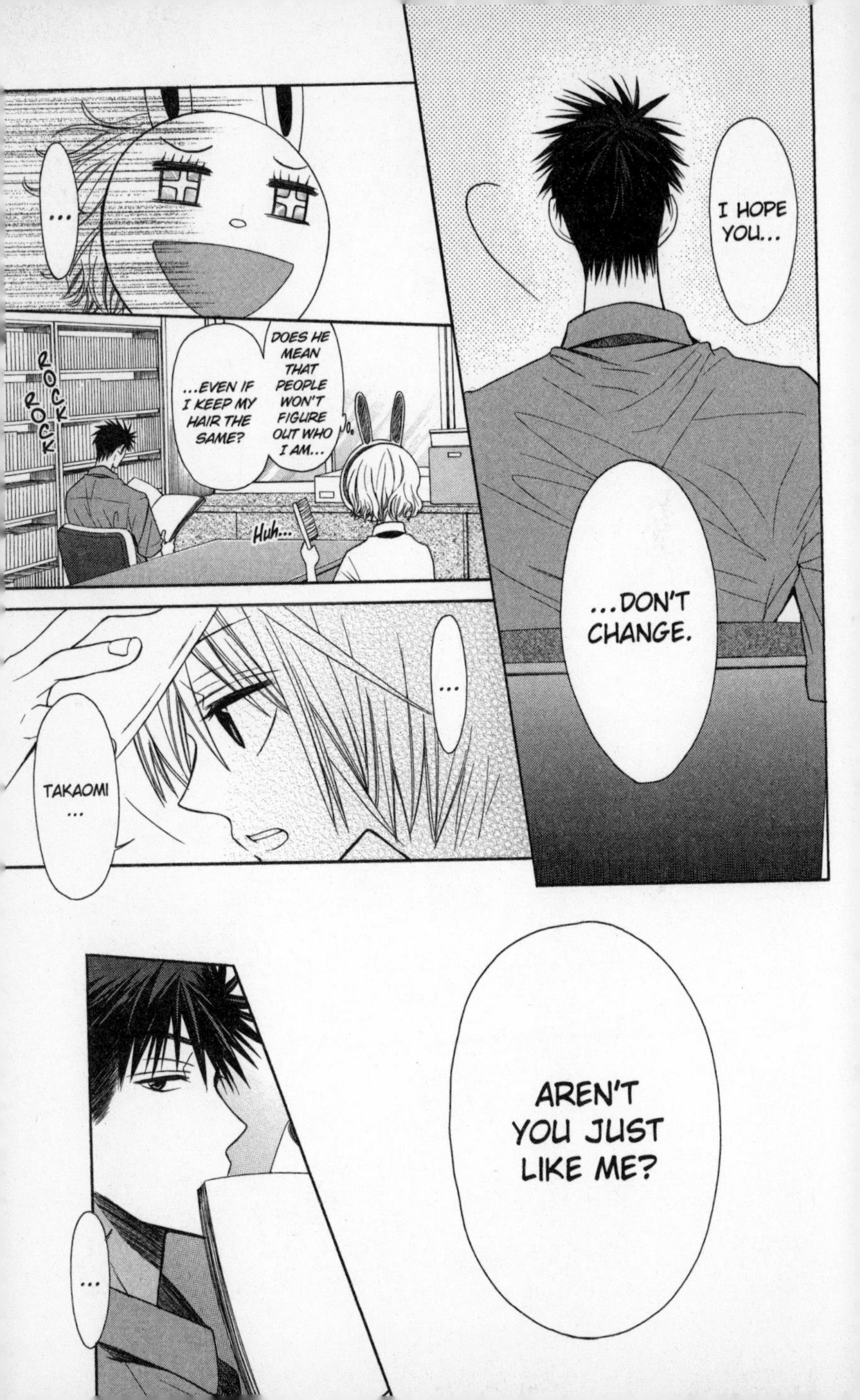
I HOPE YOU...
...DON'T CHANGE.
...
DOES HE MEAN THAT PEOPLE WON'T FIGURE OUT WHO I AM...
...EVEN IF I KEEP MY HAIR THE SAME?
ROCK ROCK
Huh...
...
TAKAOMI ...
AREN'T YOU JUST LIKE ME?
...

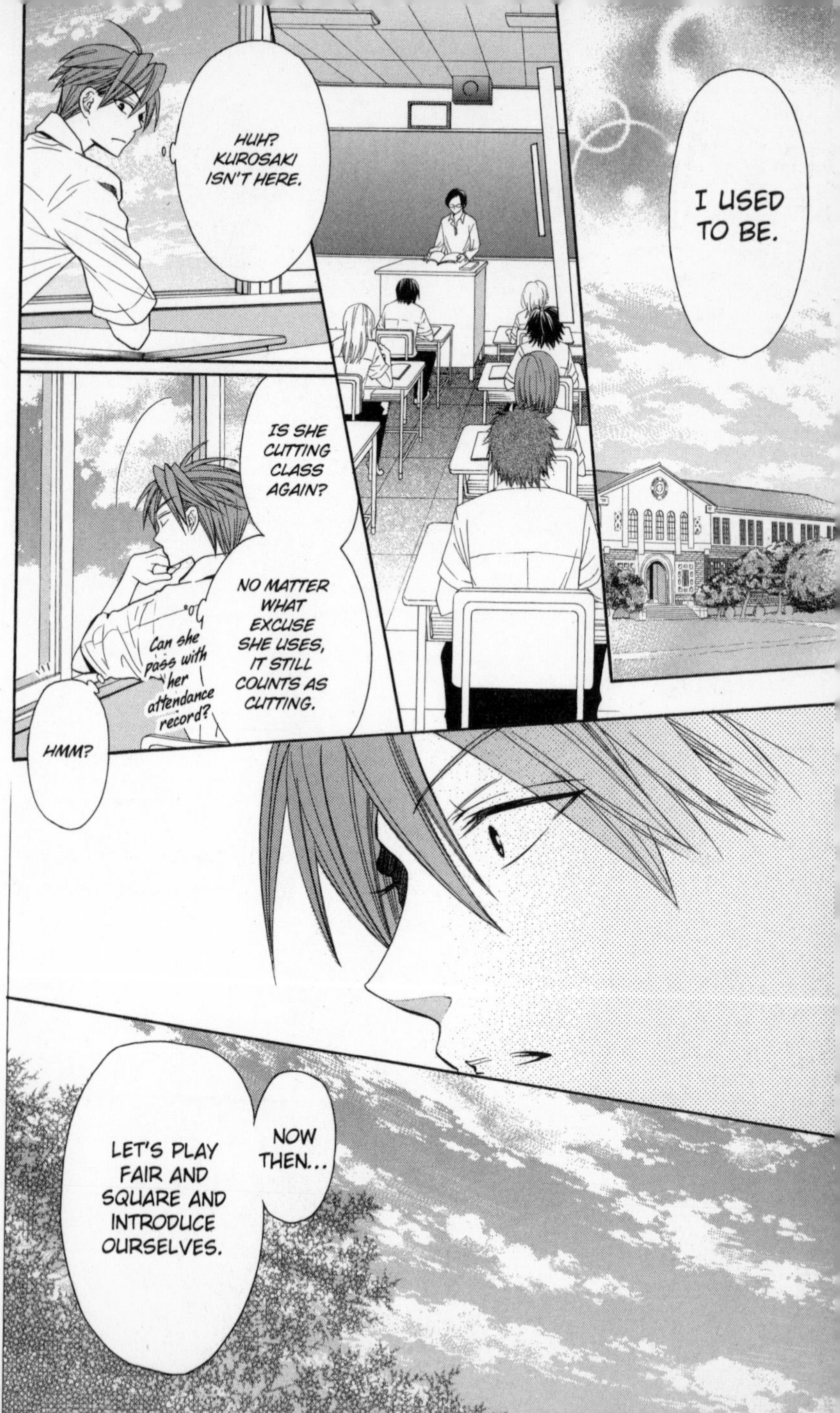
I USED TO BE.
HUH? KUROSAKI ISN'T HERE.
IS SHE CUTTING CLASS AGAIN?
NO MATTER WHAT EXCUSE SHE USES, IT STILL COUNTS AS CUTTING.
Can she pass with her attendance record?
HMM?
NOW THEN...
LET'S PLAY FAIR AND SQUARE AND INTRODUCE OURSELVES.

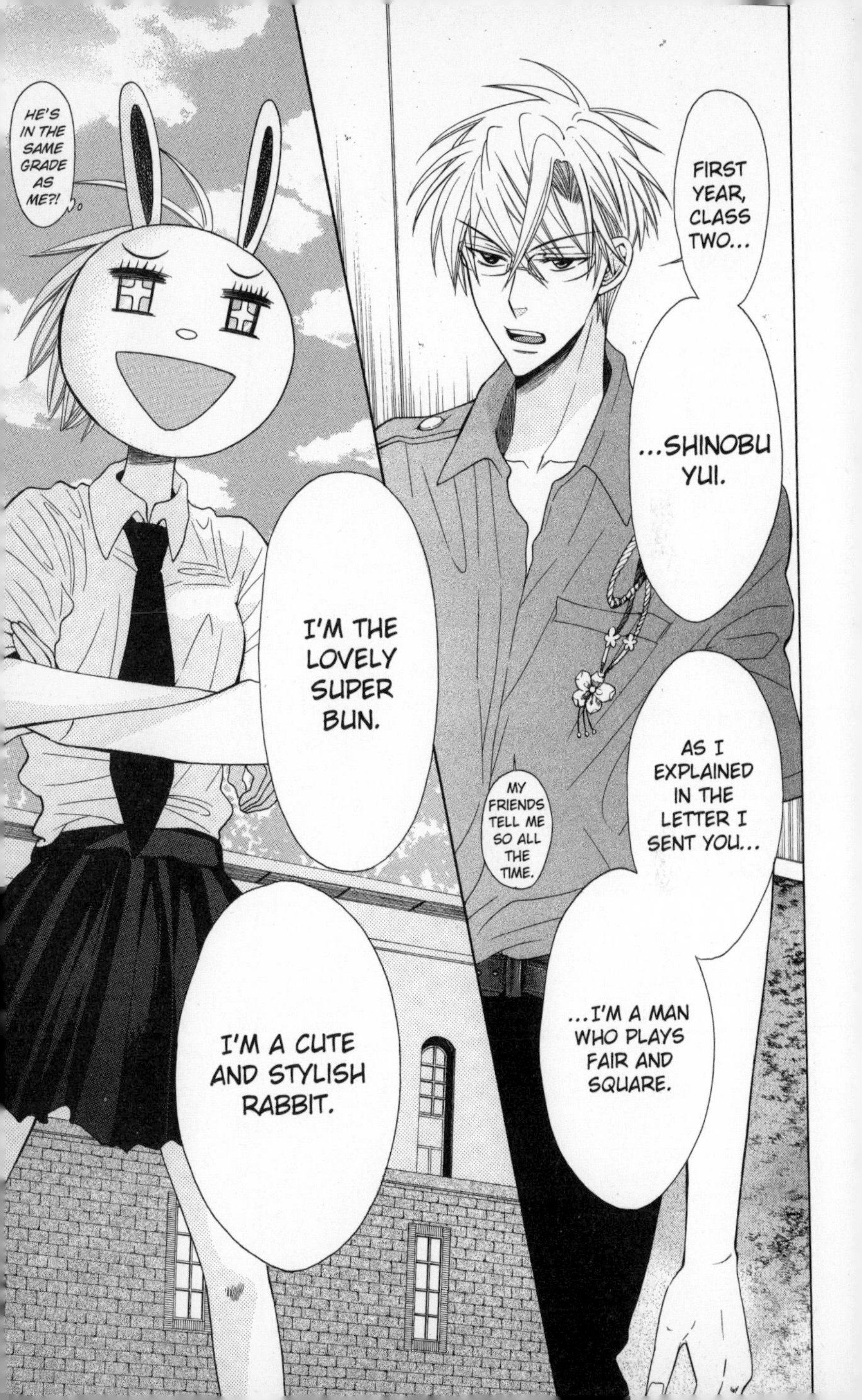
FIRST YEAR, CLASS TWO...
...SHINOBU YUI.
AS I EXPLAINED IN THE LETTER I SENT YOU...
...I'M A MAN WHO PLAYS FAIR AND SQUARE.
HE'S IN THE SAME GRADE AS ME?!
I'M THE LOVELY SUPER BUN.
MY FRIENDS TELL ME SO ALL THE TIME.
I'M A CUTE AND STYLISH RABBIT.

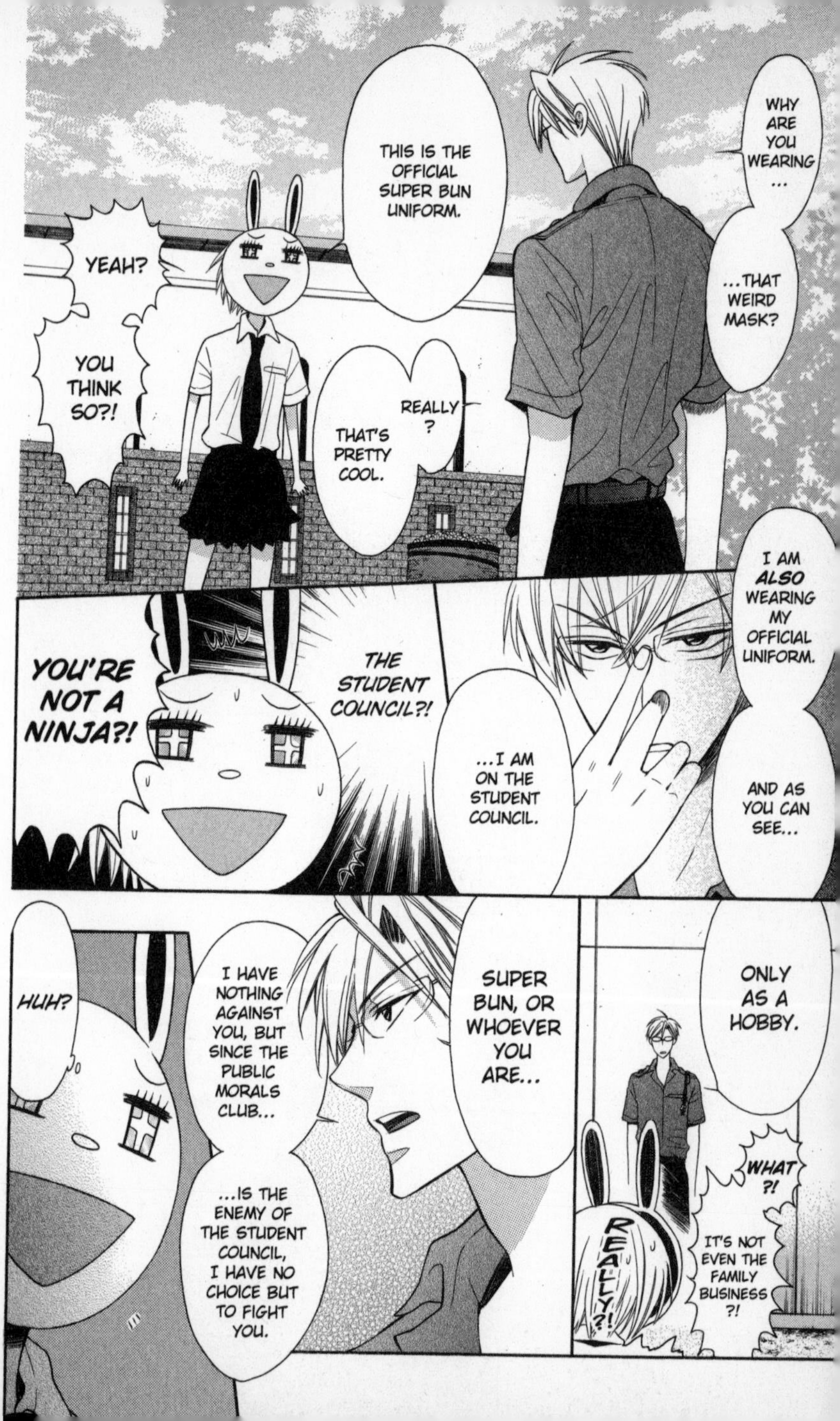
WHY ARE YOU WEARING...
...THAT WEIRD MASK?
THIS IS THE OFFICIAL SUPER BUN UNIFORM.
REALLY?
THAT'S PRETTY COOL.
YEAH? YOU THINK SO?!
I AM ALSO WEARING MY OFFICIAL UNIFORM.
AND AS YOU CAN SEE...
...I AM ON THE STUDENT COUNCIL.
THE STUDENT COUNCIL?!
YOU'RE NOT A NINJA?!
ONLY AS A HOBBY.
WHAT?!
IT'S NOT EVEN THE FAMILY BUSINESS?!
REALLY?!
SUPER BUN, OR WHOEVER YOU ARE...
I HAVE NOTHING AGAINST YOU, BUT SINCE THE PUBLIC MORALS CLUB...
...IS THE ENEMY OF THE STUDENT COUNCIL, I HAVE NO CHOICE BUT TO FIGHT YOU.
HUH?

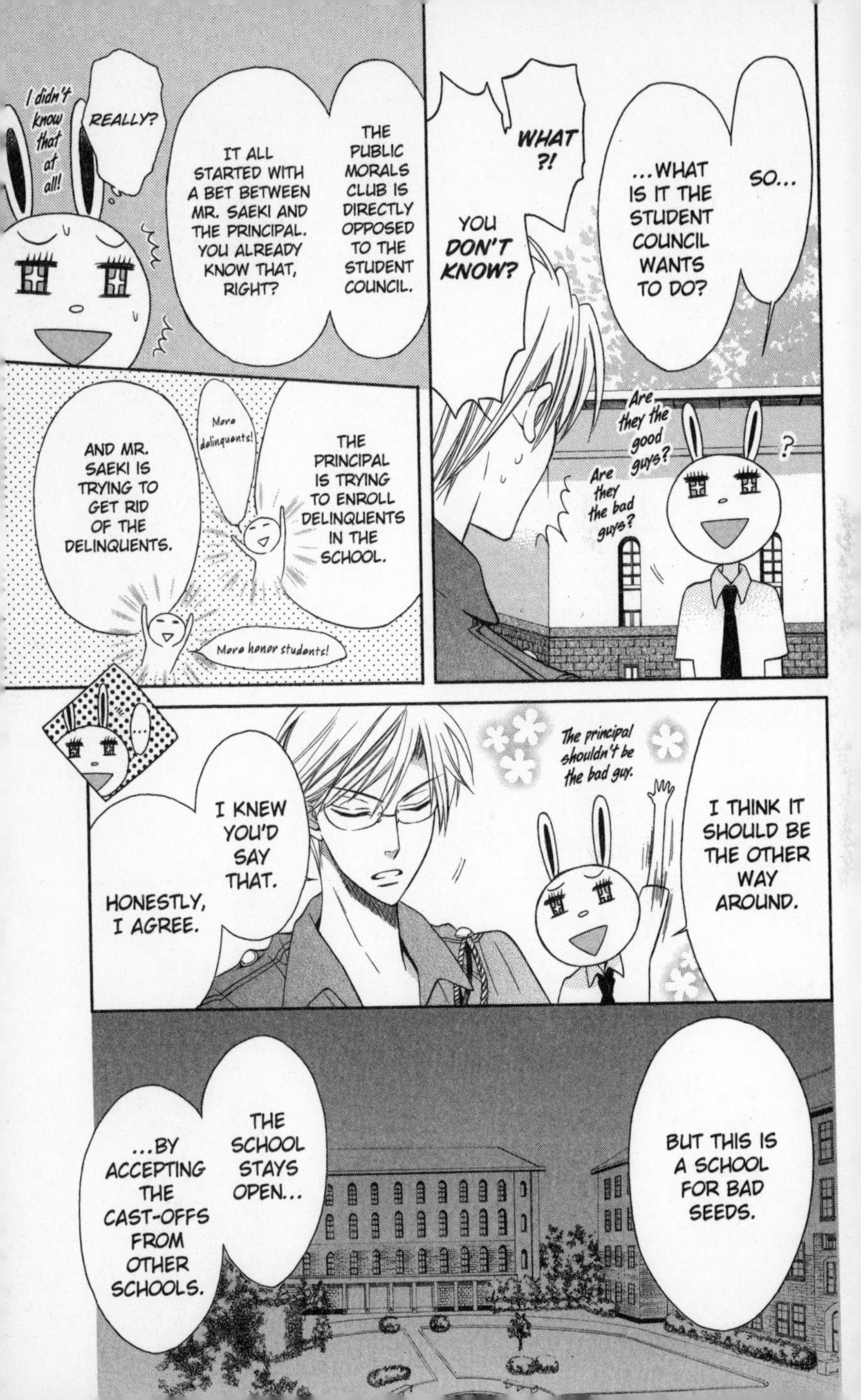
SO...
...WHAT IS IT THE STUDENT COUNCIL WANTS TO DO?
WHAT ?!
YOU DON'T KNOW?
Are they the good guys?
Are they the bad guys?
?
THE PUBLIC MORALS CLUB IS DIRECTLY OPPOSED TO THE STUDENT COUNCIL.
IT ALL STARTED WITH A BET BETWEEN MR. SAEKI AND THE PRINCIPAL. YOU ALREADY KNOW THAT, RIGHT?
REALLY?
I didn't know that at all!
THE PRINCIPAL IS TRYING TO ENROLL DELINQUENTS IN THE SCHOOL.
More delinquents!
AND MR. SAEKI IS TRYING TO GET RID OF THE DELINQUENTS.
More honor students!
I THINK IT SHOULD BE THE OTHER WAY AROUND.
The principal shouldn't be the bad guy.
I KNEW YOU'D SAY THAT.
HONESTLY, I AGREE.
...
BUT THIS IS A SCHOOL FOR BAD SEEDS.
THE SCHOOL STAYS OPEN...
...BY ACCEPTING THE CAST-OFFS FROM OTHER SCHOOLS.

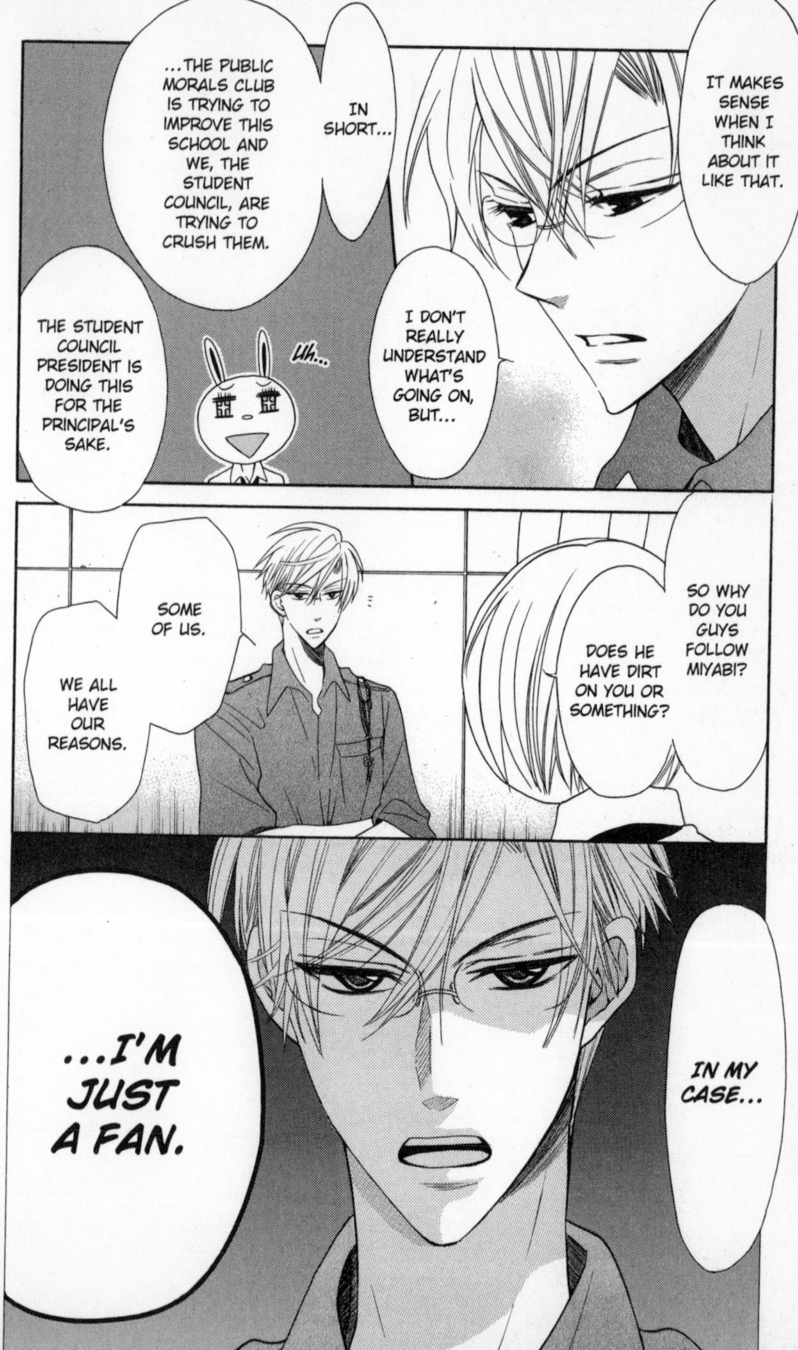
IT MAKES SENSE WHEN I THINK ABOUT IT LIKE THAT.
IN SHORT...
...THE PUBLIC MORALS CLUB IS TRYING TO IMPROVE THIS SCHOOL AND WE, THE STUDENT COUNCIL, ARE TRYING TO CRUSH THEM.
I DON'T REALLY UNDERSTAND WHAT'S GOING ON, BUT...
Uh...
THE STUDENT COUNCIL PRESIDENT IS DOING THIS FOR THE PRINCIPAL'S SAKE.
SO WHY DO YOU GUYS FOLLOW MIYABI?
DOES HE HAVE DIRT ON YOU OR SOMETHING?
SOME OF US.
WE ALL HAVE OUR REASONS.
IN MY CASE...
...I'M JUST A FAN.

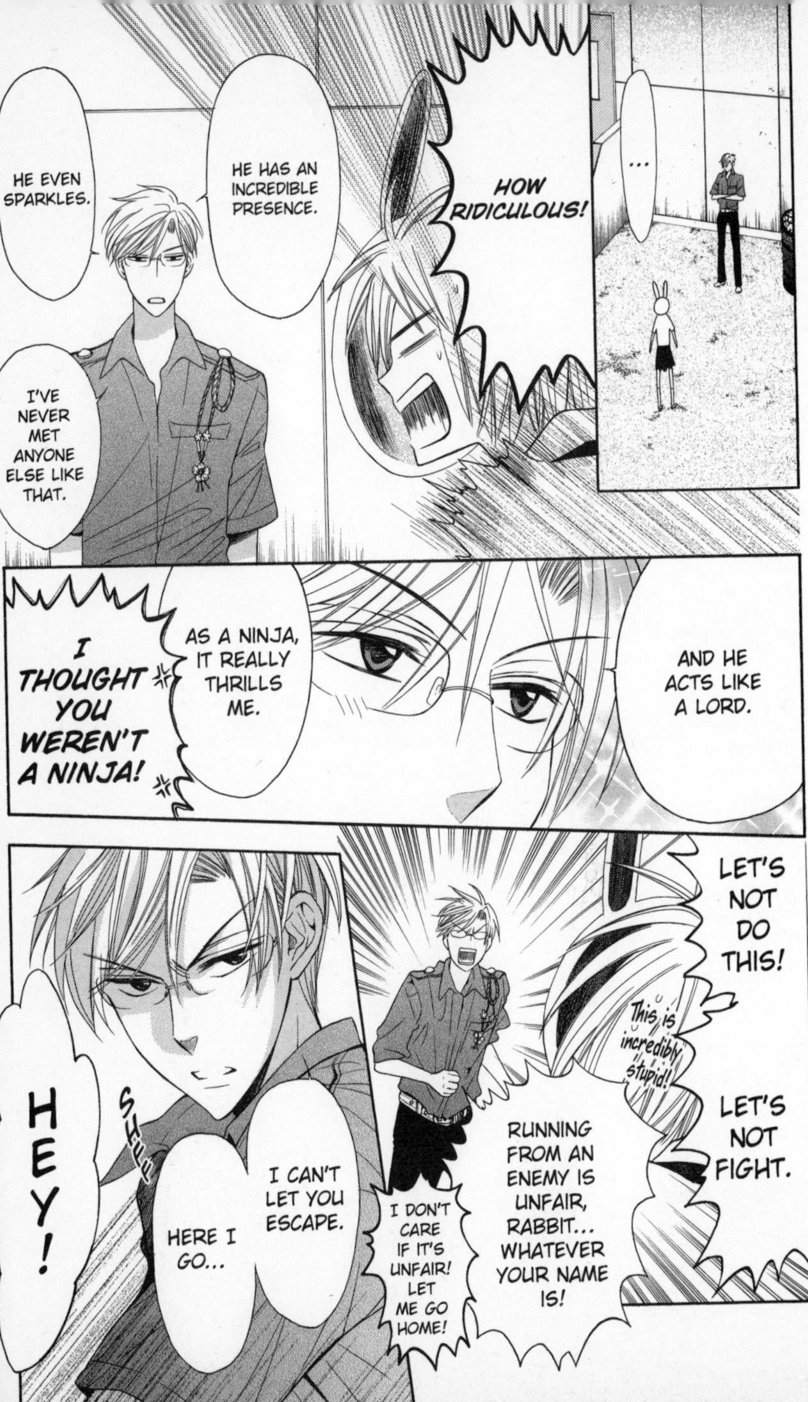
...
HOW RIDICULOUS!
HE HAS AN INCREDIBLE PRESENCE.
HE EVEN SPARKLES.
I'VE NEVER MET ANYONE ELSE LIKE THAT.
AND HE ACTS LIKE A LORD.
AS A NINJA, IT REALLY THRILLS ME.
I THOUGHT YOU WEREN'T A NINJA!
LET'S NOT DO THIS!
This is incredibly stupid!
LET'S NOT FIGHT.
RUNNING FROM AN ENEMY IS UNFAIR, RABBIT... WHATEVER YOUR NAME IS!
I DON'T CARE IF IT'S UNFAIR! LET ME GO HOME!
I CAN'T LET YOU ESCAPE.
HERE I GO...
SHF
HEY!

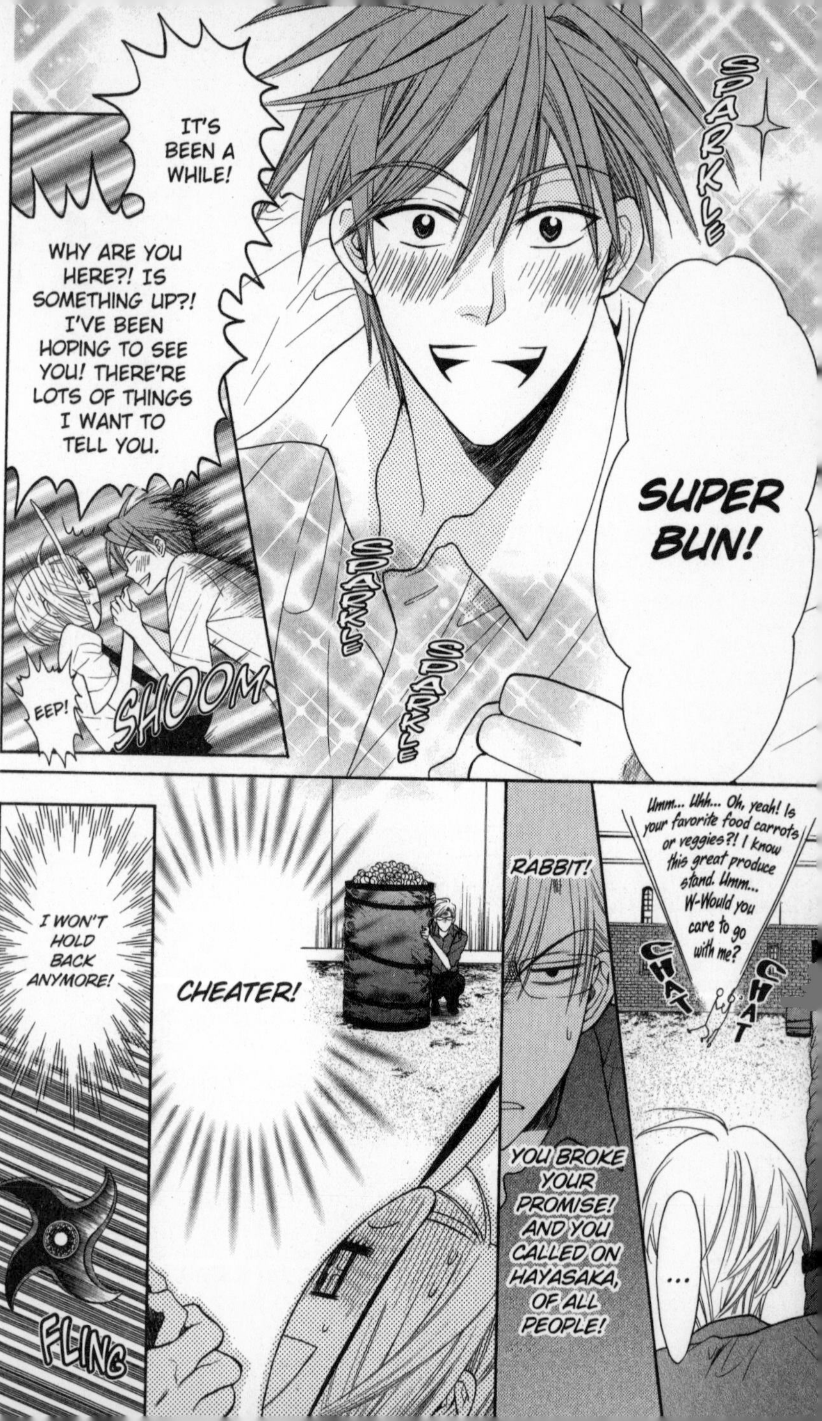
SPARKLE
SUPER BUN!
SPARKLE
SPARKLE
IT'S BEEN A WHILE!
WHY ARE YOU HERE?! IS SOMETHING UP?! I'VE BEEN HOPING TO SEE YOU! THERE'RE LOTS OF THINGS I WANT TO TELL YOU.
SHOOM
EEP!
Umm... Uhh... Oh, yeah! Is your favorite food carrots or veggies?! I know this great produce stand. Umm... W-Would you care to go with me?
CHAT
CHAT
RABBIT!
YOU BROKE YOUR PROMISE! AND YOU CALLED ON HAYASAKA, OF ALL PEOPLE!
...
CHEATER!
I WON'T HOLD BACK ANYMORE!
FLING

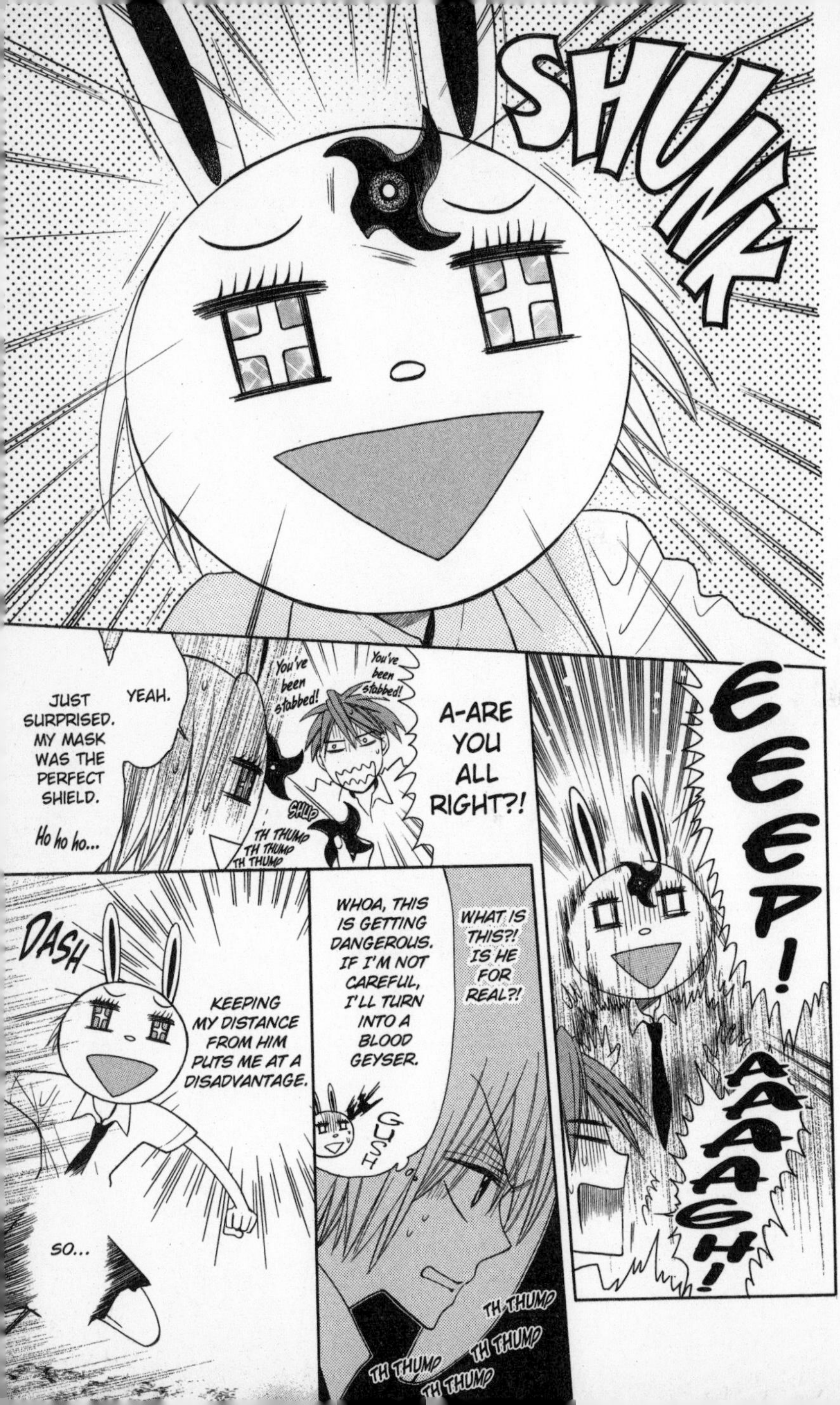

SHUNK
EEEP! AAAAAGH!
A-ARE YOU ALL RIGHT?!
You've been stabbed!
You've been stabbed!
SHUP
TH THUMP TH THUMP TH THUMP
YEAH.
JUST SURPRISED. MY MASK WAS THE PERFECT SHIELD.
Ho ho ho...
WHAT IS THIS?! IS HE FOR REAL?!
WHOA, THIS IS GETTING DANGEROUS. IF I'M NOT CAREFUL, I'LL TURN INTO A BLOOD GEYSER.
GUSH
TH THUMP TH THUMP TH THUMP TH THUMP
DASH
KEEPING MY DISTANCE FROM HIM PUTS ME AT A DISADVANTAGE.
SO...

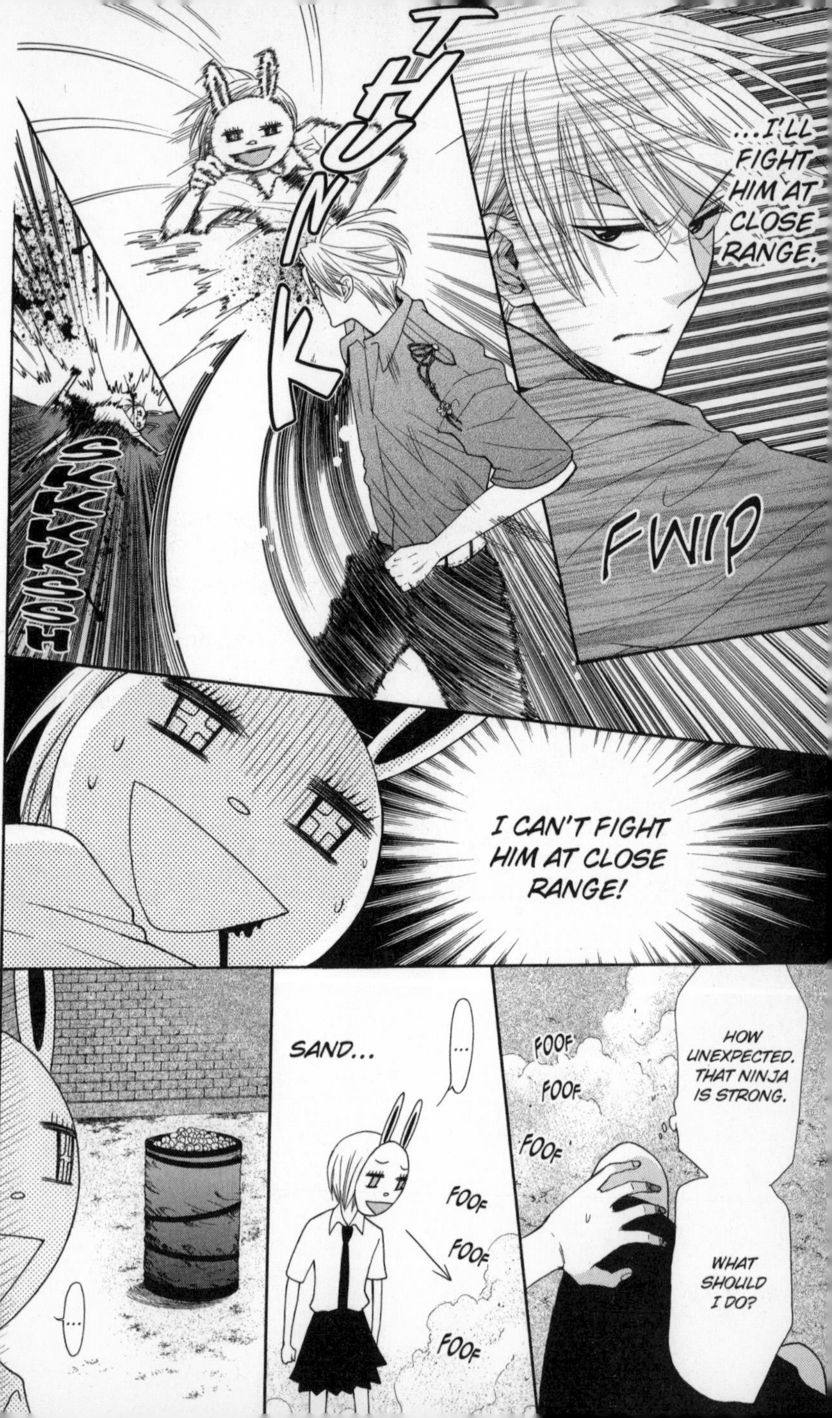
...I'LL FIGHT HIM AT CLOSE RANGE.
FWIP
THUNK
I CAN'T FIGHT HIM AT CLOSE RANGE!
HOW UNEXPECTED. THAT NINJA IS STRONG.
WHAT SHOULD I DO?
FOOF
FOOF
FOOF
FOOF
FOOF
FOOF
SAND...
...
...

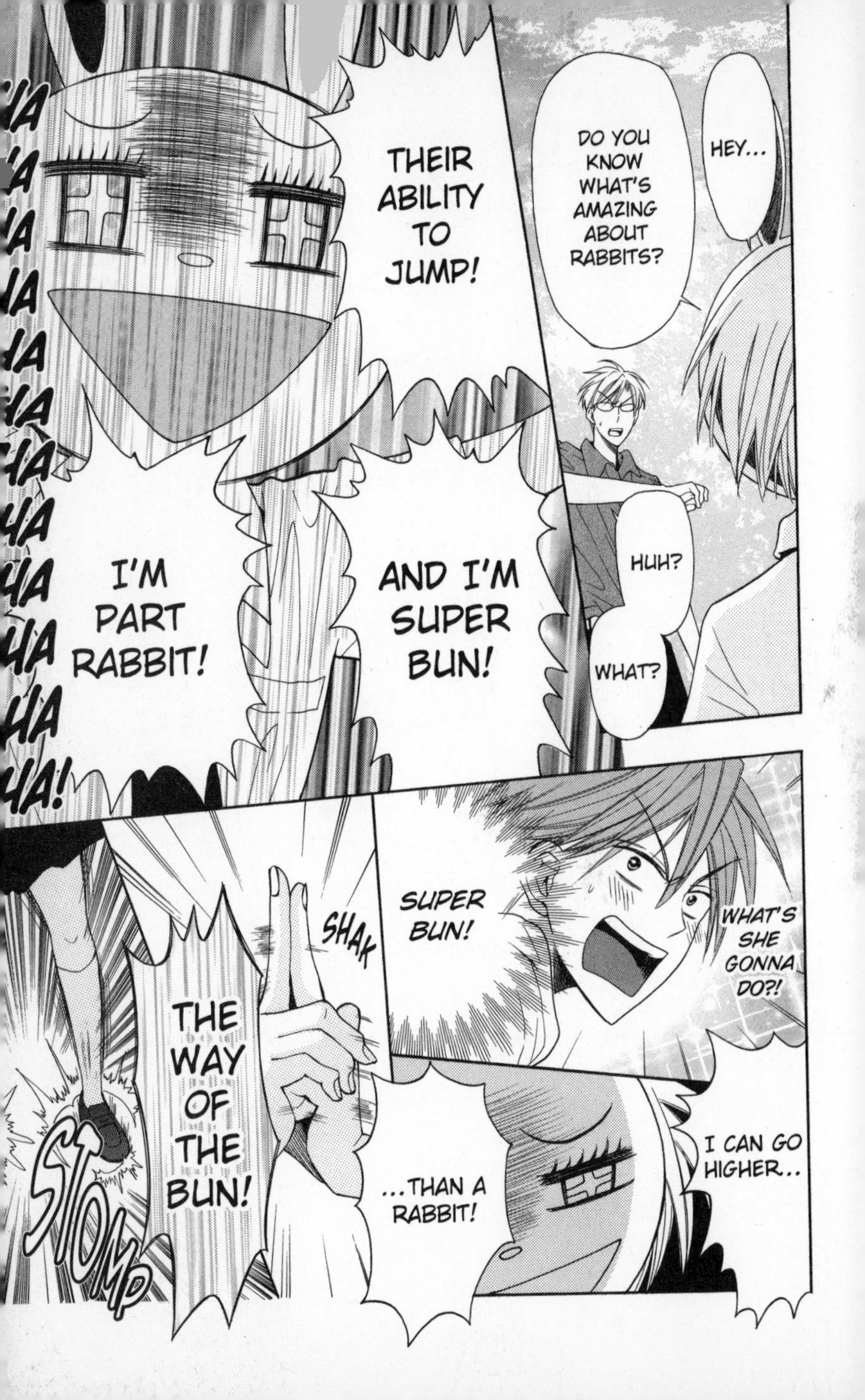
HEY...
DO YOU KNOW WHAT'S AMAZING ABOUT RABBITS?
HUH?
WHAT?
THEIR ABILITY TO JUMP!
AND I'M SUPER BUN!
I'M PART RABBIT!
HA HA HA HA HA HA HA HA HA HA HA HA HA HA!
WHAT'S SHE GONNA DO?!
SUPER BUN!
I CAN GO HIGHER...
...THAN A RABBIT!
SHAK
THE WAY OF THE BUN!
STOMP

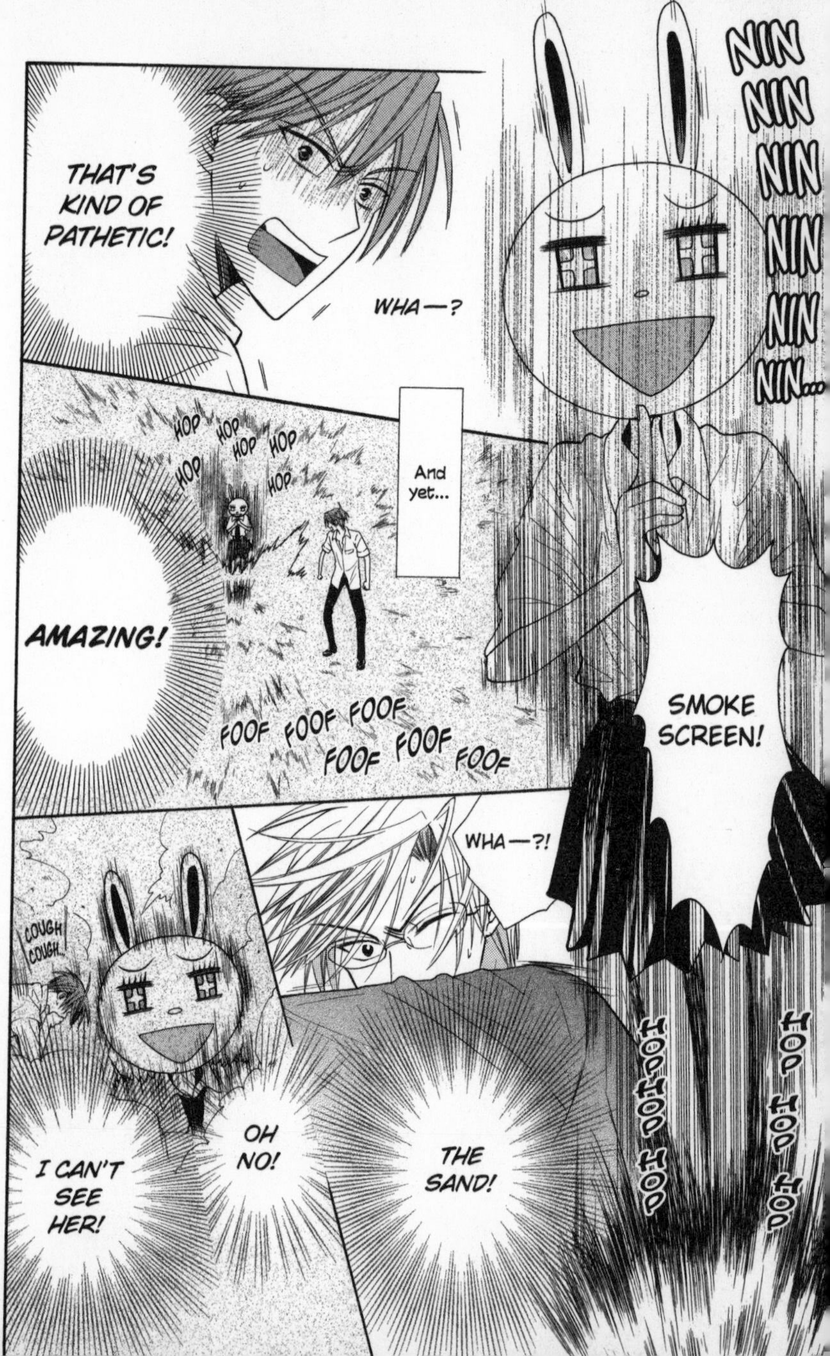

NIN NIN NIN NIN NIN NIN...
SMOKE SCREEN!
HOP HOP HOP
HOP HOP HOP
THAT'S KIND OF PATHETIC!
WHA—?
And yet...
HOP HOP HOP HOP HOP HOP
AMAZING!
FOOF FOOF FOOF FOOF FOOF FOOF
WHA—?!
THE SAND!
OH NO!
I CAN'T SEE HER!
COUGH COUGH...

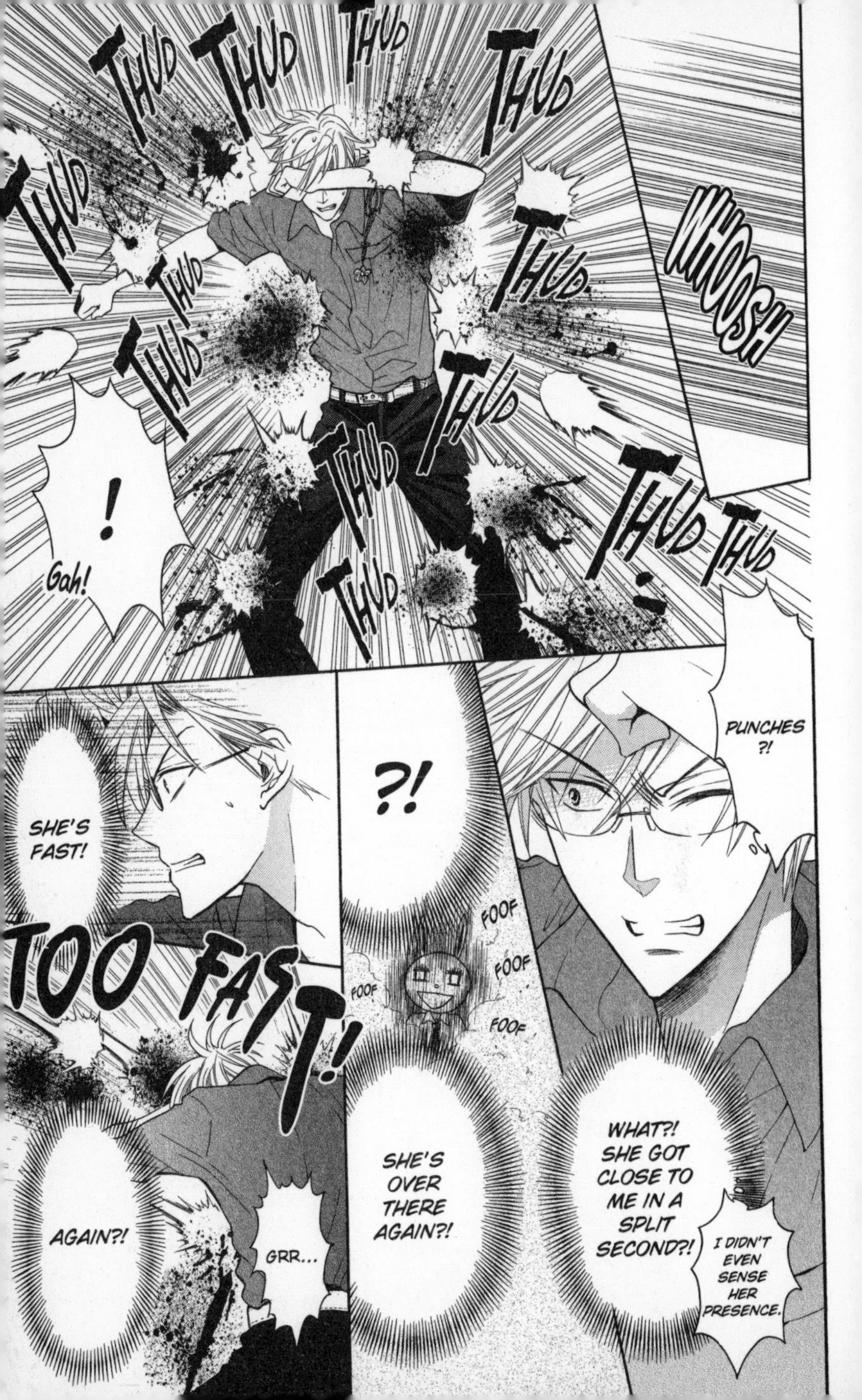
WHOOSH
THUD
THUD
THUD
THUD
THUD
THUD
THUD THUD
THUD
THUD
THUD
THUD THUD
THUD
THUD
!
Gah!
PUNCHES?!
WHAT?! SHE GOT CLOSE TO ME IN A SPLIT SECOND?!
I DIDN'T EVEN SENSE HER PRESENCE.
?!
FOOF
FOOF
FOOF
FOOF
SHE'S OVER THERE AGAIN?!
SHE'S FAST!
TOO FAST!
AGAIN?!
GRR...

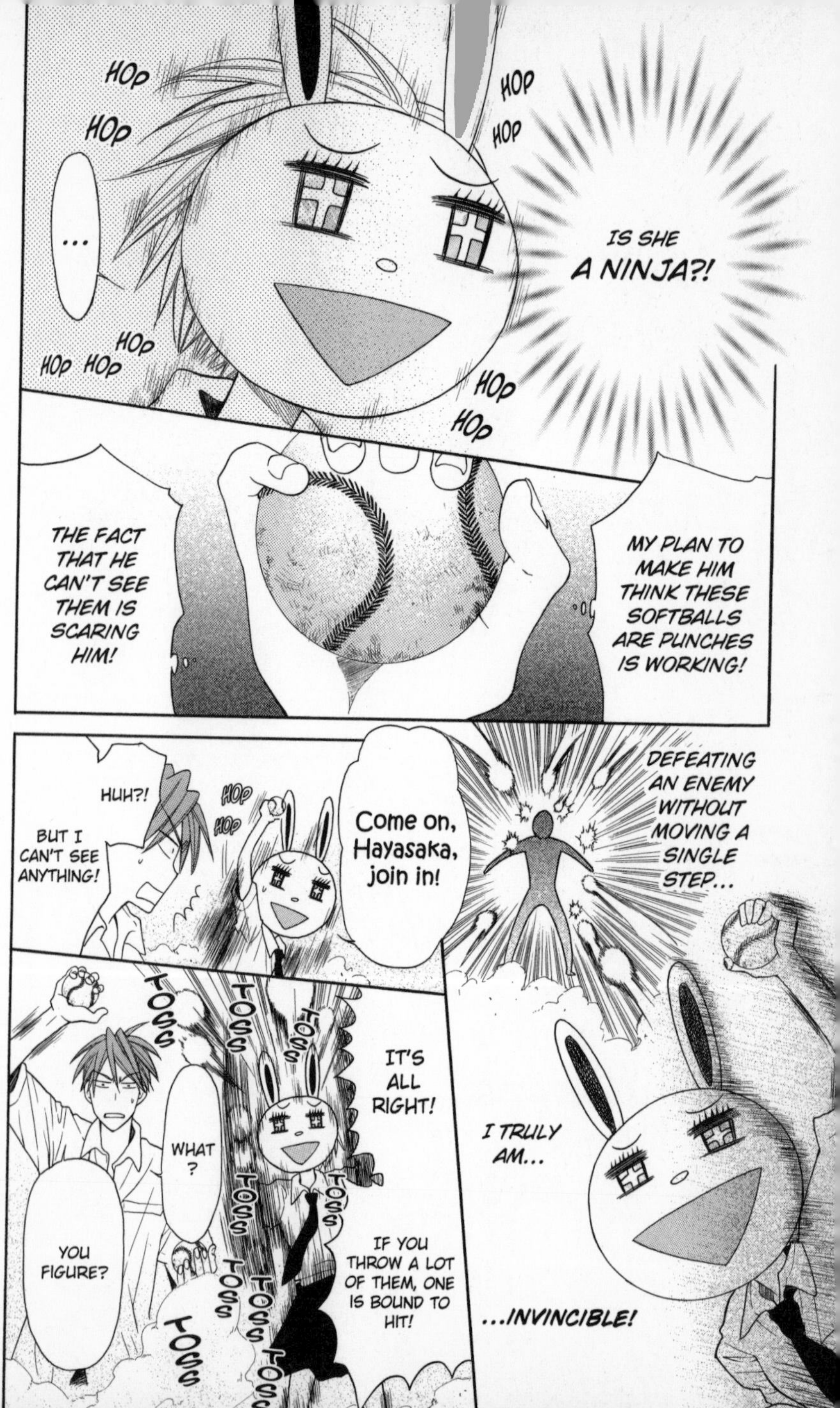
HOP
HOP
IS SHE A NINJA?!
HOP
HOP
...
HOP
HOP HOP
HOP
HOP
MY PLAN TO MAKE HIM THINK THESE SOFTBALLS ARE PUNCHES IS WORKING!
THE FACT THAT HE CAN'T SEE THEM IS SCARING HIM!
DEFEATING AN ENEMY WITHOUT MOVING A SINGLE STEP...
Come on, Hayasaka, join in!
HOP
HOP
HUH?!
BUT I CAN'T SEE ANYTHING!
I TRULY AM...
...INVINCIBLE!
IT'S ALL RIGHT!
TOSS
TOSS
TOSS
WHAT?
IF YOU THROW A LOT OF THEM, ONE IS BOUND TO HIT!
TOSS
TOSS
TOSS
TOSS
TOSS
YOU FIGURE?
TOSS

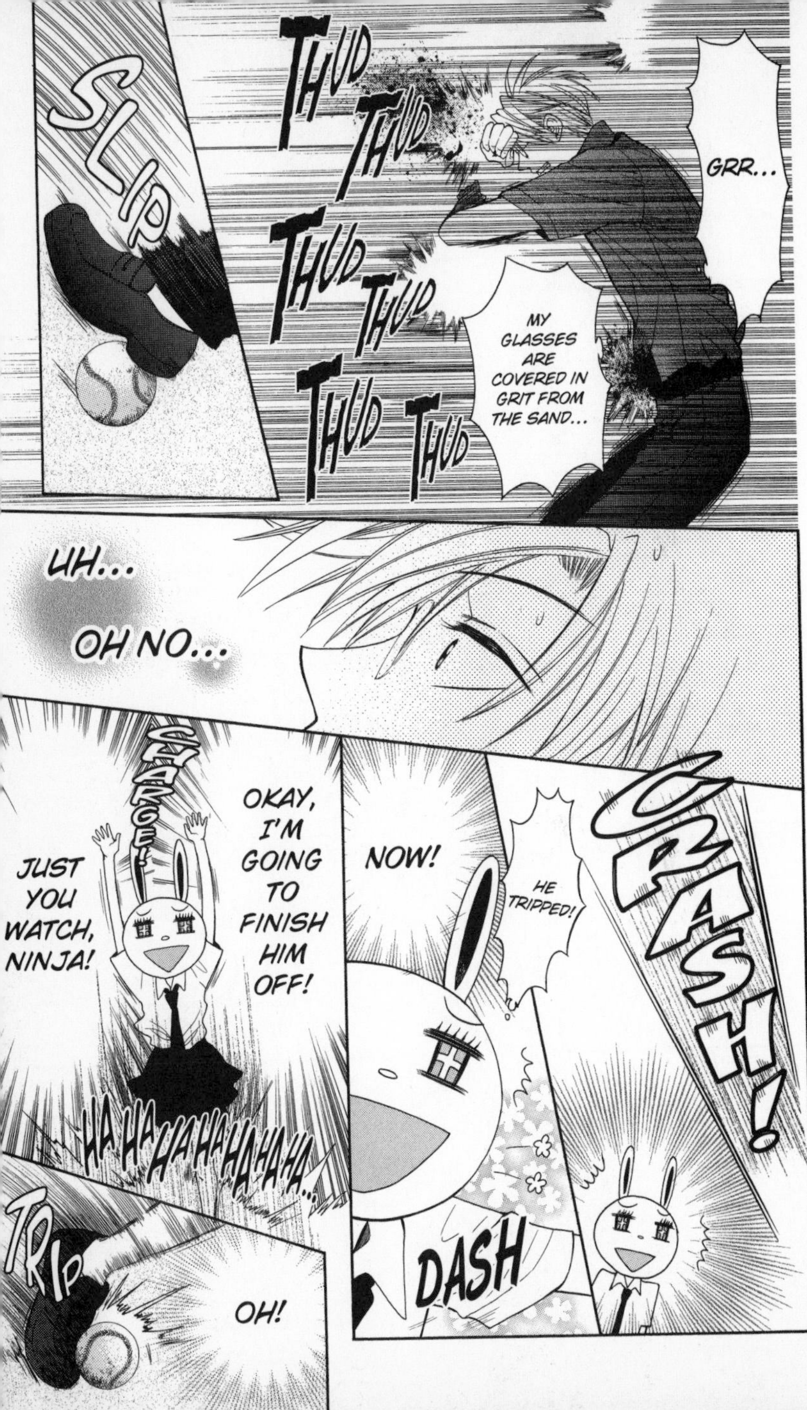
GRR...
MY GLASSES ARE COVERED IN GRIT FROM THE SAND...
THUD THUD THUD THUD THUD THUD
SLIP
UH...
OH NO...
CRASH!
HE TRIPPED!
NOW!
DASH
OKAY, I'M GOING TO FINISH HIM OFF!
CHARGE!
JUST YOU WATCH, NINJA!
HA HA HA HA HA HA HA HA...
TRIP
OH!

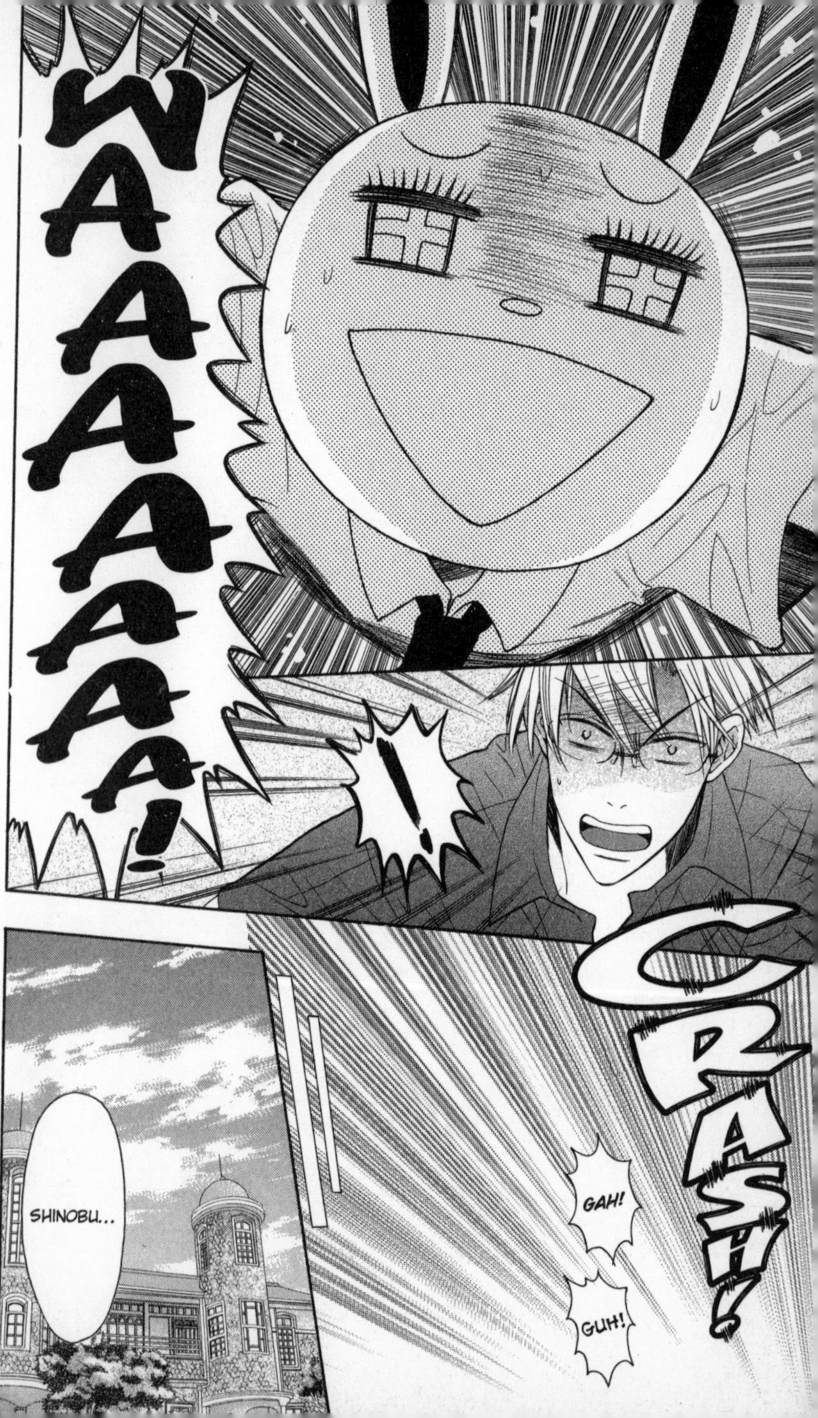
WAAAAAAAA!
!
CRASH!
GAH!
GUH!
SHINOBU...

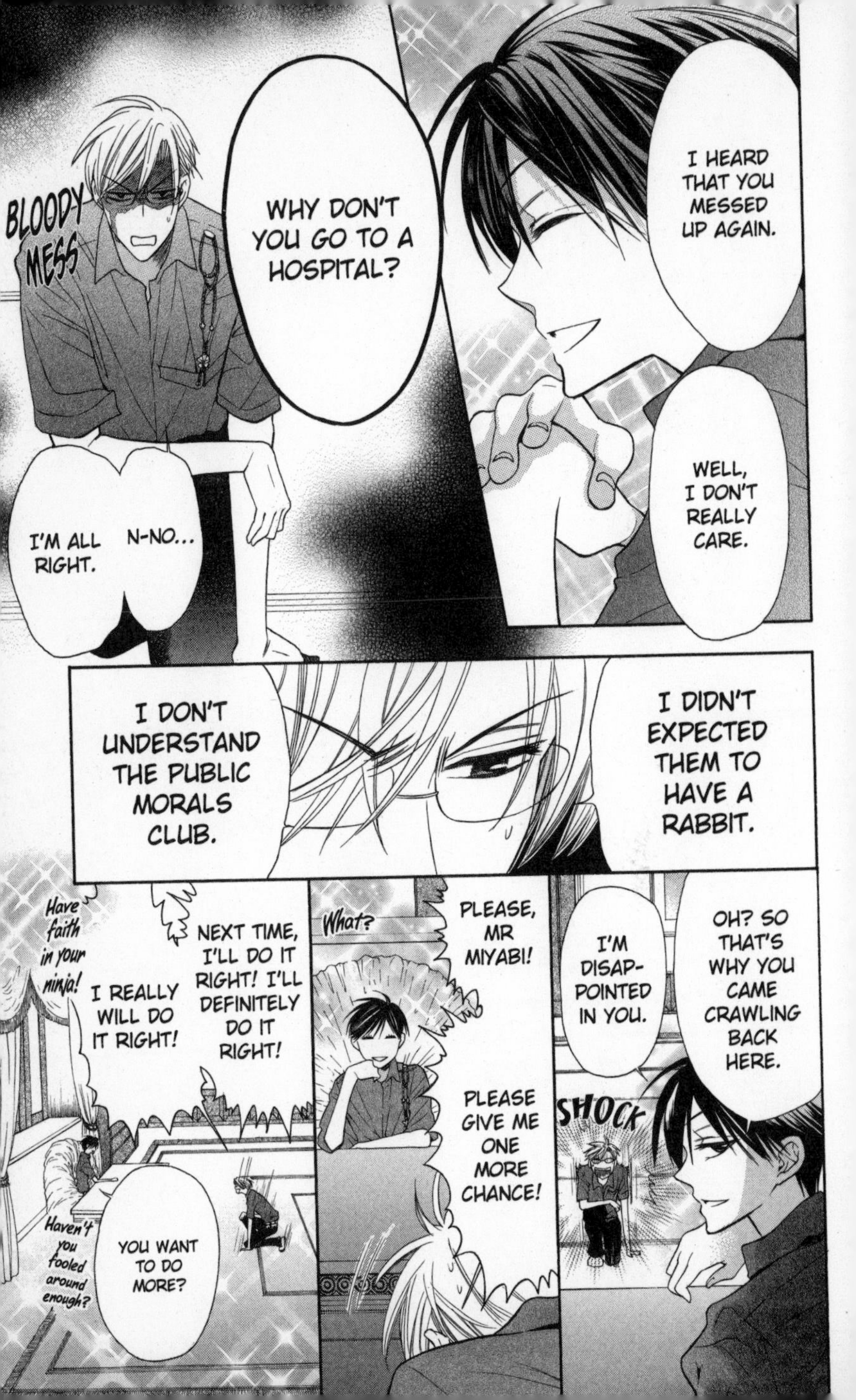
I HEARD THAT YOU MESSED UP AGAIN.
WELL, I DON'T REALLY CARE.
WHY DON'T YOU GO TO A HOSPITAL?
BLOODY MESS
N-NO...
I'M ALL RIGHT.
I DIDN'T EXPECTED THEM TO HAVE A RABBIT.
I DON'T UNDERSTAND THE PUBLIC MORALS CLUB.
OH? SO THAT'S WHY YOU CAME CRAWLING BACK HERE.
I'M DISAP-POINTED IN YOU.
SHOCK
PLEASE, MR MIYABI!
PLEASE GIVE ME ONE MORE CHANCE!
What?
NEXT TIME, I'LL DO IT RIGHT! I'LL DEFINITELY DO IT RIGHT!
I REALLY WILL DO IT RIGHT!
Have faith in your ninja!
YOU WANT TO DO MORE?
Haven't you fooled around enough?

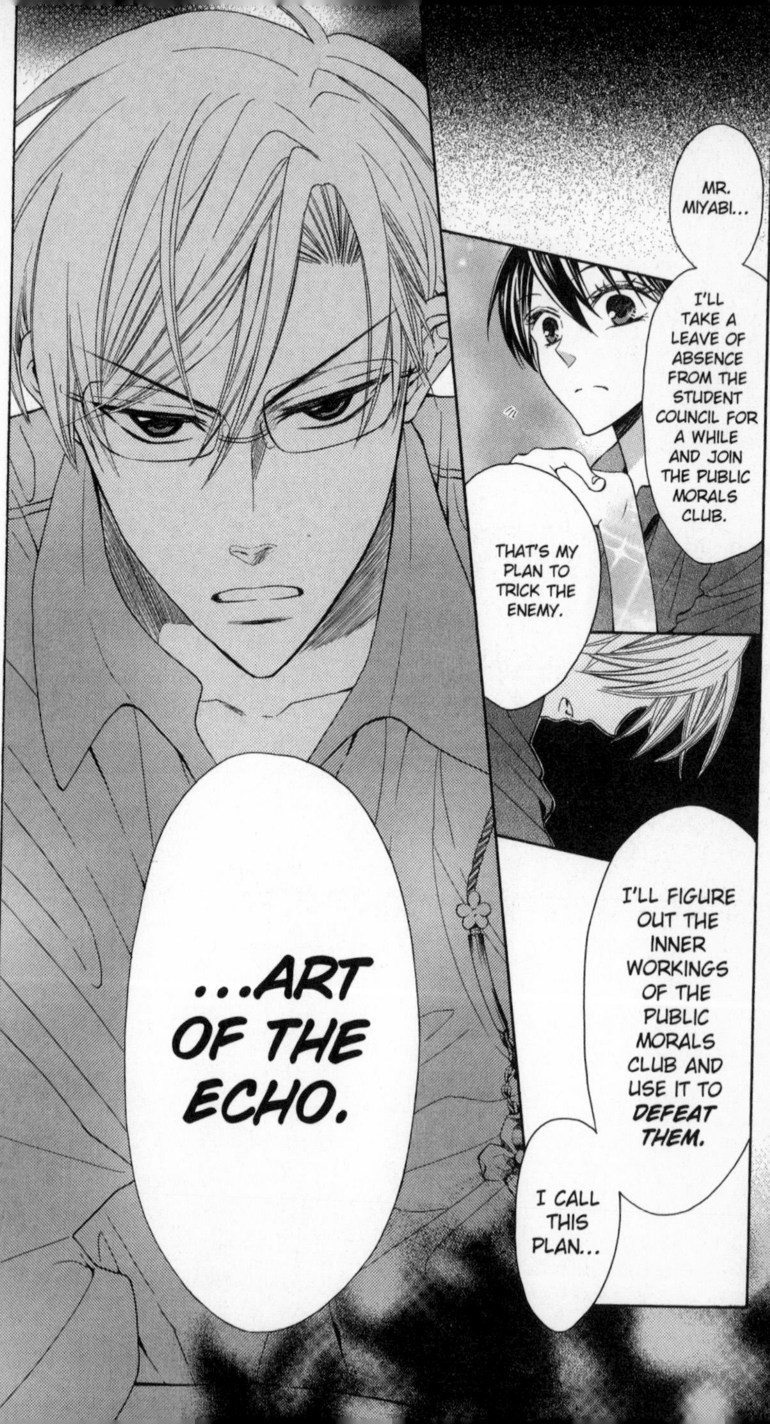
MR. MIYABI...
I'LL TAKE A LEAVE OF ABSENCE FROM THE STUDENT COUNCIL FOR A WHILE AND JOIN THE PUBLIC MORALS CLUB.
THAT'S MY PLAN TO TRICK THE ENEMY.
I'LL FIGURE OUT THE INNER WORKINGS OF THE PUBLIC MORALS CLUB AND USE IT TO DEFEAT THEM.
I CALL THIS PLAN...
...ART OF THE ECHO.

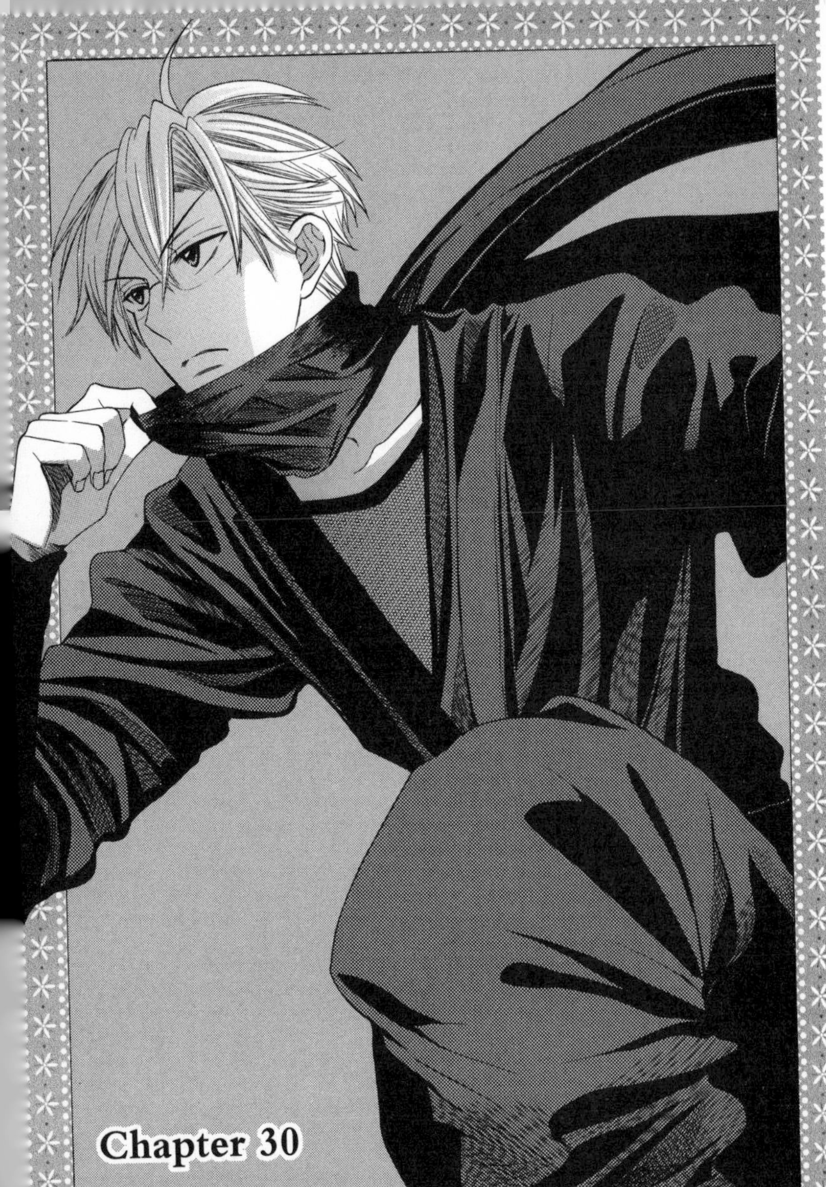
Chapter 30

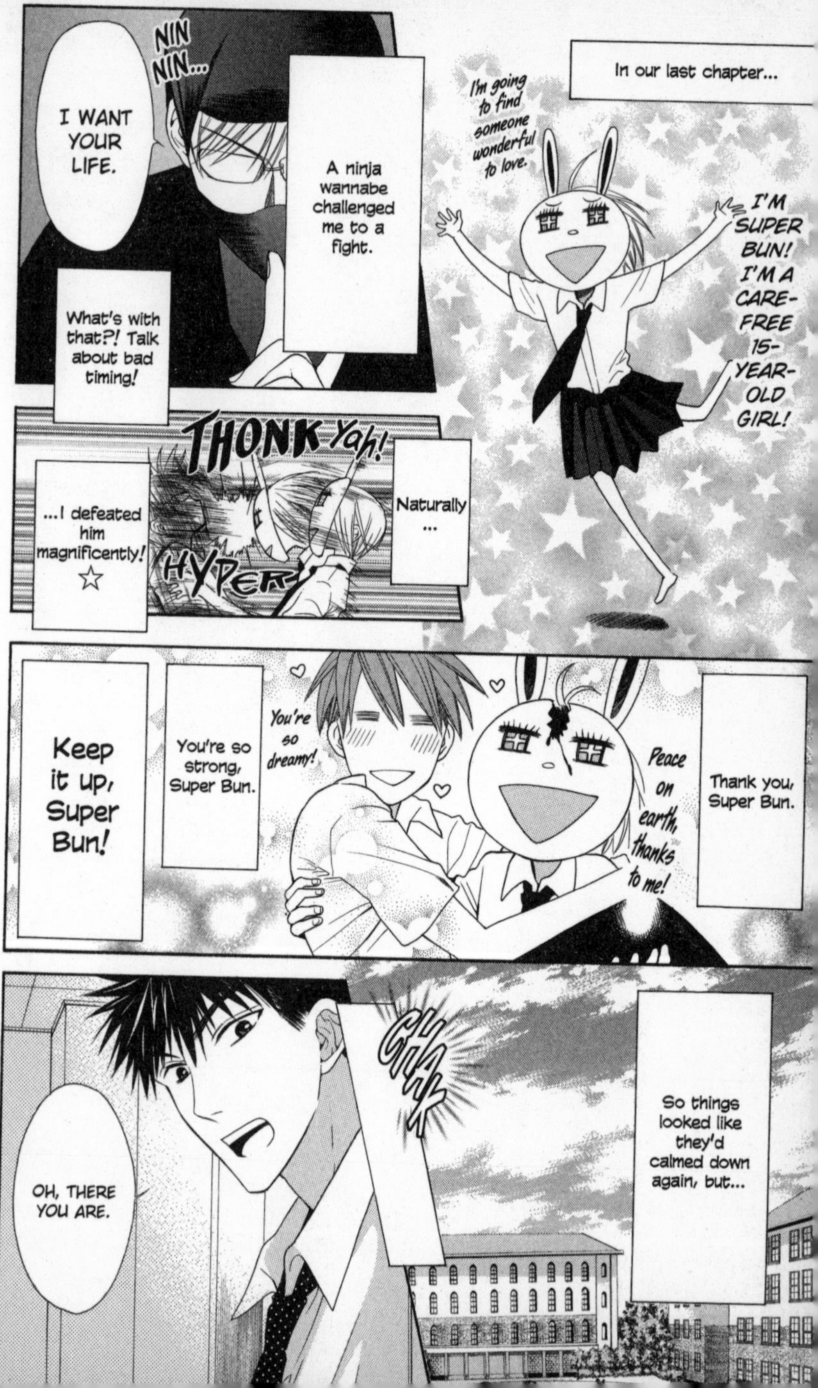

In our last chapter...
I'm going to find someone wonderful to love.
I'M SUPER BUN! I'M A CARE-FREE 15-YEAR-OLD GIRL!
NIN NIN...
A ninja wannabe challenged me to a fight.
I WANT YOUR LIFE.
What's with that?! Talk about bad timing!
Naturally...
THONK
Yah!
HYPER
...I defeated him magnificently! ☆
Thank you, Super Bun.
Peace on earth, thanks to me!
You're so dreamy!
You're so strong, Super Bun.
Keep it up, Super Bun!
So things looked like they'd calmed down again, but...
CHAK
OH, THERE YOU ARE.

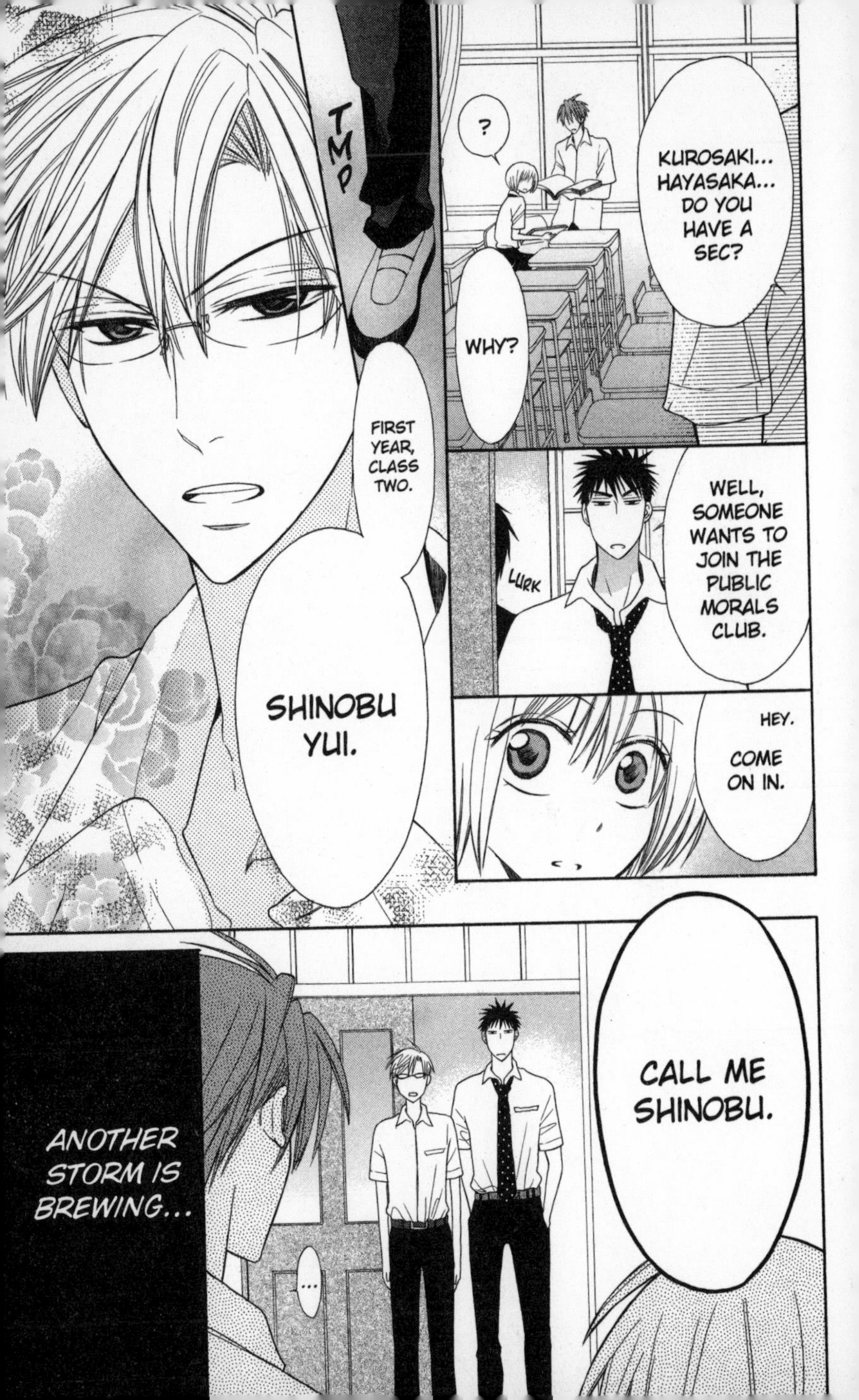
KUROSAKI... HAYASAKA... DO YOU HAVE A SEC?
?
WHY?
WELL, SOMEONE WANTS TO JOIN THE PUBLIC MORALS CLUB.
LURK
HEY.
COME ON IN.
TMP
FIRST YEAR, CLASS TWO.
SHINOBU YUI.
CALL ME SHINOBU.
...
ANOTHER STORM IS BREWING...

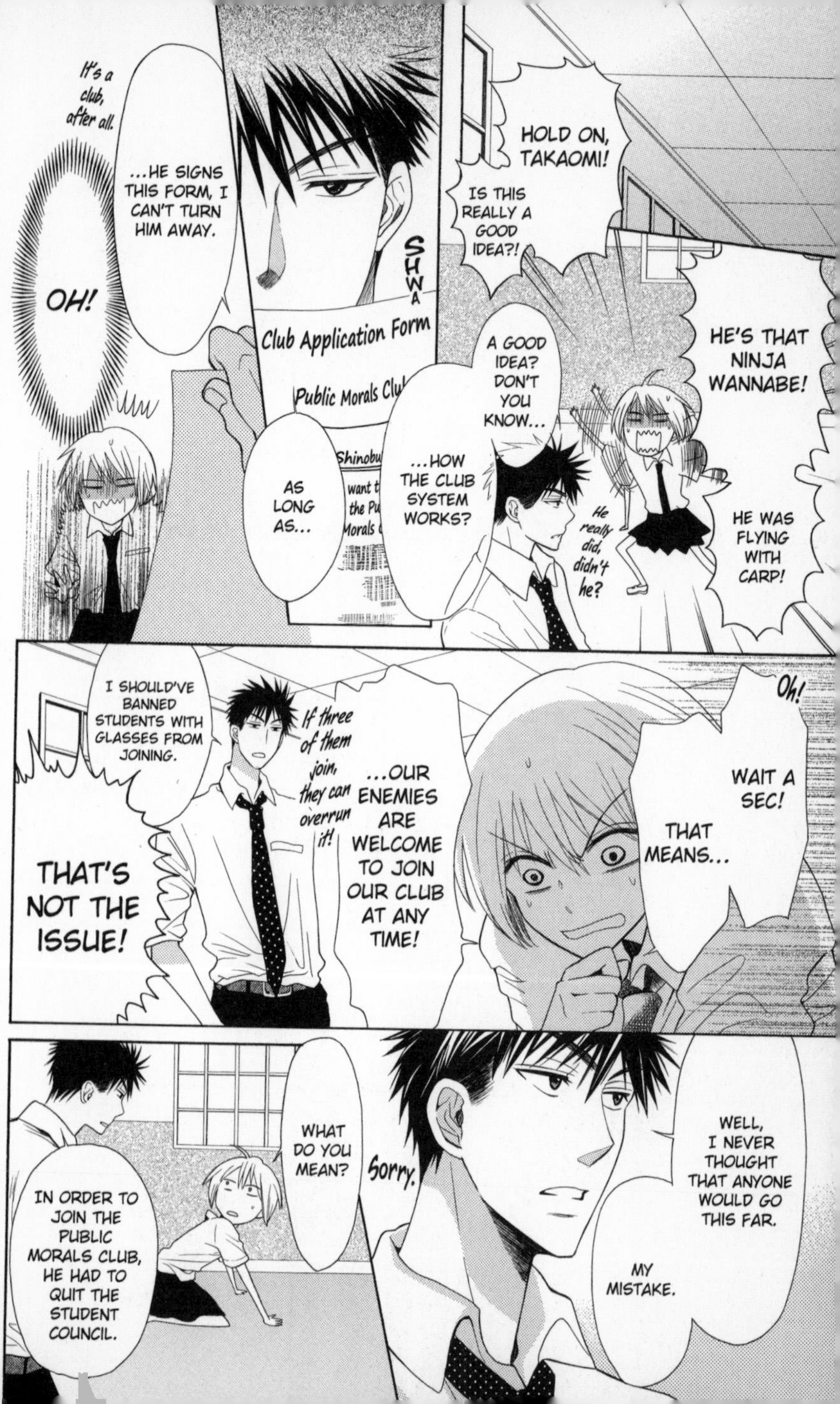
HOLD ON, TAKAOMI!
IS THIS REALLY A GOOD IDEA?!
HE'S THAT NINJA WANNABE!
HE WAS FLYING WITH CARP!
A GOOD IDEA? DON'T YOU KNOW...
...HOW THE CLUB SYSTEM WORKS?
He really did, didn't he?
SHWA
Club Application Form
AS LONG AS...
...HE SIGNS THIS FORM, I CAN'T TURN HIM AWAY.
It's a club, after all.
OH!
Oh!
WAIT A SEC!
THAT MEANS...
...OUR ENEMIES ARE WELCOME TO JOIN OUR CLUB AT ANY TIME!
If three of them join, they can overrun it!
I SHOULD'VE BANNED STUDENTS WITH GLASSES FROM JOINING.
THAT'S NOT THE ISSUE!
WELL, I NEVER THOUGHT THAT ANYONE WOULD GO THIS FAR.
MY MISTAKE.
Sorry.
WHAT DO YOU MEAN?
IN ORDER TO JOIN THE PUBLIC MORALS CLUB, HE HAD TO QUIT THE STUDENT COUNCIL.

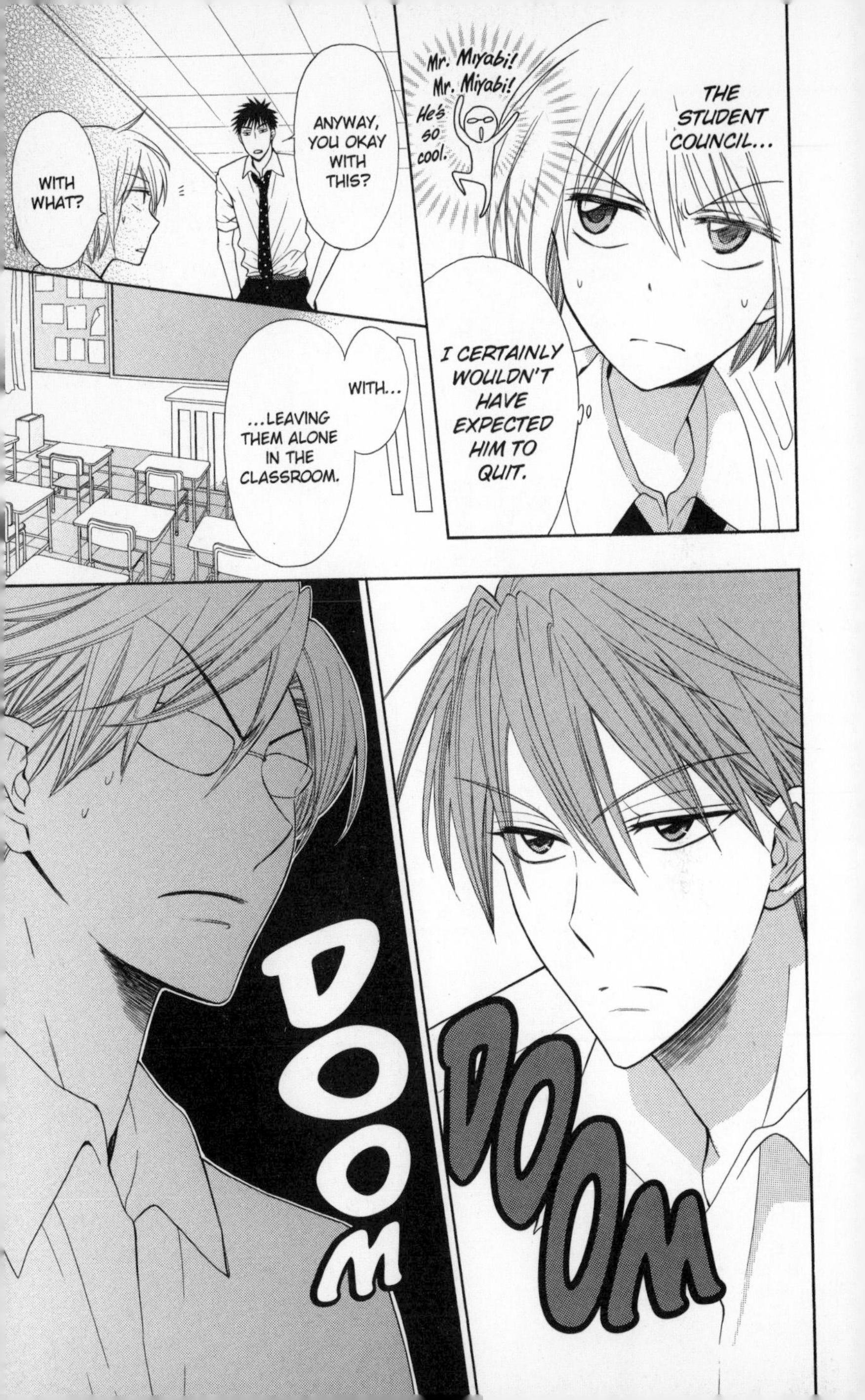
THE STUDENT COUNCIL...
Mr. Miyabi! Mr. Miyabi!
He's so cool.
I CERTAINLY WOULDN'T HAVE EXPECTED HIM TO QUIT.
ANYWAY, YOU OKAY WITH THIS?
WITH WHAT?
WITH...
...LEAVING THEM ALONE IN THE CLASSROOM.
DOOOM
DOOM

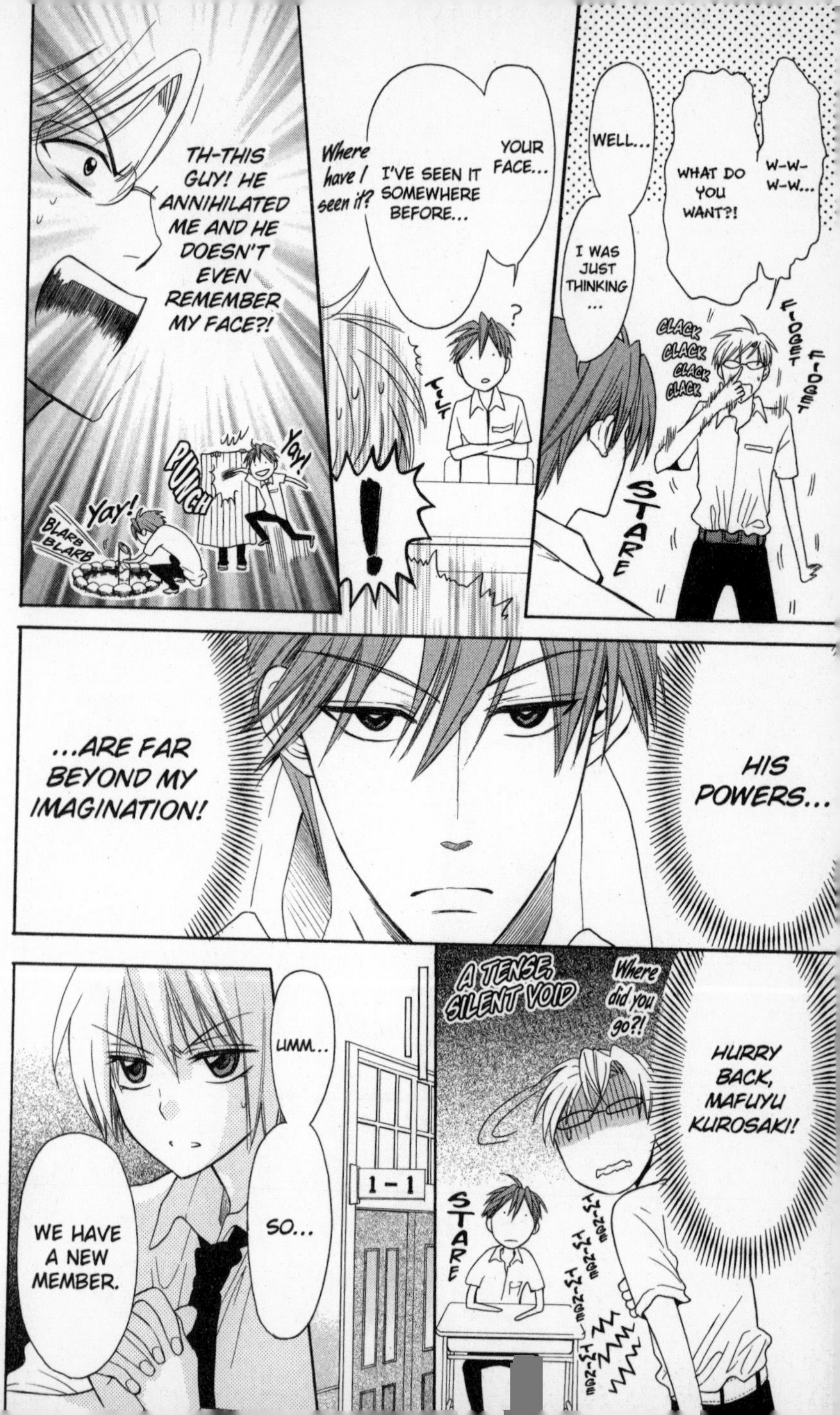
W-W-W-W...
WHAT DO YOU WANT?!
WELL...
I WAS JUST THINKING...
CLACK CLACK CLACK CLACK
FIDGET FIDGET
STARE
YOUR FACE...
I'VE SEEN IT SOMEWHERE BEFORE...
Where have I seen it?
?
TILT
!
TH-THIS GUY! HE ANNIHILATED ME AND HE DOESN'T EVEN REMEMBER MY FACE?!
Yay!
PUNCH
Yay!
BLARB BLARB
HIS POWERS...
...ARE FAR BEYOND MY IMAGINATION!
A TENSE, SILENT VOID
Where did you go?!
HURRY BACK, MAFUYU KUROSAKI!
STARE
UMM...
SO...
1-1
WE HAVE A NEW MEMBER.

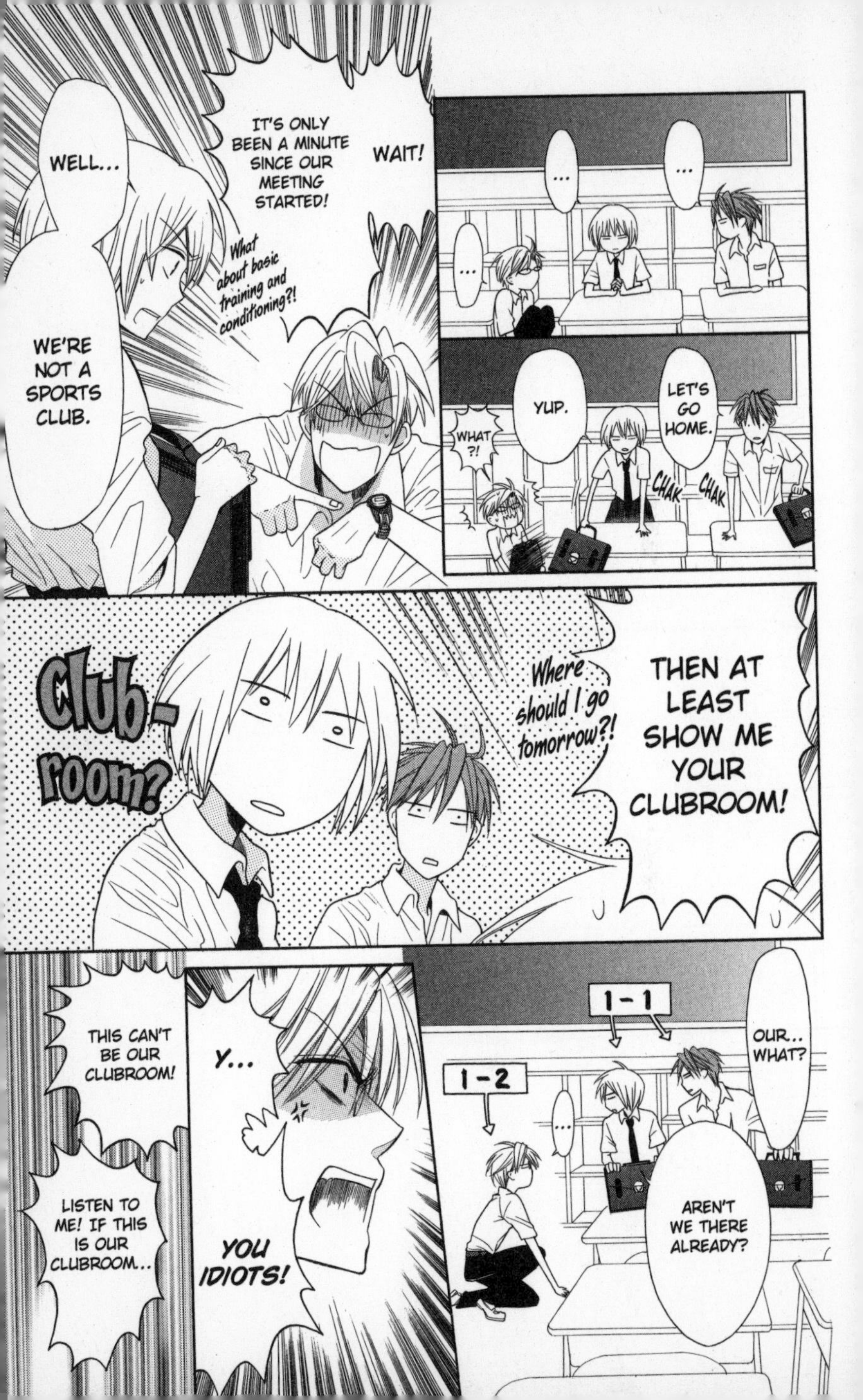
...
...
...
LET'S GO HOME.
YUP.
WHAT?!
CHAK
CHAK
WAIT!
IT'S ONLY BEEN A MINUTE SINCE OUR MEETING STARTED!
What about basic training and conditioning?!
WELL...
WE'RE NOT A SPORTS CLUB.
THEN AT LEAST SHOW ME YOUR CLUBROOM!
Where should I go tomorrow?!
Club-room?
OUR.. WHAT?
1-1
AREN'T WE THERE ALREADY?
...
1-2
Y...
YOU IDIOTS!
THIS CAN'T BE OUR CLUBROOM!
LISTEN TO ME! IF THIS IS OUR CLUBROOM...

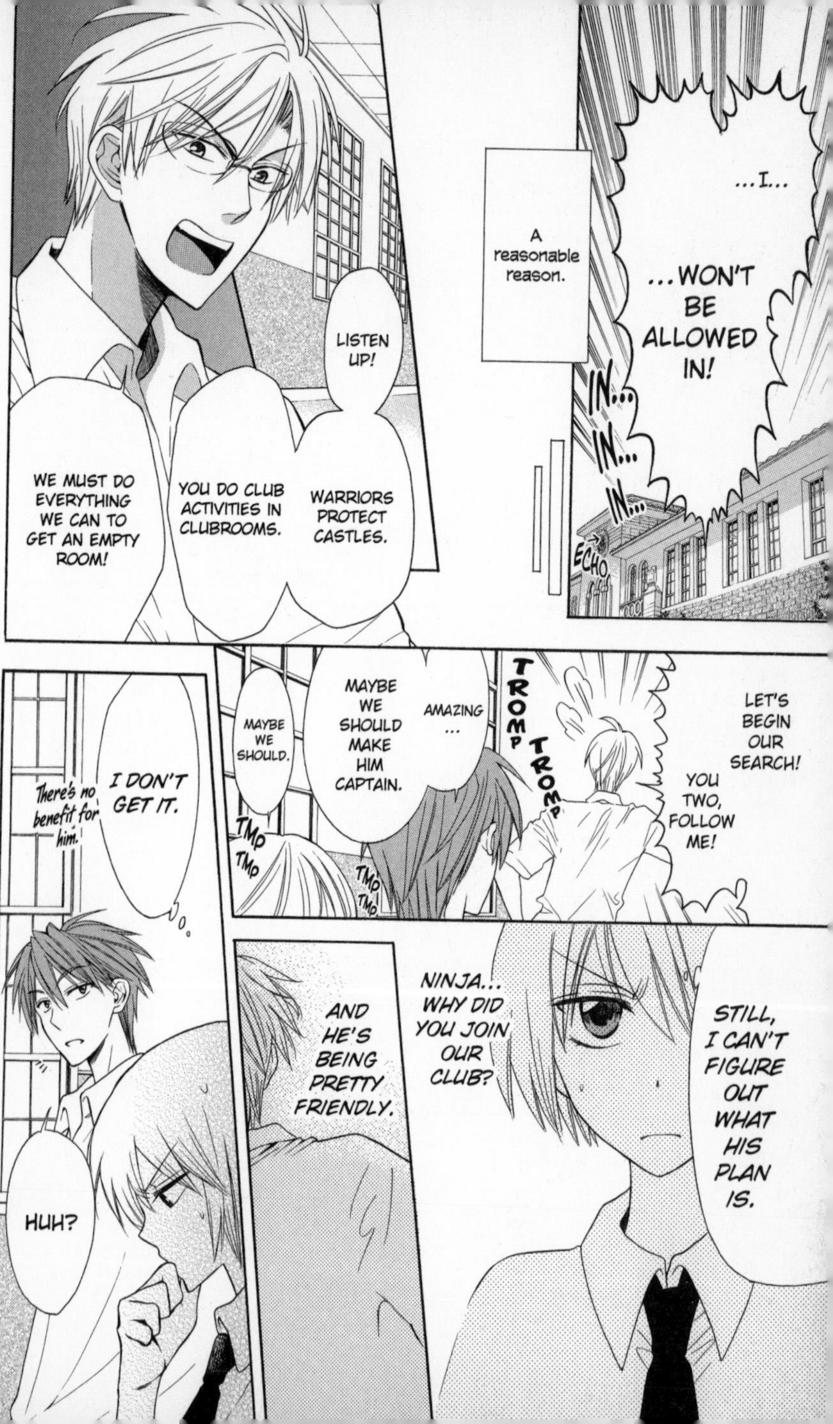
...I...
...WON'T BE ALLOWED IN!
IN... IN... IN...
ECHO
A reasonable reason.
LISTEN UP!
WARRIORS PROTECT CASTLES.
YOU DO CLUB ACTIVITIES IN CLUBROOMS.
WE MUST DO EVERYTHING WE CAN TO GET AN EMPTY ROOM!
LET'S BEGIN OUR SEARCH!
YOU TWO, FOLLOW ME!
TROMP TROMP
AMAZING...
MAYBE WE SHOULD MAKE HIM CAPTAIN.
MAYBE WE SHOULD.
TMP TMP
TMP TMP
STILL, I CAN'T FIGURE OUT WHAT HIS PLAN IS.
NINJA... WHY DID YOU JOIN OUR CLUB?
AND HE'S BEING PRETTY FRIENDLY.
I DON'T GET IT.
There's no benefit for him.
HUH?

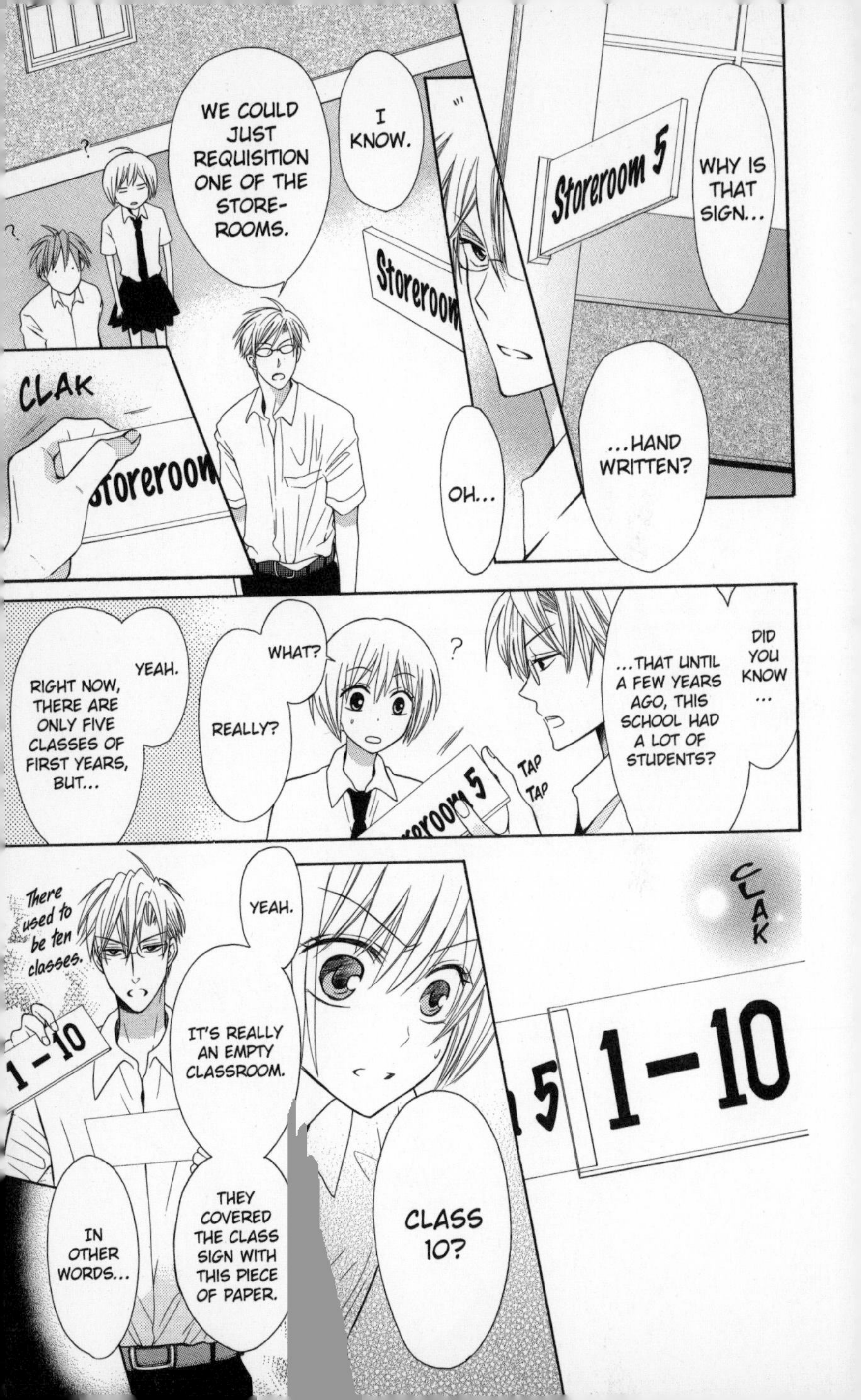
WHY IS THAT SIGN...
Storeroom 5
...HAND WRITTEN?
OH...
I KNOW.
Storeroom
WE COULD JUST REQUISITION ONE OF THE STOREROOMS.
CLAK
Storeroom
DID YOU KNOW...
...THAT UNTIL A FEW YEARS AGO, THIS SCHOOL HAD A LOT OF STUDENTS?
TAP TAP
Storeroom 5
WHAT?
REALLY?
YEAH.
RIGHT NOW, THERE ARE ONLY FIVE CLASSES OF FIRST YEARS, BUT...
CLAK
1-10
CLASS 10?
YEAH.
IT'S REALLY AN EMPTY CLASSROOM.
There used to be ten classes.
1-10
THEY COVERED THE CLASS SIGN WITH THIS PIECE OF PAPER.
IN OTHER WORDS...

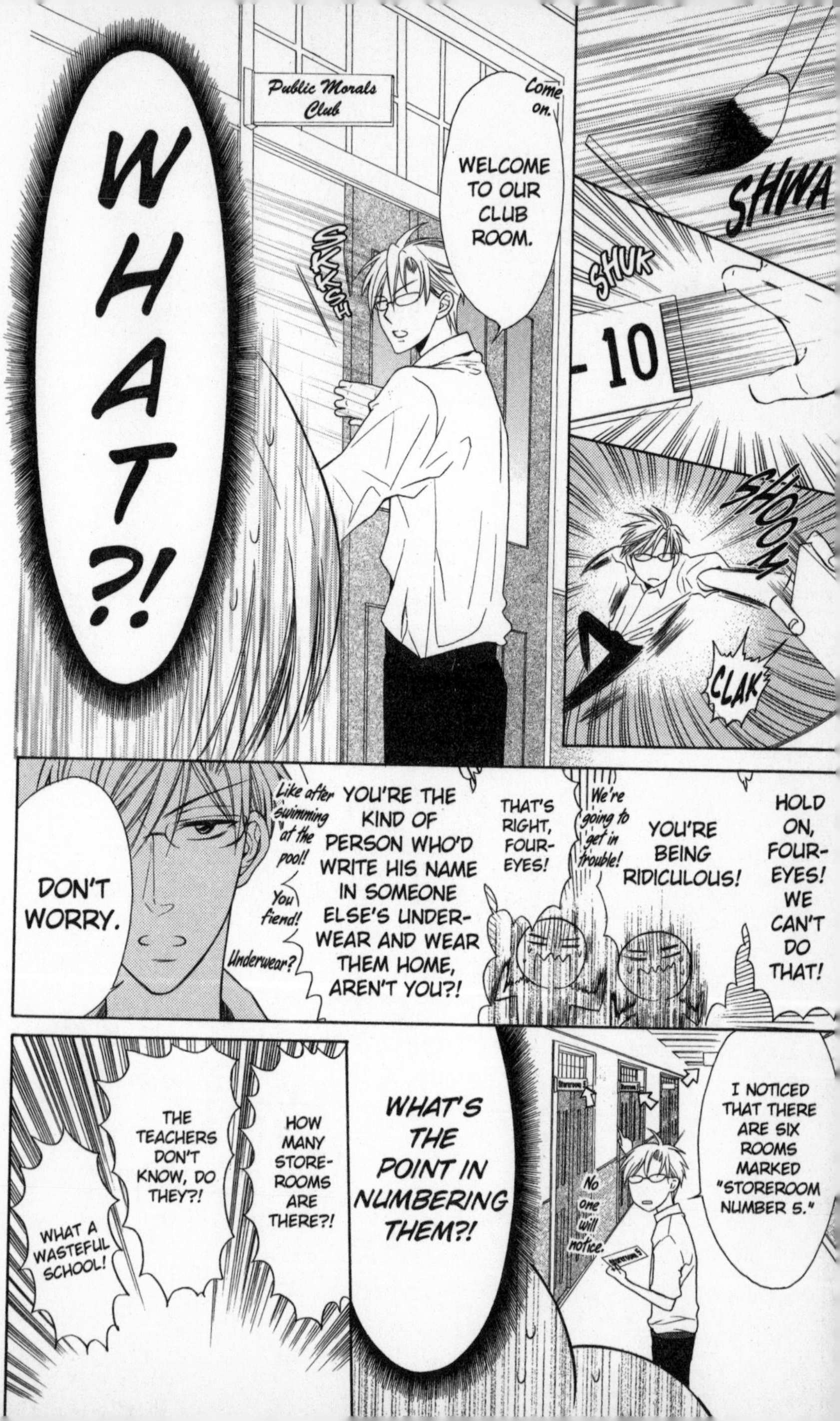
SHWA
SHUK
-10
SHOOM
CLAK
Public Morals Club
Come on.
WELCOME TO OUR CLUB ROOM.
SKRSH
WHAT?!
HOLD ON, FOUR-EYES! WE CAN'T DO THAT!
YOU'RE BEING RIDICULOUS!
We're going to get in trouble!
THAT'S RIGHT, FOUR-EYES!
YOU'RE THE KIND OF PERSON WHO'D WRITE HIS NAME IN SOMEONE ELSE'S UNDERWEAR AND WEAR THEM HOME, AREN'T YOU?!
Like after swimming at the pool!
You fiend!
Underwear?
DON'T WORRY.
I NOTICED THAT THERE ARE SIX ROOMS MARKED "STOREROOM NUMBER 5."
No one will notice.
WHAT'S THE POINT IN NUMBERING THEM?!
HOW MANY STOREROOMS ARE THERE?!
THE TEACHERS DON'T KNOW, DO THEY?!
WHAT A WASTEFUL SCHOOL!

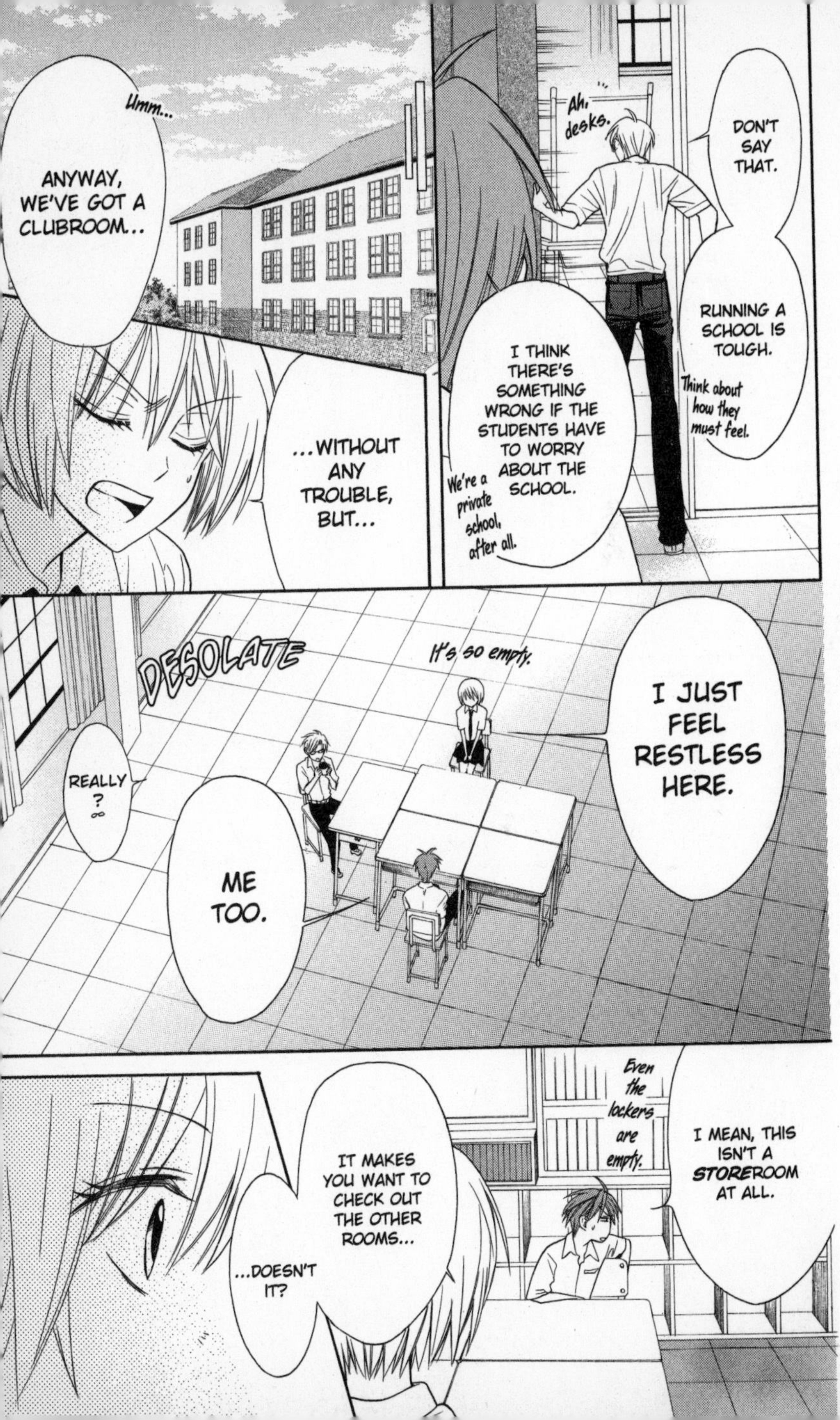
Ah, desks.
DON'T SAY THAT.
RUNNING A SCHOOL IS TOUGH.
Think about how they must feel.
I THINK THERE'S SOMETHING WRONG IF THE STUDENTS HAVE TO WORRY ABOUT THE SCHOOL.
We're a private school, after all.
Umm...
ANYWAY, WE'VE GOT A CLUBROOM...
...WITHOUT ANY TROUBLE, BUT...
I JUST FEEL RESTLESS HERE.
It's so empty.
DESOLATE
ME TOO.
REALLY?
Even the lockers are empty.
I MEAN, THIS ISN'T A STOREROOM AT ALL.
IT MAKES YOU WANT TO CHECK OUT THE OTHER ROOMS...
...DOESN'T IT?

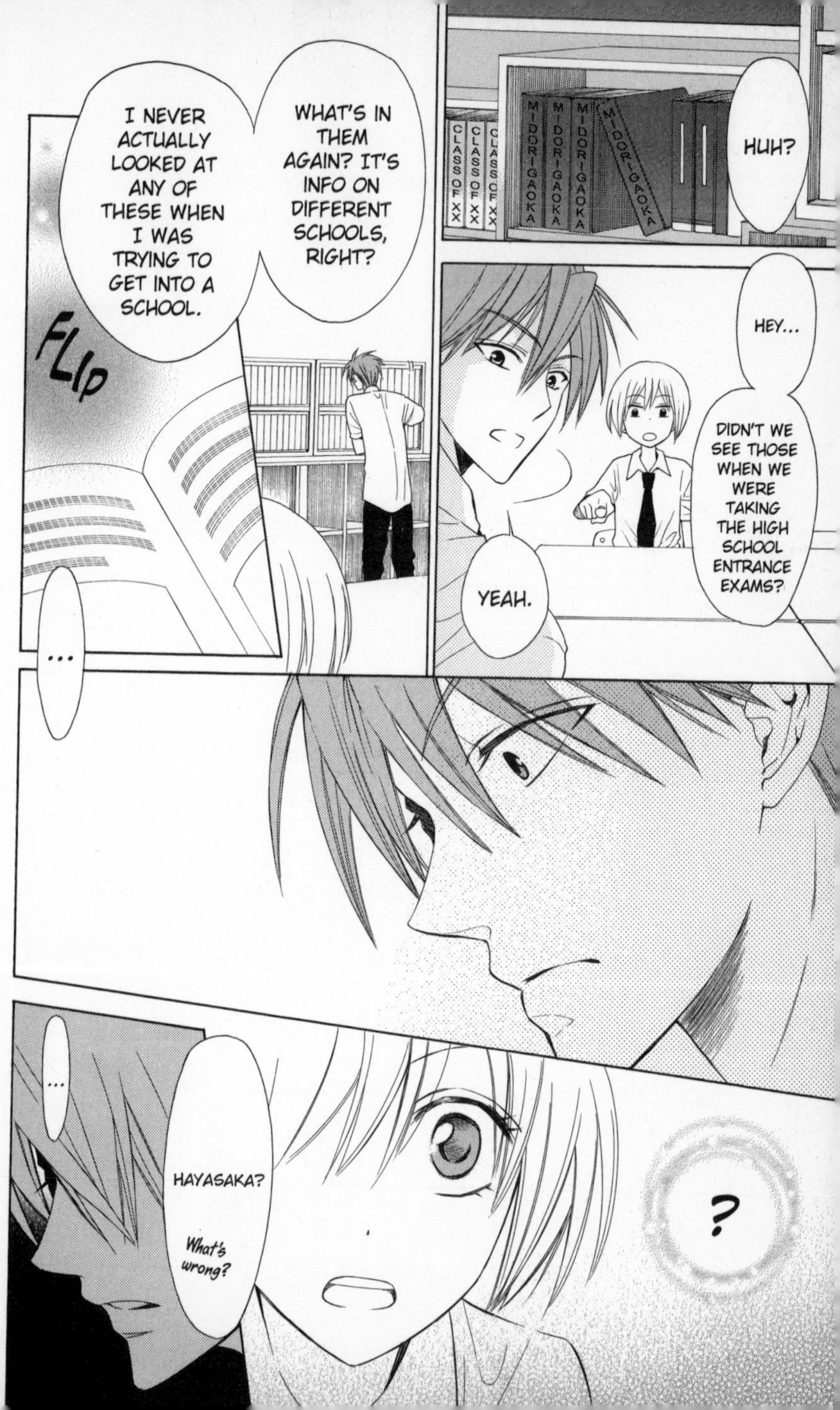
HUH?
MIDORIGAOKA
MIDORIGAOKA
MIDORIGAOKA
MIDORIGAOKA
CLASS OF XX
CLASS OF XX
CLASS OF XX
HEY...
DIDN'T WE SEE THOSE WHEN WE WERE TAKING THE HIGH SCHOOL ENTRANCE EXAMS?
YEAH.
WHAT'S IN THEM AGAIN? IT'S INFO ON DIFFERENT SCHOOLS, RIGHT?
I NEVER ACTUALLY LOOKED AT ANY OF THESE WHEN I WAS TRYING TO GET INTO A SCHOOL.
FLIP
...
?
HAYASAKA?
What's wrong?
...

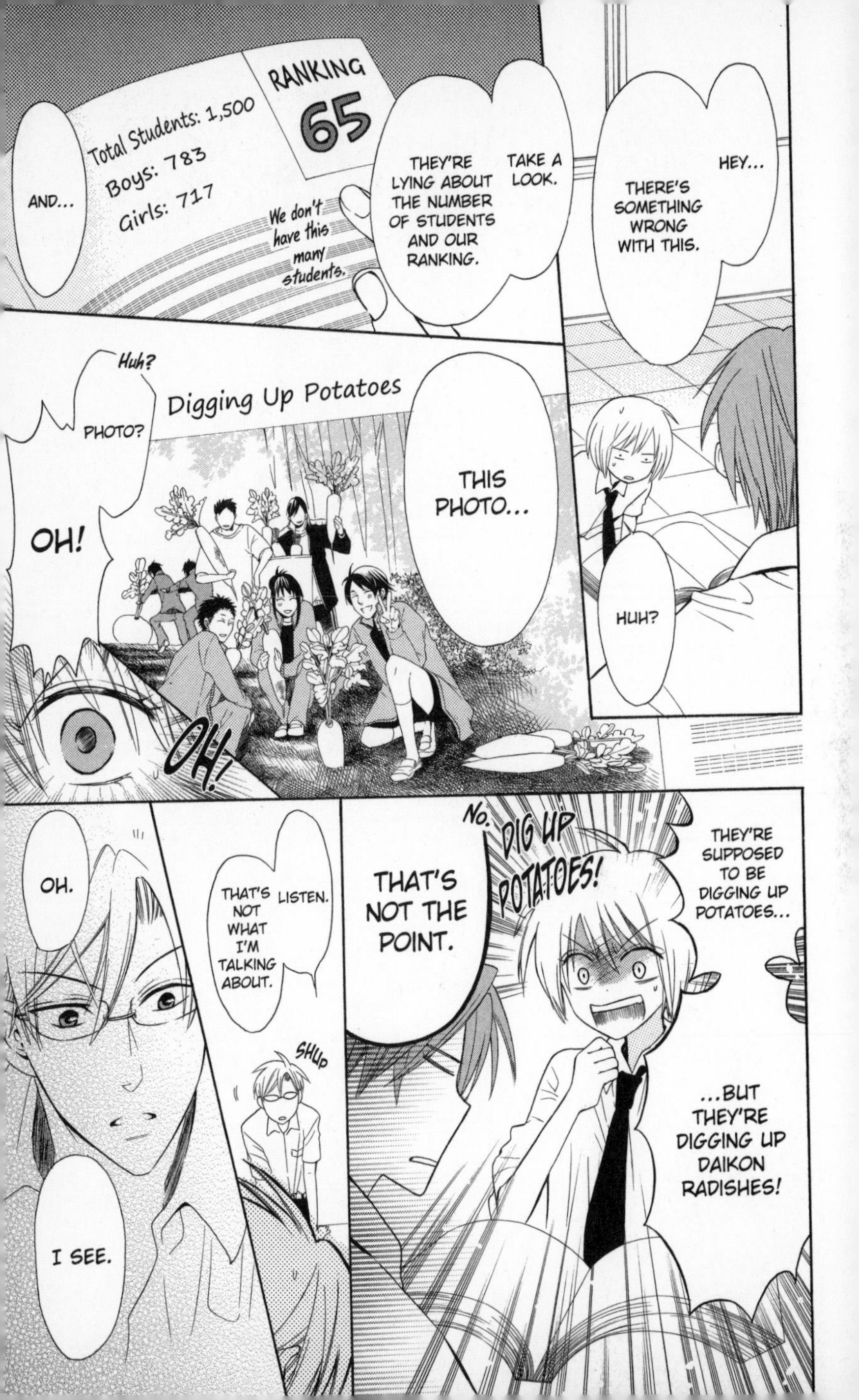
HEY...
THERE'S SOMETHING WRONG WITH THIS.
TAKE A LOOK.
THEY'RE LYING ABOUT THE NUMBER OF STUDENTS AND OUR RANKING.
RANKING
65
Total Students: 1,500
Boys: 783
Girls: 717
We don't have this many students.
AND...
HUH?
THIS PHOTO...
Digging Up Potatoes
Huh?
PHOTO?
OH!
OH!
THEY'RE SUPPOSED TO BE DIGGING UP POTATOES...
...BUT THEY'RE DIGGING UP DAIKON RADISHES!
DIG UP POTATOES!
No.
THAT'S NOT THE POINT.
LISTEN.
THAT'S NOT WHAT I'M TALKING ABOUT.
SHUP
OH.
I SEE.

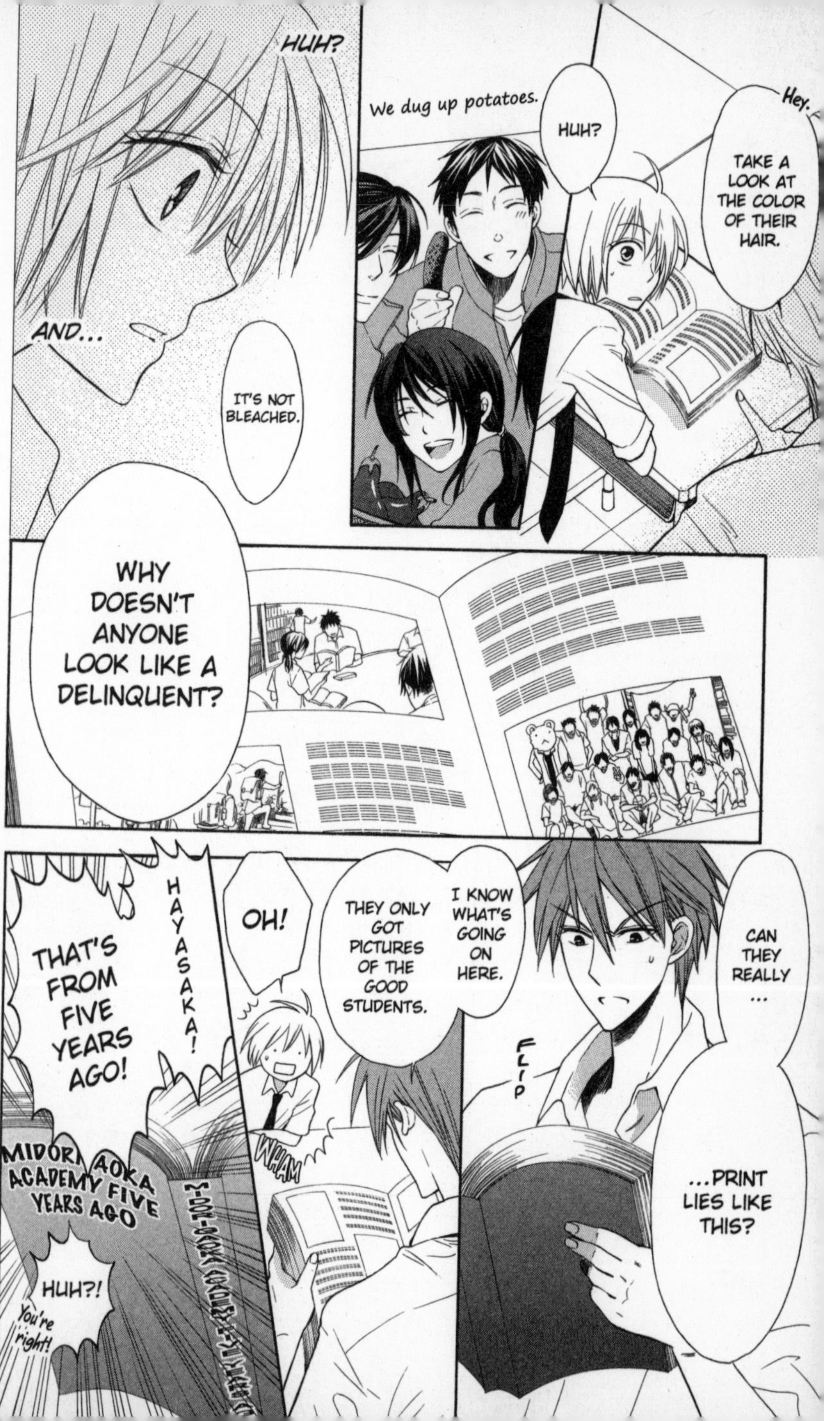
Hey.
TAKE A LOOK AT THE COLOR OF THEIR HAIR.
HUH?
We dug up potatoes.
HUH?
IT'S NOT BLEACHED.
AND...
WHY DOESN'T ANYONE LOOK LIKE A DELINQUENT?
CAN THEY REALLY...
...PRINT LIES LIKE THIS?
FLIP
I KNOW WHAT'S GOING ON HERE.
THEY ONLY GOT PICTURES OF THE GOOD STUDENTS.
OH!
HAYASAKA!
WHAM
THAT'S FROM FIVE YEARS AGO!
MIDORI AOKA ACADEMY FIVE YEARS AGO
HUH?!
You're right!

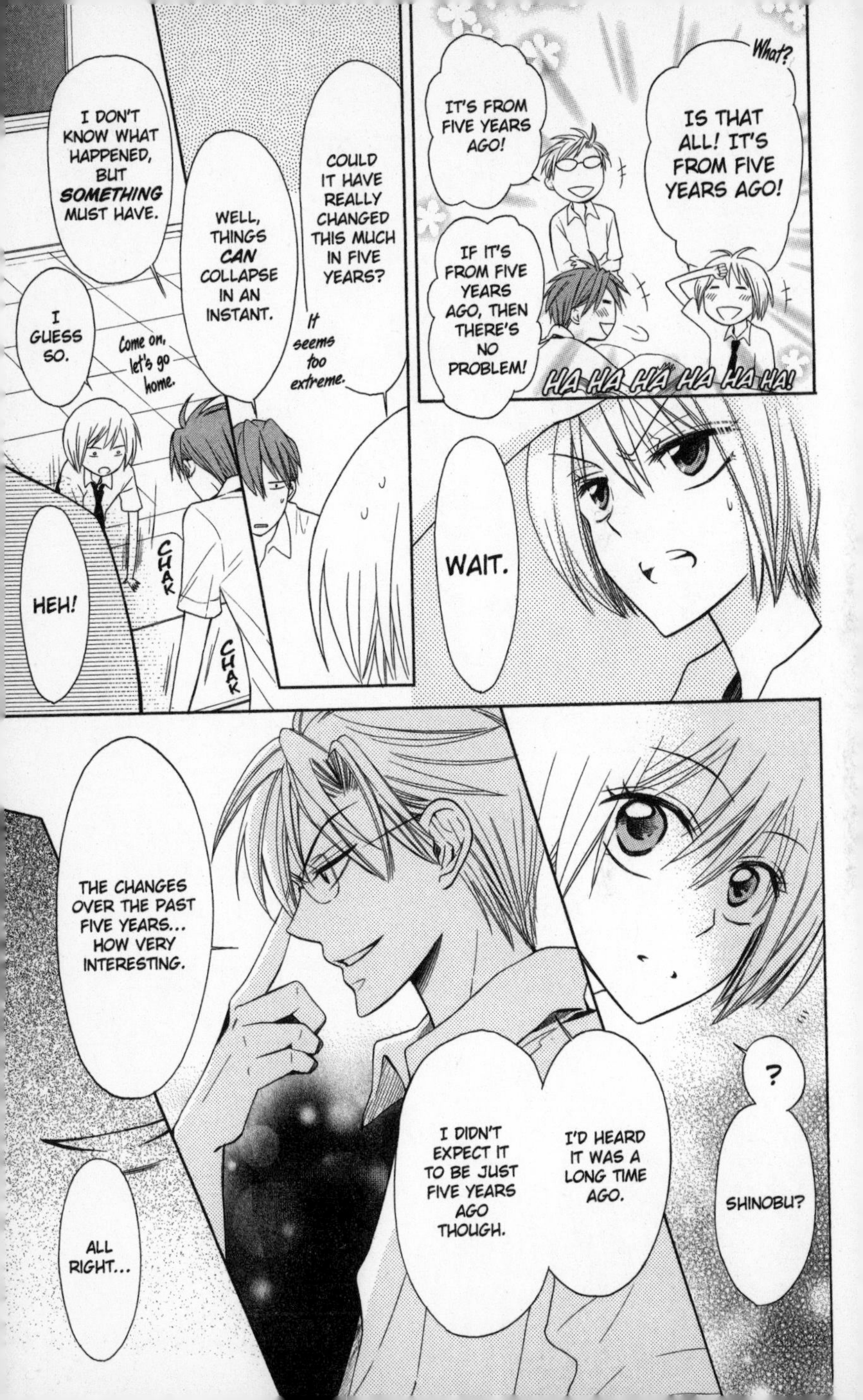
What?
IS THAT ALL! IT'S FROM FIVE YEARS AGO!
IT'S FROM FIVE YEARS AGO!
IF IT'S FROM FIVE YEARS AGO, THEN THERE'S NO PROBLEM!
HA HA HA HA HA HA!
COULD IT HAVE REALLY CHANGED THIS MUCH IN FIVE YEARS?
It seems too extreme.
WELL, THINGS CAN COLLAPSE IN AN INSTANT.
I DON'T KNOW WHAT HAPPENED, BUT SOMETHING MUST HAVE.
I GUESS SO.
Come on, let's go home.
CHAK
CHAK
HEH!
WAIT.
?
SHINOBU?
I'D HEARD IT WAS A LONG TIME AGO.
I DIDN'T EXPECT IT TO BE JUST FIVE YEARS AGO THOUGH.
THE CHANGES OVER THE PAST FIVE YEARS... HOW VERY INTERESTING.
ALL RIGHT...

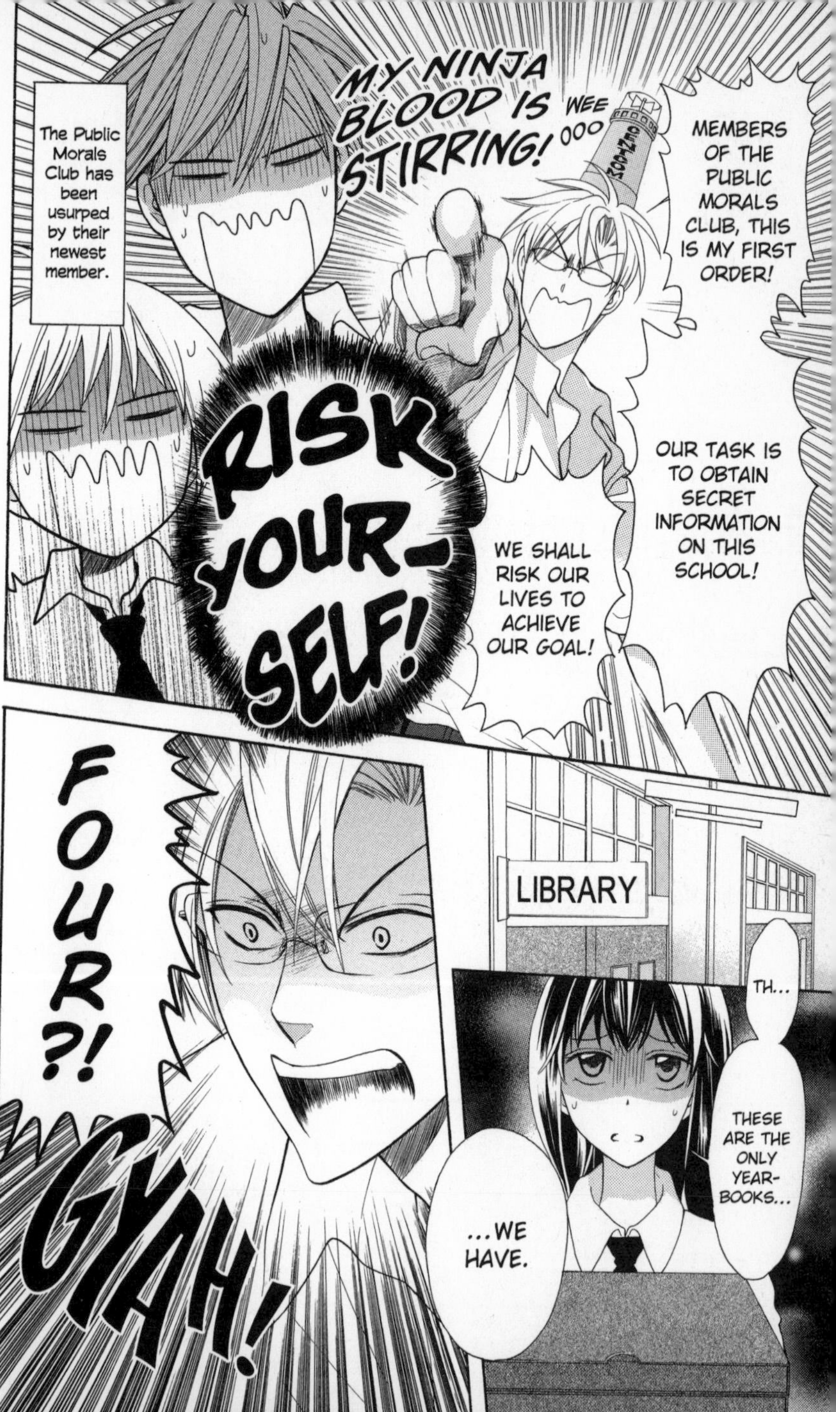
MEMBERS OF THE PUBLIC MORALS CLUB, THIS IS MY FIRST ORDER!
WEE OOO
MY NINJA BLOOD IS STIRRING!
The Public Morals Club has been usurped by their newest member.
OUR TASK IS TO OBTAIN SECRET INFORMATION ON THIS SCHOOL!
WE SHALL RISK OUR LIVES TO ACHIEVE OUR GOAL!
RISK YOUR-SELF!
LIBRARY
TH...
THESE ARE THE ONLY YEAR-BOOKS...
...WE HAVE.
FOUR?!
GYAH!

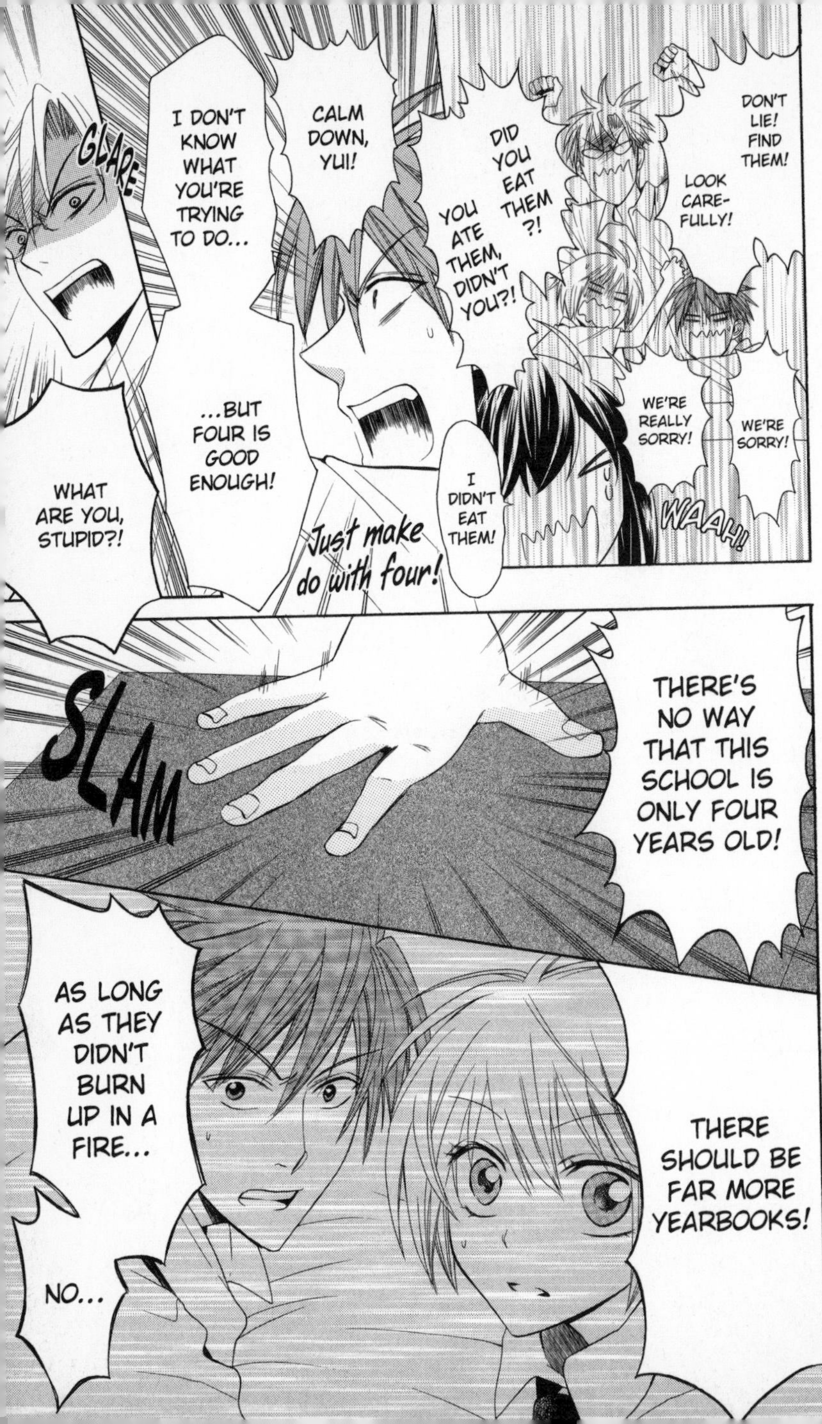
DON'T LIE! FIND THEM!
LOOK CARE-FULLY!
DID YOU EAT THEM?!
YOU ATE THEM, DIDN'T YOU?!
WE'RE SORRY!
WE'RE REALLY SORRY!
WAAAH!
I DIDN'T EAT THEM!
CALM DOWN, YUI!
Just make do with four!
I DON'T KNOW WHAT YOU'RE TRYING TO DO...
...BUT FOUR IS GOOD ENOUGH!
GLARE
WHAT ARE YOU, STUPID?!
THERE'S NO WAY THAT THIS SCHOOL IS ONLY FOUR YEARS OLD!
SLAM
THERE SHOULD BE FAR MORE YEARBOOKS!
AS LONG AS THEY DIDN'T BURN UP IN A FIRE...
NO...

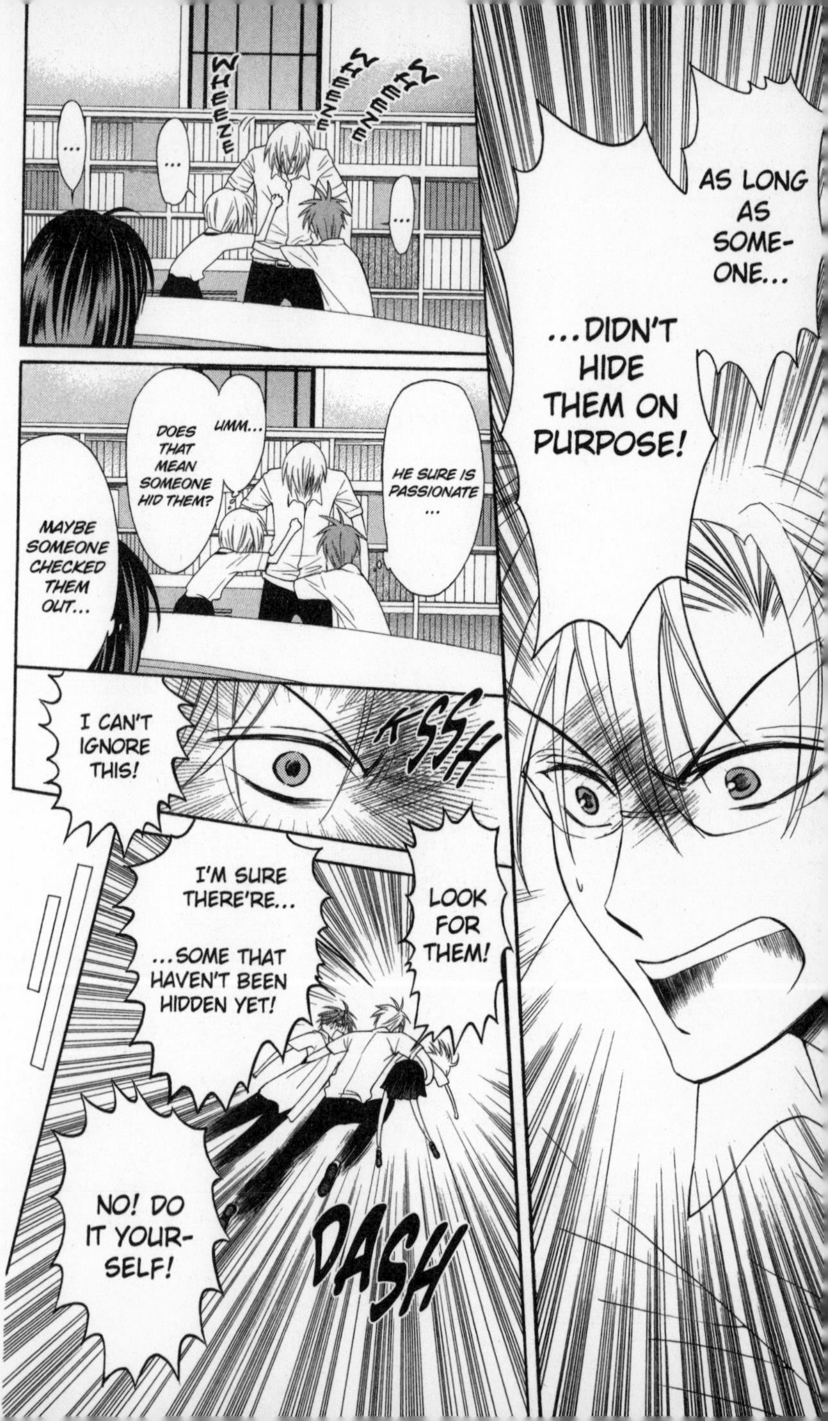
AS LONG AS SOME-ONE...
...DIDN'T HIDE THEM ON PURPOSE!
WHEEZE
WHEEZE
WHEEZE
...
...
...
HE SURE IS PASSIONATE ...
UMM...
DOES THAT MEAN SOMEONE HID THEM?
MAYBE SOMEONE CHECKED THEM OUT...
KSSH
I CAN'T IGNORE THIS!
LOOK FOR THEM!
I'M SURE THERE'RE...
...SOME THAT HAVEN'T BEEN HIDDEN YET!
NO! DO IT YOUR-SELF!
DASH

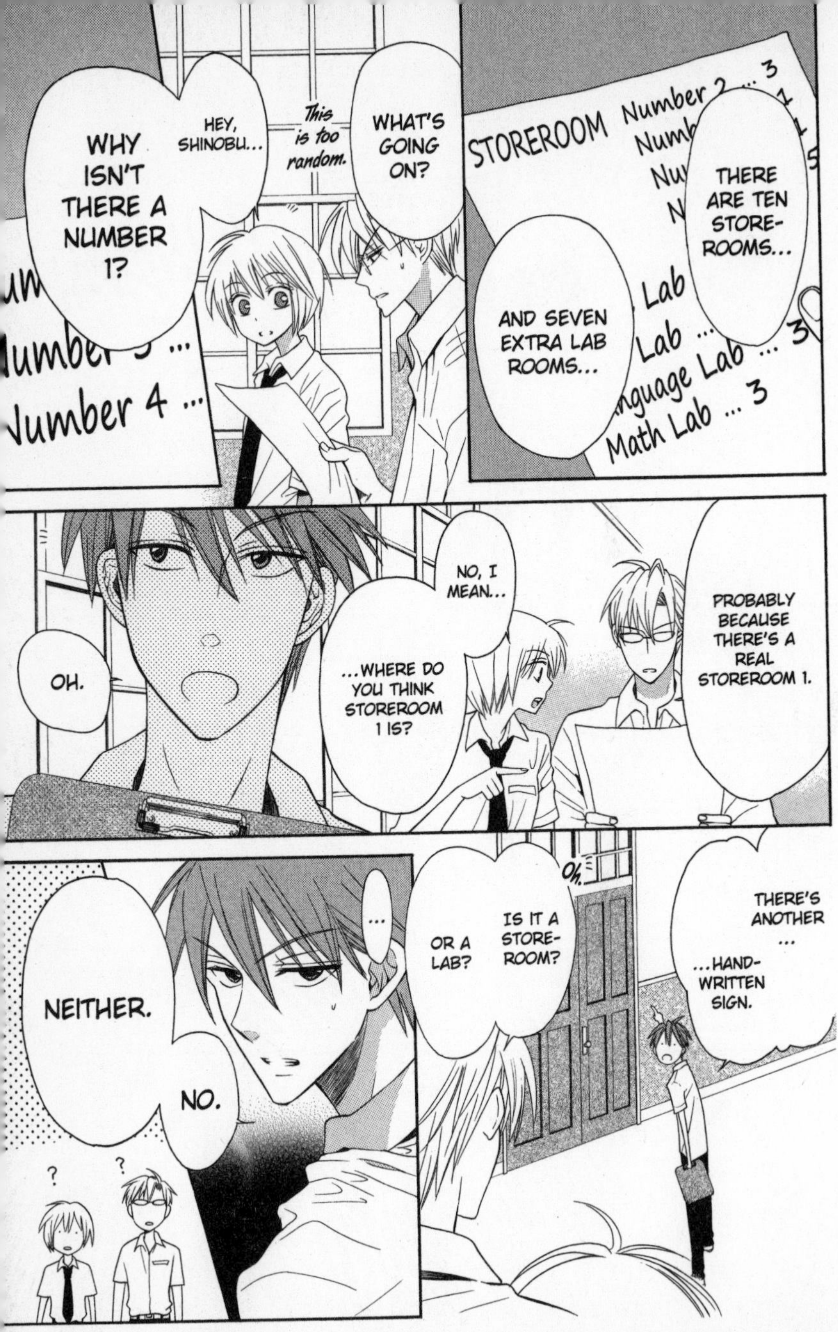
STOREROOM Number 2 ... 3
THERE ARE TEN STOREROOMS...
AND SEVEN EXTRA LAB ROOMS...
Math Lab ... 3
WHAT'S GOING ON?
This is too random.
HEY, SHINOBU...
WHY ISN'T THERE A NUMBER 1?
Number 4 ...
PROBABLY BECAUSE THERE'S A REAL STOREROOM 1.
NO, I MEAN...
...WHERE DO YOU THINK STOREROOM 1 IS?
OH.
THERE'S ANOTHER ...
...HAND-WRITTEN SIGN.
Oh.
IS IT A STOREROOM?
OR A LAB?
...
NEITHER.
NO.
?
?

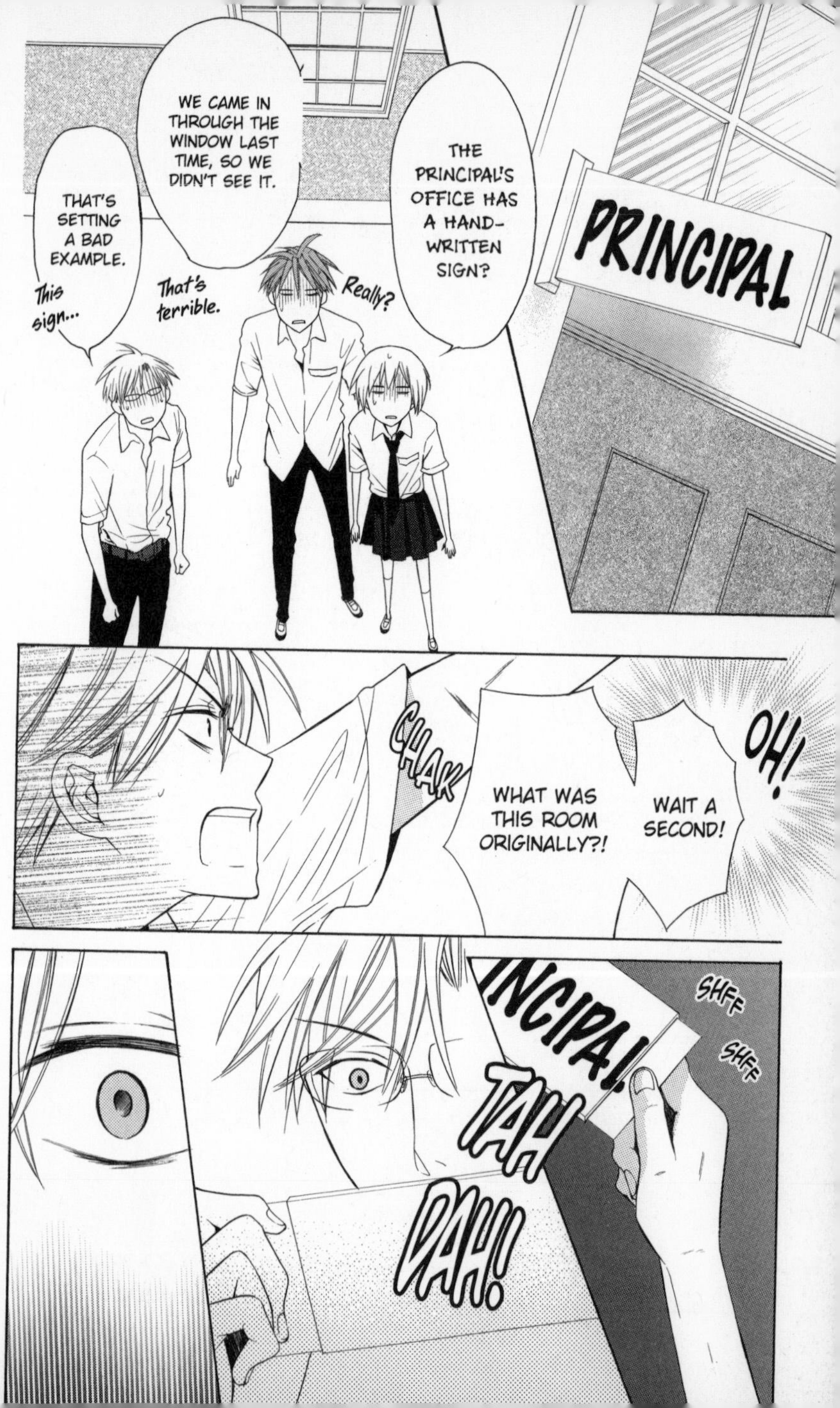
PRINCIPAL
THE PRINCIPAL'S OFFICE HAS A HAND-WRITTEN SIGN?
Really?
WE CAME IN THROUGH THE WINDOW LAST TIME, SO WE DIDN'T SEE IT.
That's terrible.
THAT'S SETTING A BAD EXAMPLE.
This sign...
OH!
WAIT A SECOND!
WHAT WAS THIS ROOM ORIGINALLY?!
CHAK
SHFF
SHFF
INCIPAL
TAH DAH!

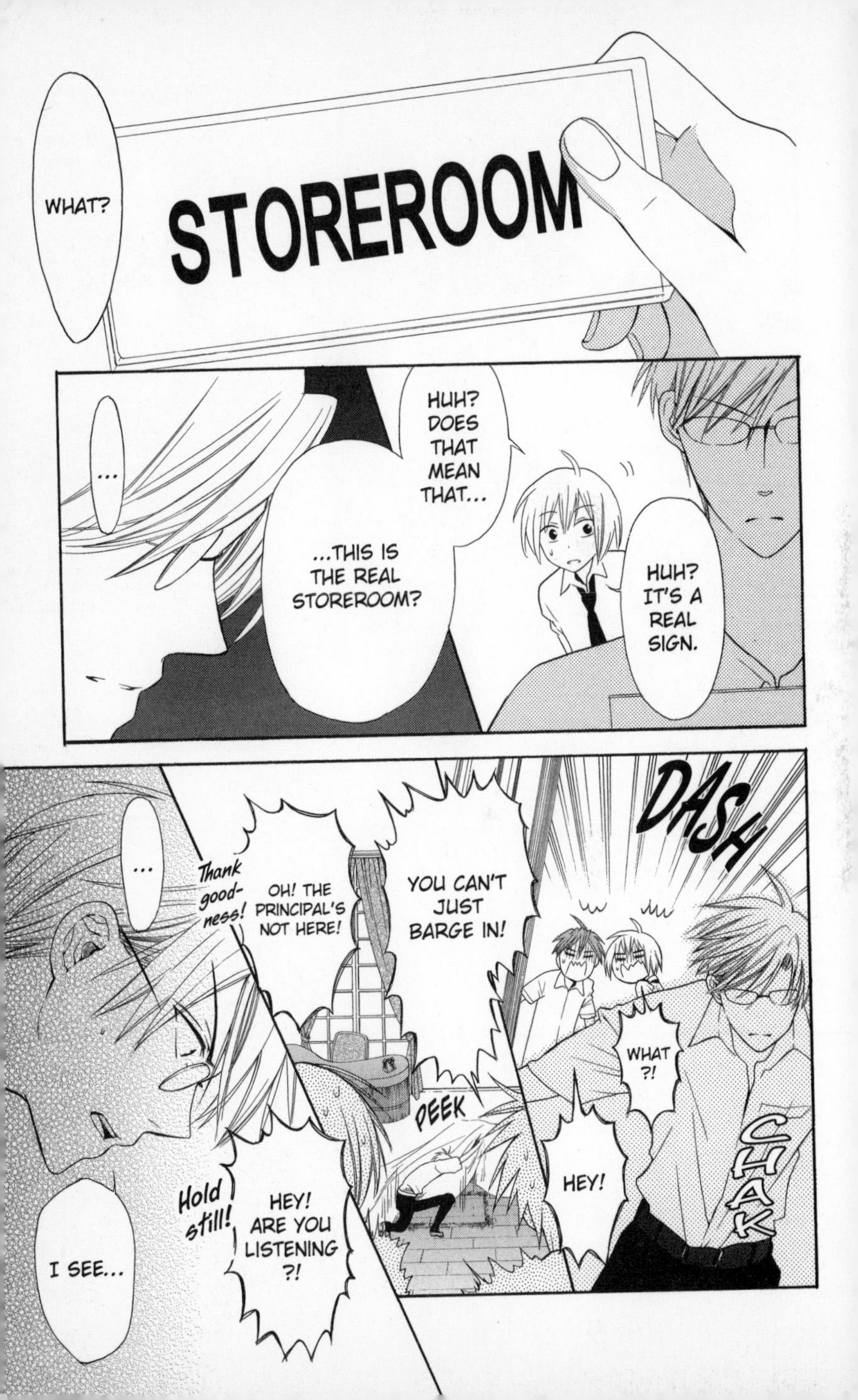
STOREROOM
WHAT?
HUH? IT'S A REAL SIGN.
HUH? DOES THAT MEAN THAT...
...THIS IS THE REAL STOREROOM?
...
DASH
WHAT ?!
CHAK
HEY!
YOU CAN'T JUST BARGE IN!
OH! THE PRINCIPAL'S NOT HERE!
Thank goodness!
PEEK
HEY! ARE YOU LISTENING ?!
Hold still!
...
I SEE...

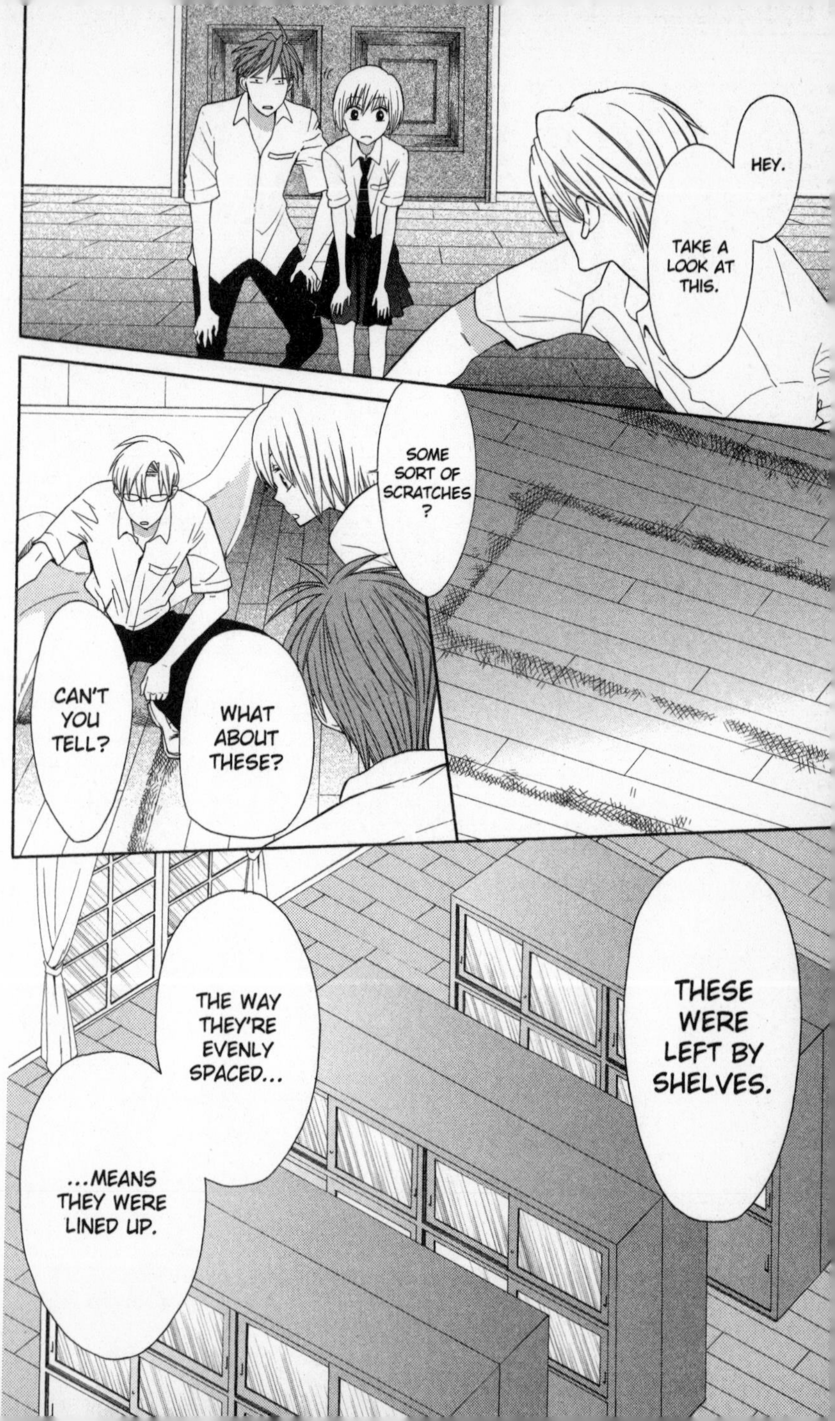
HEY.
TAKE A LOOK AT THIS.
SOME SORT OF SCRATCHES?
WHAT ABOUT THESE?
CAN'T YOU TELL?
THESE WERE LEFT BY SHELVES.
THE WAY THEY'RE EVENLY SPACED...
...MEANS THEY WERE LINED UP.

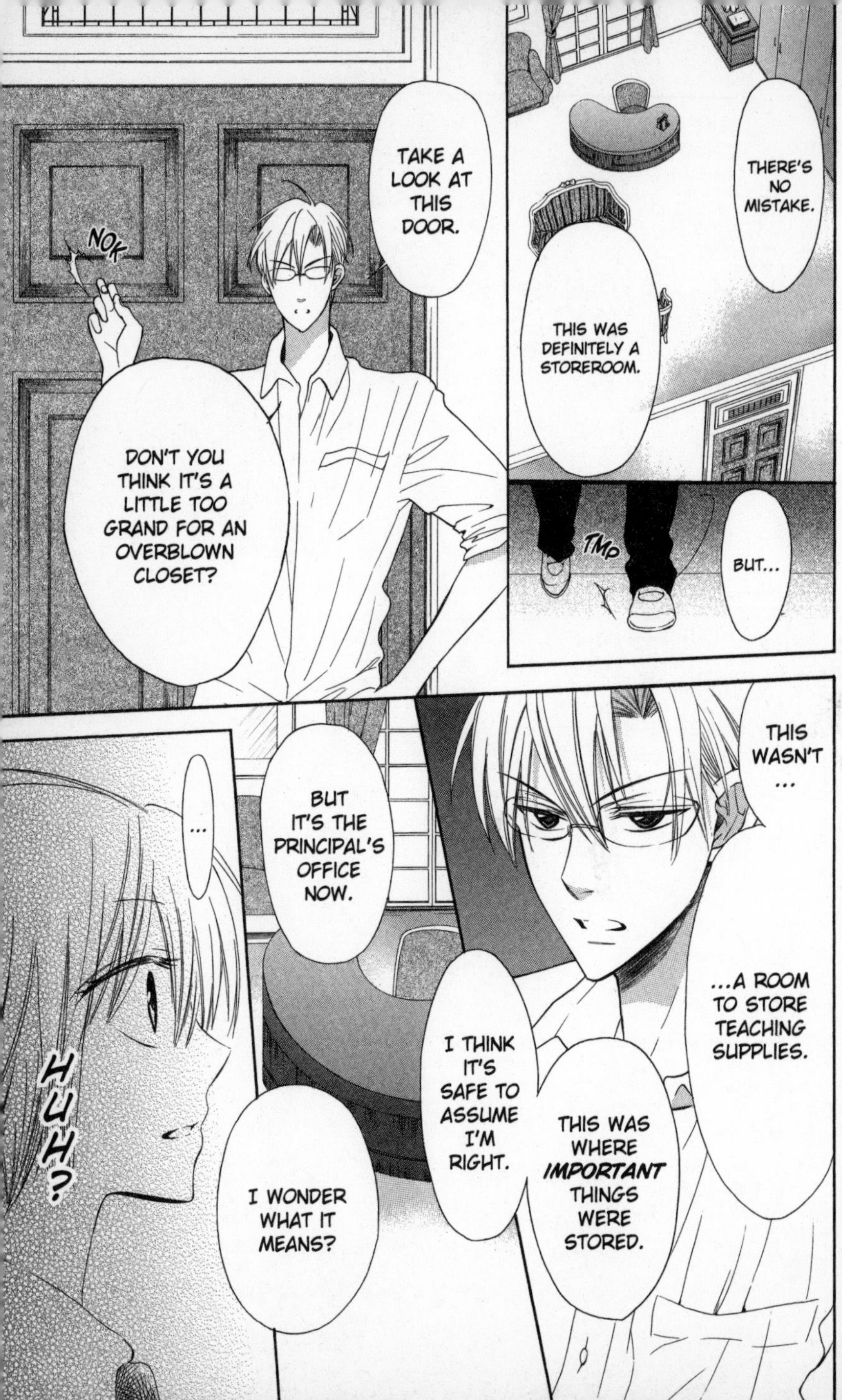
THERE'S NO MISTAKE.
THIS WAS DEFINITELY A STOREROOM.
TMP
BUT...
TAKE A LOOK AT THIS DOOR.
NOK
DON'T YOU THINK IT'S A LITTLE TOO GRAND FOR AN OVERBLOWN CLOSET?
THIS WASN'T ...
...A ROOM TO STORE TEACHING SUPPLIES.
BUT IT'S THE PRINCIPAL'S OFFICE NOW.
THIS WAS WHERE *IMPORTANT* THINGS WERE STORED.
I THINK IT'S SAFE TO ASSUME I'M RIGHT.
...
HUH?
I WONDER WHAT IT MEANS?

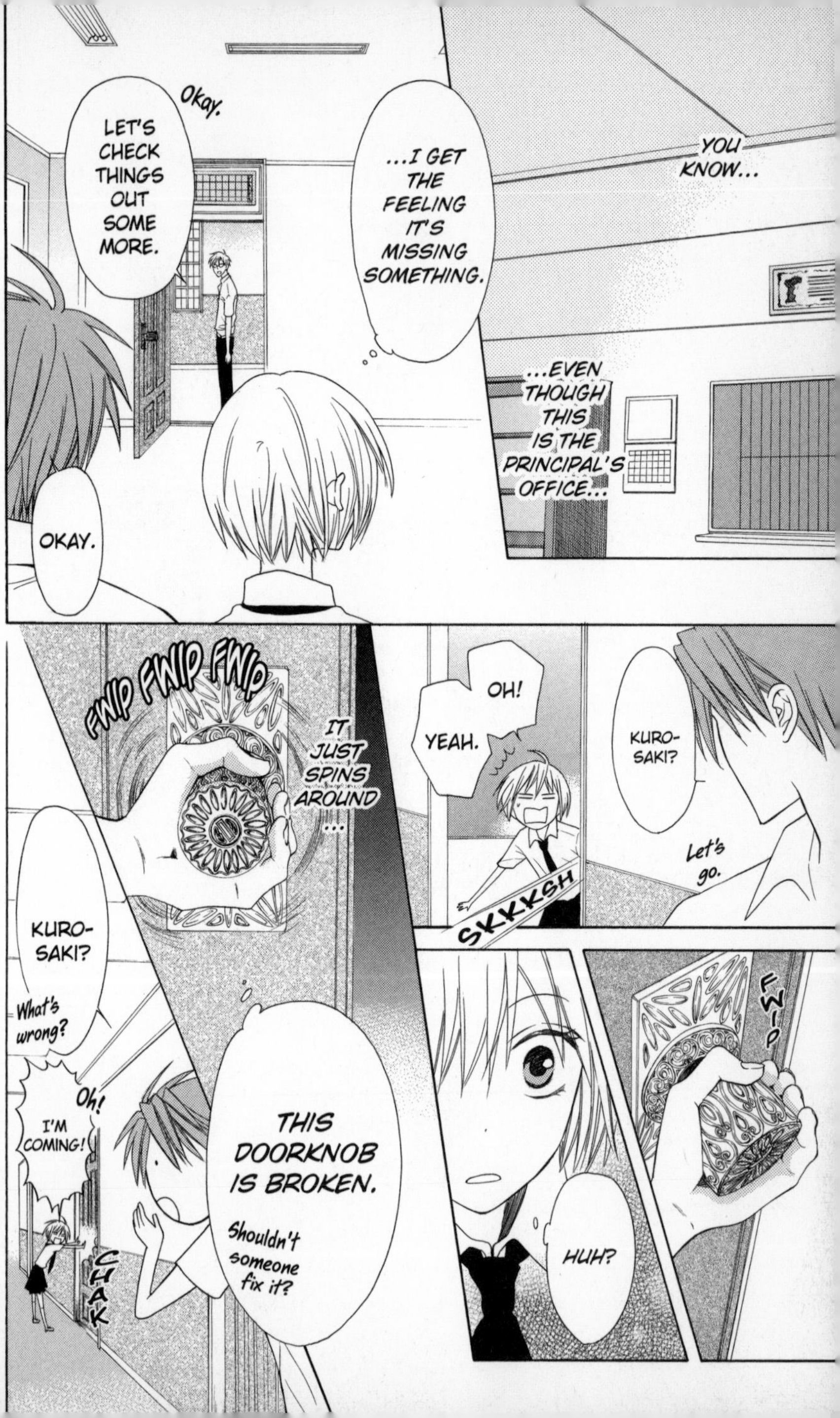
YOU KNOW...
...EVEN THOUGH THIS IS THE PRINCIPAL'S OFFICE...
...I GET THE FEELING IT'S MISSING SOMETHING.
Okay.
LET'S CHECK THINGS OUT SOME MORE.
OKAY.
KURO-SAKI?
Let's go.
OH!
YEAH.
SKKKSH
FWIP
HUH?
FWIP FWIP FWIP
IT JUST SPINS AROUND...
THIS DOORKNOB IS BROKEN.
Shouldn't someone fix it?
KURO-SAKI?
What's wrong?
Oh!
I'M COMING!
CHAK

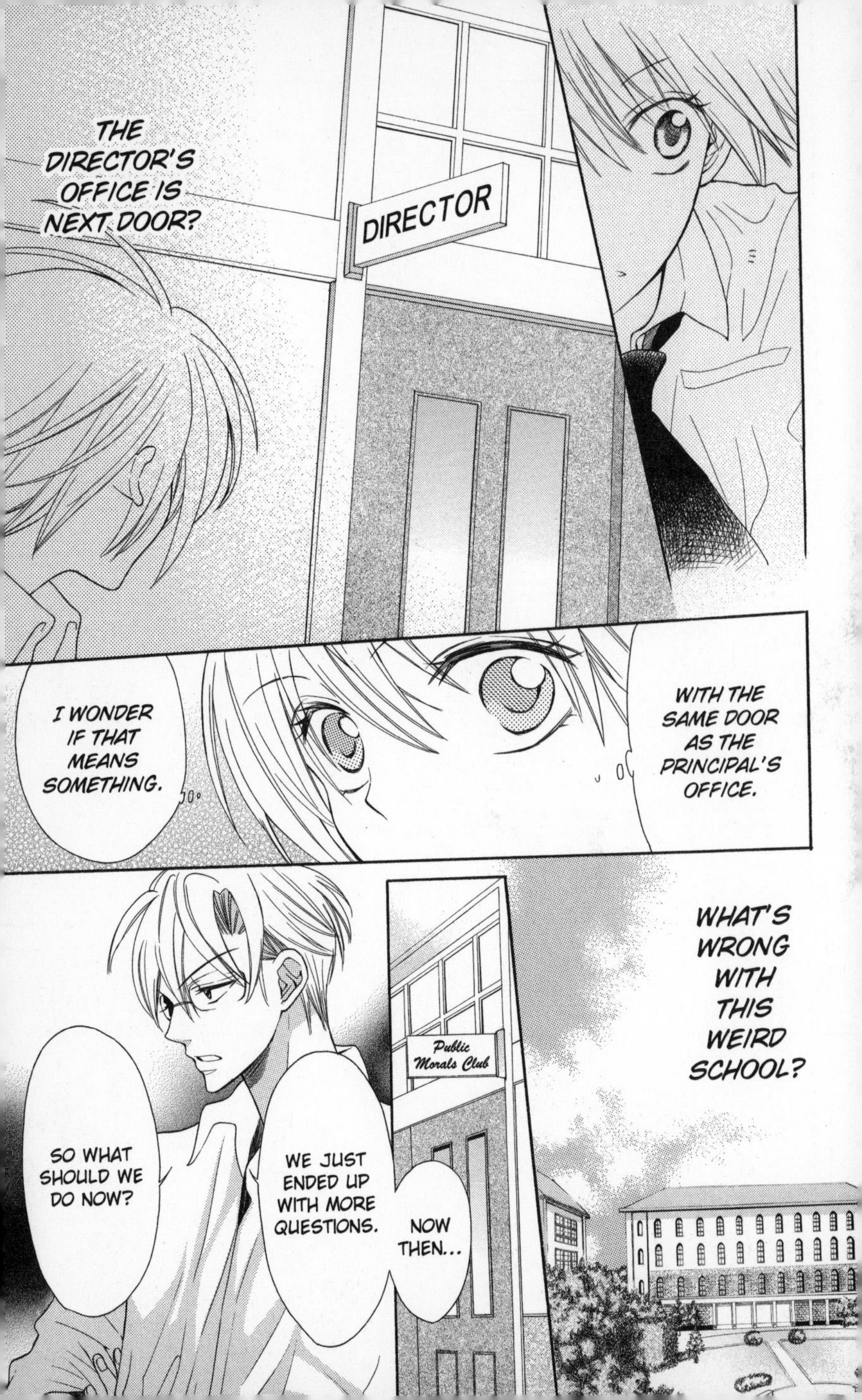
DIRECTOR
THE DIRECTOR'S OFFICE IS NEXT DOOR?
WITH THE SAME DOOR AS THE PRINCIPAL'S OFFICE.
I WONDER IF THAT MEANS SOMETHING.
WHAT'S WRONG WITH THIS WEIRD SCHOOL?
Public Morals Club
NOW THEN...
WE JUST ENDED UP WITH MORE QUESTIONS.
SO WHAT SHOULD WE DO NOW?

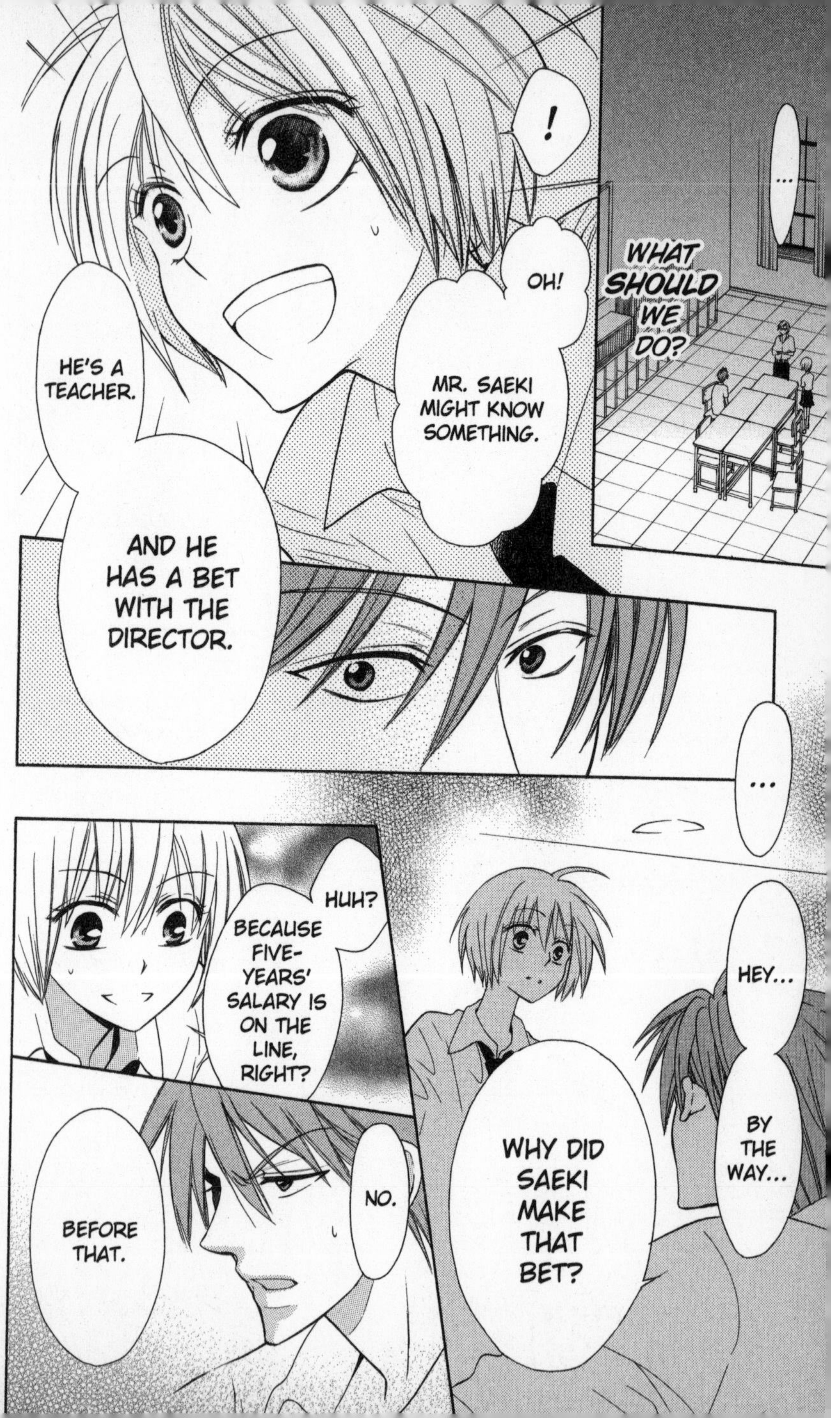

...
WHAT SHOULD WE DO?
!
OH!
MR. SAEKI MIGHT KNOW SOMETHING.
HE'S A TEACHER.
AND HE HAS A BET WITH THE DIRECTOR.
...
HEY...
BY THE WAY...
WHY DID SAEKI MAKE THAT BET?
HUH?
BECAUSE FIVE-YEARS' SALARY IS ON THE LINE, RIGHT?
NO.
BEFORE THAT.

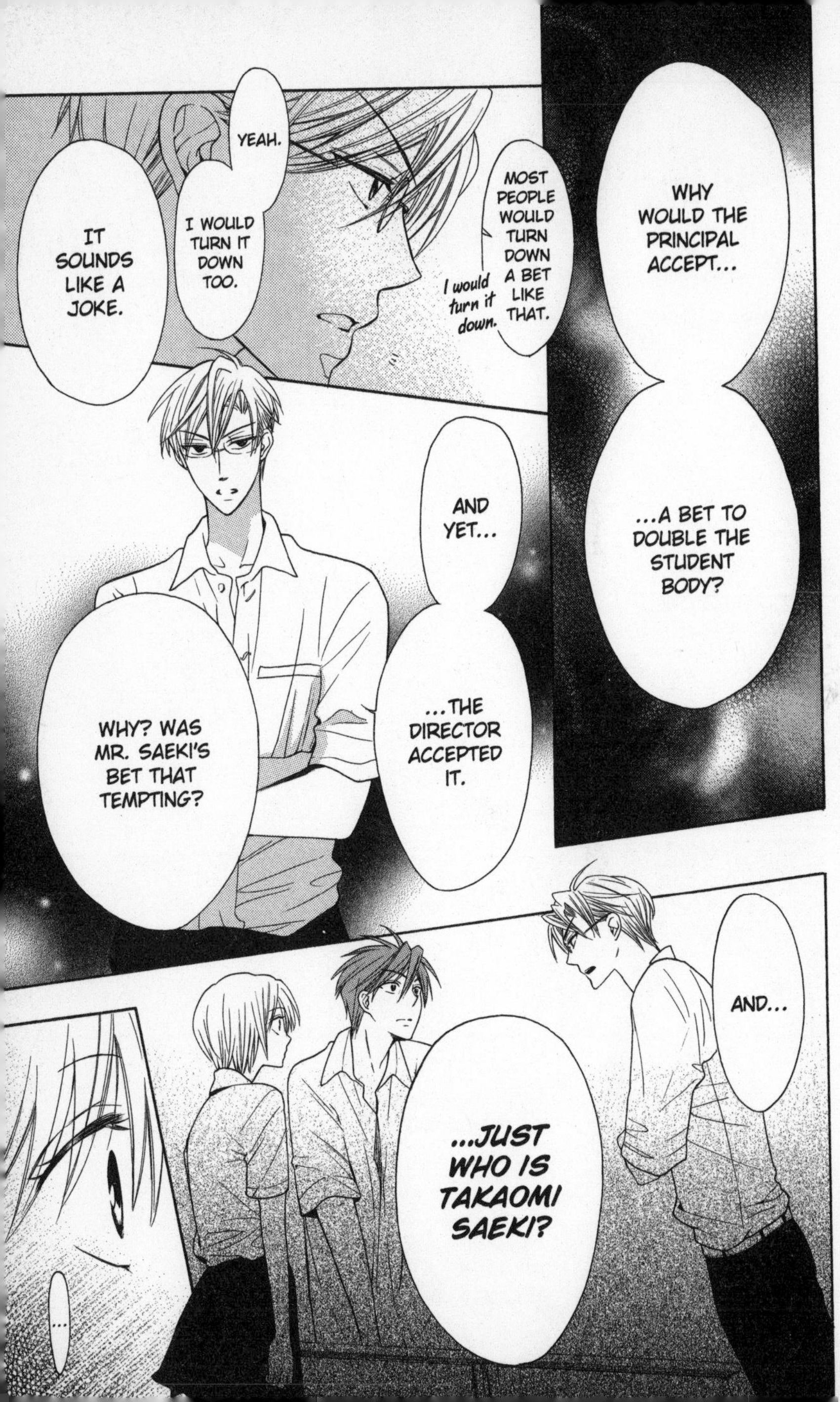
WHY WOULD THE PRINCIPAL ACCEPT...
...A BET TO DOUBLE THE STUDENT BODY?
MOST PEOPLE WOULD TURN DOWN A BET LIKE THAT.
I would turn it down.
YEAH.
I WOULD TURN IT DOWN TOO.
IT SOUNDS LIKE A JOKE.
AND YET...
...THE DIRECTOR ACCEPTED IT.
WHY? WAS MR. SAEKI'S BET THAT TEMPTING?
AND...
...JUST WHO IS TAKAOMI SAEKI?
...

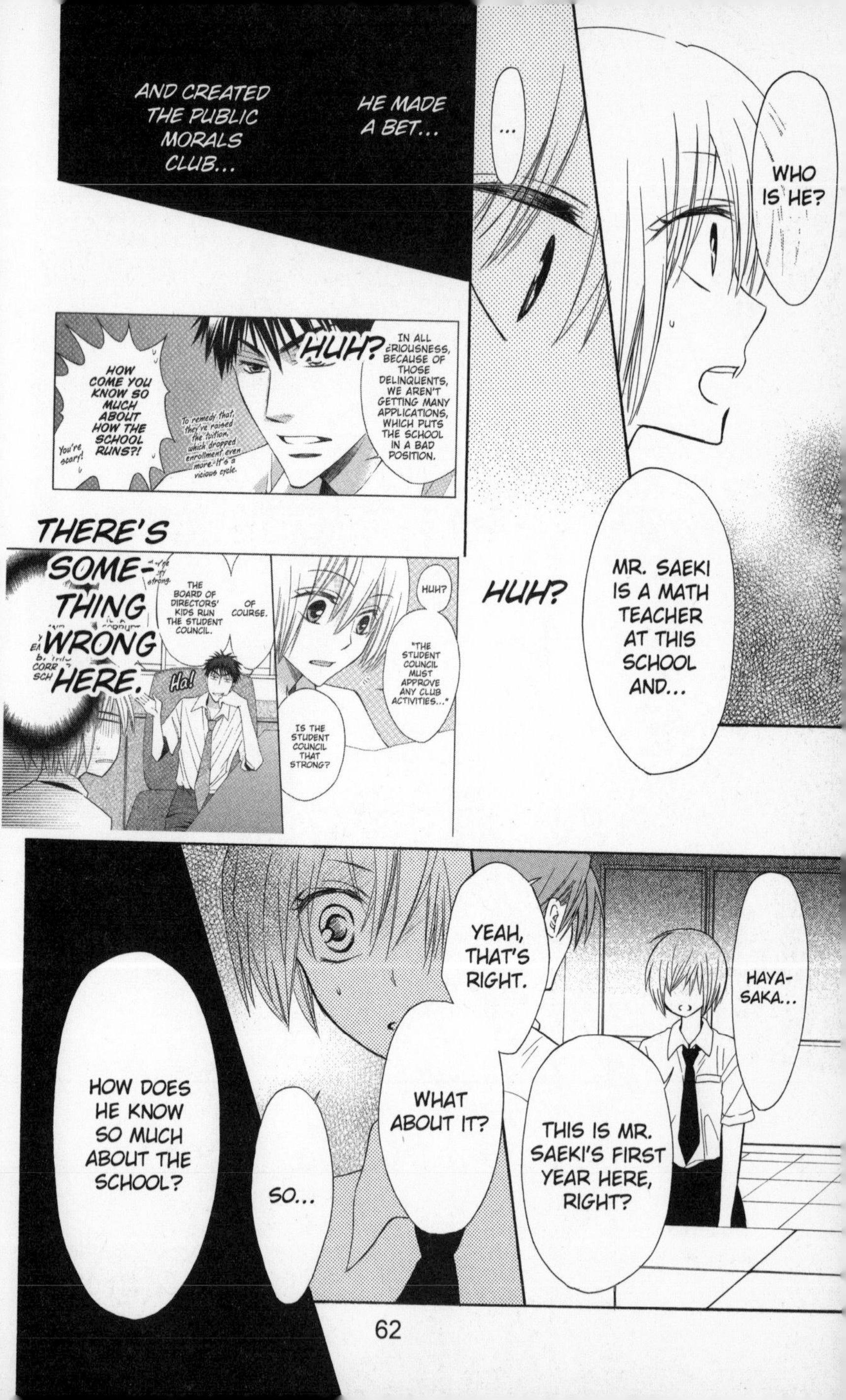
WHO IS HE?
...
HUH?
MR. SAEKI IS A MATH TEACHER AT THIS SCHOOL AND...
HE MADE A BET...
AND CREATED THE PUBLIC MORALS CLUB...
HUH?
IN ALL SERIOUSNESS, BECAUSE OF THOSE DELINQUENTS, WE AREN'T GETTING MANY APPLICATIONS, WHICH PUTS THE SCHOOL IN A BAD POSITION.
To remedy that, they've raised the tuition, which dropped enrollment even more. It's a vicious cycle.
HOW COME YOU KNOW SO MUCH ABOUT HOW THE SCHOOL RUNS?!
You're scary!
HUH?
"THE STUDENT COUNCIL MUST APPROVE ANY CLUB ACTIVITIES..."
IS THE STUDENT COUNCIL THAT STRONG?
OF COURSE.
THE BOARD OF DIRECTORS' KIDS RUN THE STUDENT COUNCIL.
Ha!
THERE'S SOMETHING WRONG HERE.
HAYA-SAKA...
THIS IS MR. SAEKI'S FIRST YEAR HERE, RIGHT?
YEAH, THAT'S RIGHT.
WHAT ABOUT IT?
SO...
HOW DOES HE KNOW SO MUCH ABOUT THE SCHOOL?

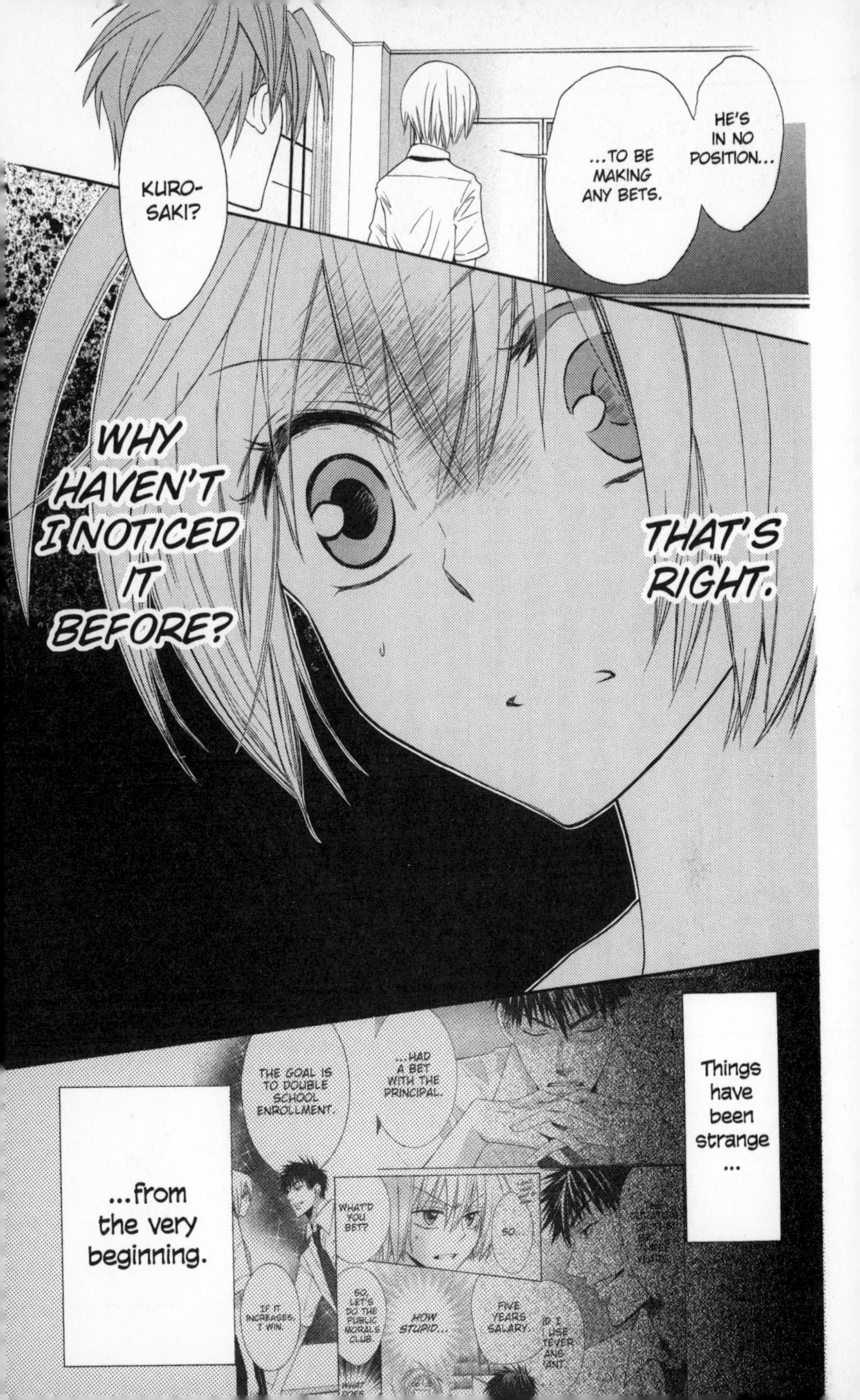
HE'S IN NO POSITION...
...TO BE MAKING ANY BETS.
KURO-SAKI?
THAT'S RIGHT.
WHY HAVEN'T I NOTICED IT BEFORE?
Things have been strange ...
...HAD A BET WITH THE PRINCIPAL.
THE GOAL IS TO DOUBLE SCHOOL ENROLLMENT.
SO.
WHAT'D YOU BET?
FIVE YEARS SALARY.
HOW STUPID...
SO, LET'S DO THE PUBLIC MORALS CLUB.
IF IT INCREASES, I WIN.
...from the very beginning.

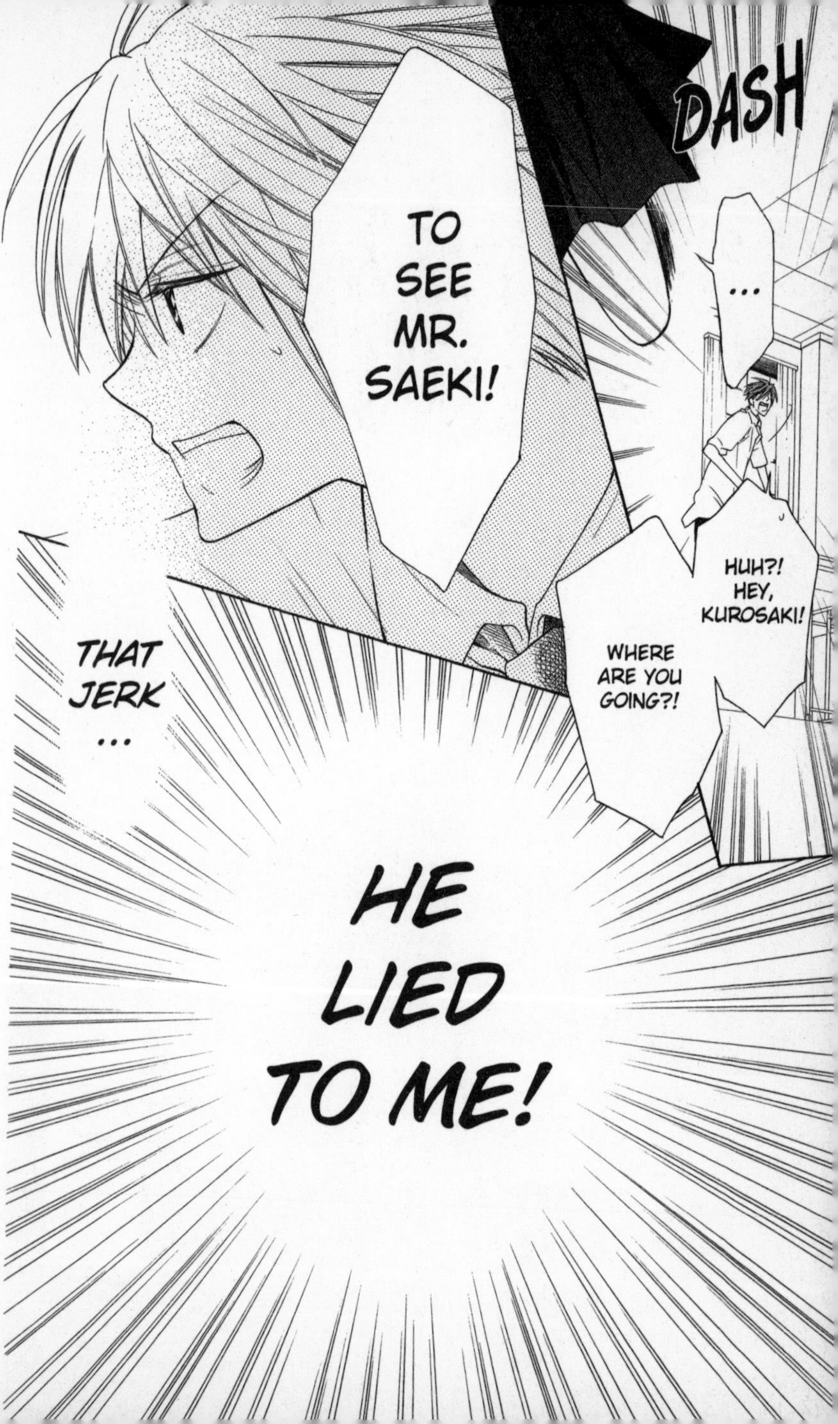
DASH
...
HUH?! HEY, KUROSAKI!
WHERE ARE YOU GOING?!
TO SEE MR. SAEKI!
THAT JERK ...
HE LIED TO ME!

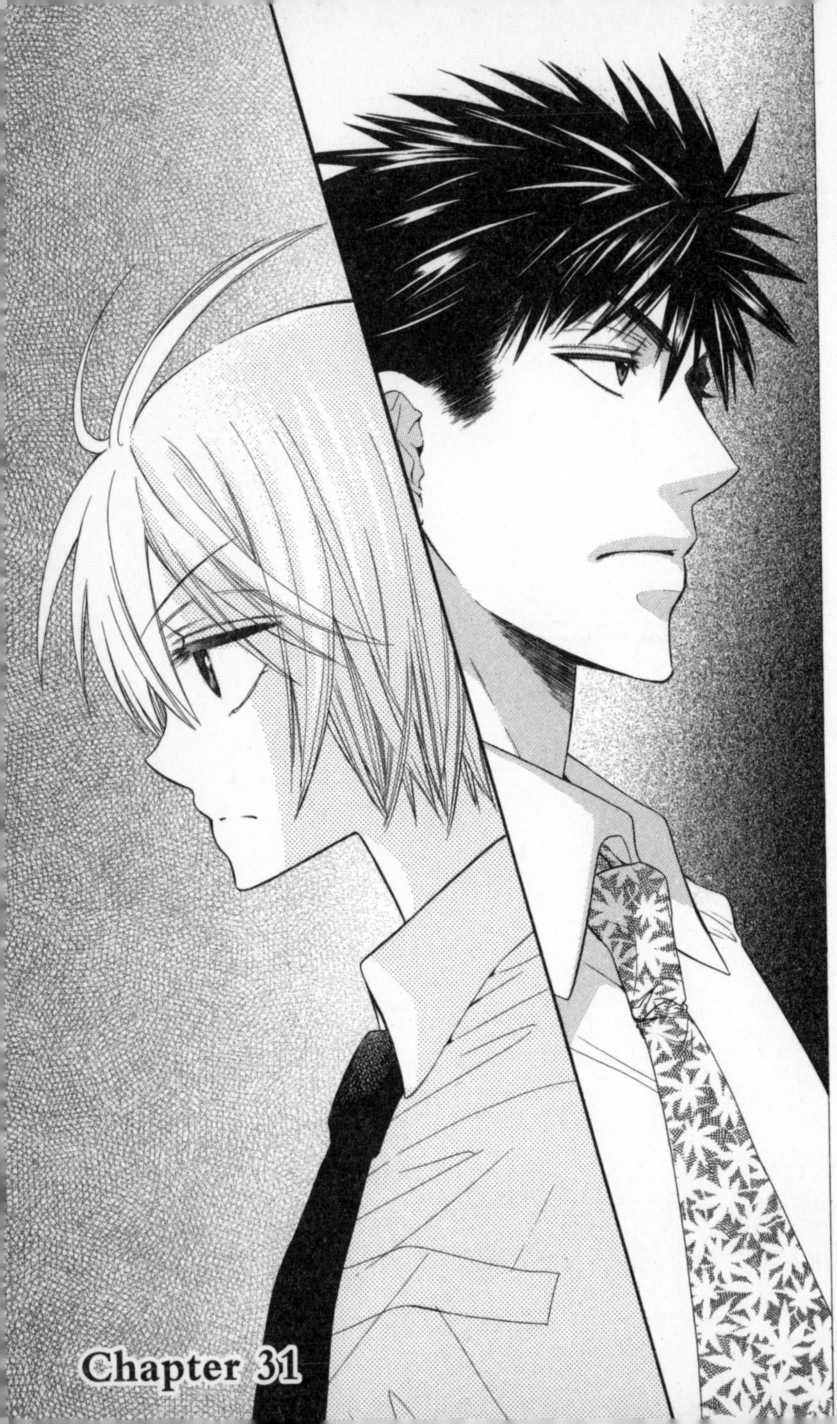

Chapter 31

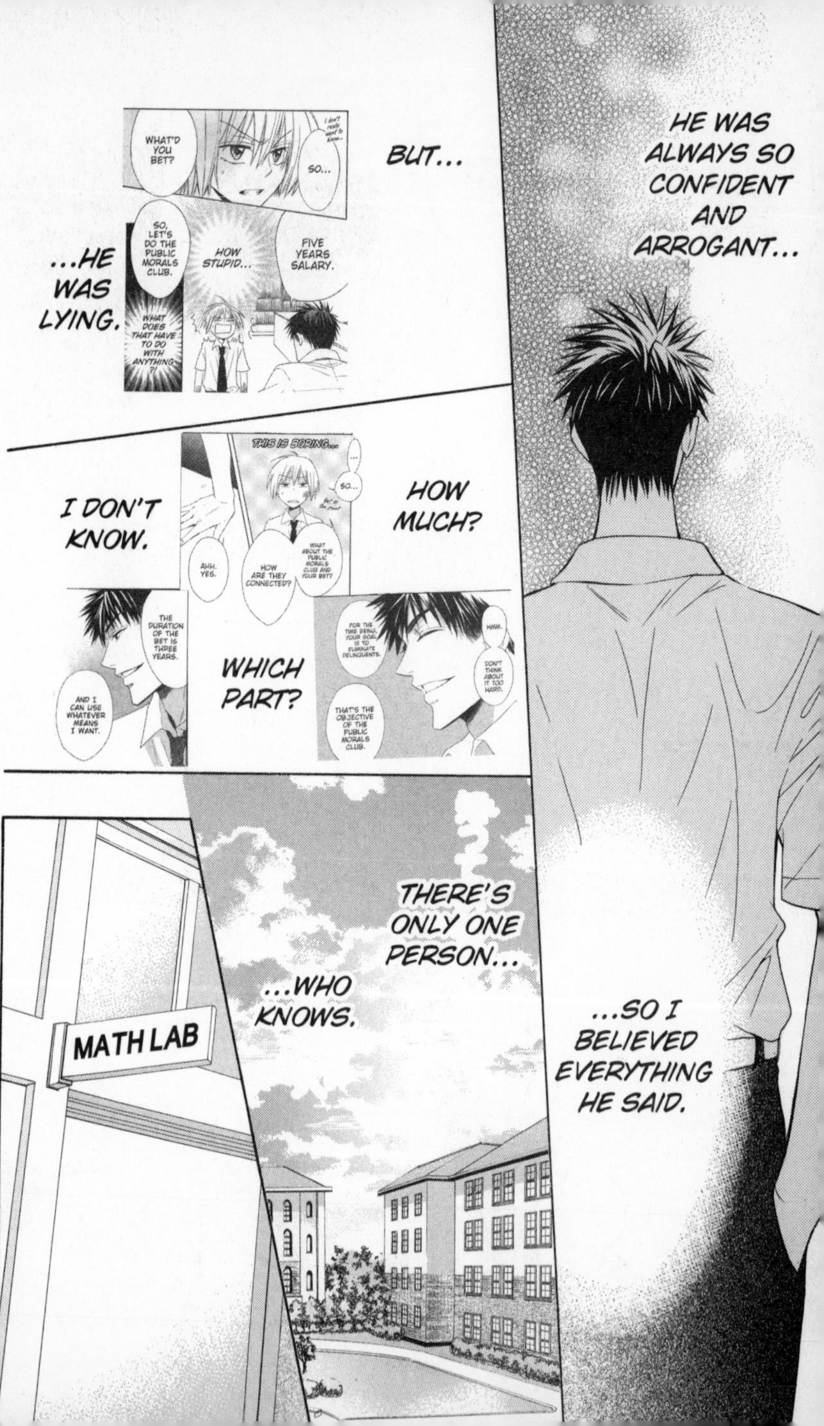
HE WAS ALWAYS SO CONFIDENT AND ARROGANT...
...SO I BELIEVED EVERYTHING HE SAID.
BUT...
I don't really want to know...
SO...
WHAT'D YOU BET?
FIVE YEARS SALARY.
HOW STUPID...
SO, LET'S DO THE PUBLIC MORALS CLUB.
WHAT DOES THAT HAVE TO DO WITH ANYTHING?!
...HE WAS LYING.
HOW MUCH?
...
SO...
Get to the point
THIS IS BORING...
WHAT ABOUT THE PUBLIC MORALS CLUB AND YOUR BET?
HOW ARE THEY CONNECTED?
AHH. YES.
I DON'T KNOW.
HMM.
DON'T THINK ABOUT IT TOO HARD.
FOR THE TIME BEING, YOUR GOAL IS TO ELIMINATE DELINQUENTS.
THAT'S THE OBJECTIVE OF THE PUBLIC MORALS CLUB.
WHICH PART?
THE DURATION OF THE BET IS THREE YEARS.
AND I CAN USE WHATEVER MEANS I WANT.
THERE'S ONLY ONE PERSON...
...WHO KNOWS.
MATH LAB

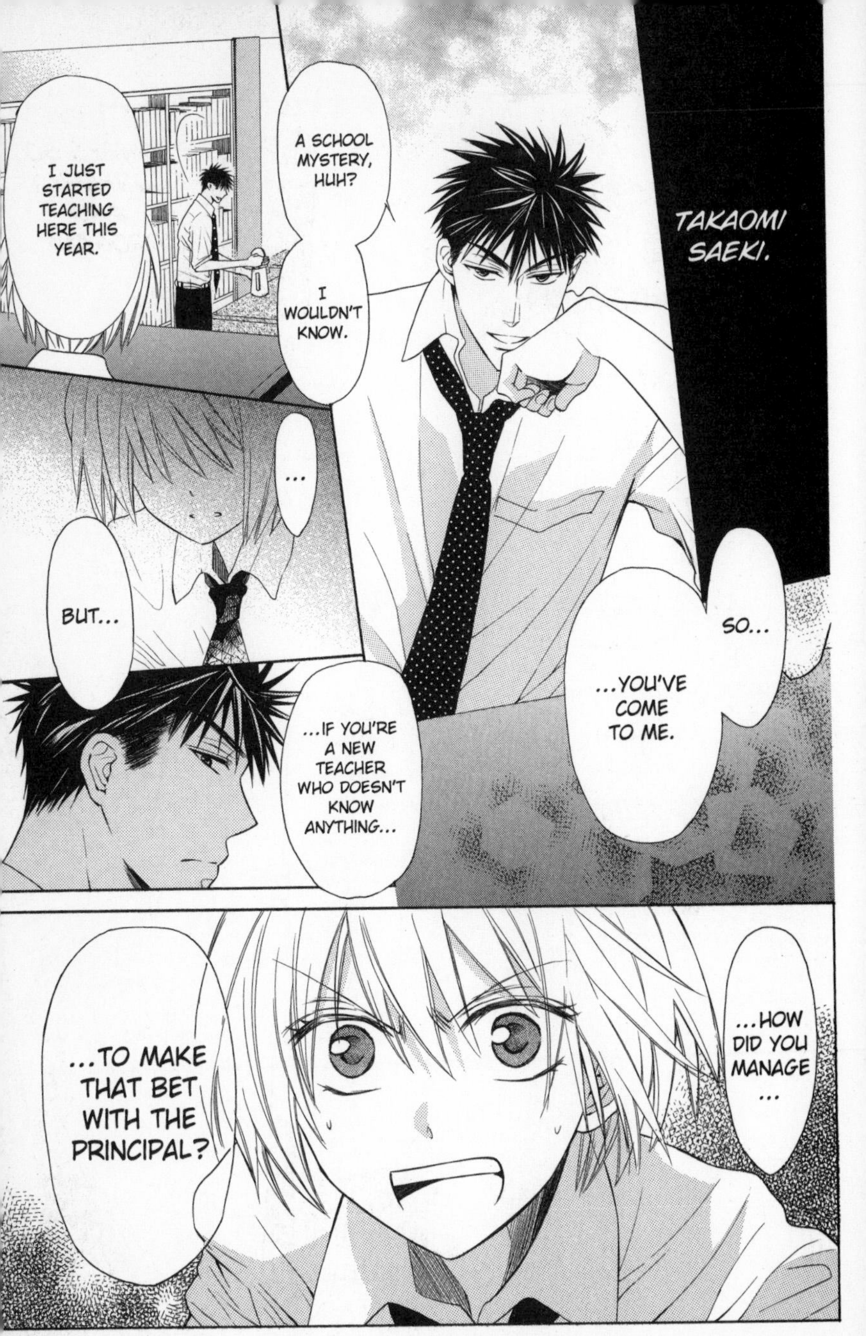
TAKAOMI SAEKI.
SO...
...YOU'VE COME TO ME.
A SCHOOL MYSTERY, HUH?
I WOULDN'T KNOW.
I JUST STARTED TEACHING HERE THIS YEAR.
...
BUT...
...IF YOU'RE A NEW TEACHER WHO DOESN'T KNOW ANYTHING...
...HOW DID YOU MANAGE...
...TO MAKE THAT BET WITH THE PRINCIPAL?

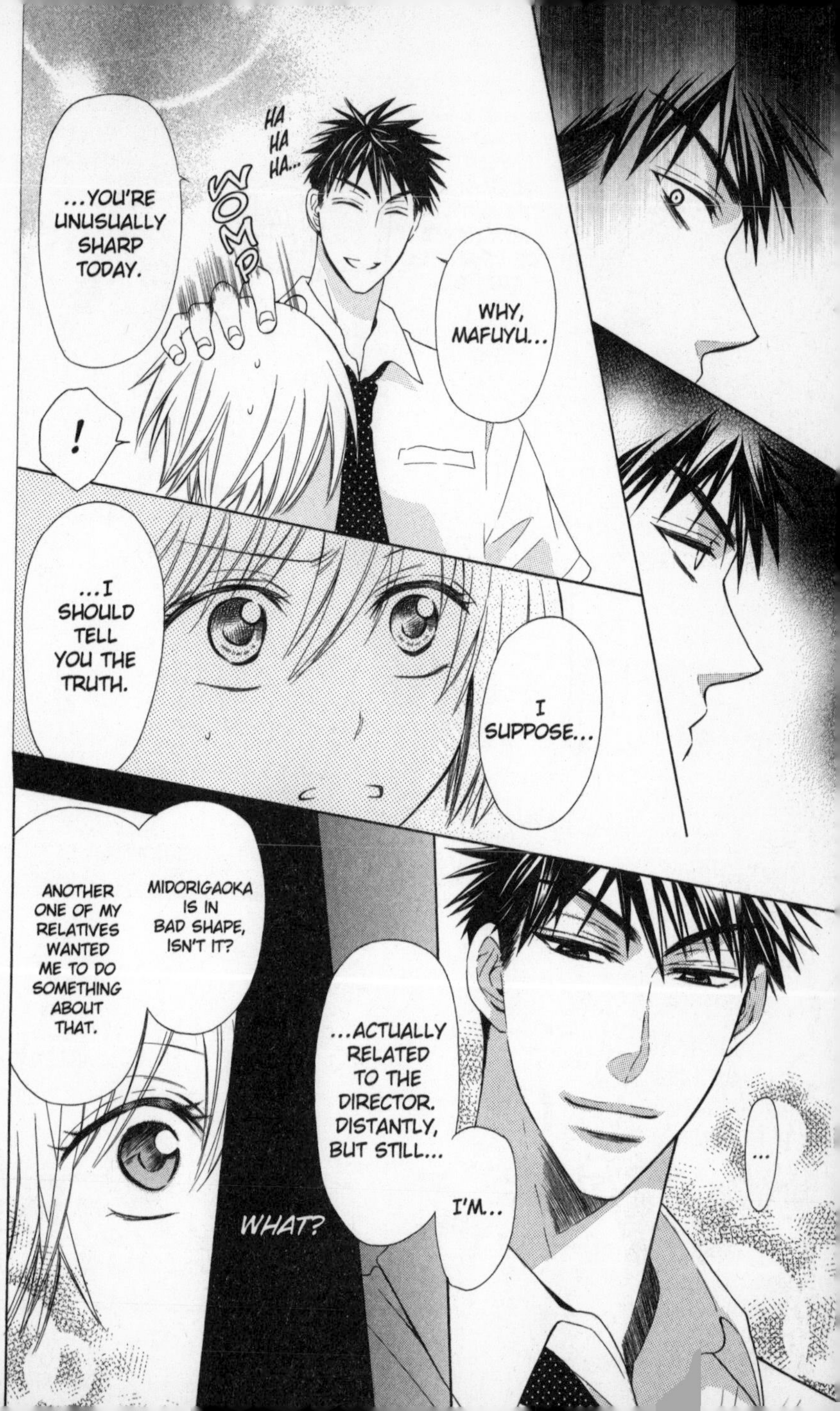
WHY, MAFUYU...
HA HA HA...
WOMP
...YOU'RE UNUSUALLY SHARP TODAY.
!
I SUPPOSE...
...I SHOULD TELL YOU THE TRUTH.
...
I'M...
...ACTUALLY RELATED TO THE DIRECTOR. DISTANTLY, BUT STILL...
WHAT?
MIDORIGAOKA IS IN BAD SHAPE, ISN'T IT?
ANOTHER ONE OF MY RELATIVES WANTED ME TO DO SOMETHING ABOUT THAT.

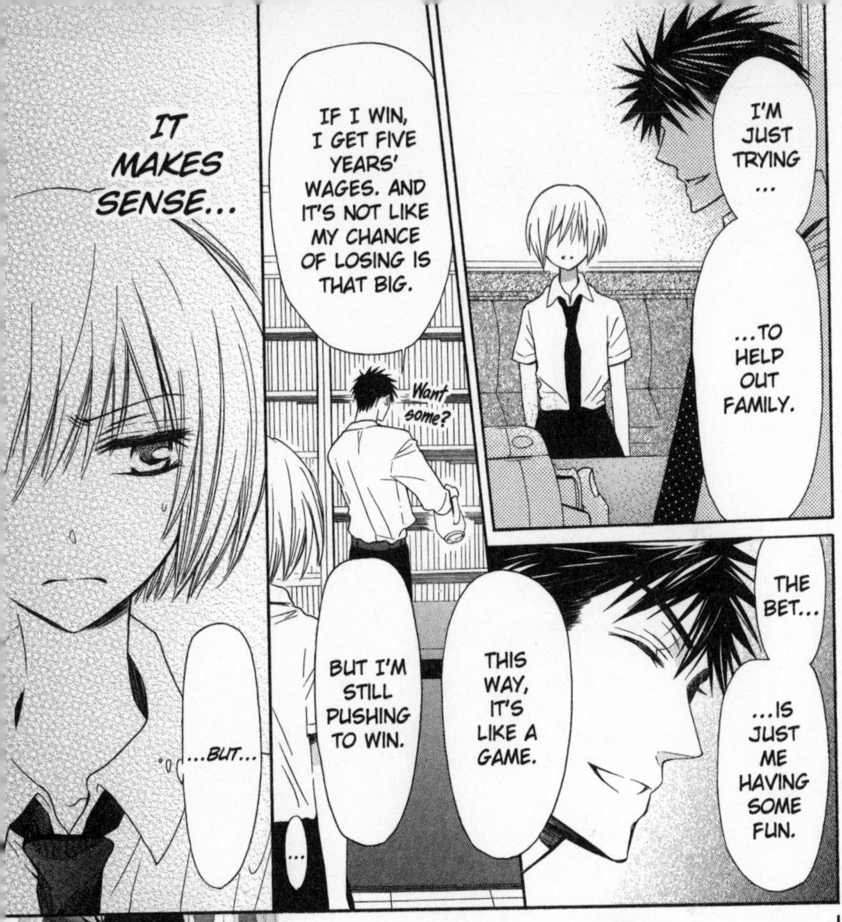
I'M JUST TRYING ...
...TO HELP OUT FAMILY.
IF I WIN, I GET FIVE YEARS' WAGES. AND IT'S NOT LIKE MY CHANCE OF LOSING IS THAT BIG.
Want some?
THE BET...
...IS JUST ME HAVING SOME FUN.
THIS WAY, IT'S LIKE A GAME.
BUT I'M STILL PUSHING TO WIN.
...
IT MAKES SENSE...
...BUT...

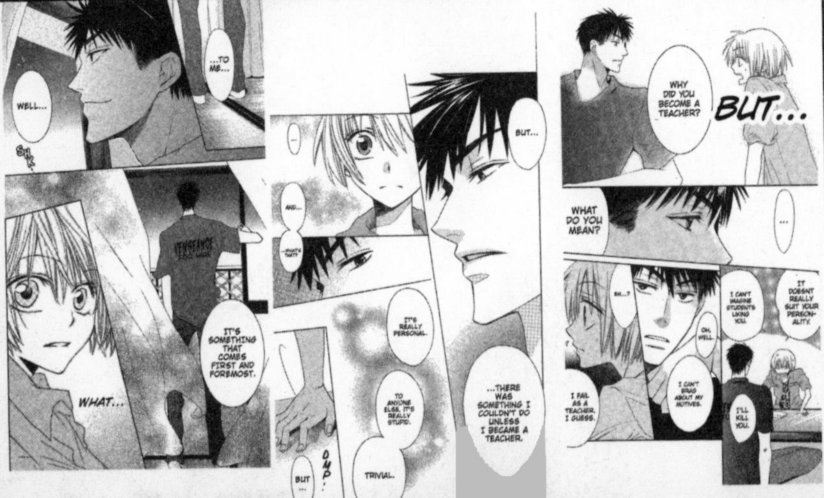
WHY DID YOU BECOME A TEACHER?
BUT...
...
WHAT DO YOU MEAN?
IT DOESN'T REALLY SUIT YOUR PERSONALITY.
I CAN'T IMAGINE STUDENTS LIKING YOU.
OH, WELL.
I'LL KILL YOU.
I CAN'T BRAG ABOUT MY MOTIVES.
EH...?
I FAIL AS A TEACHER, I GUESS.
...TO ME...
WELL...
SHK
BUT...
...
AND...
IT'S REALLY PERSONAL.
TO ANYONE ELSE, IT'S REALLY STUPID.
TRIVIAL.
BUT
...THERE WAS SOMETHING I COULDN'T DO UNLESS I BECAME A TEACHER.
IT'S SOMETHING THAT COMES FIRST AND FOREMOST.
WHAT...

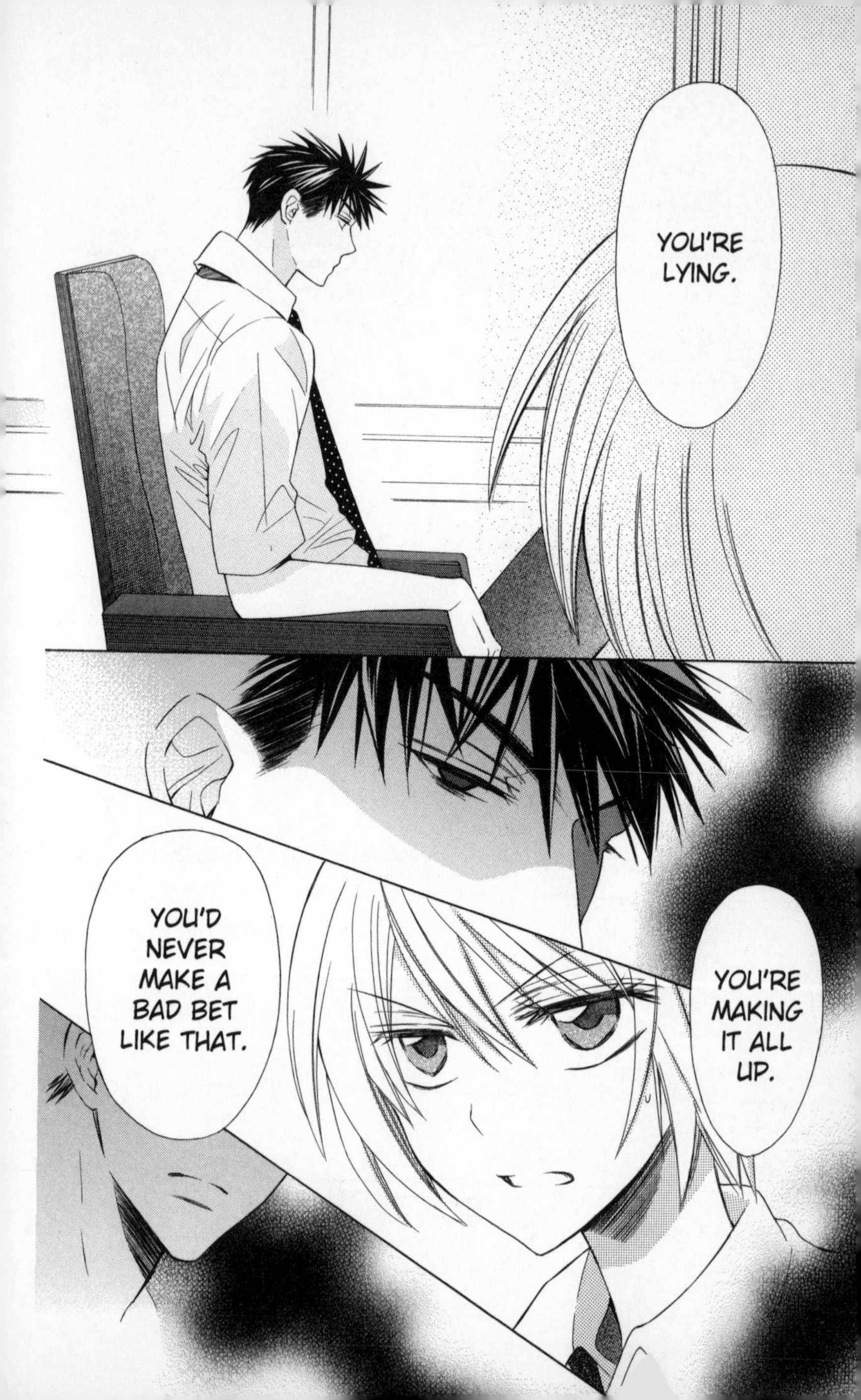
YOU'RE LYING.
YOU'RE MAKING IT ALL UP.
YOU'D NEVER MAKE A BAD BET LIKE THAT.

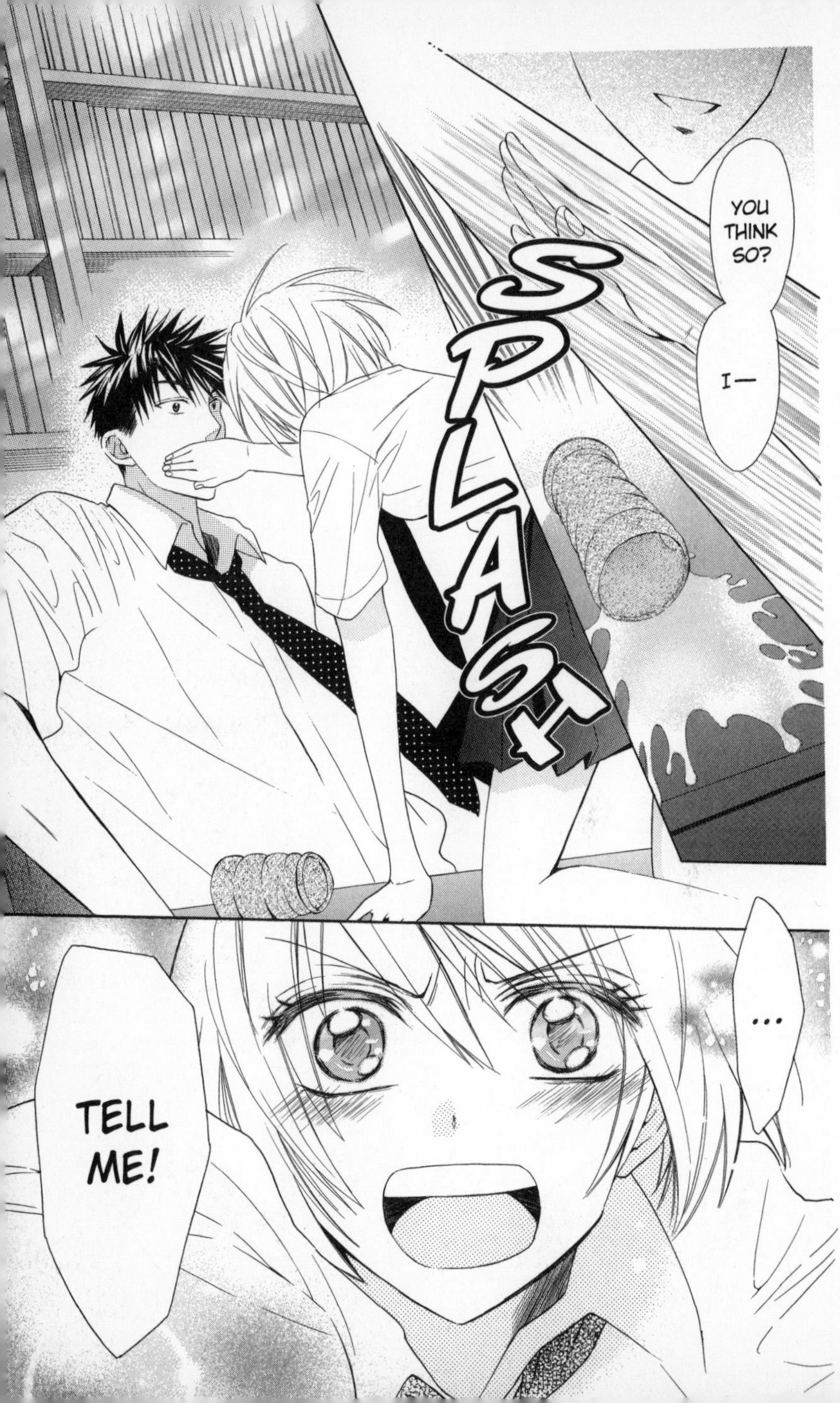
YOU THINK SO?
I—
SPLASH
...
TELL ME!

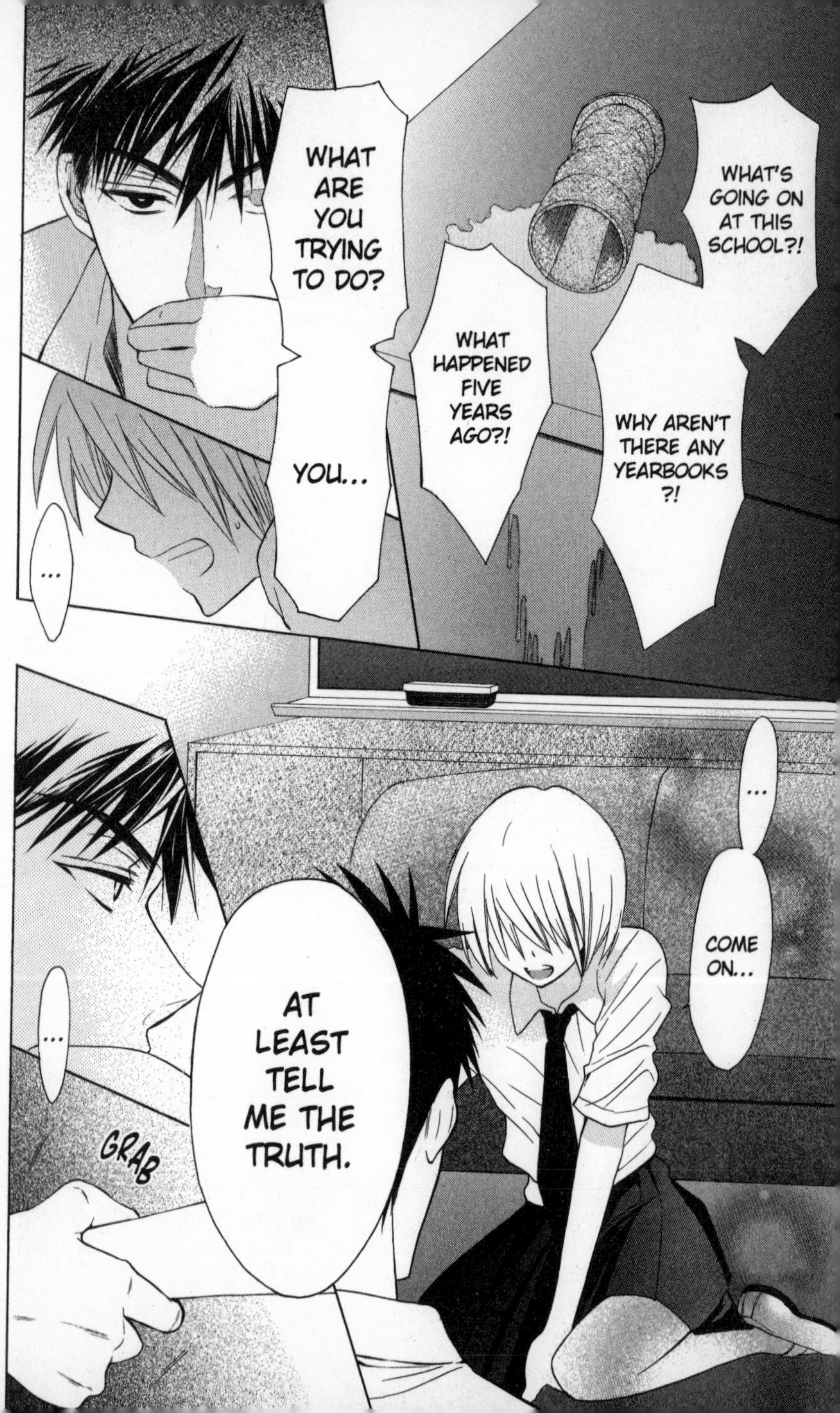
WHAT'S GOING ON AT THIS SCHOOL?!
WHY AREN'T THERE ANY YEARBOOKS?!
WHAT HAPPENED FIVE YEARS AGO?!
WHAT ARE YOU TRYING TO DO?
YOU...
...
...
COME ON...
AT LEAST TELL ME THE TRUTH.
...
GRAB

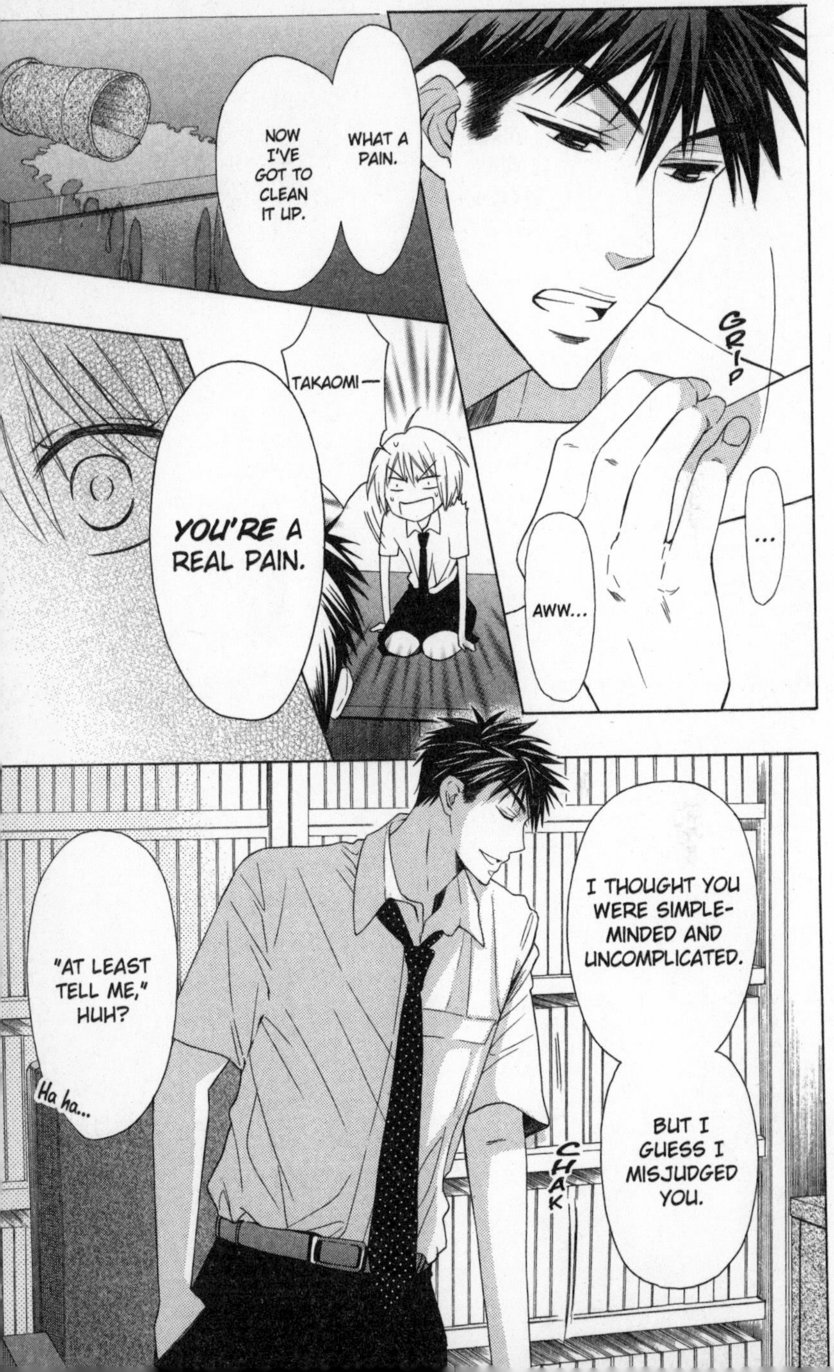
WHAT A PAIN.
NOW I'VE GOT TO CLEAN IT UP.
GRIP
...
AWW...
TAKAOMI—
YOU'RE A REAL PAIN.
I THOUGHT YOU WERE SIMPLE-MINDED AND UNCOMPLICATED.
BUT I GUESS I MISJUDGED YOU.
CHAK
"AT LEAST TELL ME," HUH?
Ha ha...

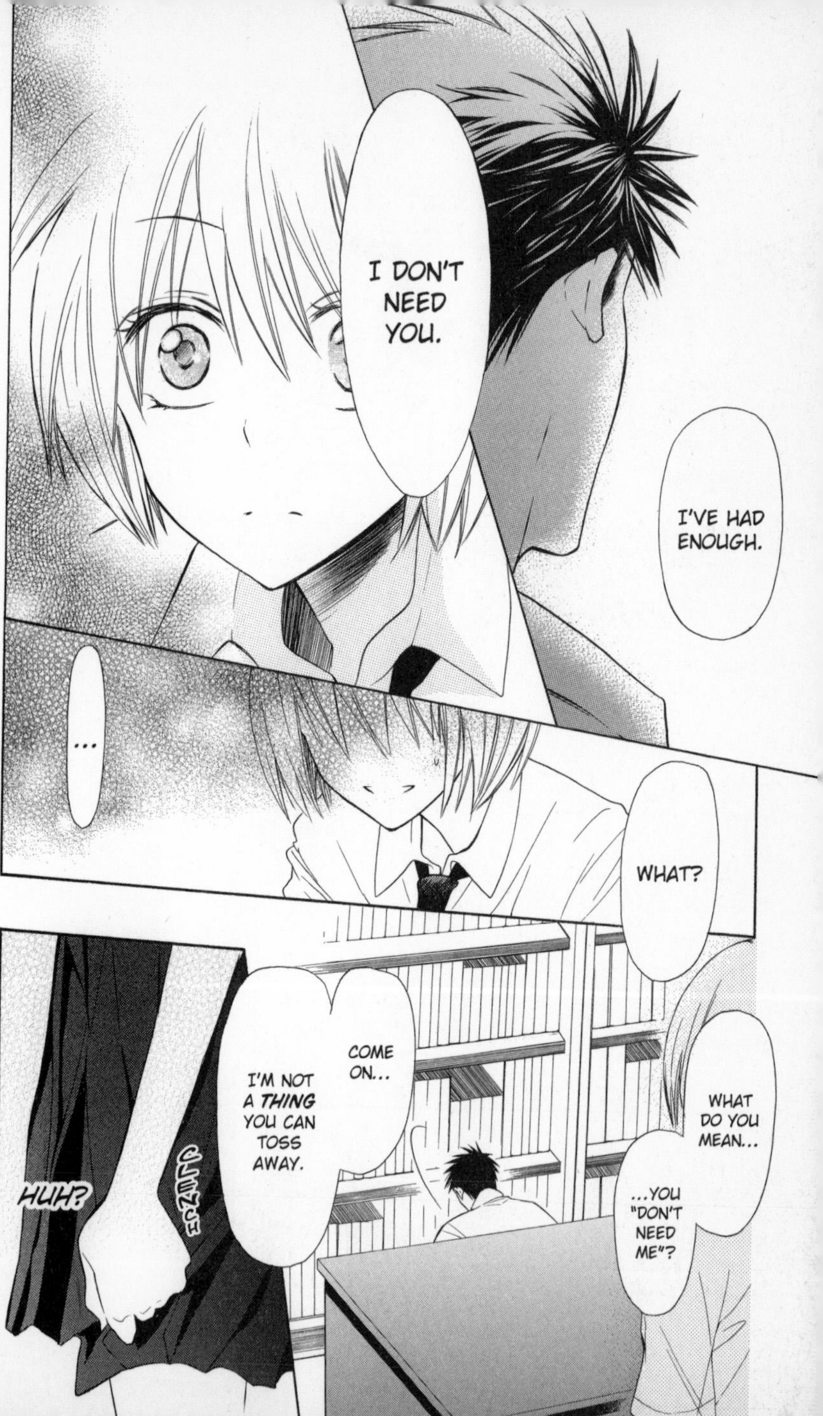

I'VE HAD ENOUGH.
I DON'T NEED YOU.
WHAT?
...
WHAT DO YOU MEAN...
...YOU "DON'T NEED ME"?
COME ON...
I'M NOT A *THING* YOU CAN TOSS AWAY.
CLENCH
HUH?

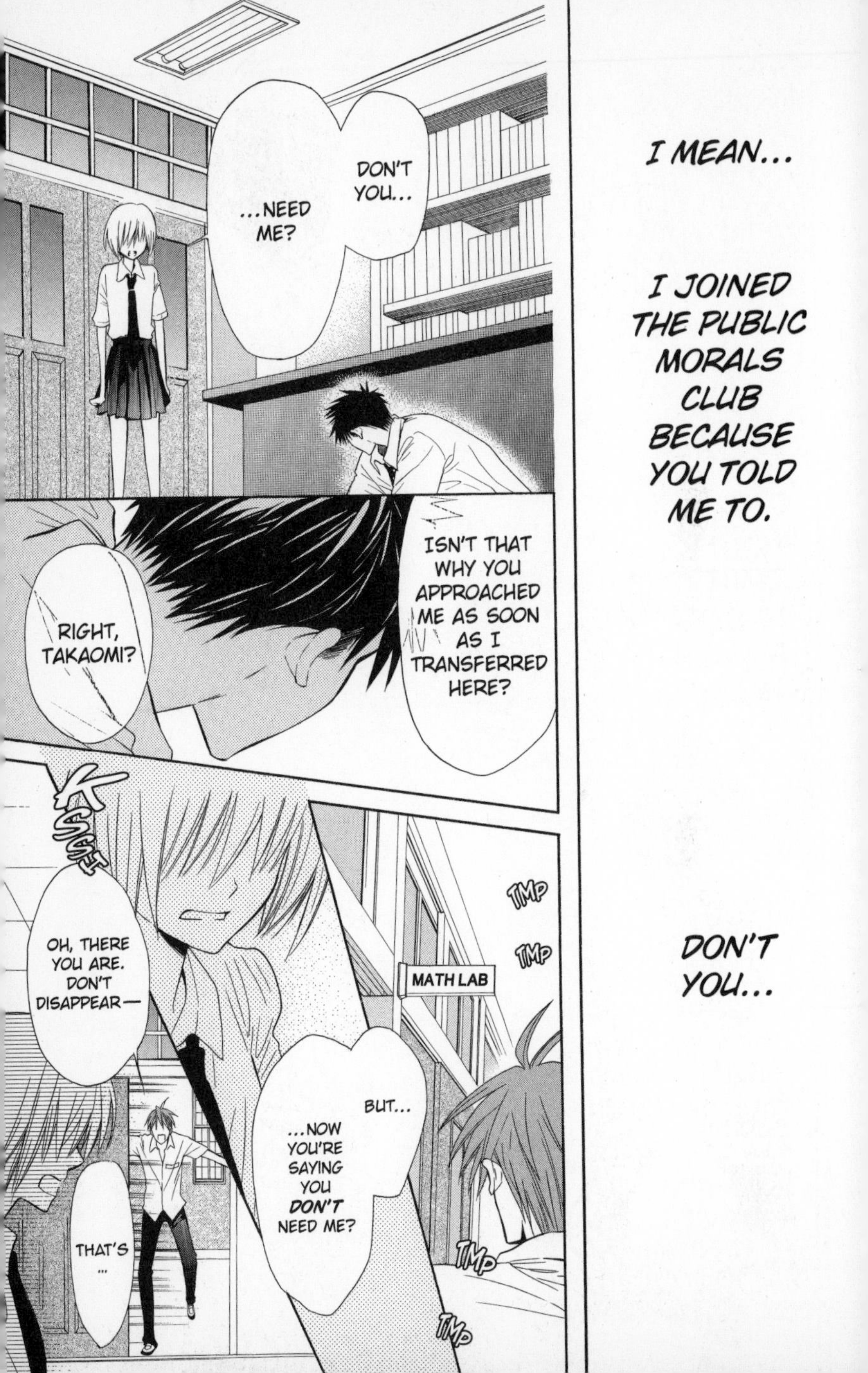
I MEAN...
I JOINED THE PUBLIC MORALS CLUB BECAUSE YOU TOLD ME TO.
DON'T YOU...
DON'T YOU...
...NEED ME?
ISN'T THAT WHY YOU APPROACHED ME AS SOON AS I TRANSFERRED HERE?
RIGHT, TAKAOMI?
TMP
TMP
MATH LAB
BUT...
...NOW YOU'RE SAYING YOU *DON'T* NEED ME?
TMP
TMP
KSSH
OH, THERE YOU ARE. DON'T DISAPPEAR—
THAT'S ...

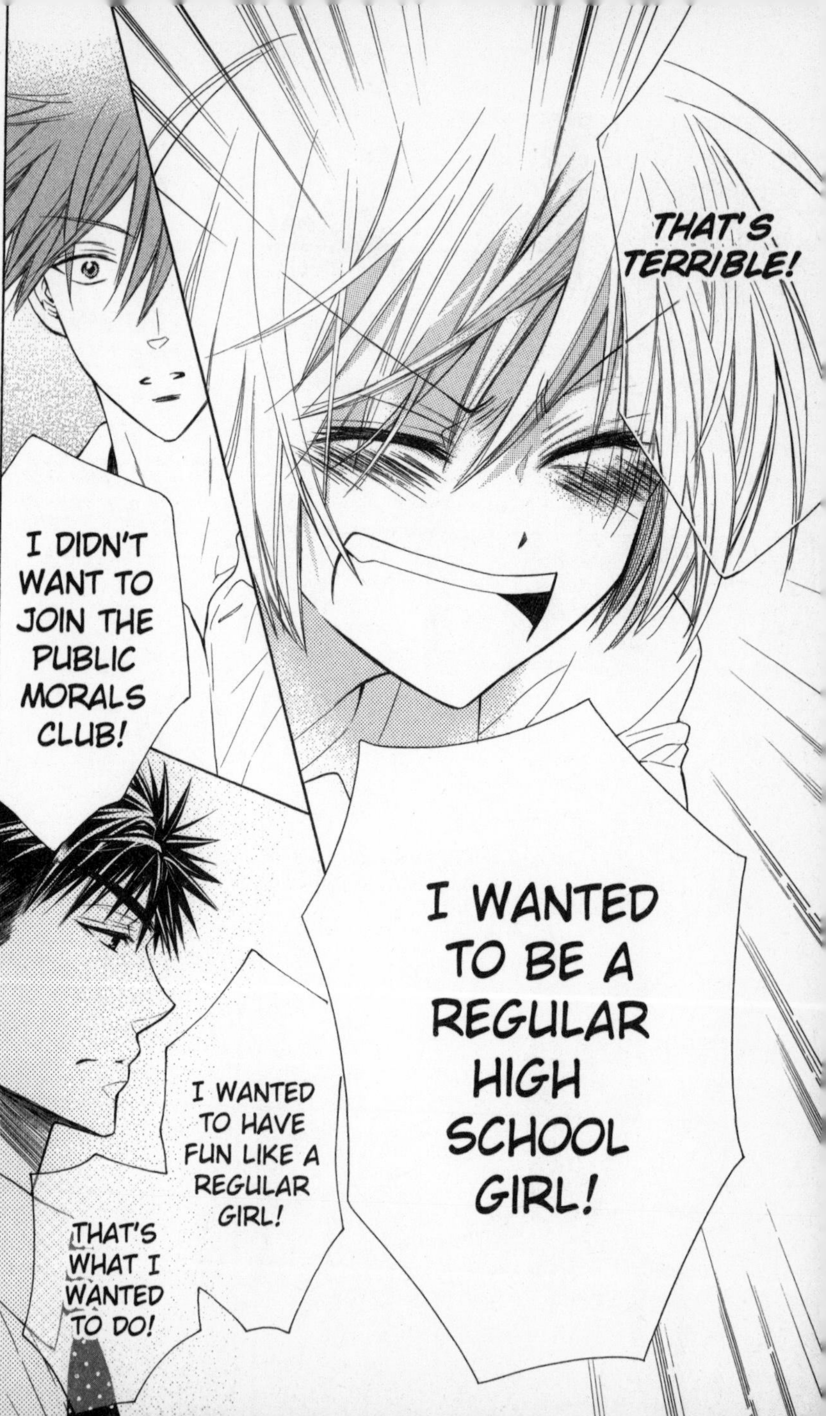
THAT'S TERRIBLE!
I DIDN'T WANT TO JOIN THE PUBLIC MORALS CLUB!
I WANTED TO BE A REGULAR HIGH SCHOOL GIRL!
I WANTED TO HAVE FUN LIKE A REGULAR GIRL!
THAT'S WHAT I WANTED TO DO!

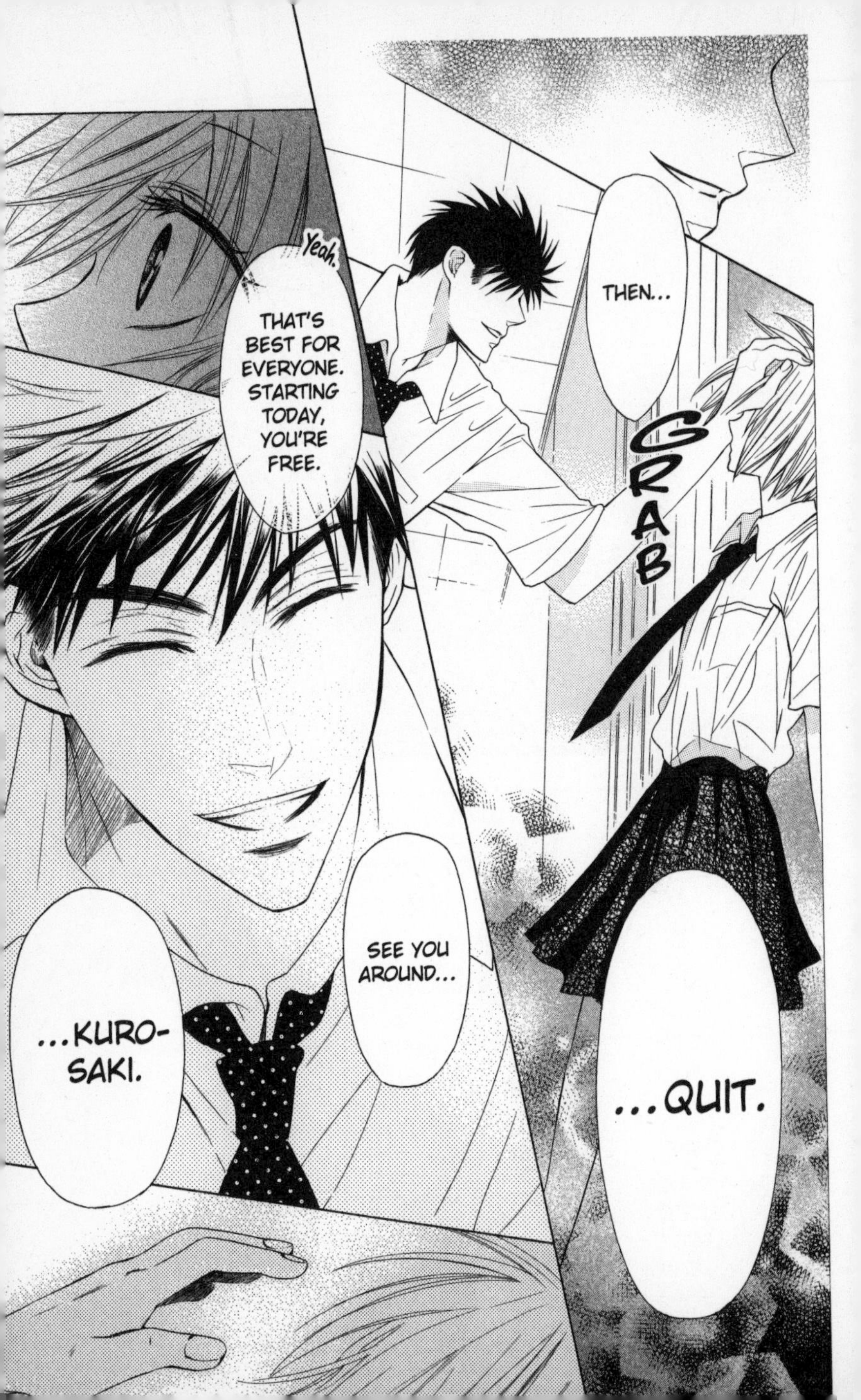
THEN...
GRAB
...QUIT.
Yeah.
THAT'S BEST FOR EVERYONE. STARTING TODAY, YOU'RE FREE.
SEE YOU AROUND...
...KURO-SAKI.

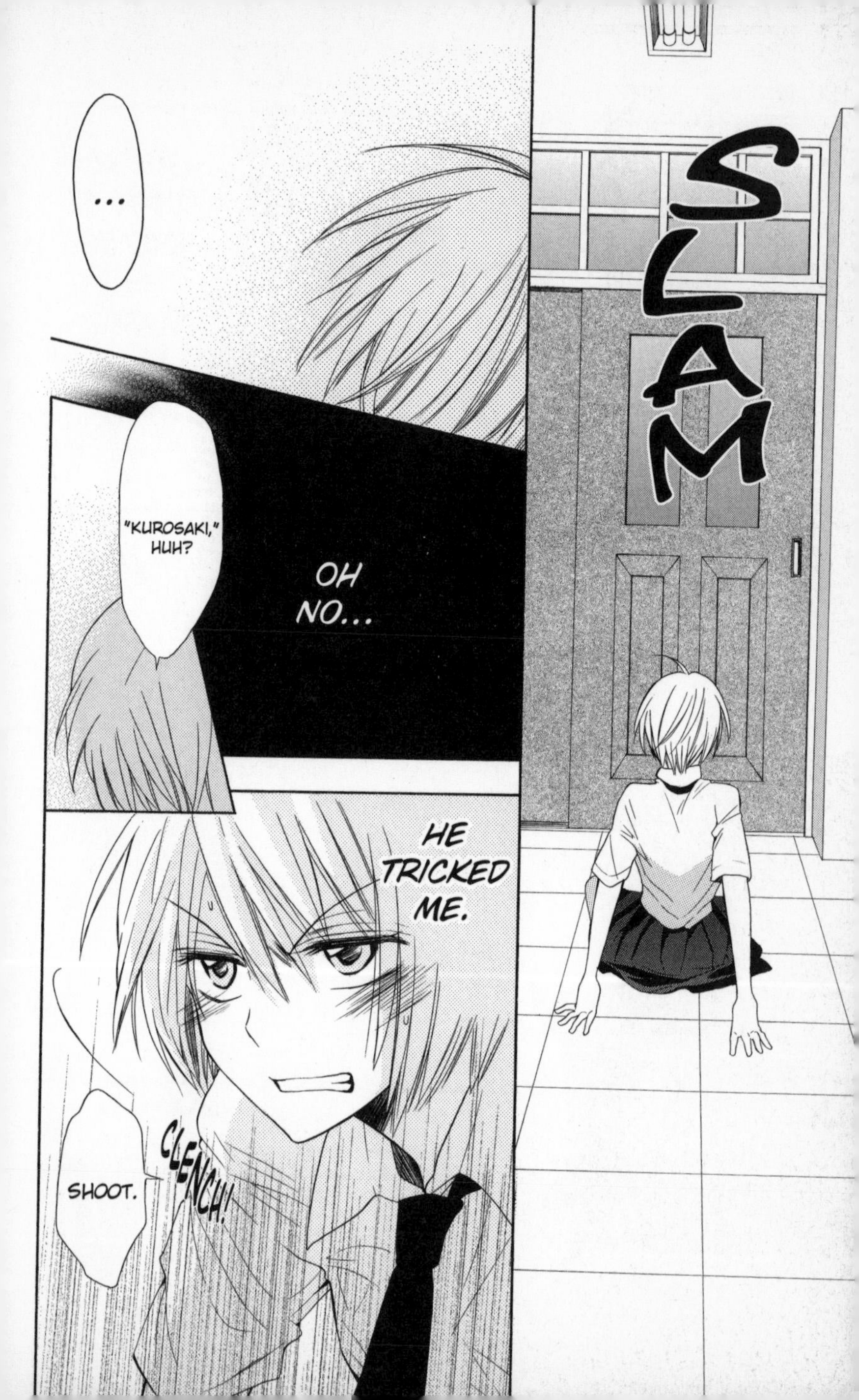
SLAM
...
OH NO...
"KUROSAKI," HUH?
HE TRICKED ME.
CLENCH!
SHOOT.

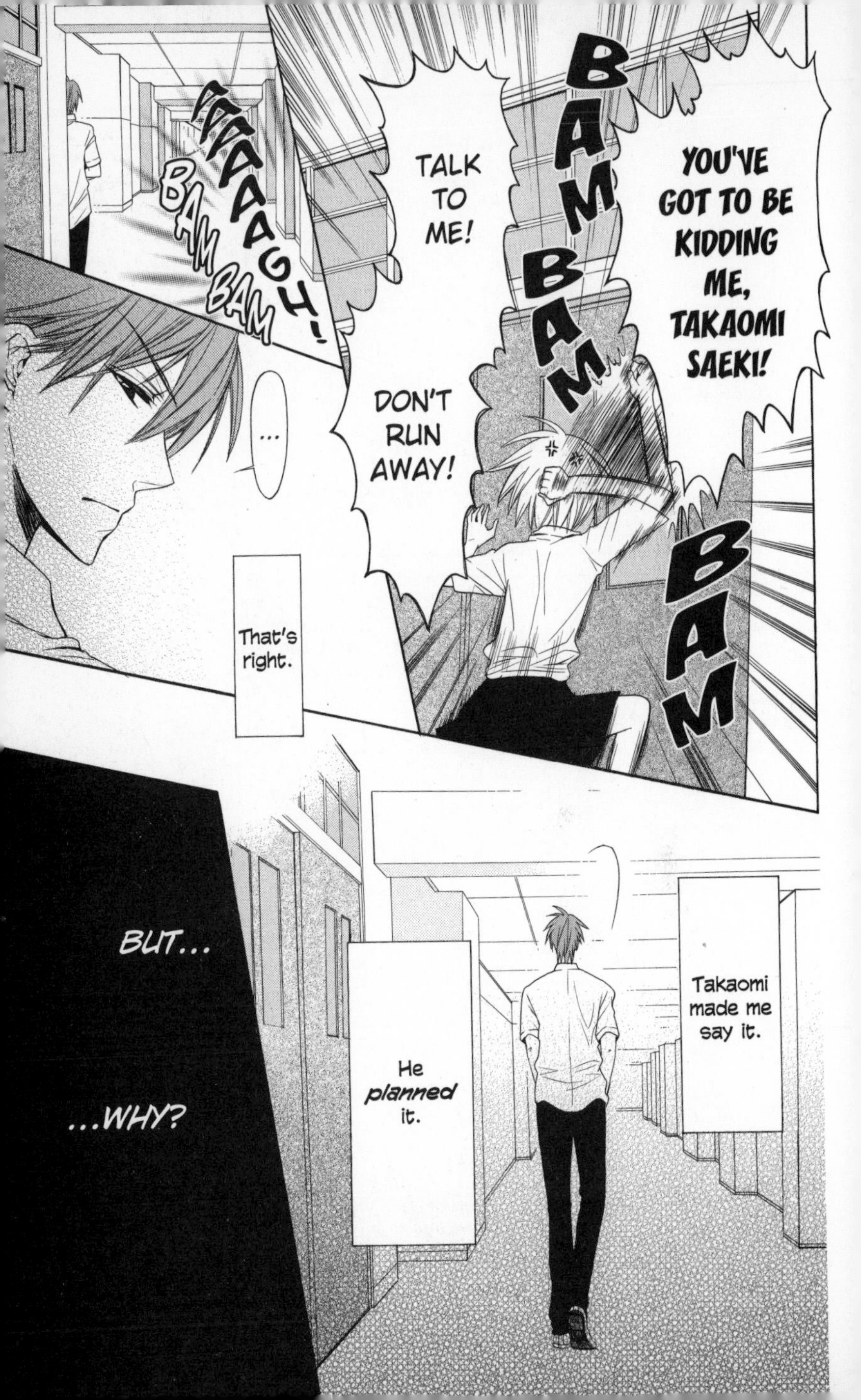
YOU'VE GOT TO BE KIDDING ME, TAKAOMI SAEKI!
BAM BAM
TALK TO ME!
DON'T RUN AWAY!
BAM BAM
WAAAAGH!
BAM BAM BAM
...
That's right.
Takaomi made me say it.
He *planned* it.
BUT...
...WHY?

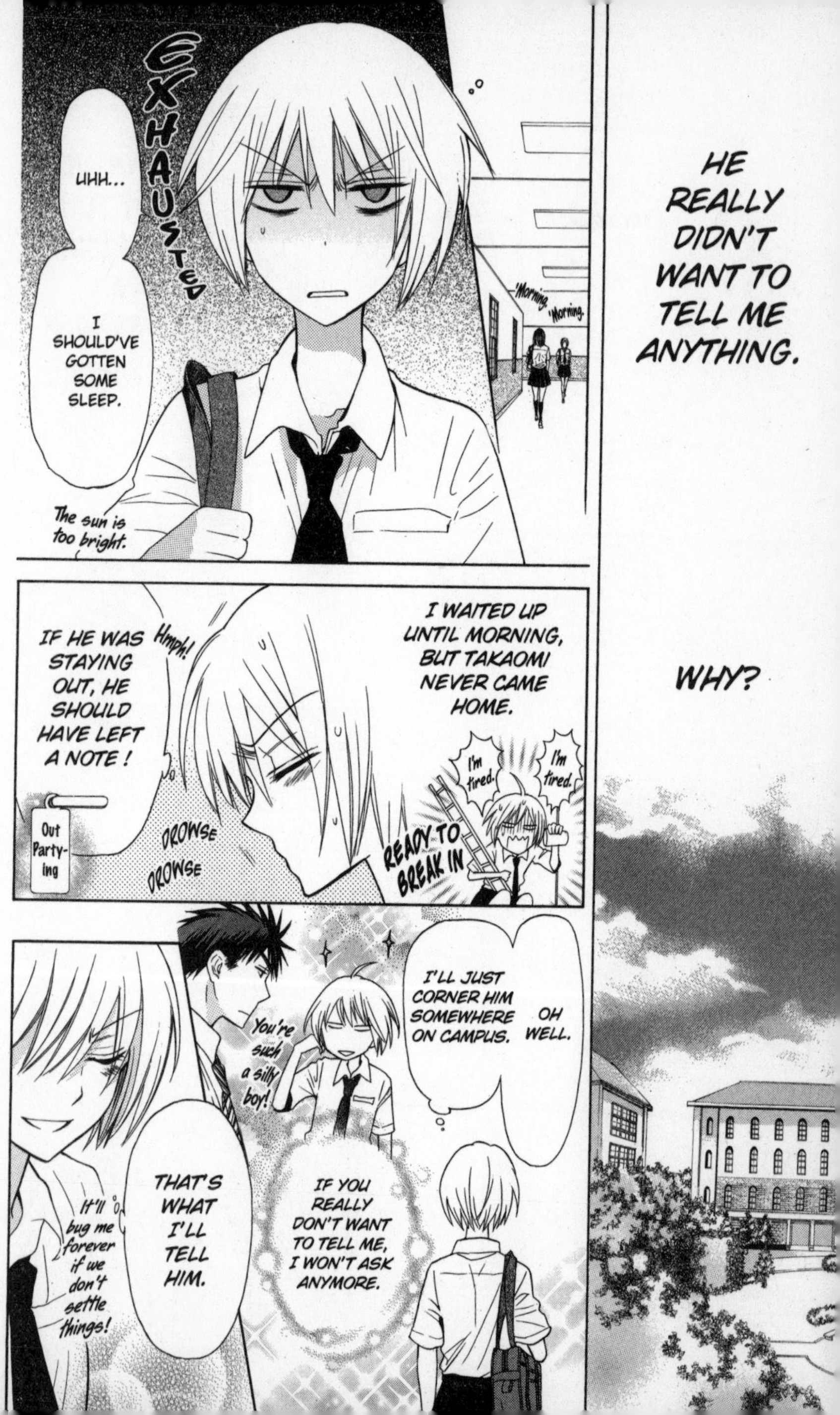
HE REALLY DIDN'T WANT TO TELL ME ANYTHING.
WHY?
'Morning.
'Morning.
EXHAUSTED
UHH...
I SHOULD'VE GOTTEN SOME SLEEP.
The sun is too bright.
I WAITED UP UNTIL MORNING, BUT TAKAOMI NEVER CAME HOME.
I'm tired.
I'm tired.
READY TO BREAK IN
Hmph!
IF HE WAS STAYING OUT, HE SHOULD HAVE LEFT A NOTE !
DROWSE
DROWSE
Out Party-ing
OH WELL.
I'LL JUST CORNER HIM SOMEWHERE ON CAMPUS.
You're such a silly boy!
IF YOU REALLY DON'T WANT TO TELL ME, I WON'T ASK ANYMORE.
THAT'S WHAT I'LL TELL HIM.
It'll bug me forever if we don't settle things!

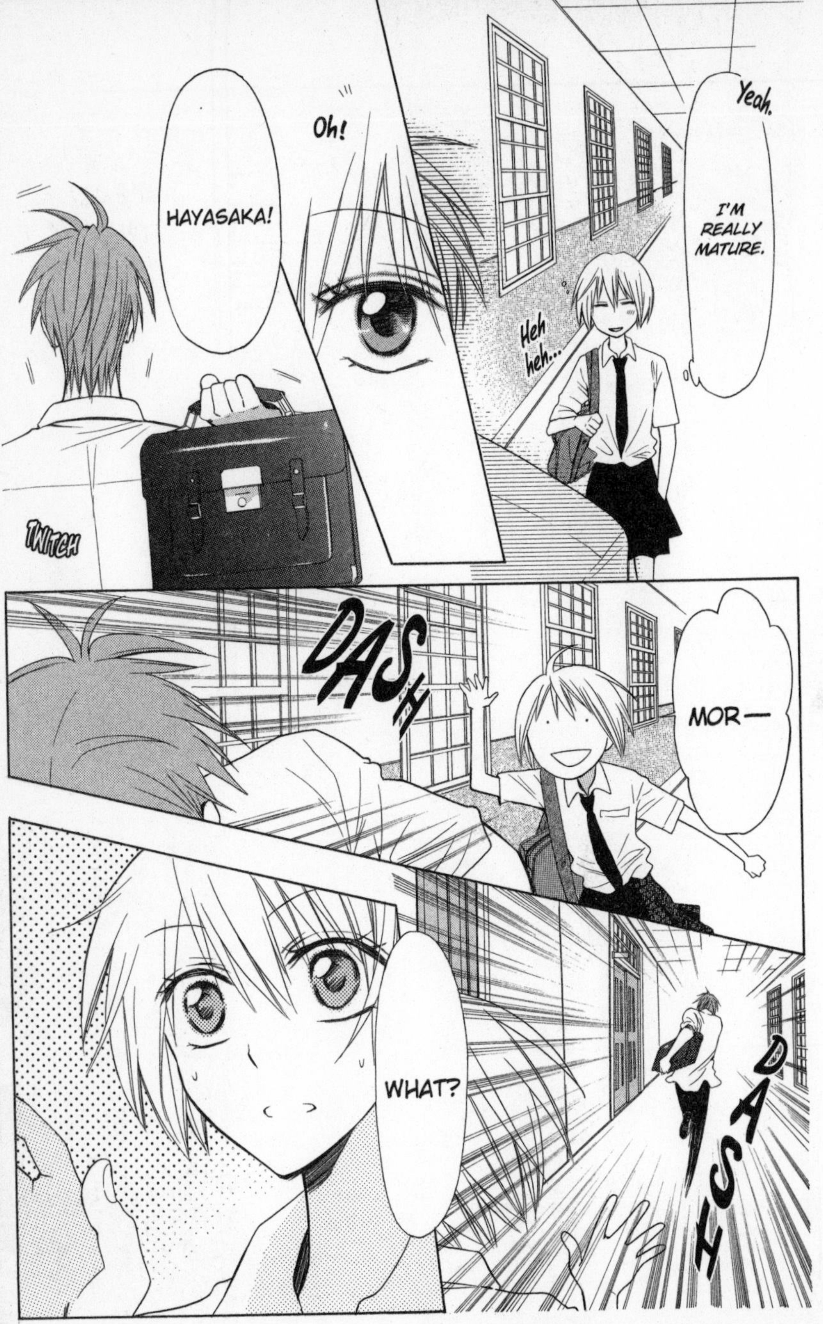
Yeah.
I'M REALLY MATURE.
Heh heh...
Oh!
HAYASAKA!
TWITCH
MOR—
DASH
DASH
WHAT?

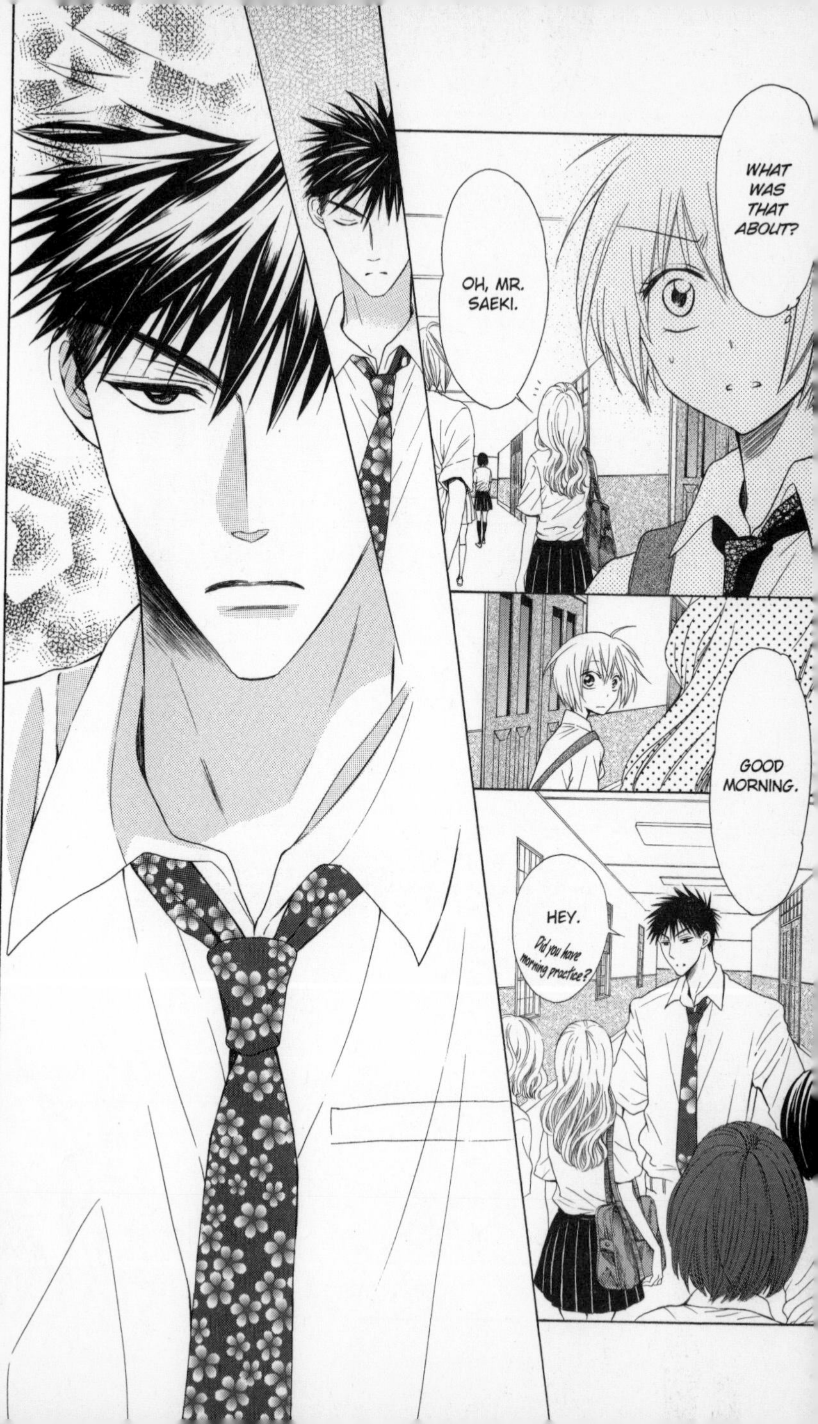
WHAT WAS THAT ABOUT?
OH, MR. SAEKI.
GOOD MORNING.
HEY.
Did you have morning practice?

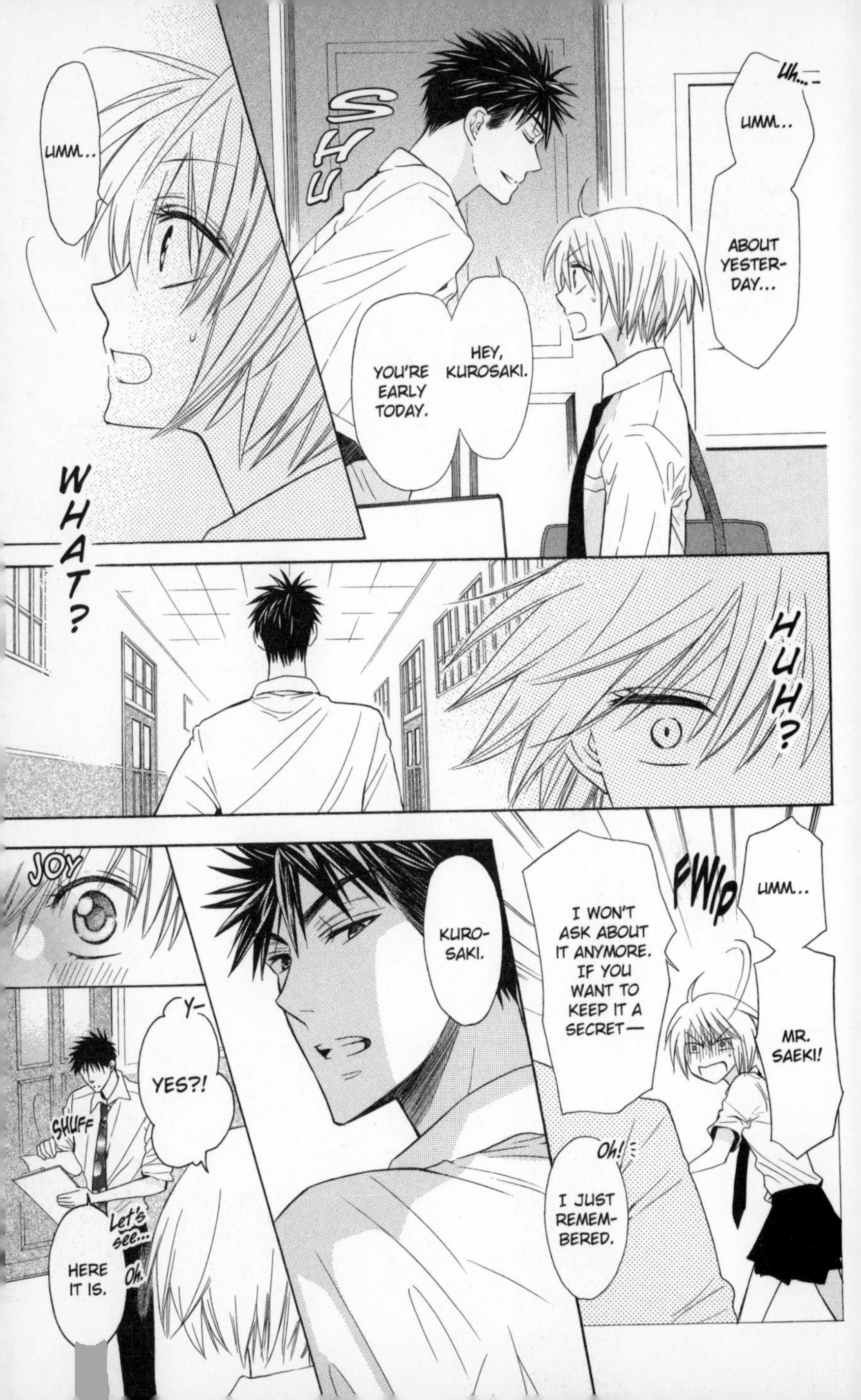
Uh...
UMM...
ABOUT YESTER-DAY...
SHU
HEY, KUROSAKI.
YOU'RE EARLY TODAY.
UMM...
WHAT?
HUH?
UMM...
MR. SAEKI!
FWIP
I WON'T ASK ABOUT IT ANYMORE. IF YOU WANT TO KEEP IT A SECRET—
Oh!
I JUST REMEMBERED.
KURO-SAKI.
JOY
Y-
YES?!
SHUFF
Let's see...
Oh.
HERE IT IS.

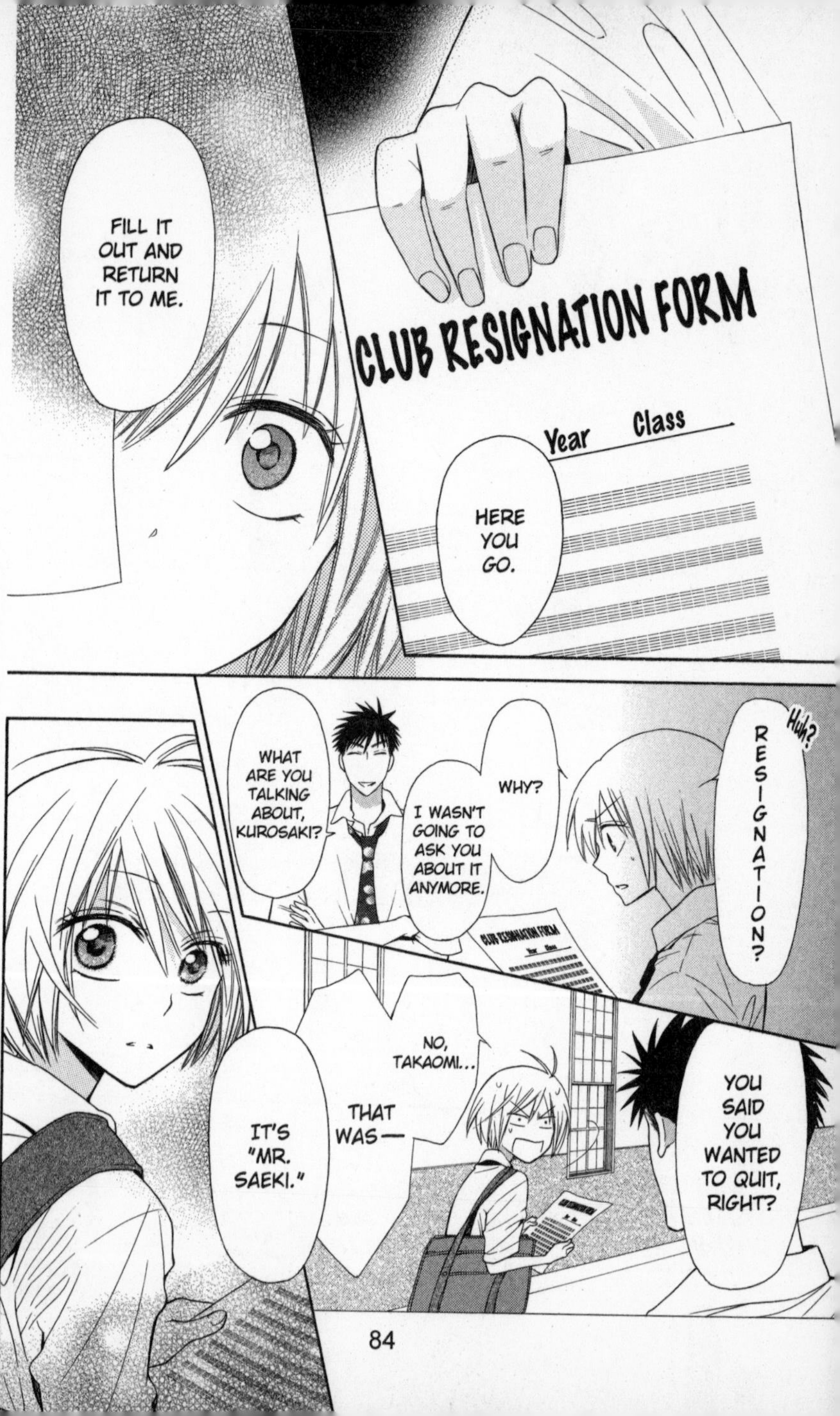
CLUB RESIGNATION FORM
Year Class
HERE YOU GO.
FILL IT OUT AND RETURN IT TO ME.
Huh?
RESIGNATION?
WHY?
I WASN'T GOING TO ASK YOU ABOUT IT ANYMORE.
WHAT ARE YOU TALKING ABOUT, KUROSAKI?
CLUB RESIGNATION FORM
YOU SAID YOU WANTED TO QUIT, RIGHT?
NO, TAKAOMI...
THAT WAS—
IT'S "MR. SAEKI."

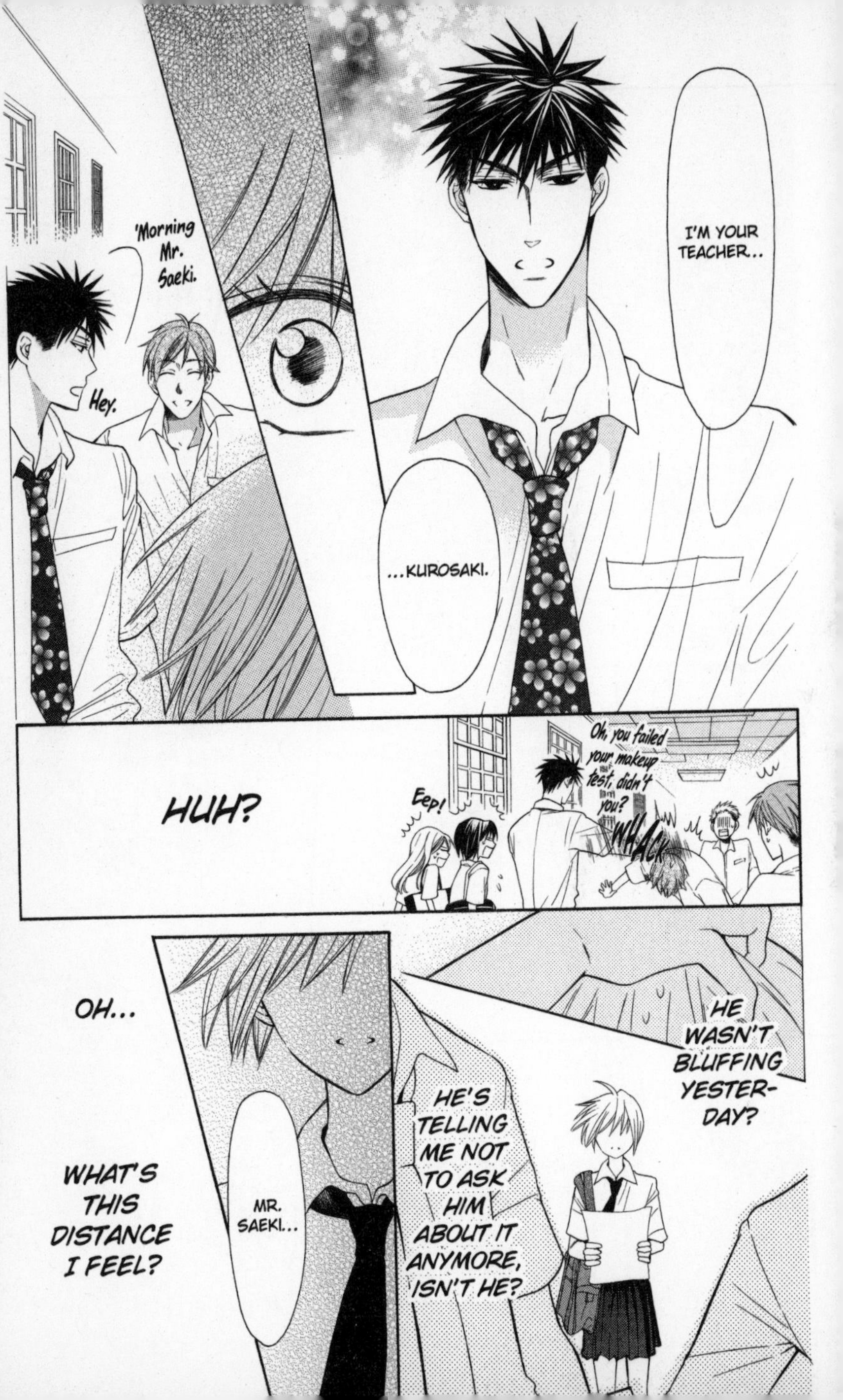
I'M YOUR TEACHER...
...KUROSAKI.
'Morning Mr. Saeki.
Hey.
Oh, you failed your makeup test, didn't you?
WHACK
Eep!
HUH?
HE WASN'T BLUFFING YESTER-DAY?
HE'S TELLING ME NOT TO ASK HIM ABOUT IT ANYMORE, ISN'T HE?
MR. SAEKI...
OH...
WHAT'S THIS DISTANCE I FEEL?

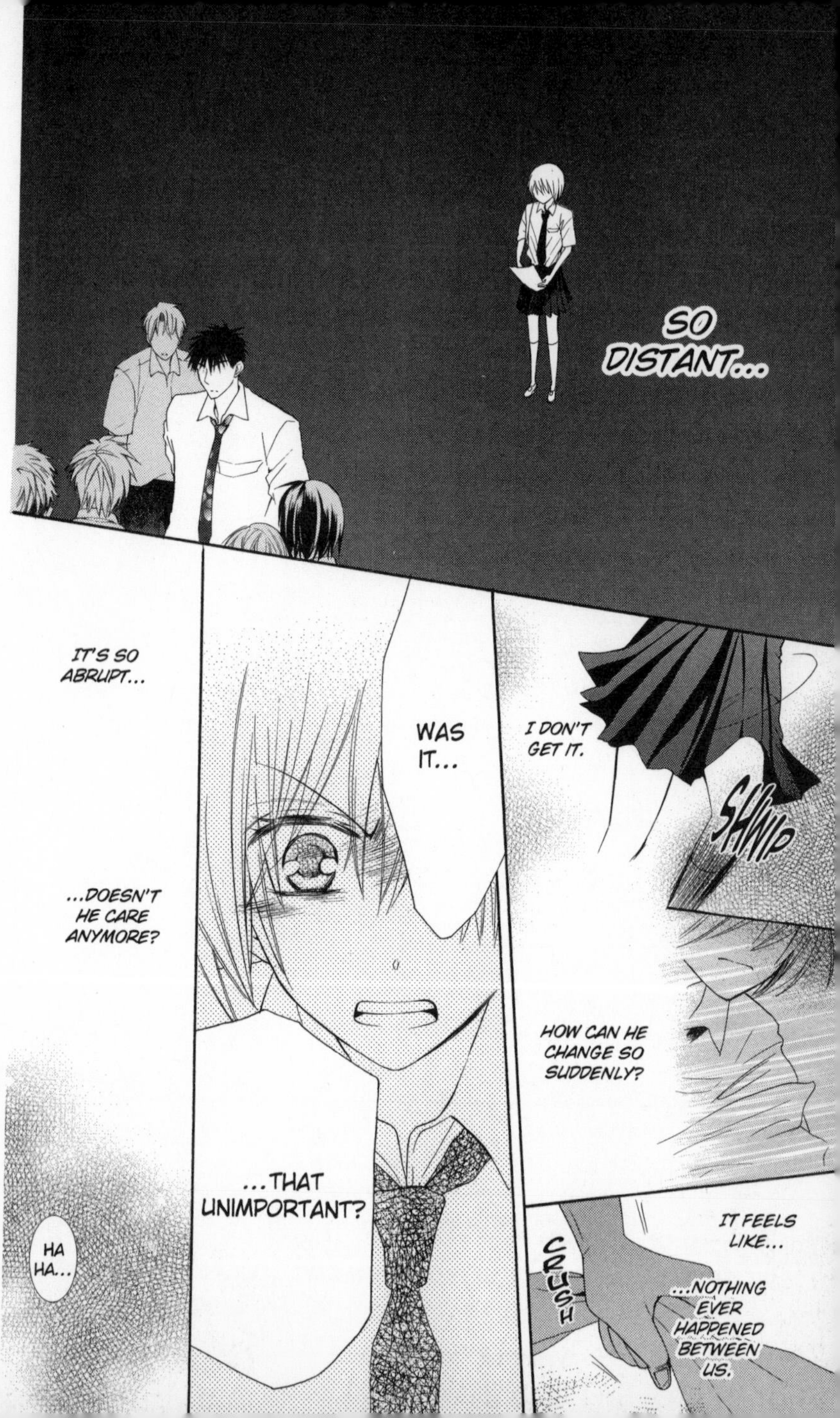
SO DISTANT...
I DON'T GET IT.
SHWIP
HOW CAN HE CHANGE SO SUDDENLY?
IT FEELS LIKE...
...NOTHING EVER HAPPENED BETWEEN US.
CRUSH
WAS IT...
...THAT UNIMPORTANT?
IT'S SO ABRUPT...
...DOESN'T HE CARE ANYMORE?
HA HA...

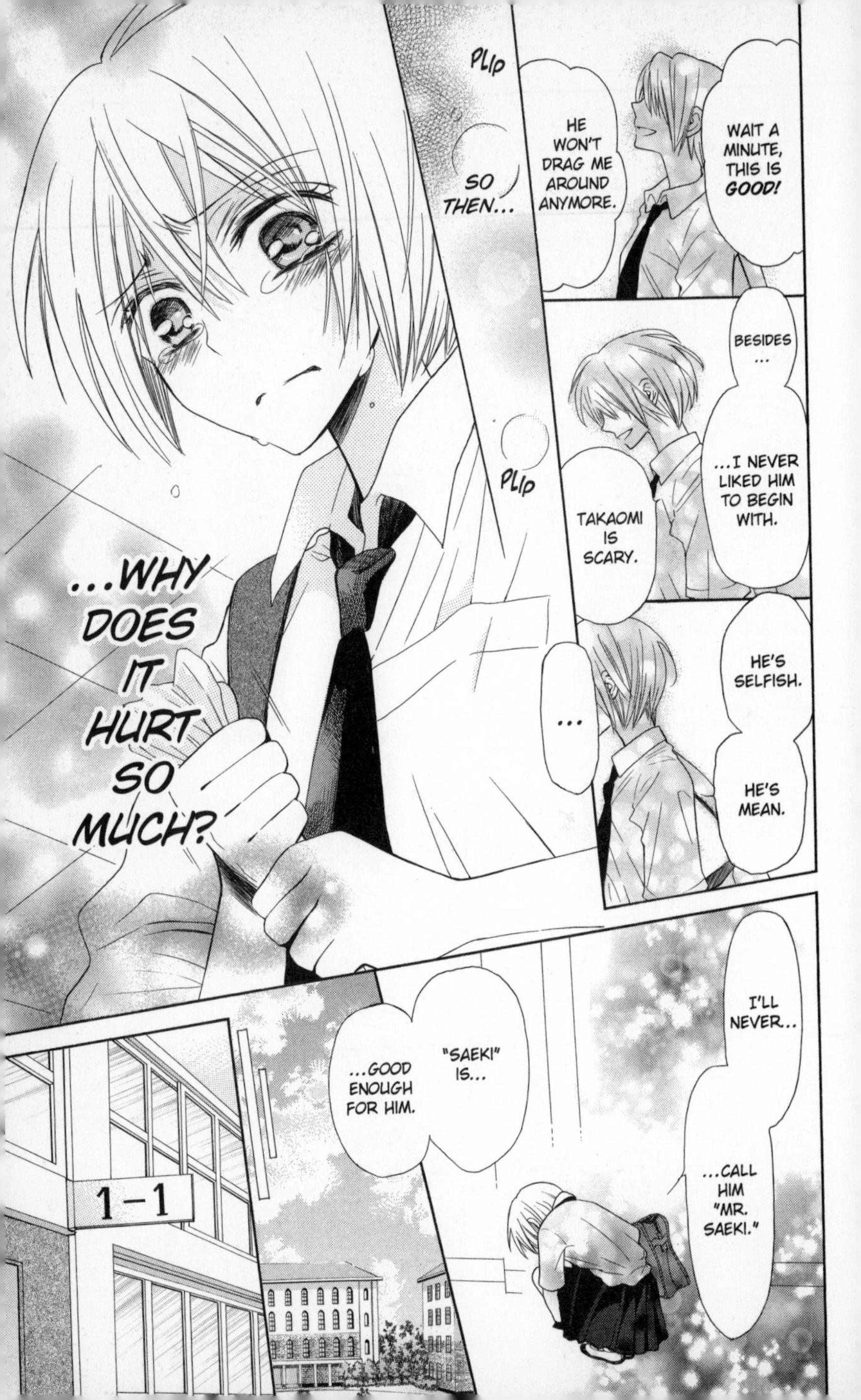

WAIT A MINUTE, THIS IS GOOD!
HE WON'T DRAG ME AROUND ANYMORE.
SO THEN...
PLIP
BESIDES...
...I NEVER LIKED HIM TO BEGIN WITH.
TAKAOMI IS SCARY.
PLIP
HE'S SELFISH.
HE'S MEAN.
...
...WHY DOES IT HURT SO MUCH?
I'LL NEVER...
...CALL HIM "MR. SAEKI."
"SAEKI" IS...
...GOOD ENOUGH FOR HIM.
1-1

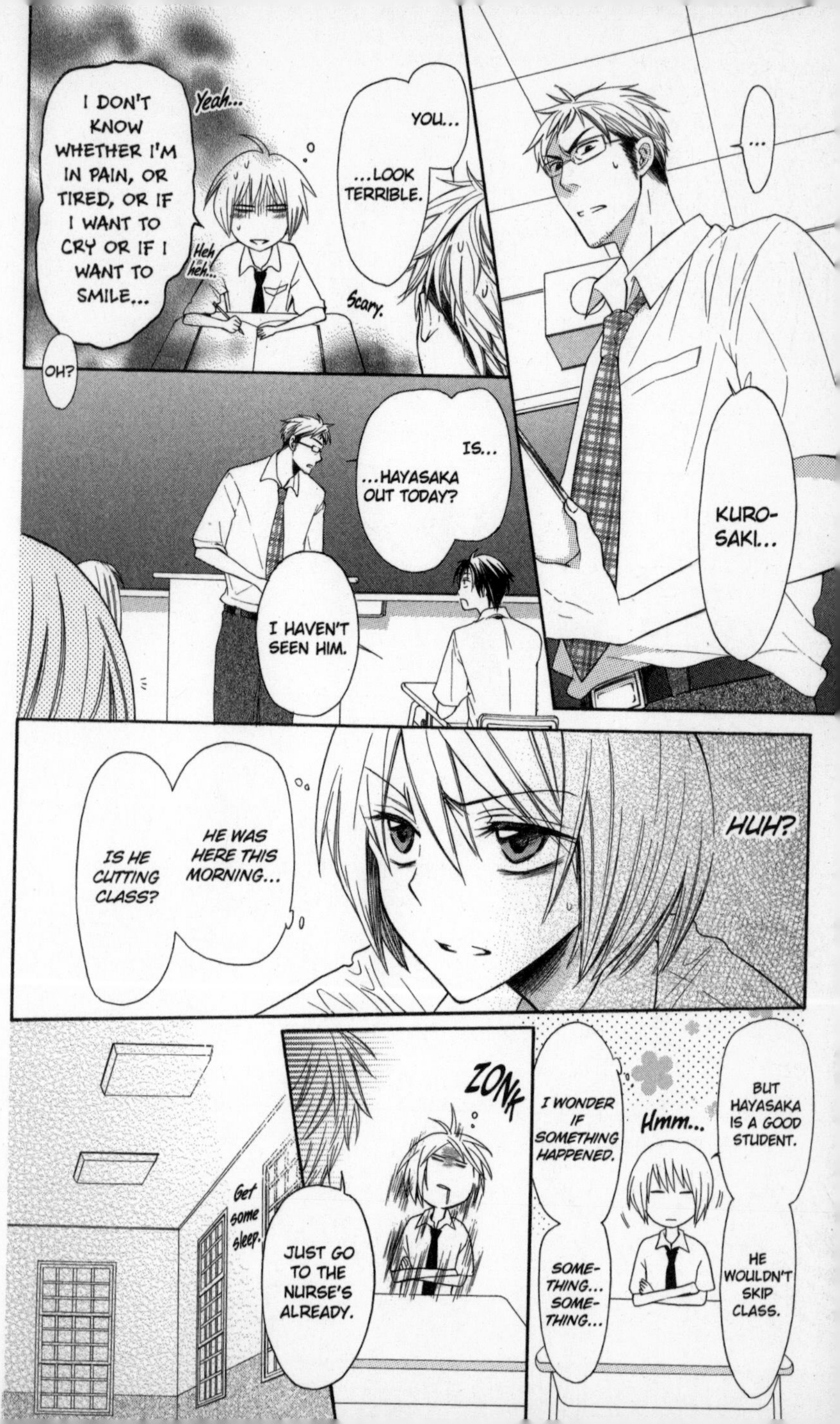
...
KURO-SAKI...
YOU... ...LOOK TERRIBLE.
Scary.
Yeah...
I DON'T KNOW WHETHER I'M IN PAIN, OR TIRED, OR IF I WANT TO CRY OR IF I WANT TO SMILE...
Heh heh...
OH?
IS... ...HAYASAKA OUT TODAY?
I HAVEN'T SEEN HIM.
HUH?
HE WAS HERE THIS MORNING...
IS HE CUTTING CLASS?
BUT HAYASAKA IS A GOOD STUDENT.
Hmm...
I WONDER IF SOMETHING HAPPENED.
HE WOULDN'T SKIP CLASS.
SOME-THING... SOME-THING...
ZONK
JUST GO TO THE NURSE'S ALREADY.
Get some sleep.

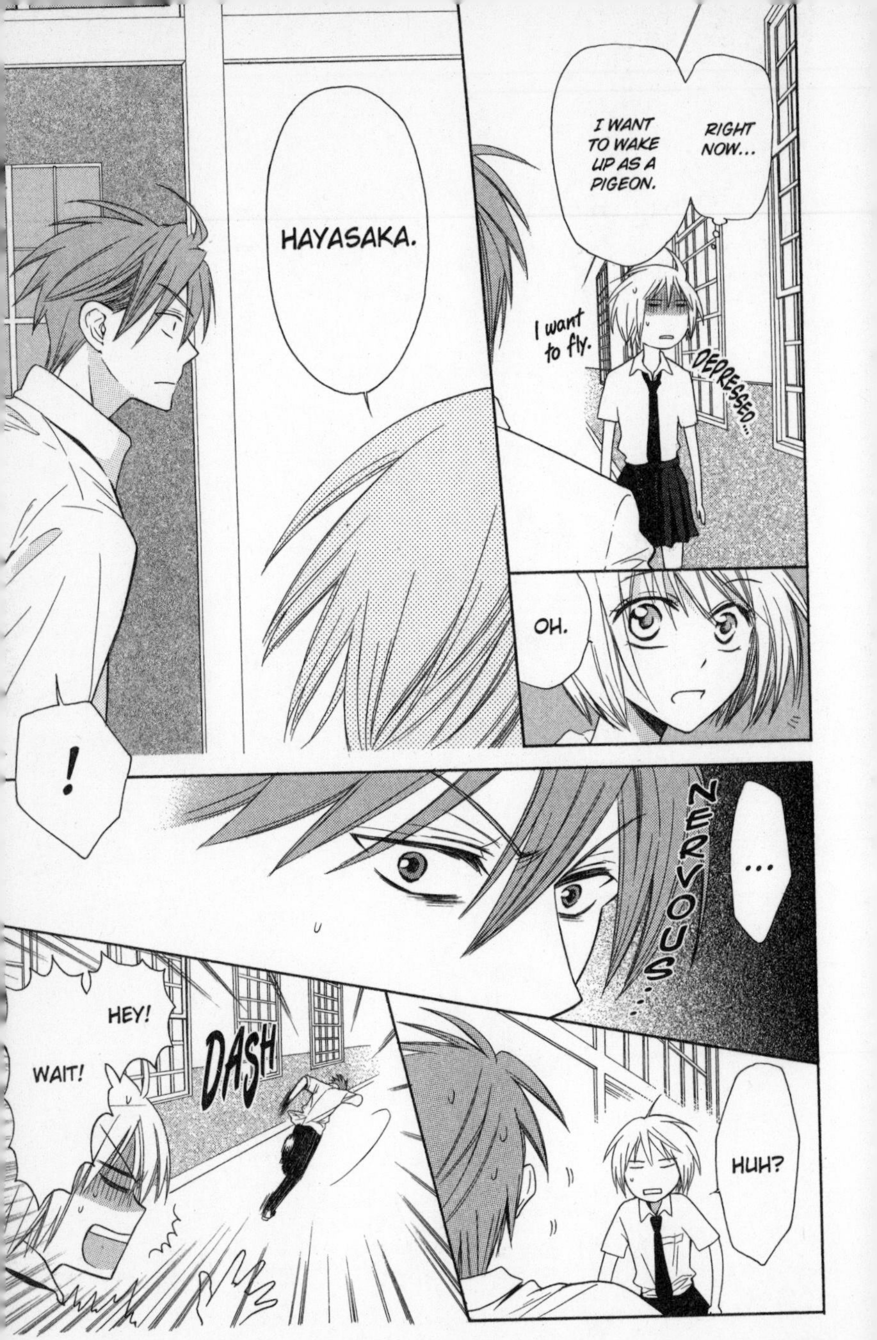
RIGHT NOW...
I WANT TO WAKE UP AS A PIGEON.
I want to fly.
DEPRESSED...
OH.
HAYASAKA.
!
...
NERVOUS...
HUH?
DASH
HEY!
WAIT!

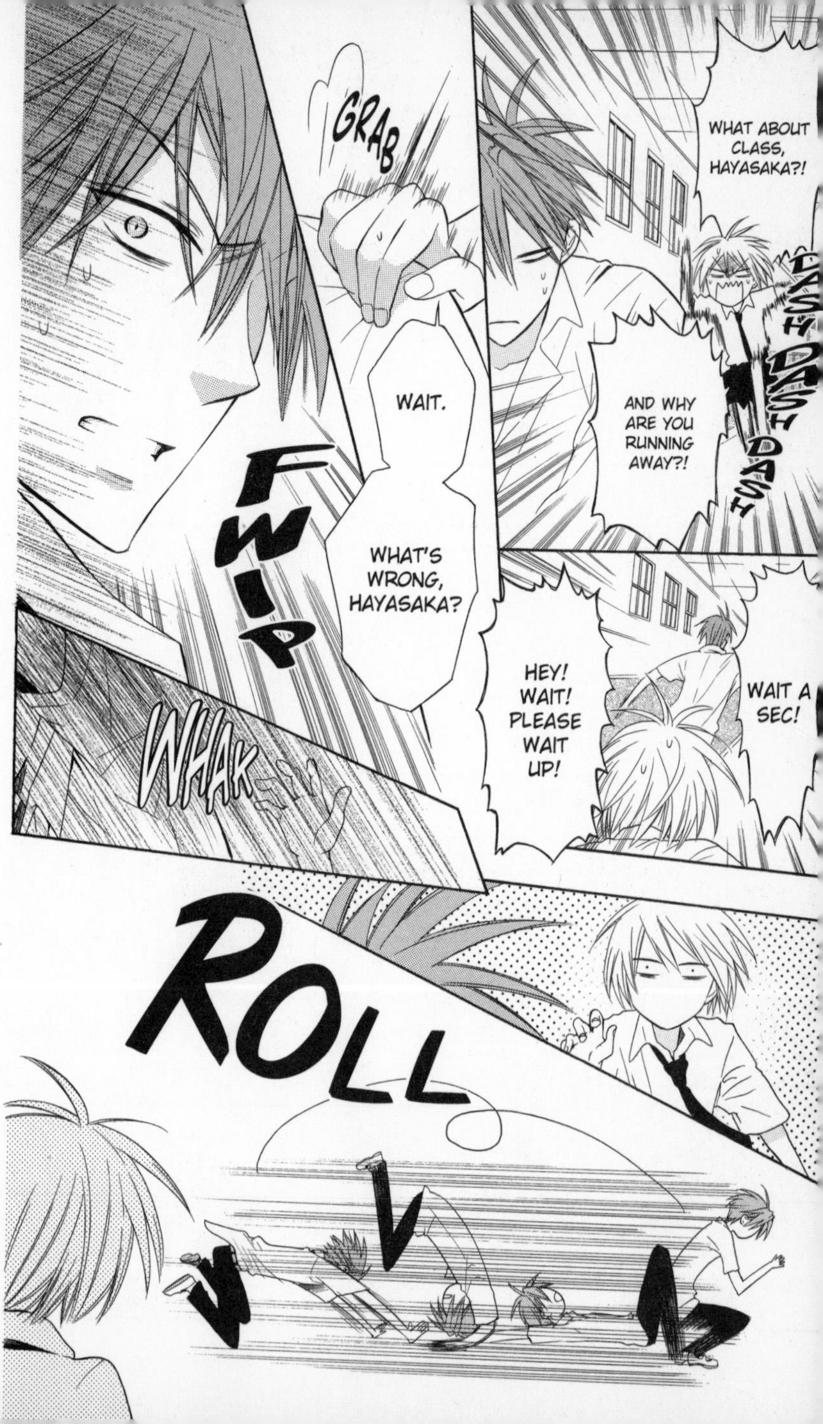
WHAT ABOUT CLASS, HAYASAKA?!
DASH DASH DASH
AND WHY ARE YOU RUNNING AWAY?!
WAIT A SEC!
HEY! WAIT! PLEASE WAIT UP!
GRAB
WAIT.
WHAT'S WRONG, HAYASAKA?
FWIP
WHAK
ROLL

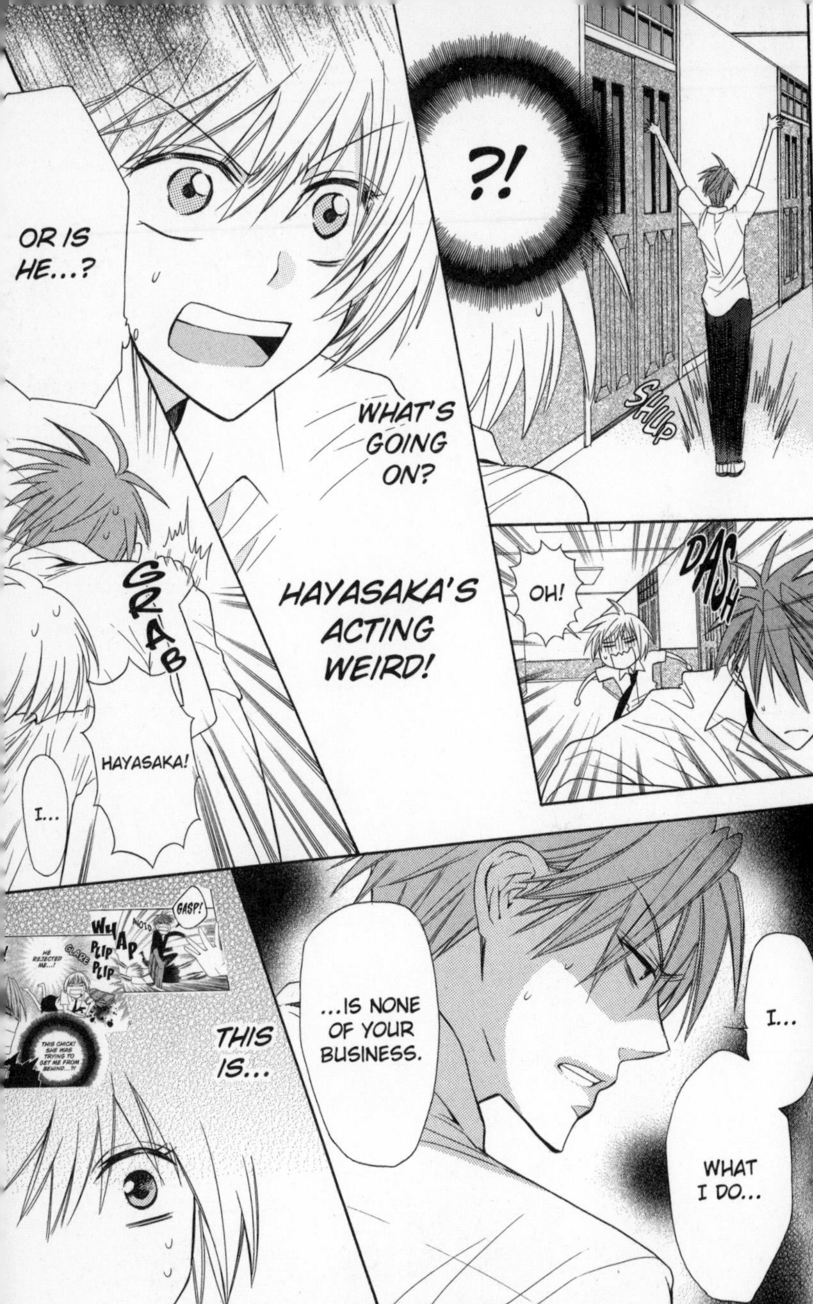
?!
SHLIP
OR IS HE...?
WHAT'S GOING ON?
OH!
DASH
HAYASAKA'S ACTING WEIRD!
GRAB
HAYASAKA!
I...
I...
WHAT I DO...
...IS NONE OF YOUR BUSINESS.
THIS IS...
GASP!
WHAP
PLIP PLIP
GLARE
HE REJECTED ME...!
THIS CHICK! SHE WAS TRYING TO GET ME FROM BEHIND...?!

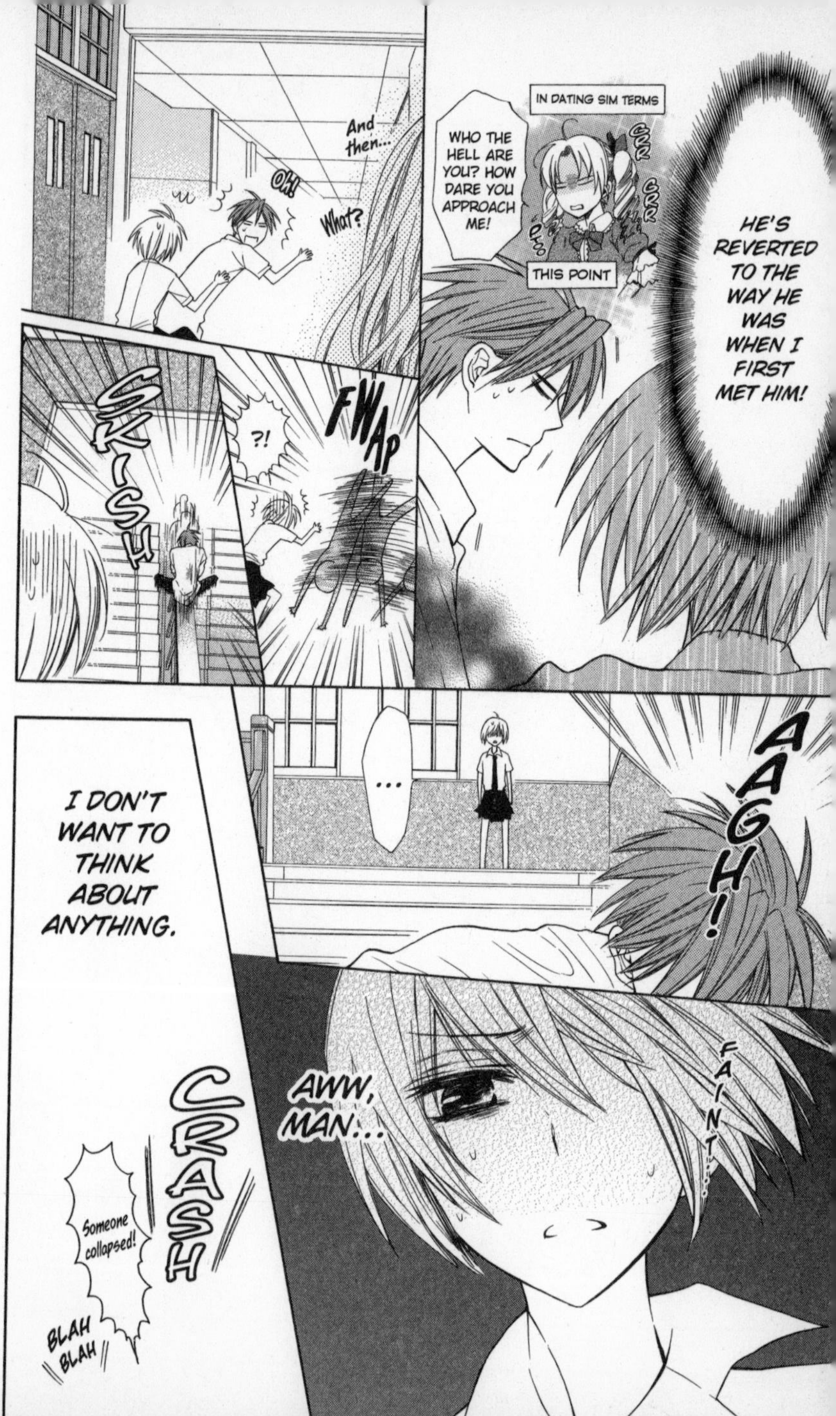
HE'S REVERTED TO THE WAY HE WAS WHEN I FIRST MET HIM!
IN DATING SIM TERMS
GRR GRR
WHO THE HELL ARE YOU? HOW DARE YOU APPROACH ME!
THIS POINT
And then...
OH!
What?
FWAP
?!
SKRISH
AAGH!
...
FAINT...
AWW, MAN...
I DON'T WANT TO THINK ABOUT ANYTHING.
CRASH
Someone collapsed!
BLAH BLAH

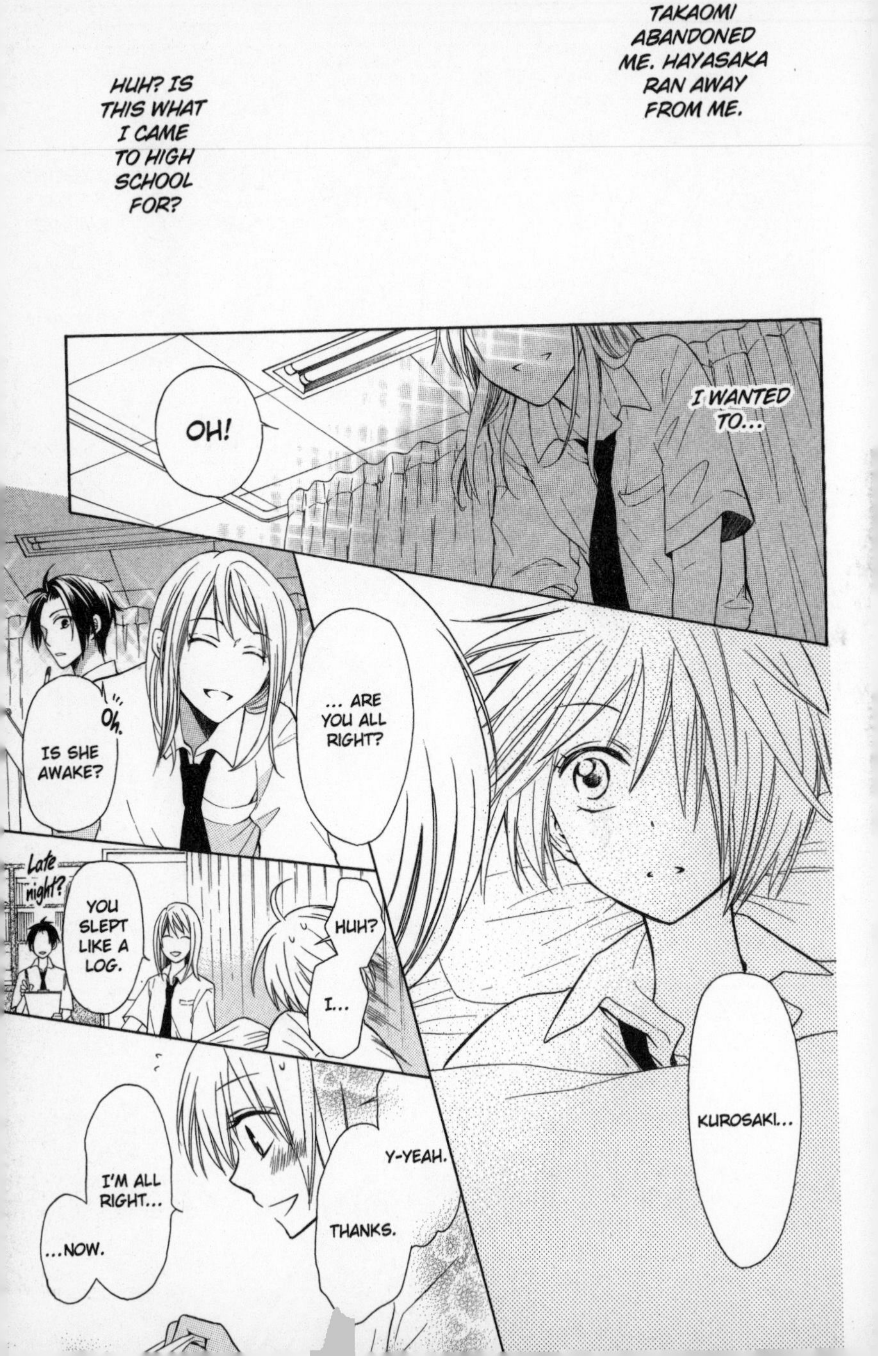
TAKAOMI ABANDONED ME. HAYASAKA RAN AWAY FROM ME.
HUH? IS THIS WHAT I CAME TO HIGH SCHOOL FOR?
I WANTED TO...
OH!
KUROSAKI...
... ARE YOU ALL RIGHT?
Oh.
IS SHE AWAKE?
HUH?
I...
Late night?
YOU SLEPT LIKE A LOG.
Y-YEAH.
THANKS.
I'M ALL RIGHT...
...NOW.

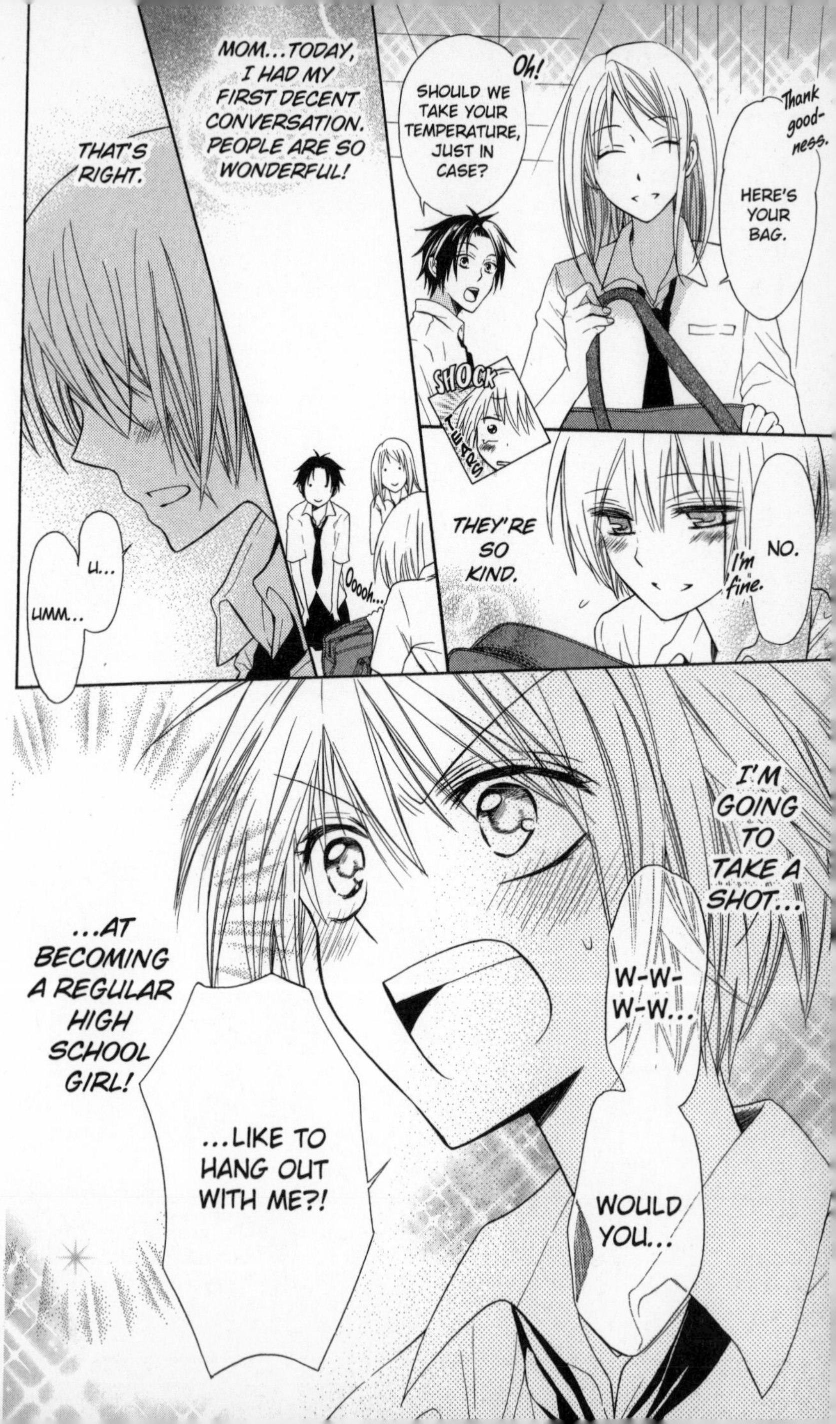
Thank goodness.
HERE'S YOUR BAG.
Oh!
SHOULD WE TAKE YOUR TEMPERATURE, JUST IN CASE?
SHOCK
NO.
I'm fine.
THEY'RE SO KIND.
MOM...TODAY, I HAD MY FIRST DECENT CONVERSATION. PEOPLE ARE SO WONDERFUL!
Ooooh...
THAT'S RIGHT.
U... UMM...
I'M GOING TO TAKE A SHOT...
...AT BECOMING A REGULAR HIGH SCHOOL GIRL!
W-W-W-W...
WOULD YOU...
...LIKE TO HANG OUT WITH ME?!

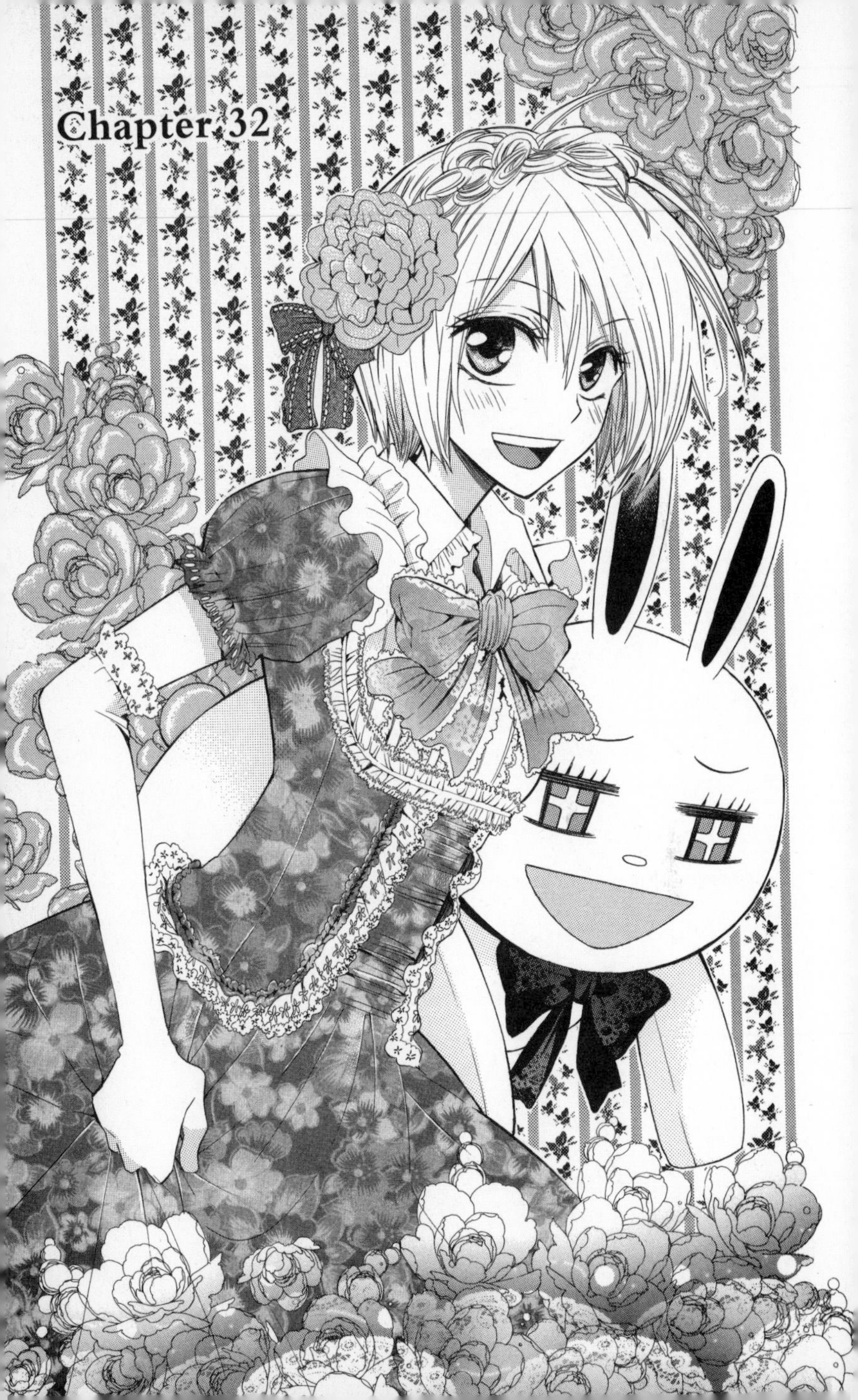
Chapter 32

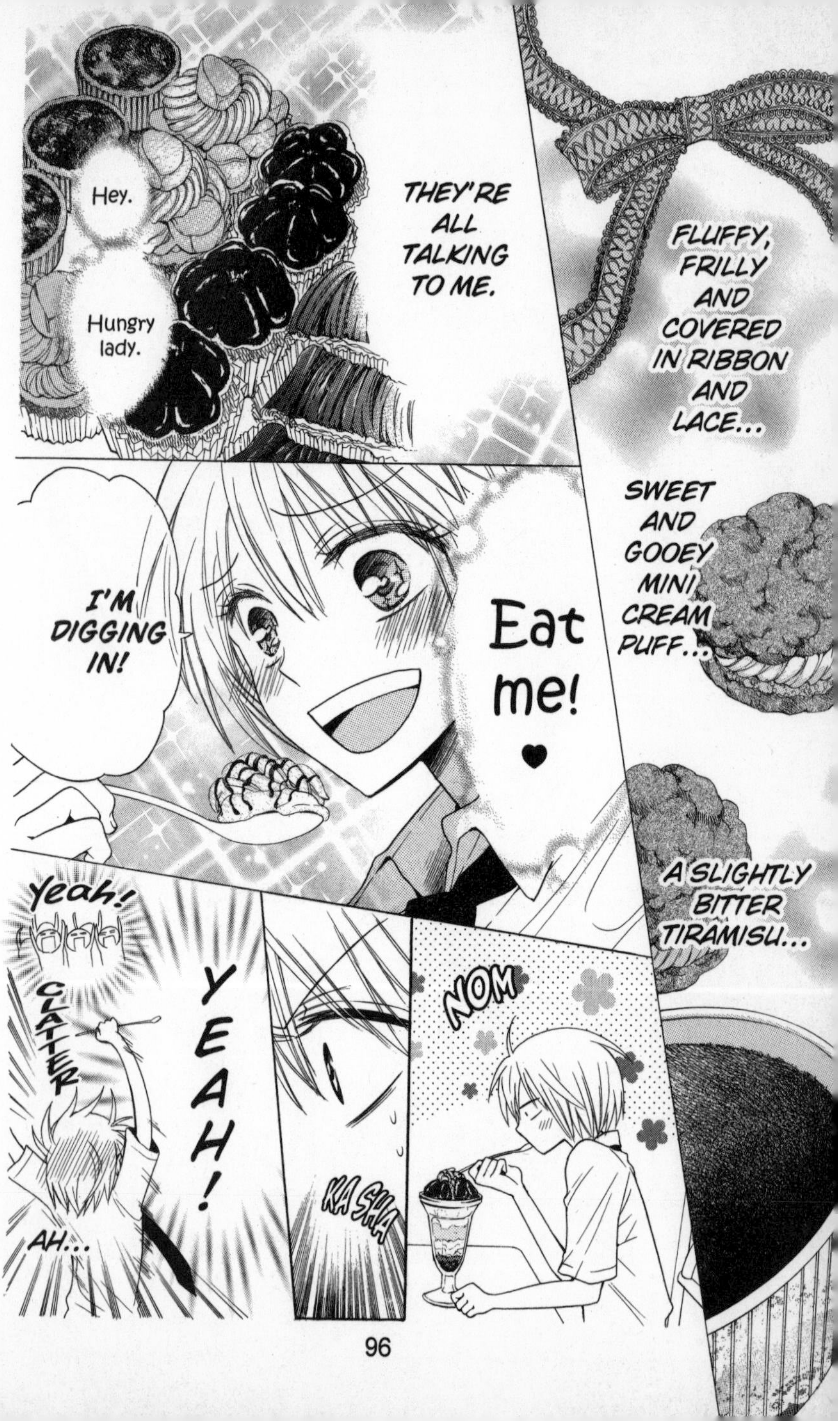

FLUFFY, FRILLY AND COVERED IN RIBBON AND LACE...
SWEET AND GOOEY MINI CREAM PUFF...
A SLIGHTLY BITTER TIRAMISU...
THEY'RE ALL TALKING TO ME.
Hey.
Hungry lady.
Eat me! ♥
I'M DIGGING IN!
NOM
KA SHA
YEAH!
Yeah!
CLATTER
AH...

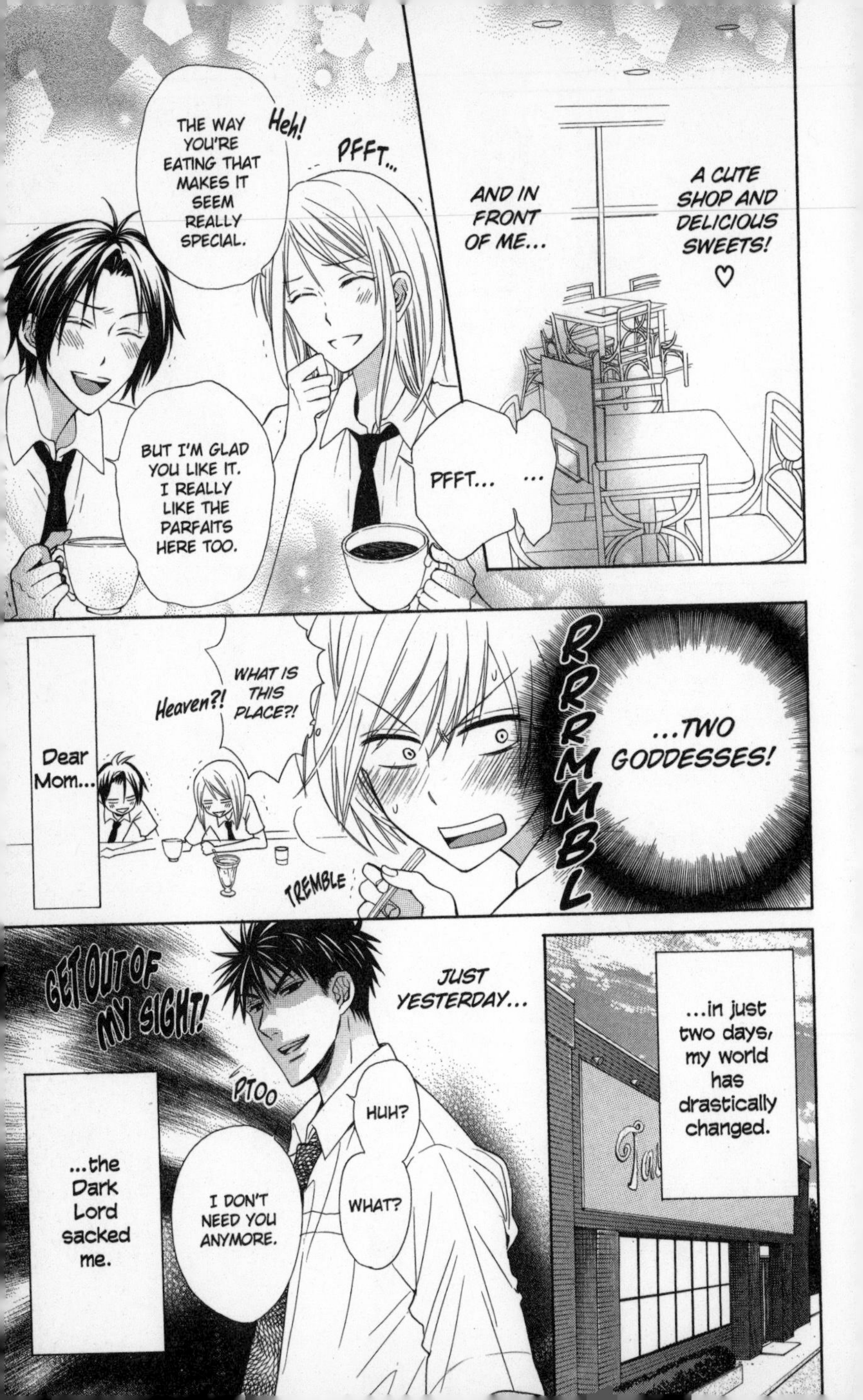
A CUTE SHOP AND DELICIOUS SWEETS! ♡
AND IN FRONT OF ME...
PFFT... ...
PFFT...
Heh!
THE WAY YOU'RE EATING THAT MAKES IT SEEM REALLY SPECIAL.
BUT I'M GLAD YOU LIKE IT. I REALLY LIKE THE PARFAITS HERE TOO.
...TWO GODDESSES!
RRRMMBL
TREMBLE
WHAT IS THIS PLACE?!
Heaven?!
Dear Mom...
...in just two days, my world has drastically changed.
JUST YESTERDAY...
HUH?
WHAT?
I DON'T NEED YOU ANYMORE.
PTOO
GET OUT OF MY SIGHT!
...the Dark Lord sacked me.

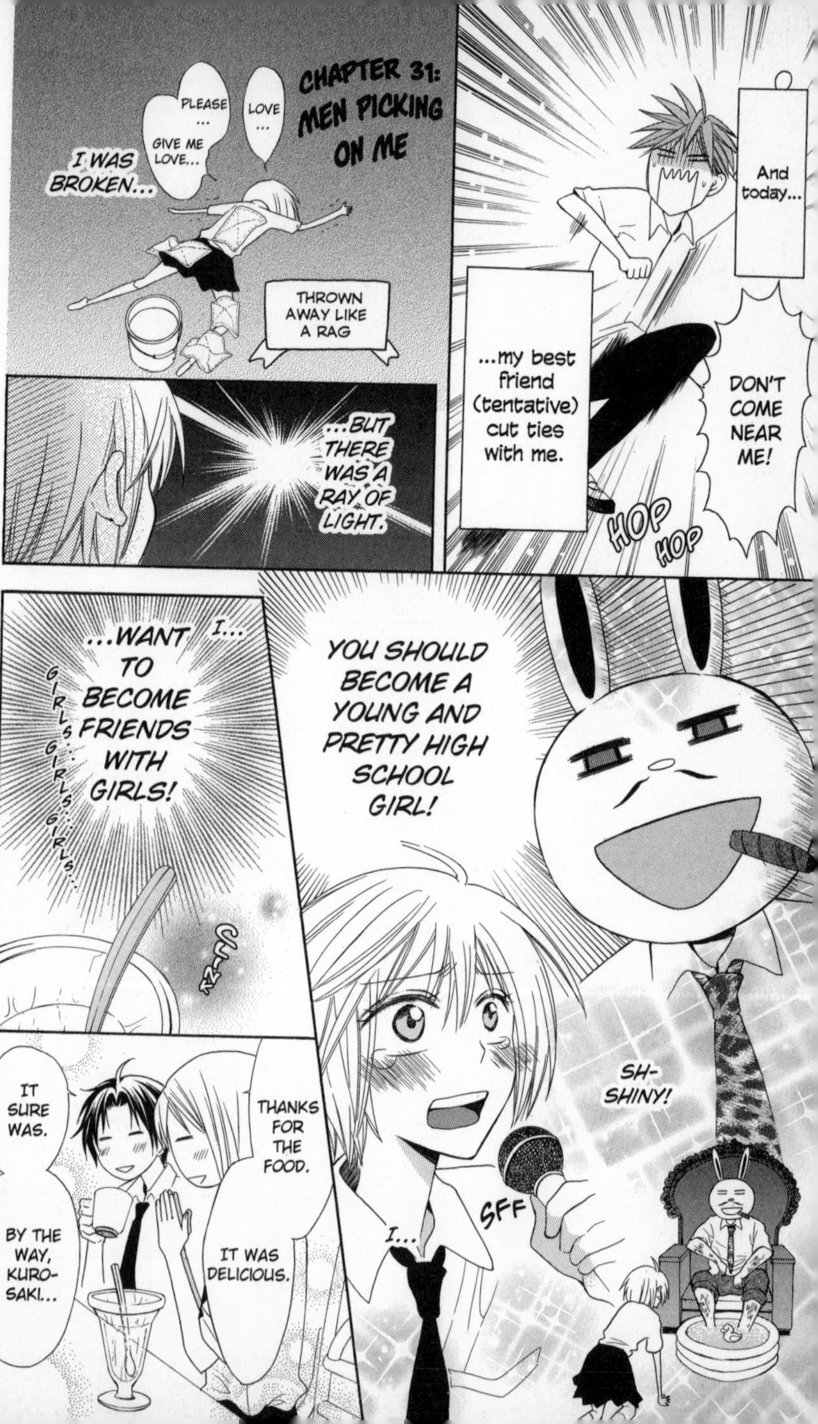
And today...
...my best friend (tentative) cut ties with me.
DON'T COME NEAR ME!
HOP HOP
CHAPTER 31: MEN PICKING ON ME
LOVE...
PLEASE... GIVE ME LOVE...
I WAS BROKEN...
THROWN AWAY LIKE A RAG
...BUT THERE WAS A RAY OF LIGHT.
YOU SHOULD BECOME A YOUNG AND PRETTY HIGH SCHOOL GIRL!
SH- SHINY!
SFF
I...
I...
...WANT TO BECOME FRIENDS WITH GIRLS!
GIRLS... GIRLS... GIRLS... GIRLS...
THANKS FOR THE FOOD.
IT SURE WAS.
IT WAS DELICIOUS.
BY THE WAY, KURO- SAKI...

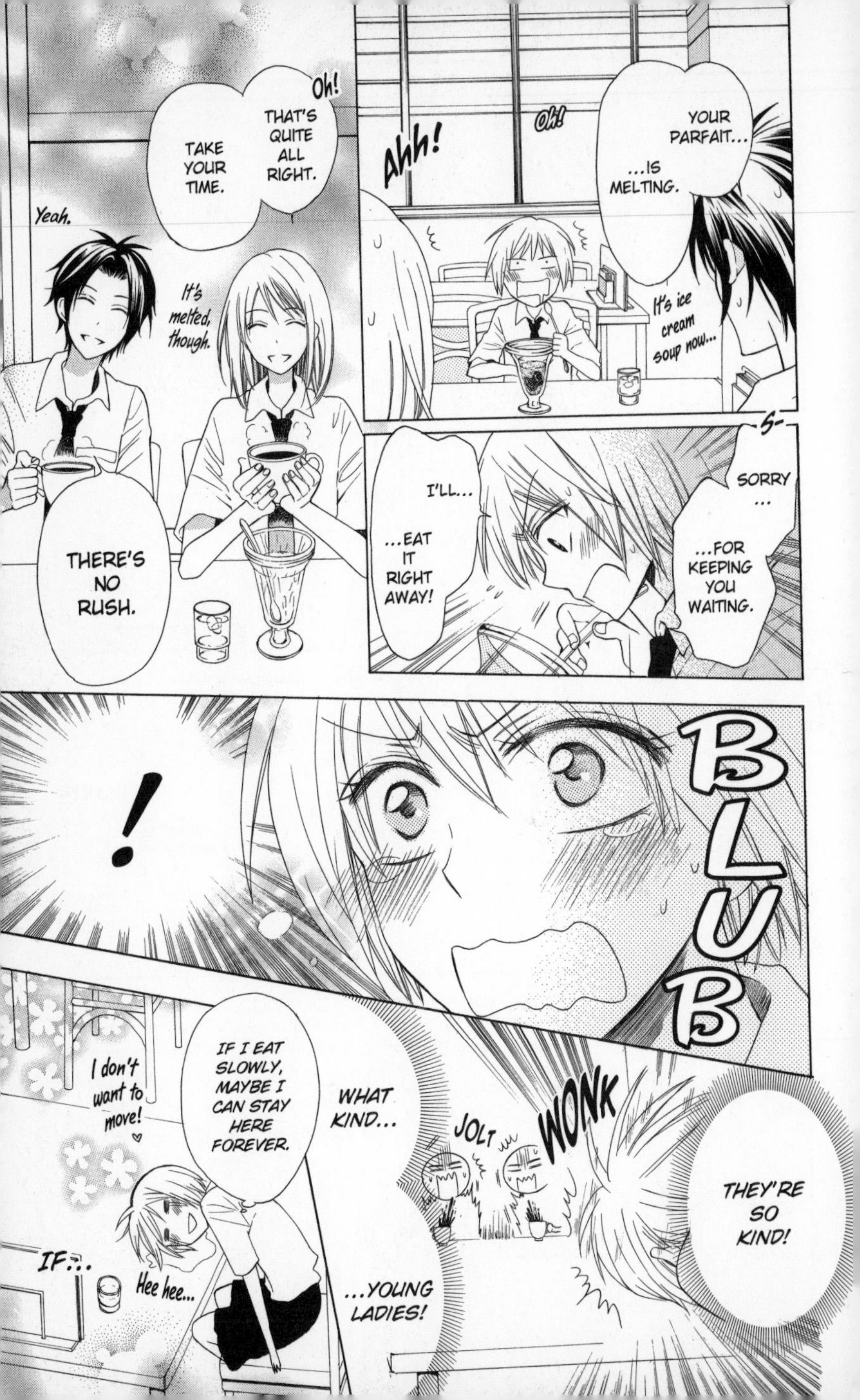
YOUR PARFAIT...
...IS MELTING.
Oh!
Ahh!
It's ice cream soup now...
SORRY...
...FOR KEEPING YOU WAITING.
I'LL...
...EAT IT RIGHT AWAY!
Oh!
THAT'S QUITE ALL RIGHT.
TAKE YOUR TIME.
Yeah.
It's melted, though.
THERE'S NO RUSH.
BLUB
!
THEY'RE SO KIND!
WONK
JOLT
WHAT KIND...
...YOUNG LADIES!
IF I EAT SLOWLY, MAYBE I CAN STAY HERE FOREVER.
I don't want to move!
IF...
Hee hee...

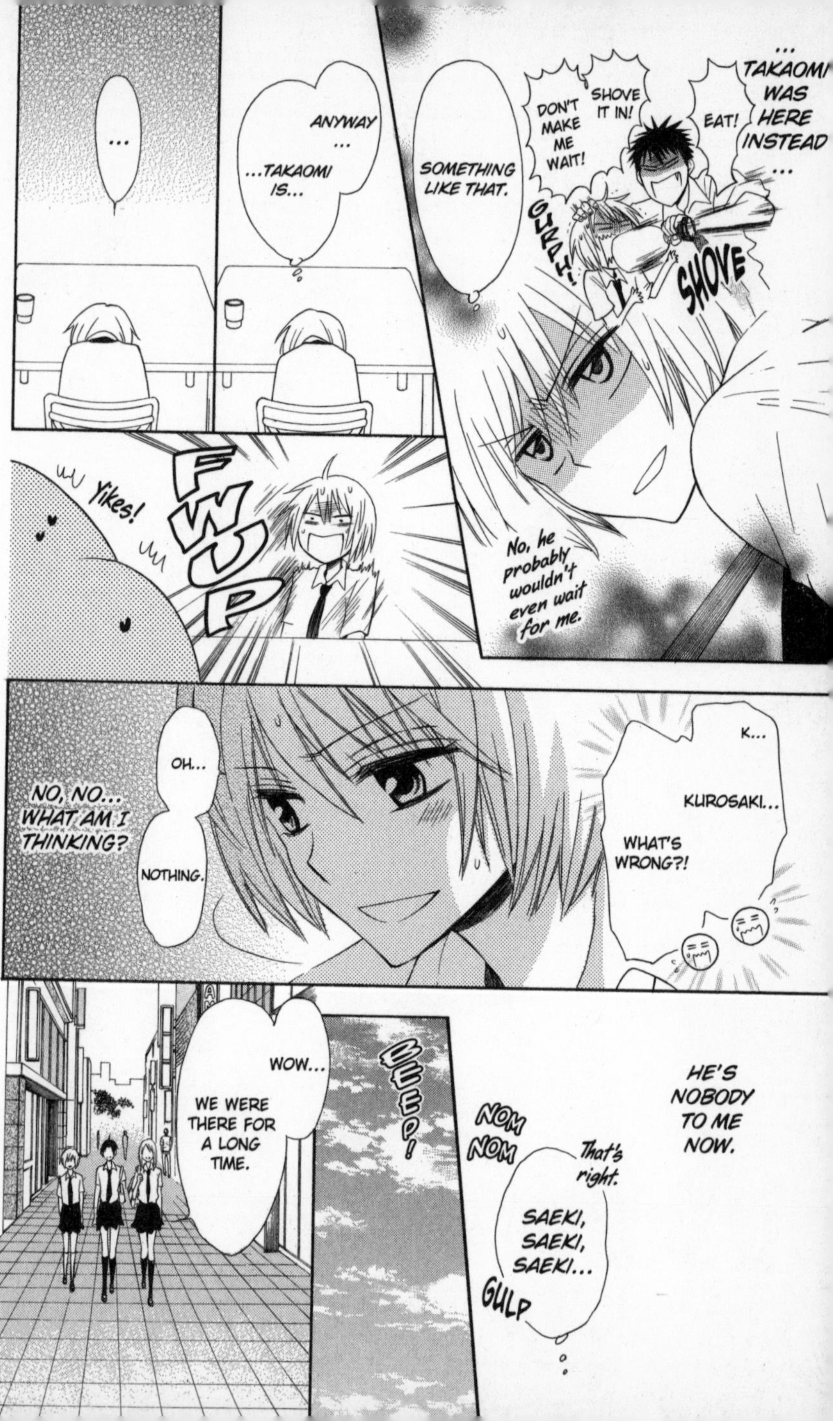
...TAKAOMI WAS HERE INSTEAD...
EAT!
SHOVE IT IN!
DON'T MAKE ME WAIT!
GURAH!
SHOVE
SOMETHING LIKE THAT.
No, he probably wouldn't even wait for me.
ANYWAY... ...TAKAOMI IS...
...
FWUP
Yikes!
K...
KUROSAKI...
WHAT'S WRONG?!
OH...
NOTHING.
NO, NO... WHAT AM I THINKING?
HE'S NOBODY TO ME NOW.
NOM NOM
That's right.
SAEKI, SAEKI, SAEKI...
GULP
BEEEP!
WOW...
WE WERE THERE FOR A LONG TIME.

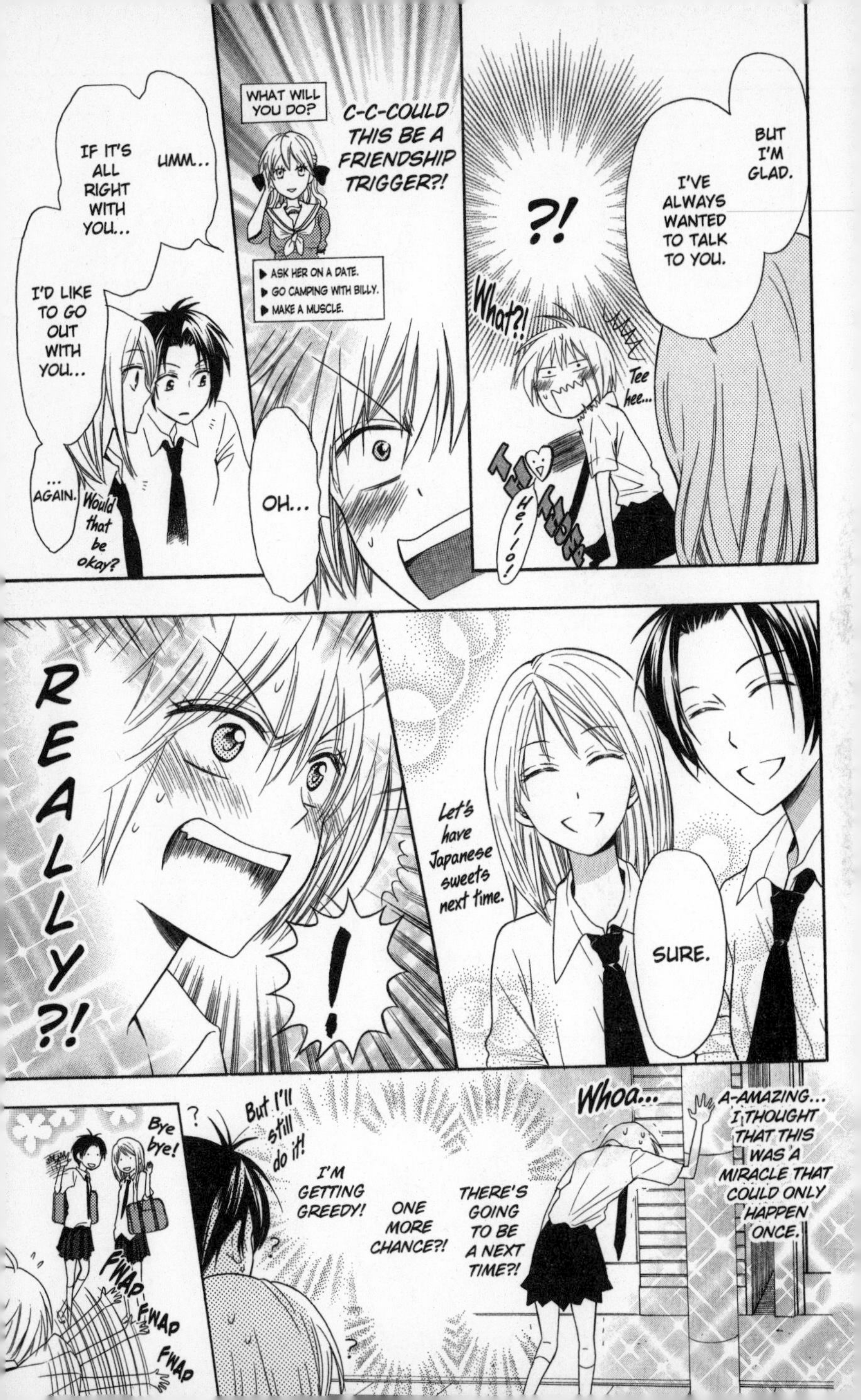
BUT I'M GLAD.
I'VE ALWAYS WANTED TO TALK TO YOU.
?!
What?!
Tee hee...
Hello!
WHAT WILL YOU DO?
C-C-COULD THIS BE A FRIENDSHIP TRIGGER?!
▶ ASK HER ON A DATE.
▶ GO CAMPING WITH BILLY.
▶ MAKE A MUSCLE.
OH...
UMM...
IF IT'S ALL RIGHT WITH YOU...
I'D LIKE TO GO OUT WITH YOU...
...AGAIN.
Would that be okay?
Let's have Japanese sweets next time.
SURE.
!
REALLY?!
A-AMAZING... I THOUGHT THAT THIS WAS A MIRACLE THAT COULD ONLY HAPPEN ONCE.
Whoa...
THERE'S GOING TO BE A NEXT TIME?!
ONE MORE CHANCE?!
I'M GETTING GREEDY!
But I'll still do it!
Bye bye!
FWAP
FWAP
FWAP

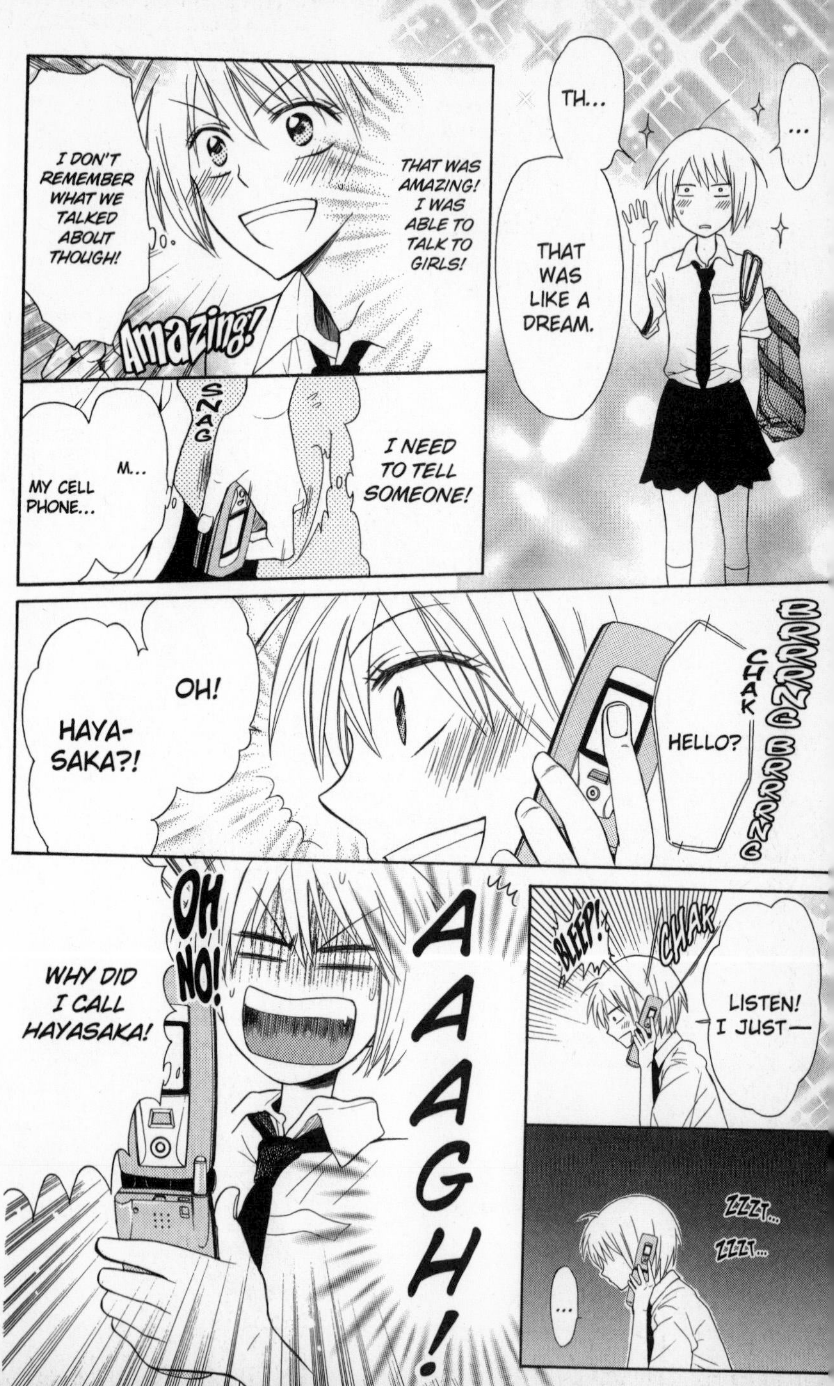
...
TH...
THAT WAS LIKE A DREAM.
THAT WAS AMAZING! I WAS ABLE TO TALK TO GIRLS!
I DON'T REMEMBER WHAT WE TALKED ABOUT THOUGH!
Amazing!
SNAG
I NEED TO TELL SOMEONE!
M...
MY CELL PHONE...
BRRRNG BRRRNG
CHAK
HELLO?
OH!
HAYA-SAKA?!
CHAK
BLEEP!
LISTEN! I JUST—
ZZZT...
ZZZT...
...
AAAGH!
OH NO!
WHY DID I CALL HAYASAKA!

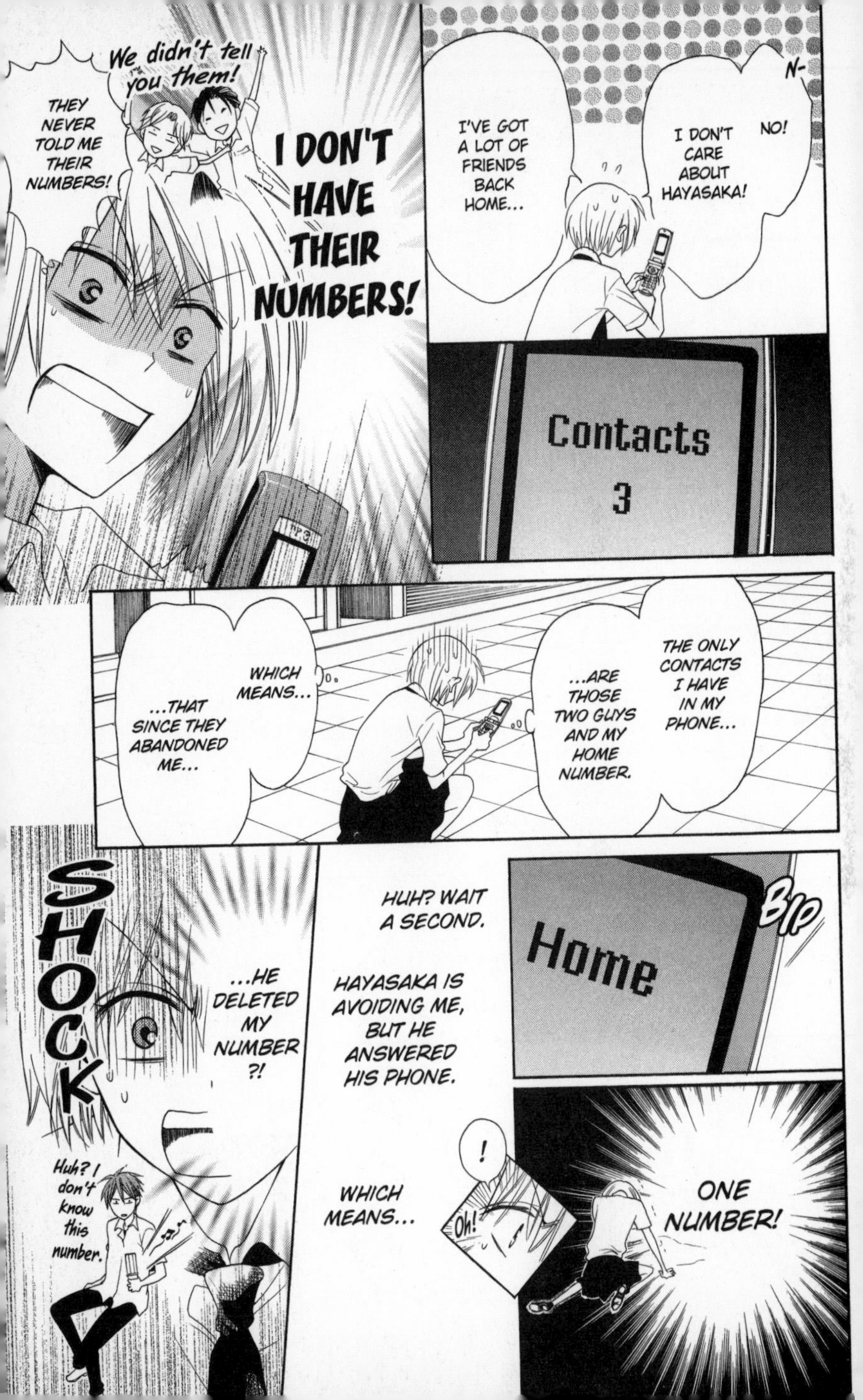
N-
NO!
I DON'T CARE ABOUT HAYASAKA!
I'VE GOT A LOT OF FRIENDS BACK HOME...
Contacts
3
I DON'T HAVE THEIR NUMBERS!
We didn't tell you them!
THEY NEVER TOLD ME THEIR NUMBERS!
THE ONLY CONTACTS I HAVE IN MY PHONE...
...ARE THOSE TWO GUYS AND MY HOME NUMBER.
WHICH MEANS...
...THAT SINCE THEY ABANDONED ME...
BIP
Home
ONE NUMBER!
!
Oh!
HUH? WAIT A SECOND.
HAYASAKA IS AVOIDING ME, BUT HE ANSWERED HIS PHONE.
WHICH MEANS...
SHOCK
...HE DELETED MY NUMBER?!
Huh? I don't know this number.

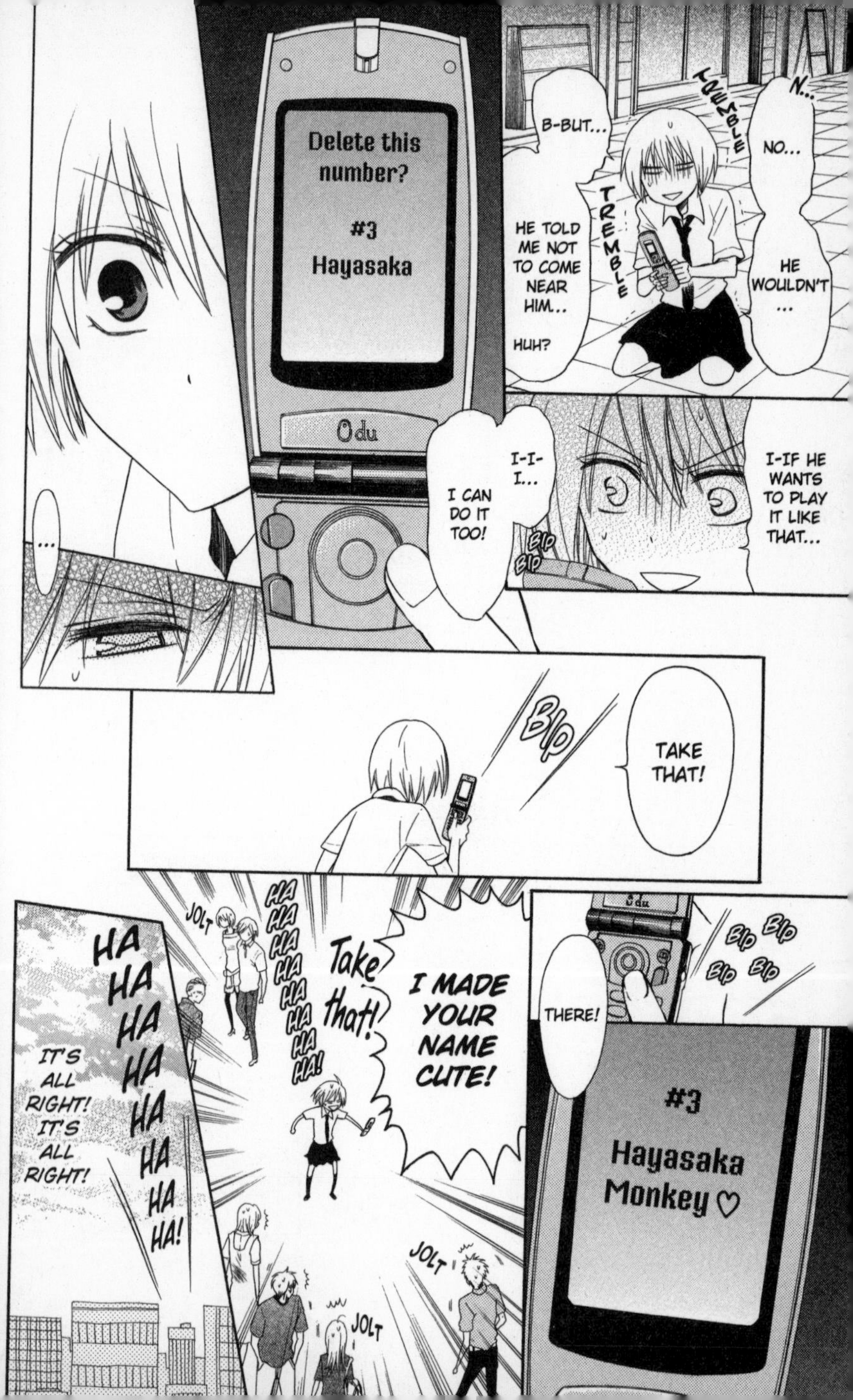
N...
NO...
HE WOULDN'T ...
TREMBLE
B-BUT...
TREMBLE
HE TOLD ME NOT TO COME NEAR HIM...
HUH?
I-IF HE WANTS TO PLAY IT LIKE THAT...
I-I-I...
I CAN DO IT TOO!
BLIP BLIP
Delete this number?
#3
Hayasaka
Odu
...
TAKE THAT!
BLIP
BLIP BLIP
BLIP BLIP
THERE!
#3
Hayasaka Monkey ♡
I MADE YOUR NAME CUTE!
Take that!
HA HA HA HA HA HA HA HA HA!
JOLT
HA HA HA HA HA HA HA HA HA!
IT'S ALL RIGHT! IT'S ALL RIGHT!
JOLT
JOLT

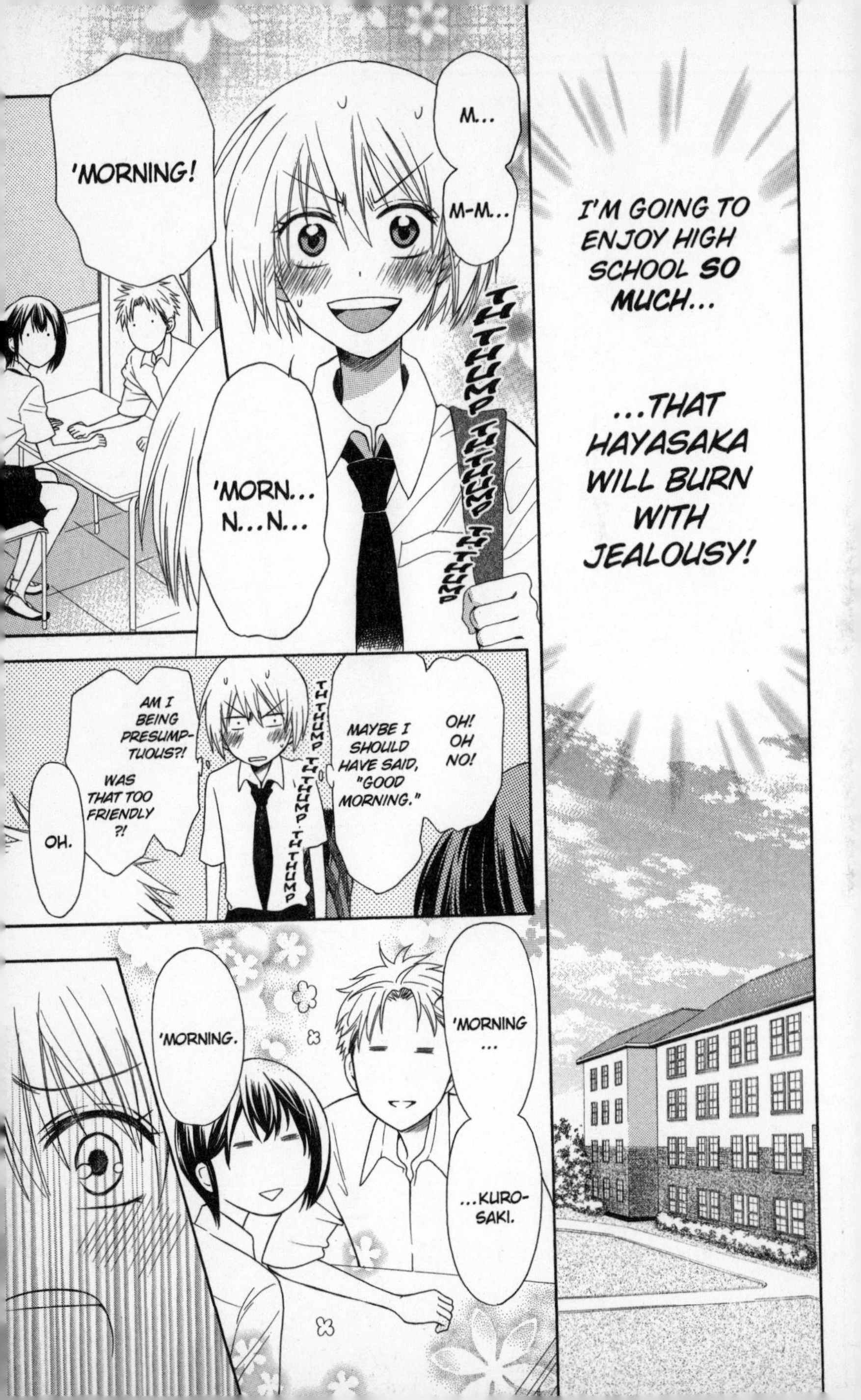
I'M GOING TO ENJOY HIGH SCHOOL SO MUCH...
...THAT HAYASAKA WILL BURN WITH JEALOUSY!
M...
M-M...
'MORNING!
THTHUMP THTHUMP THTHUMP
'MORN... N...N...
OH! OH NO!
MAYBE I SHOULD HAVE SAID, "GOOD MORNING."
THTHUMP THTHUMP THTHUMP
AM I BEING PRESUMP-TUOUS?!
WAS THAT TOO FRIENDLY ?!
OH.
'MORNING ...
...KURO-SAKI.
'MORNING.

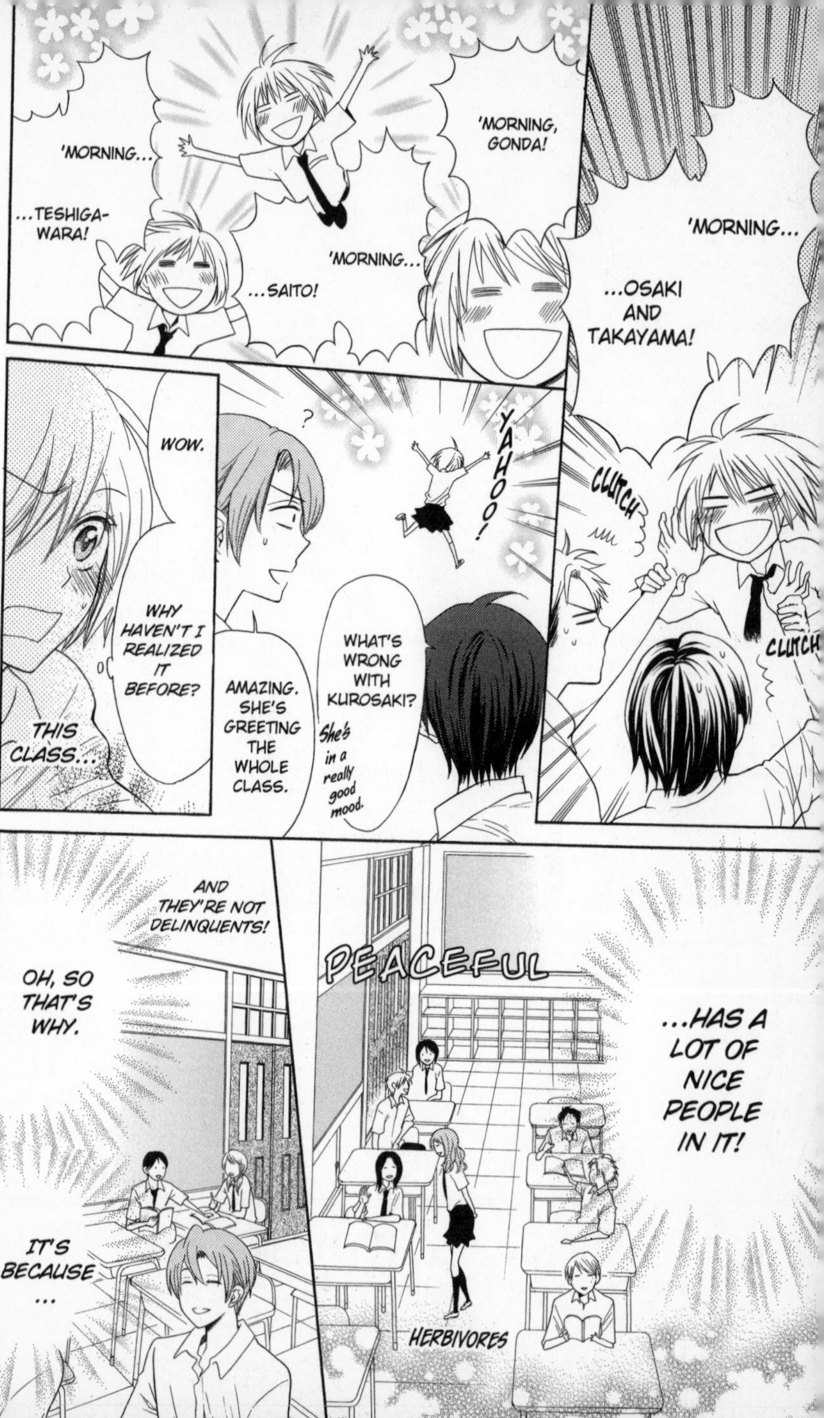
'MORNING...
...OSAKI AND TAKAYAMA!
'MORNING, GONDA!
'MORNING...
...TESHIGA-WARA!
'MORNING...
...SAITO!
CLUTCH
CLUTCH
YAHOO!
WHAT'S WRONG WITH KUROSAKI?
She's in a really good mood.
AMAZING. SHE'S GREETING THE WHOLE CLASS.
WOW.
WHY HAVEN'T I REALIZED IT BEFORE?
THIS CLASS...
PEACEFUL
...HAS A LOT OF NICE PEOPLE IN IT!
HERBIVORES
AND THEY'RE NOT DELINQUENTS!
OH, SO THAT'S WHY.
IT'S BECAUSE ...

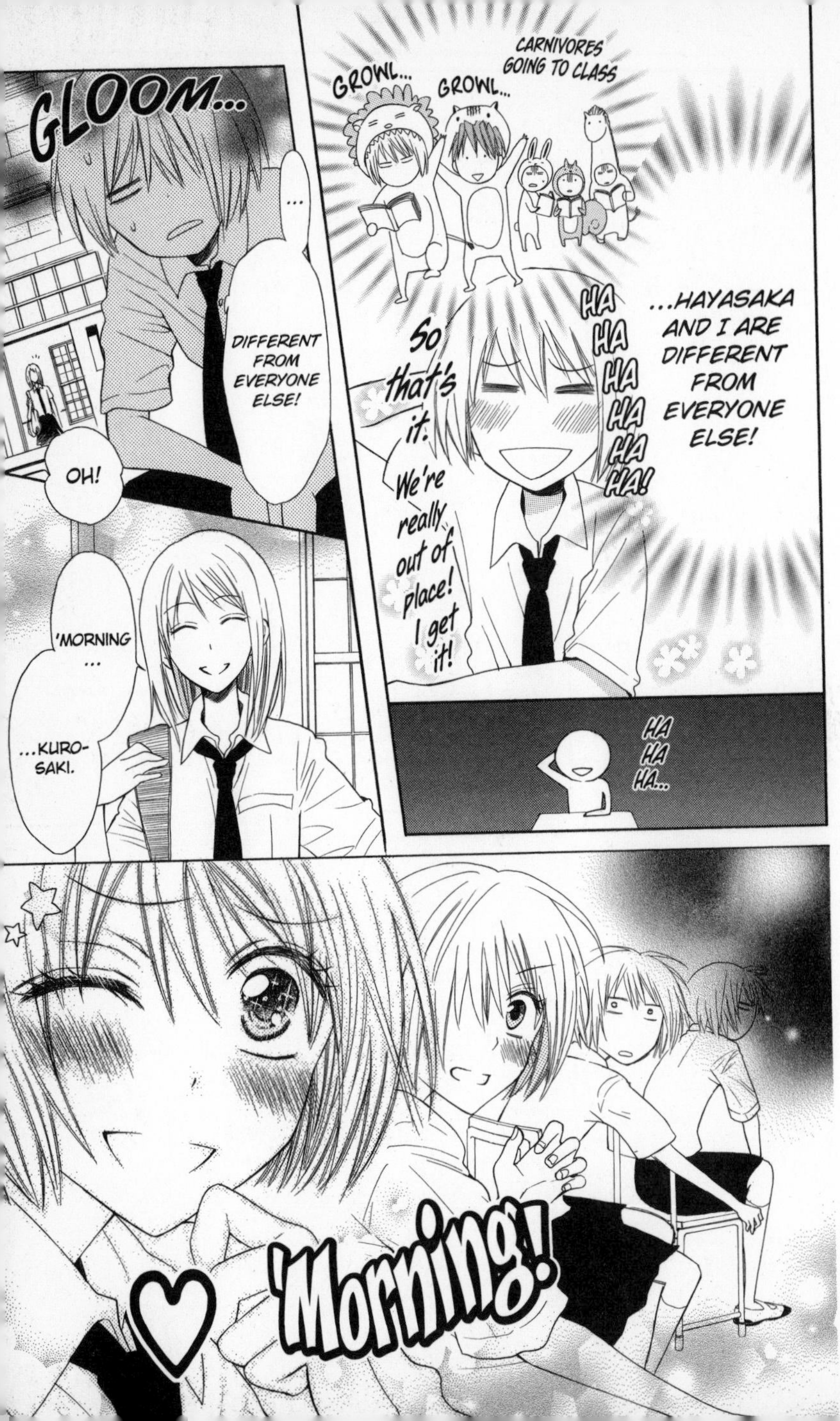
CARNIVORES GOING TO CLASS
GROWL...
GROWL...
...HAYASAKA AND I ARE DIFFERENT FROM EVERYONE ELSE!
HA HA HA HA HA HA!
So that's it.
We're really out of place! I get it!
HA HA HA...
GLOOM...
...
DIFFERENT FROM EVERYONE ELSE!
OH!
'MORNING...
...KURO-SAKI.
'Morning!

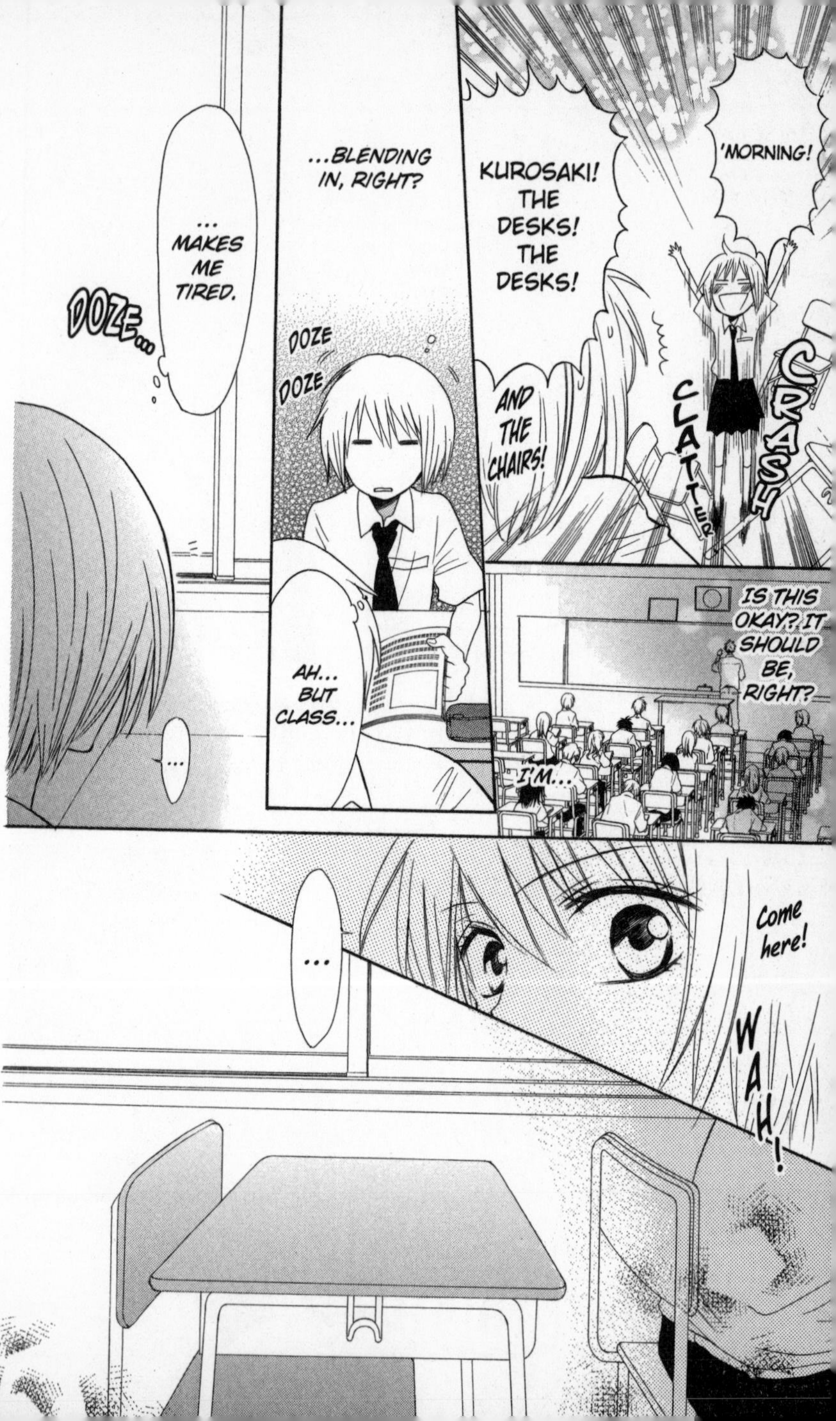

'MORNING!
CRASH
CLATTER
KUROSAKI! THE DESKS! THE DESKS!
AND THE CHAIRS!
IS THIS OKAY? IT SHOULD BE, RIGHT?
I'M...
...BLENDING IN, RIGHT?
DOZE
DOZE
AH... BUT CLASS...
... MAKES ME TIRED.
DOZE...
...
Come here!
WAH!
...

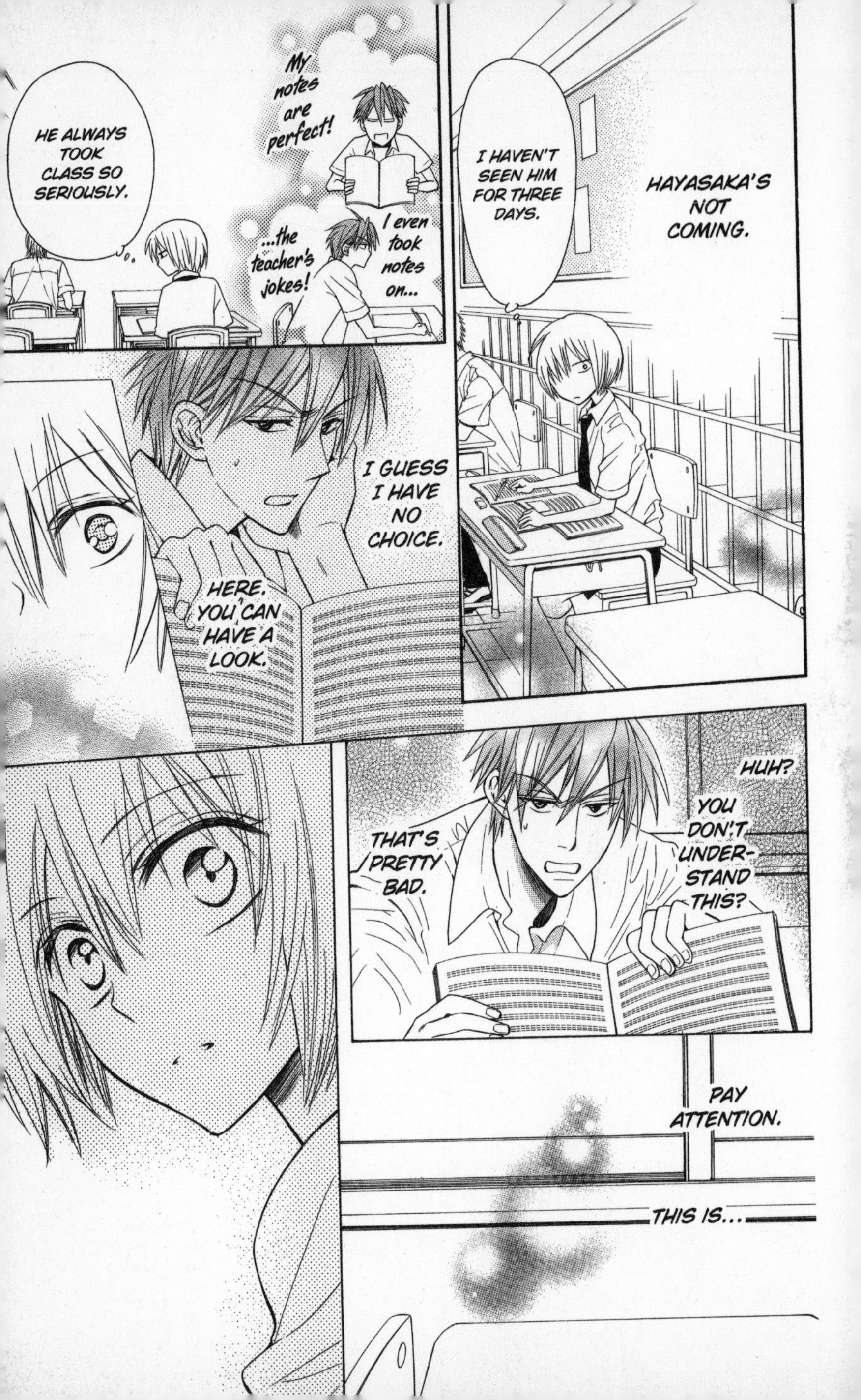
HAYASAKA'S NOT COMING.
I HAVEN'T SEEN HIM FOR THREE DAYS.
My notes are perfect!
I even took notes on...
...the teacher's jokes!
HE ALWAYS TOOK CLASS SO SERIOUSLY.
I GUESS I HAVE NO CHOICE.
HERE. YOU CAN HAVE A LOOK.
HUH?
YOU DON'T UNDER-STAND THIS?
THAT'S PRETTY BAD.
PAY ATTENTION.
THIS IS...

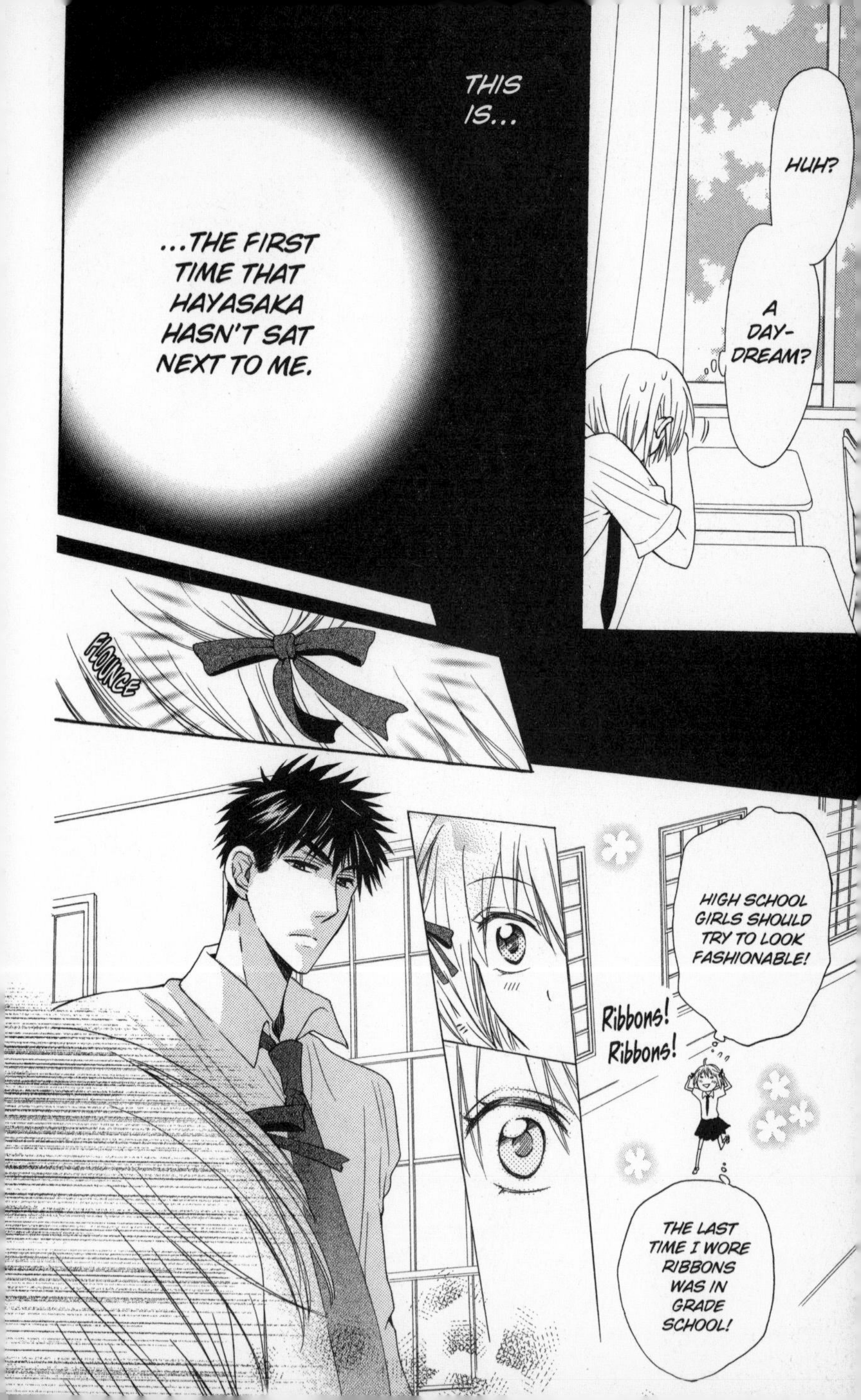
HUH?
A DAY-DREAM?
THIS IS...
...THE FIRST TIME THAT HAYASAKA HASN'T SAT NEXT TO ME.
FLOUNCE
HIGH SCHOOL GIRLS SHOULD TRY TO LOOK FASHIONABLE!
Ribbons! Ribbons!
THE LAST TIME I WORE RIBBONS WAS IN GRADE SCHOOL!

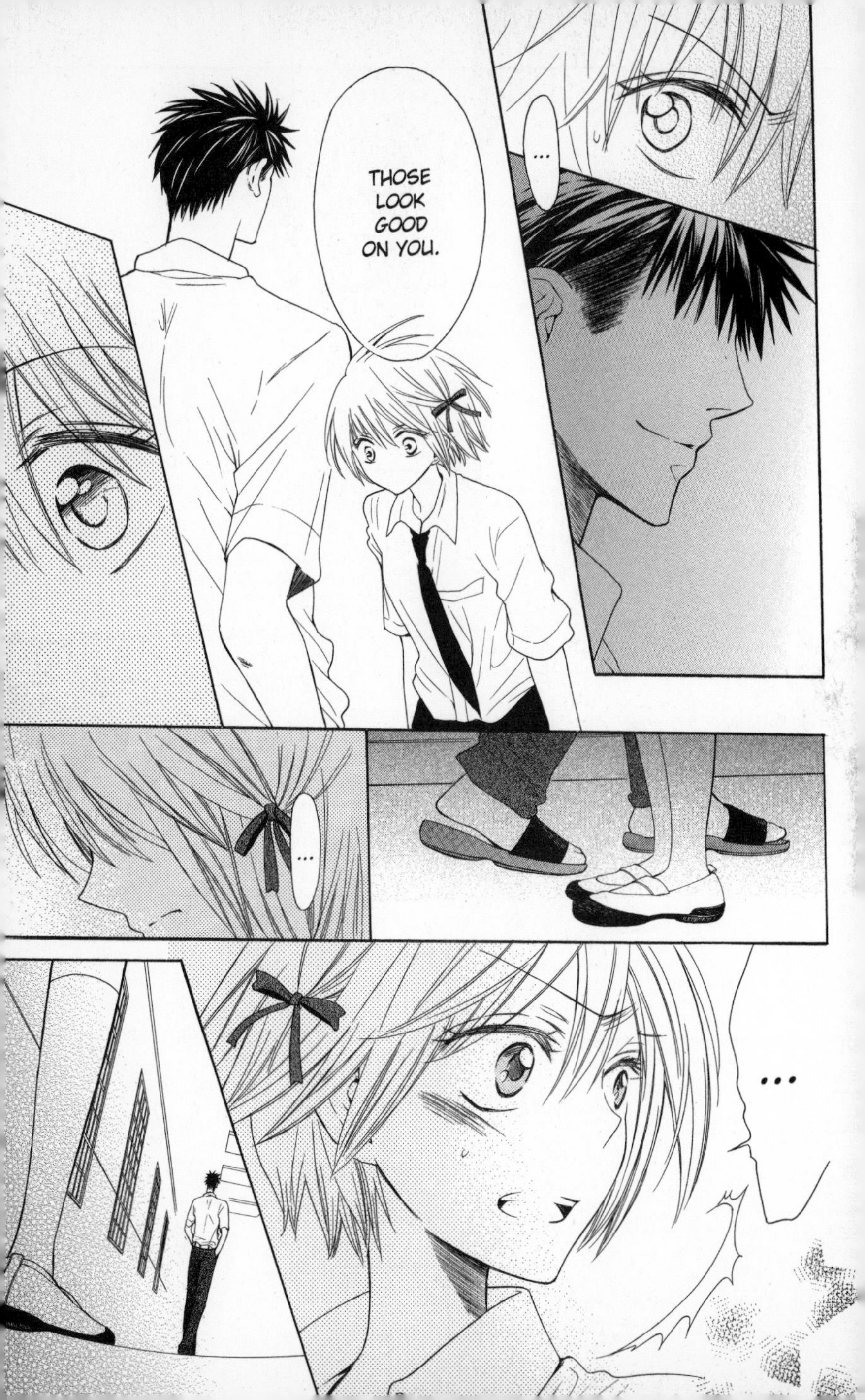
...
THOSE LOOK GOOD ON YOU.
...
...

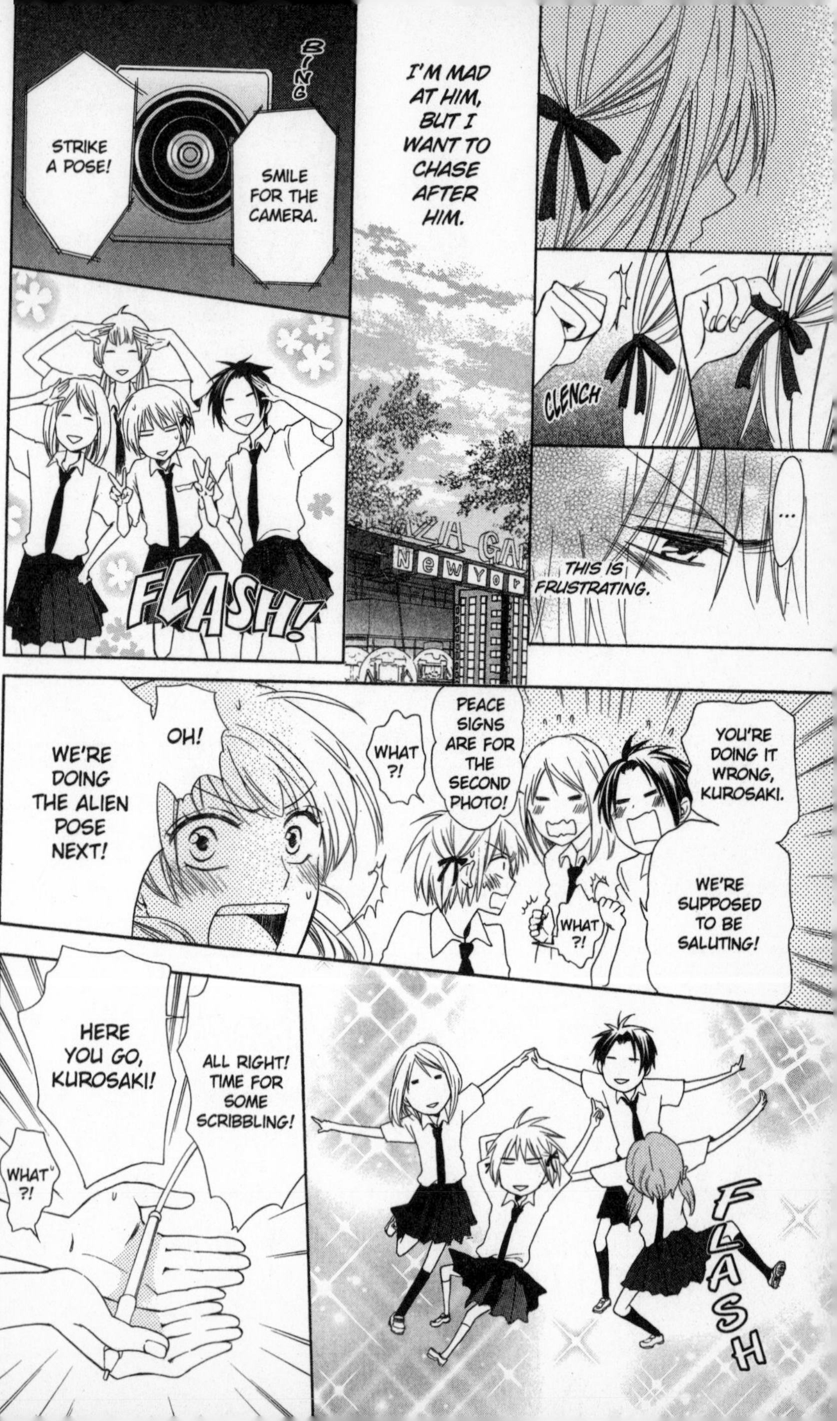
CLENCH
...
THIS IS FRUSTRATING.
I'M MAD AT HIM, BUT I WANT TO CHASE AFTER HIM.
BING
SMILE FOR THE CAMERA.
STRIKE A POSE!
FLASH!
YOU'RE DOING IT WRONG, KUROSAKI.
WE'RE SUPPOSED TO BE SALUTING!
WHAT ?!
PEACE SIGNS ARE FOR THE SECOND PHOTO!
WHAT ?!
OH!
WE'RE DOING THE ALIEN POSE NEXT!
FLASH
ALL RIGHT! TIME FOR SOME SCRIBBLING!
HERE YOU GO, KUROSAKI!
WHAT ?!

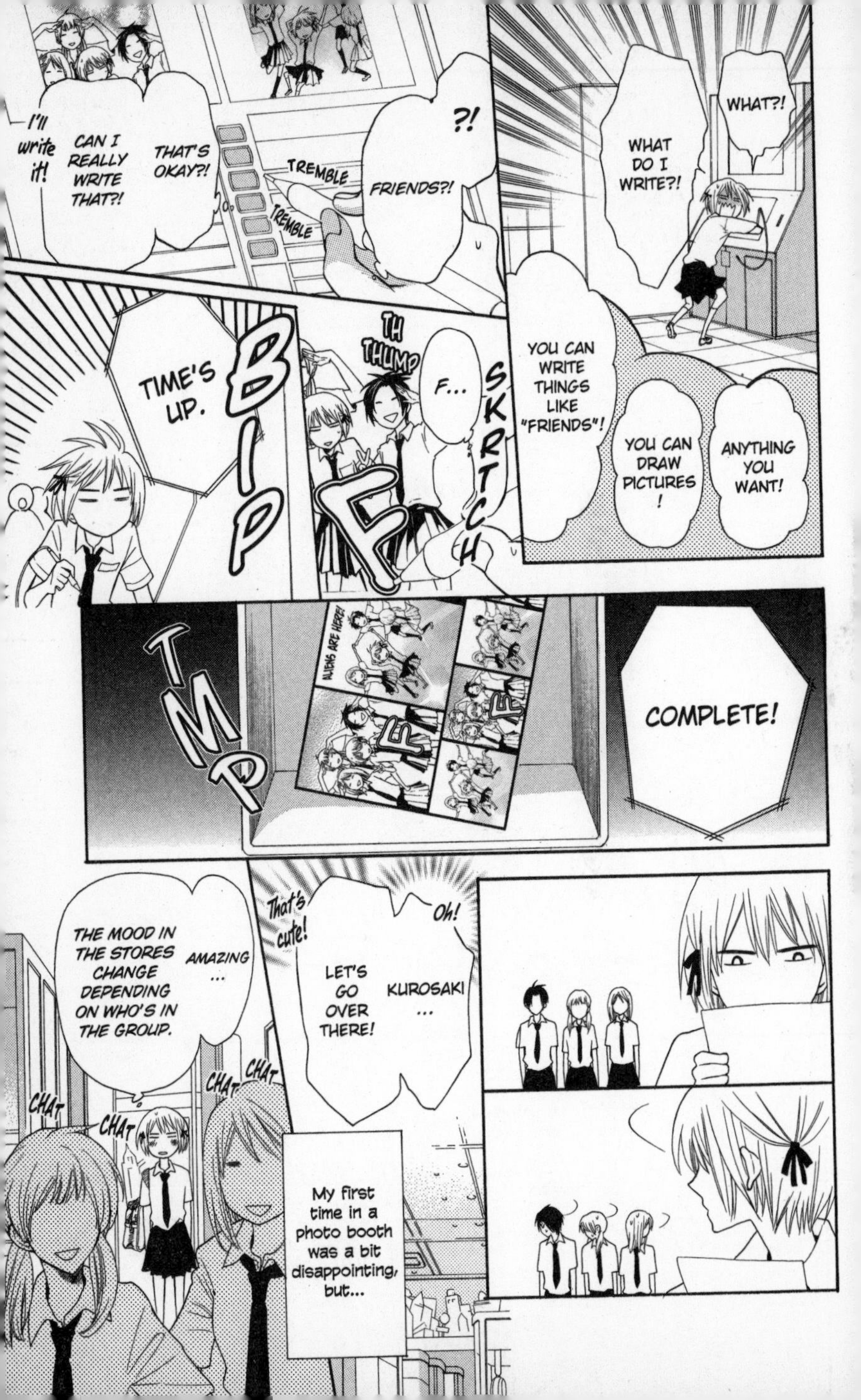
WHAT?!
WHAT DO I WRITE?!
YOU CAN WRITE THINGS LIKE "FRIENDS"!
ANYTHING YOU WANT!
YOU CAN DRAW PICTURES!
?!
FRIENDS?!
TREMBLE
TREMBLE
THAT'S OKAY?!
CAN I REALLY WRITE THAT?!
I'll write it!
SKRTCH
F...
TH THUMP
F
BIP
TIME'S UP.
COMPLETE!
ALIENS ARE HERE!
F
TMP
Oh!
KUROSAKI...
LET'S GO OVER THERE!
That's cute!
My first time in a photo booth was a bit disappointing, but...
AMAZING...
THE MOOD IN THE STORES CHANGE DEPENDING ON WHO'S IN THE GROUP.
CHAT
CHAT
CHAT
CHAT

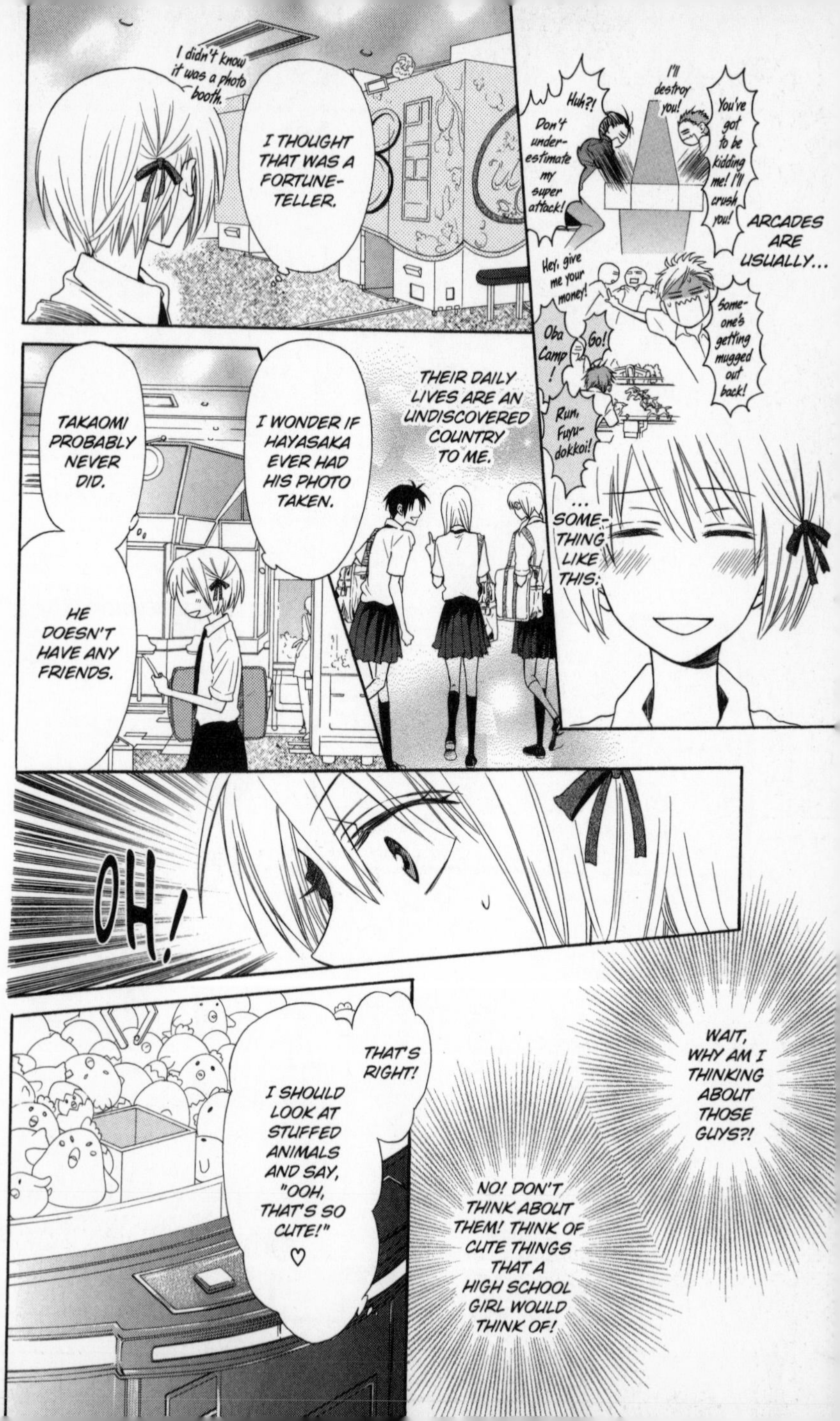
You've got to be kidding me! I'll crush you!
I'll destroy you!
Huh?!
Don't under-estimate my super attack!
ARCADES ARE USUALLY...
Some-one's getting mugged out back!
Hey, give me your money!
Go!
Oba Camp!
Run, Fuyu-dokkoi!
...SOME-THING LIKE THIS.
I THOUGHT THAT WAS A FORTUNE-TELLER.
I didn't know it was a photo booth.
THEIR DAILY LIVES ARE AN UNDISCOVERED COUNTRY TO ME.
I WONDER IF HAYASAKA EVER HAD HIS PHOTO TAKEN.
TAKAOMI PROBABLY NEVER DID.
HE DOESN'T HAVE ANY FRIENDS.
OH!
WAIT, WHY AM I THINKING ABOUT THOSE GUYS?!
NO! DON'T THINK ABOUT THEM! THINK OF CUTE THINGS THAT A HIGH SCHOOL GIRL WOULD THINK OF!
THAT'S RIGHT!
I SHOULD LOOK AT STUFFED ANIMALS AND SAY, "OOH, THAT'S SO CUTE!" ♡

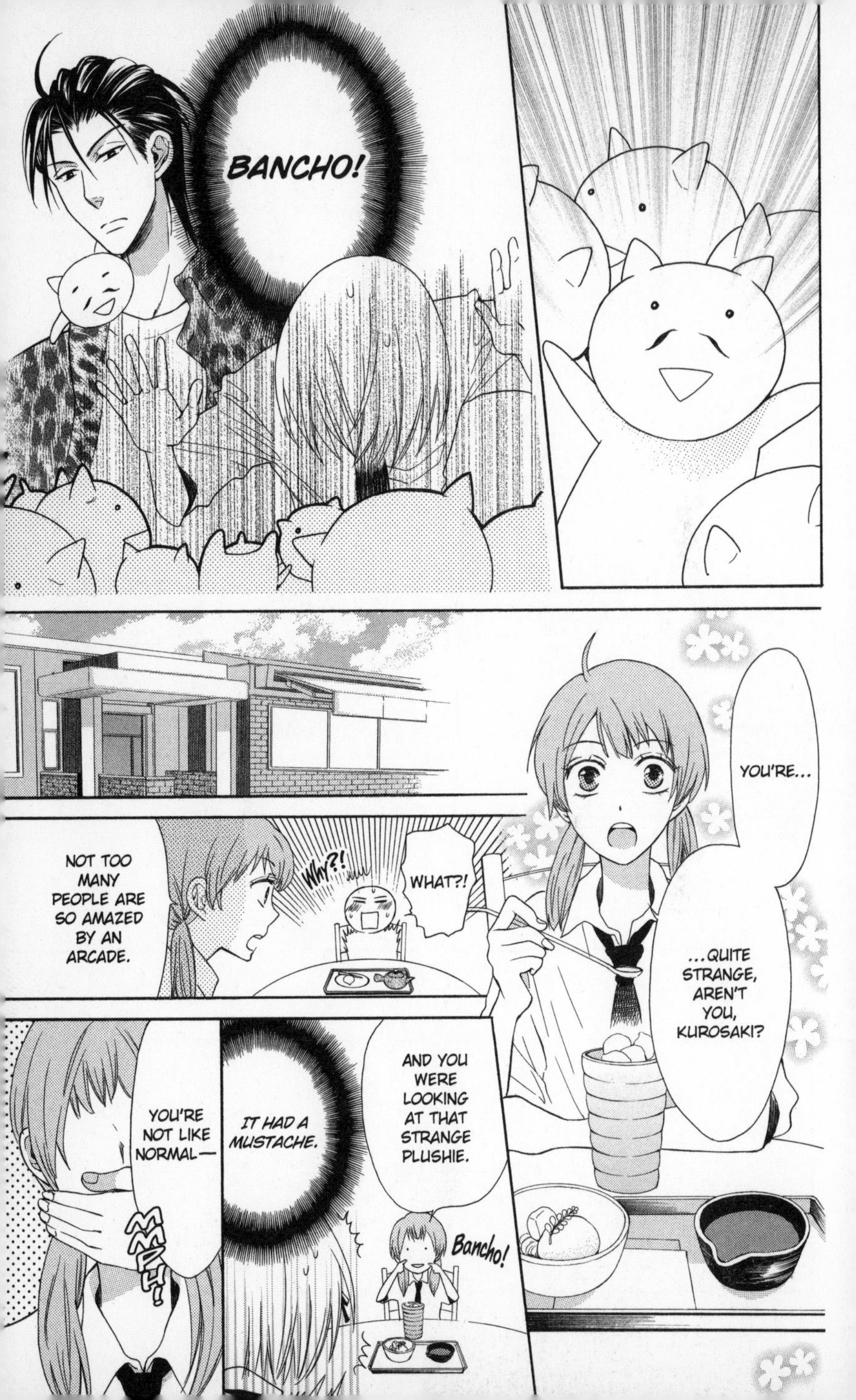
BANCHO!
YOU'RE...
...QUITE STRANGE, AREN'T YOU, KUROSAKI?
WHAT?!
Why?!
NOT TOO MANY PEOPLE ARE SO AMAZED BY AN ARCADE.
AND YOU WERE LOOKING AT THAT STRANGE PLUSHIE.
Bancho!
IT HAD A MUSTACHE.
YOU'RE NOT LIKE NORMAL—
MMPH!

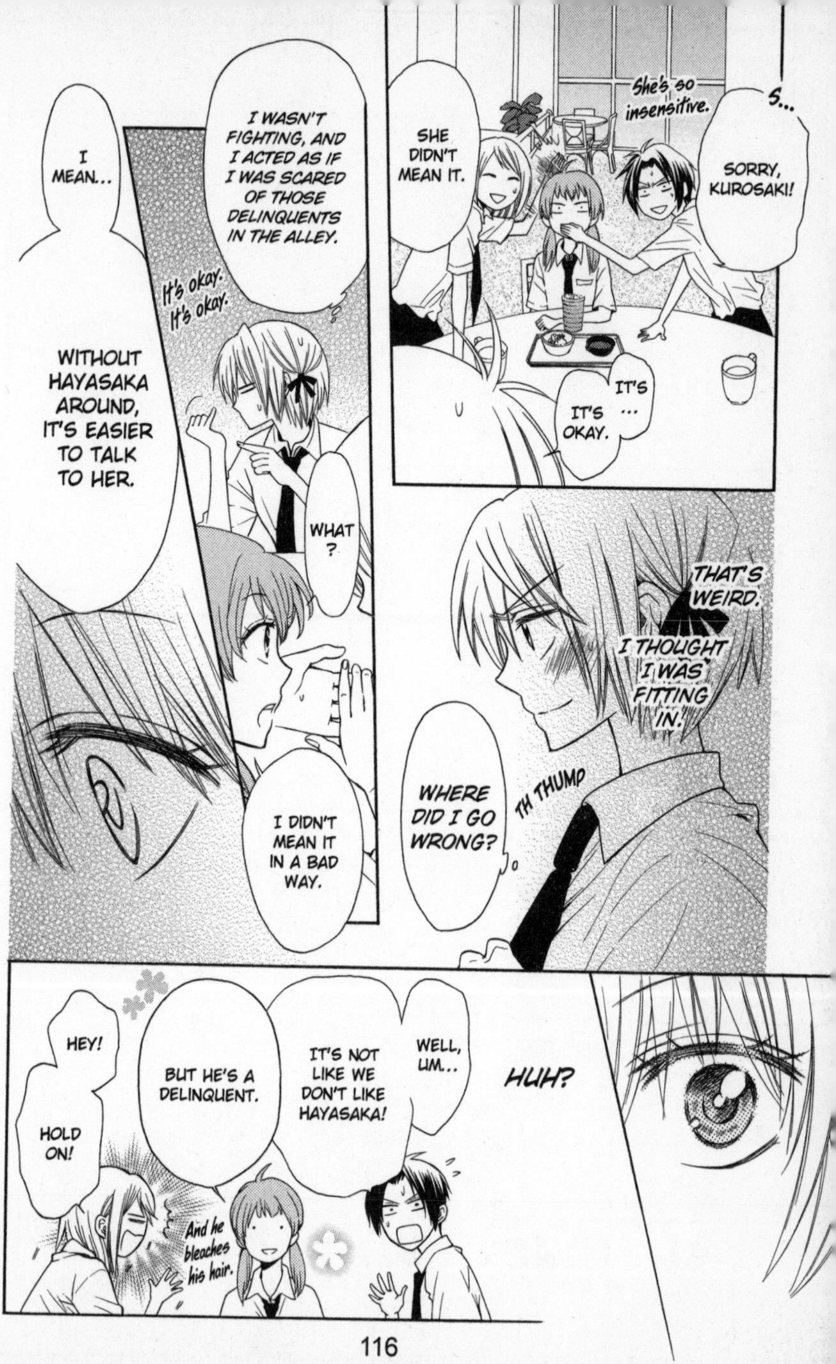
S...
SORRY, KUROSAKI!
She's so insensitive.
SHE DIDN'T MEAN IT.
IT'S ...
IT'S OKAY.
THAT'S WEIRD.
I THOUGHT I WAS FITTING IN.
WHERE DID I GO WRONG?
TH THUMP
I WASN'T FIGHTING, AND I ACTED AS IF I WAS SCARED OF THOSE DELINQUENTS IN THE ALLEY.
It's okay. It's okay.
I MEAN...
WITHOUT HAYASAKA AROUND, IT'S EASIER TO TALK TO HER.
WHAT?
I DIDN'T MEAN IT IN A BAD WAY.
HUH?
WELL, UM...
IT'S NOT LIKE WE DON'T LIKE HAYASAKA!
BUT HE'S A DELINQUENT.
And he bleaches his hair.
HEY!
HOLD ON!

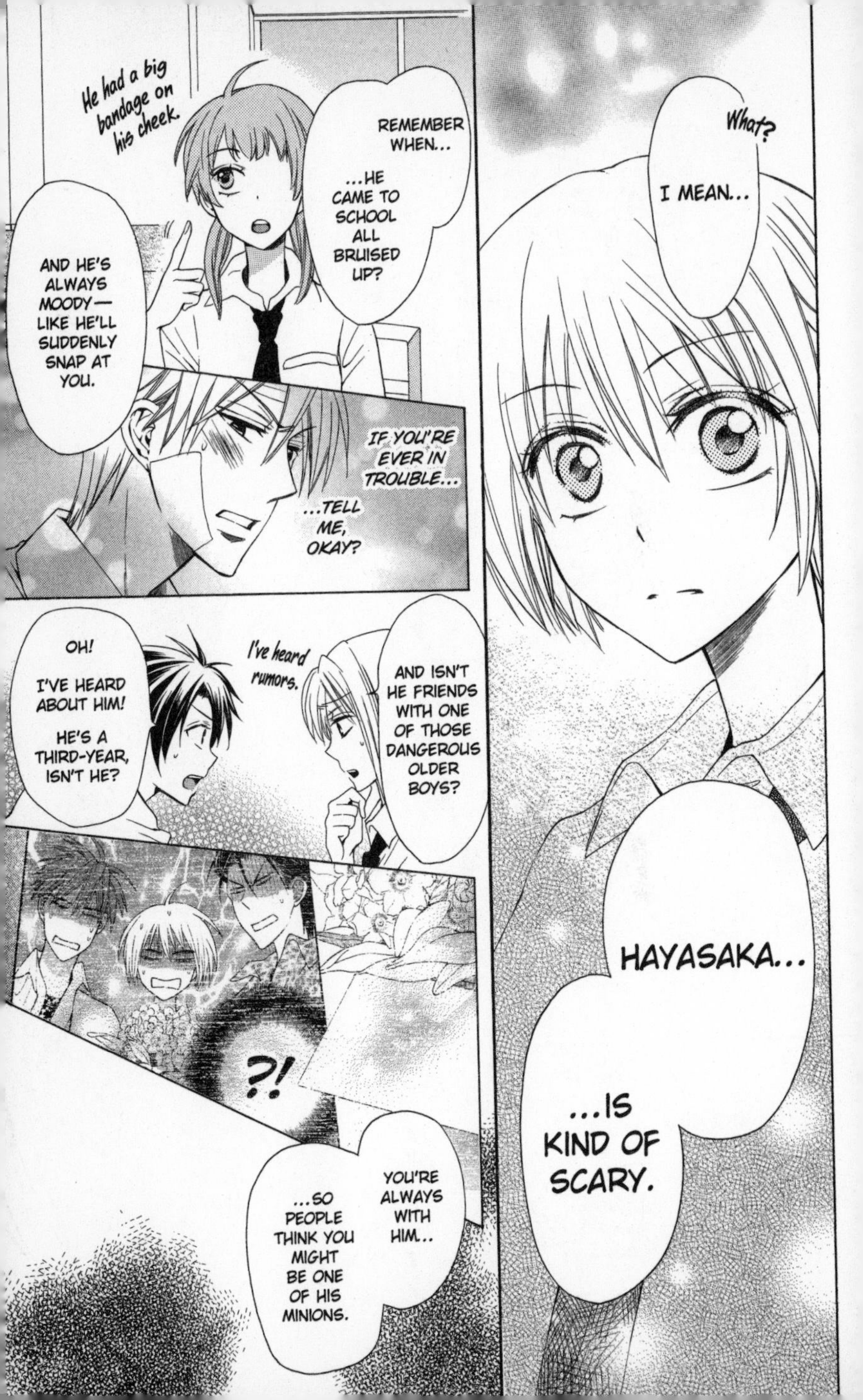
What?
I MEAN...
HAYASAKA...
...IS KIND OF SCARY.
REMEMBER WHEN...
...HE CAME TO SCHOOL ALL BRUISED UP?
He had a big bandage on his cheek.
AND HE'S ALWAYS MOODY—LIKE HE'LL SUDDENLY SNAP AT YOU.
IF YOU'RE EVER IN TROUBLE...
...TELL ME, OKAY?
AND ISN'T HE FRIENDS WITH ONE OF THOSE DANGEROUS OLDER BOYS?
I've heard rumors.
OH!
I'VE HEARD ABOUT HIM!
HE'S A THIRD-YEAR, ISN'T HE?
?!
YOU'RE ALWAYS WITH HIM..
...SO PEOPLE THINK YOU MIGHT BE ONE OF HIS MINIONS.

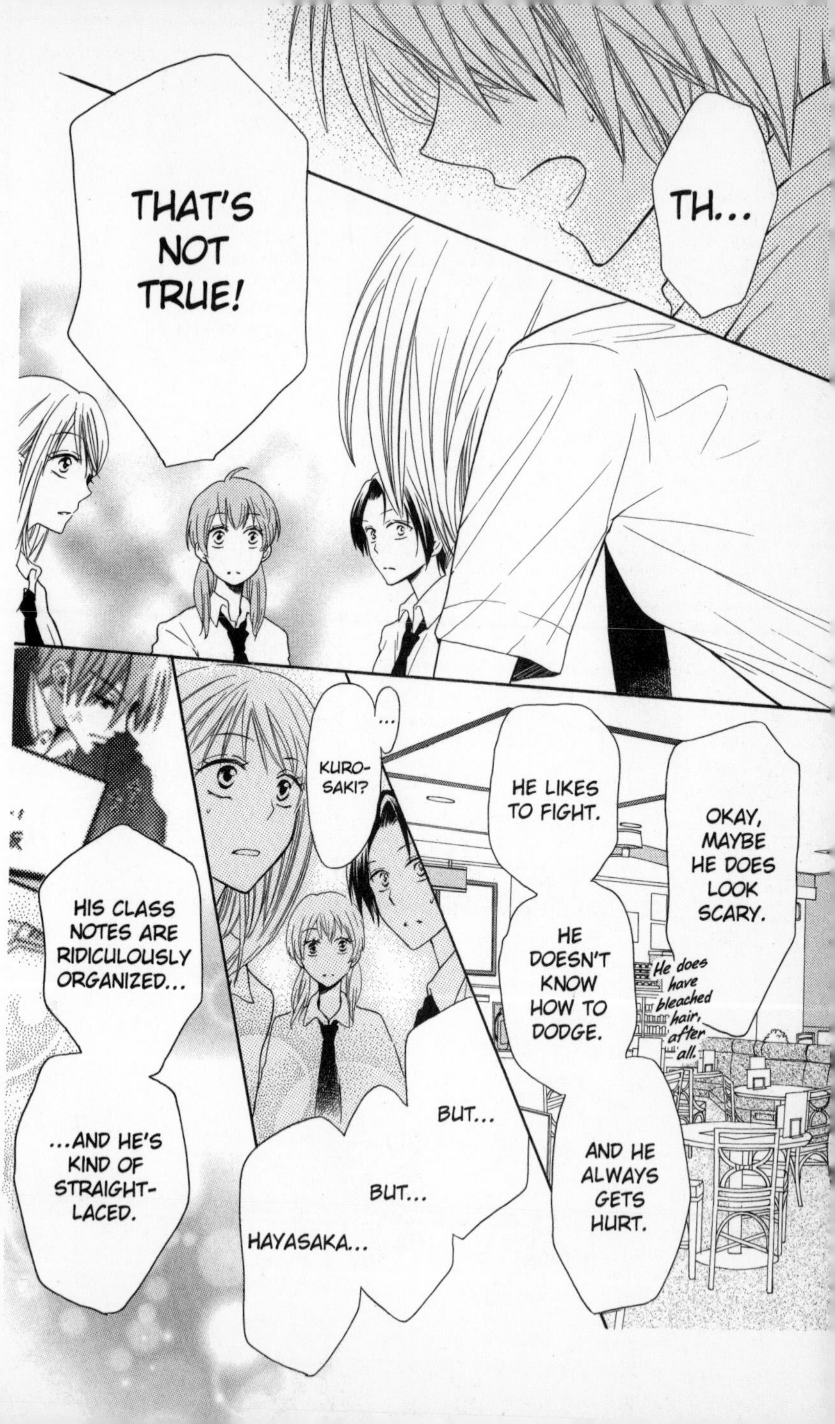
TH...
THAT'S NOT TRUE!
OKAY, MAYBE HE DOES LOOK SCARY.
He does have bleached hair, after all.
HE LIKES TO FIGHT.
HE DOESN'T KNOW HOW TO DODGE.
AND HE ALWAYS GETS HURT.
...
KURO-SAKI?
BUT...
BUT...
HAYASAKA...
HIS CLASS NOTES ARE RIDICULOUSLY ORGANIZED...
...AND HE'S KIND OF STRAIGHT-LACED.

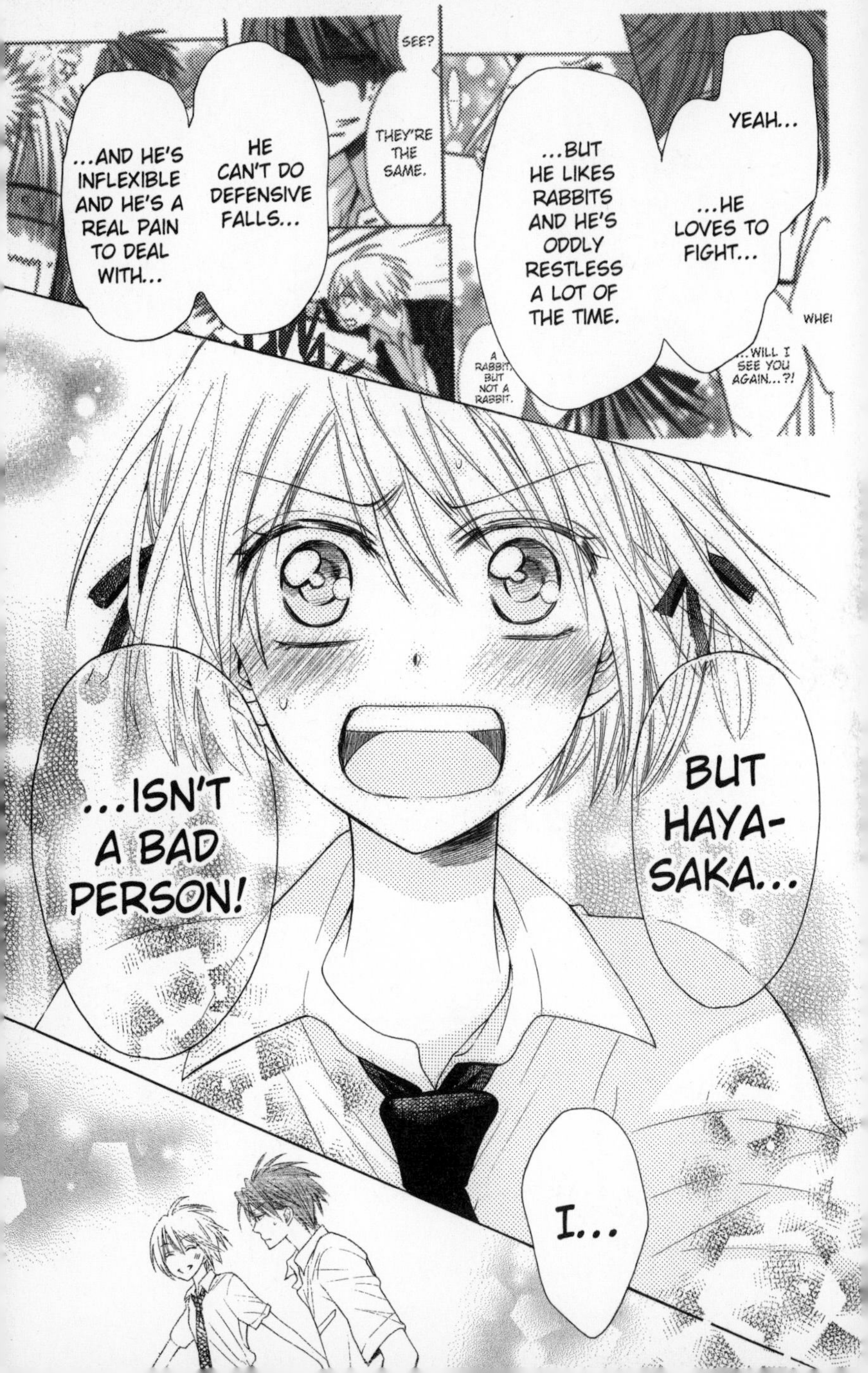
YEAH...
...HE LOVES TO FIGHT...
...WILL I SEE YOU AGAIN...?!
...BUT HE LIKES RABBITS AND HE'S ODDLY RESTLESS A LOT OF THE TIME.
A RABBIT, BUT NOT A RABBIT.
SEE?
THEY'RE THE SAME.
HE CAN'T DO DEFENSIVE FALLS...
...AND HE'S INFLEXIBLE AND HE'S A REAL PAIN TO DEAL WITH...
BUT HAYA-SAKA...
...ISN'T A BAD PERSON!
I...

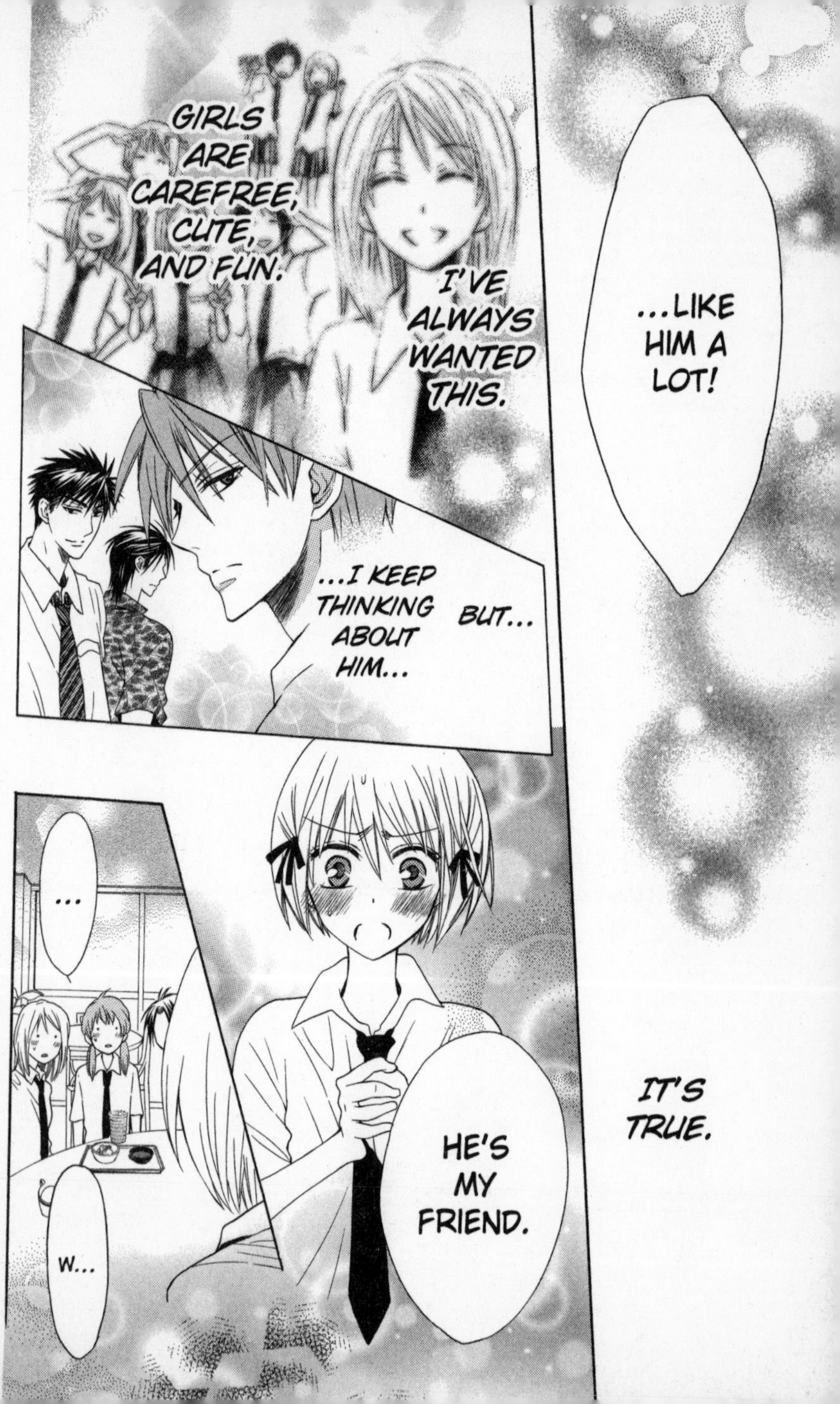
...LIKE HIM A LOT!
I'VE ALWAYS WANTED THIS.
GIRLS ARE CAREFREE, CUTE, AND FUN.
BUT...
...I KEEP THINKING ABOUT HIM...
IT'S TRUE.
HE'S MY FRIEND.
...
W...

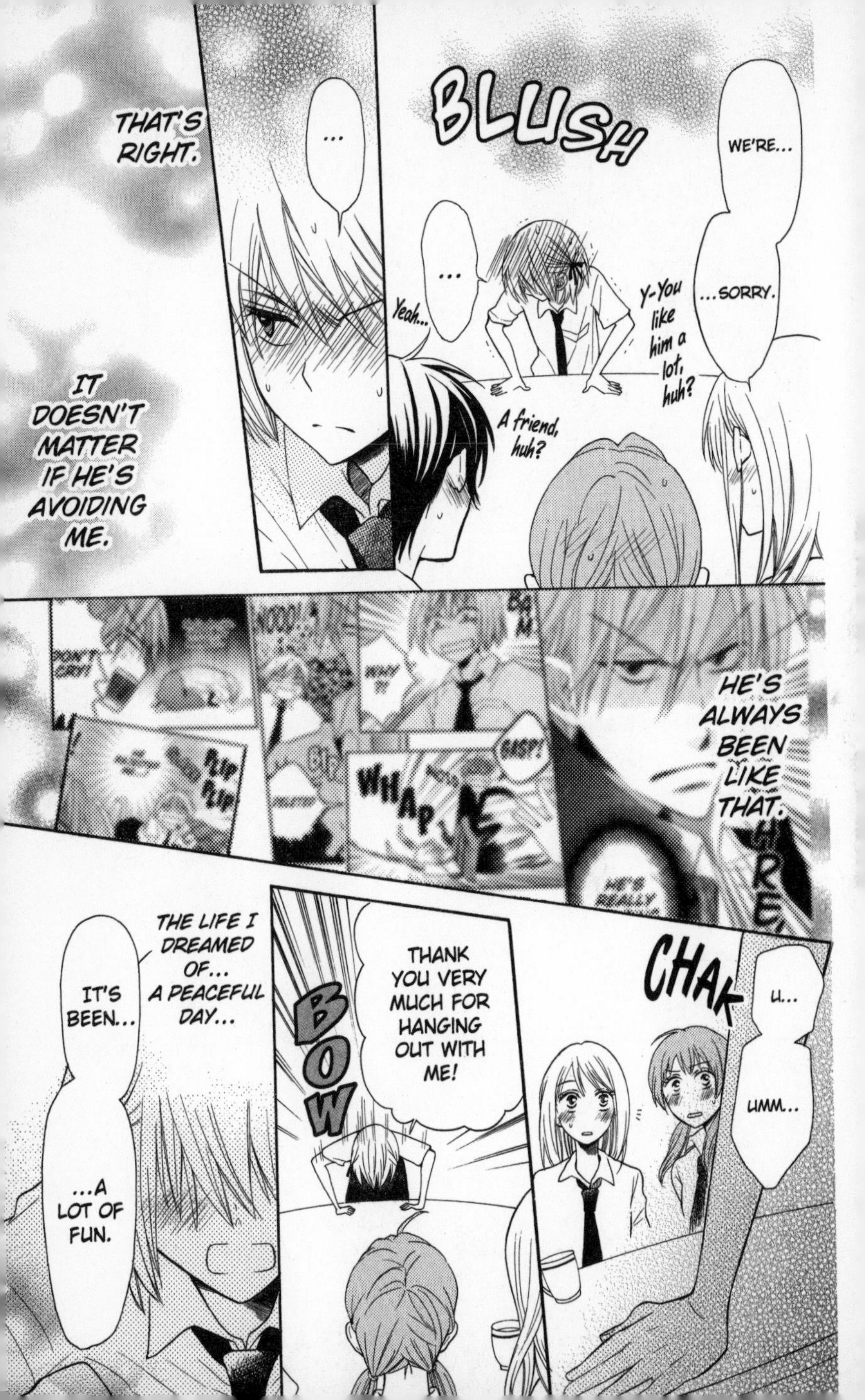
WE'RE...
...SORRY.
Y-You like him a lot, huh?
BLUSH
...
Yeah...
A friend, huh?
...
THAT'S RIGHT.
IT DOESN'T MATTER IF HE'S AVOIDING ME.
HE'S ALWAYS BEEN LIKE THAT.
CHAK
U...
UMM...
THANK YOU VERY MUCH FOR HANGING OUT WITH ME!
BOW
THE LIFE I DREAMED OF... A PEACEFUL DAY...
IT'S BEEN...
...A LOT OF FUN.

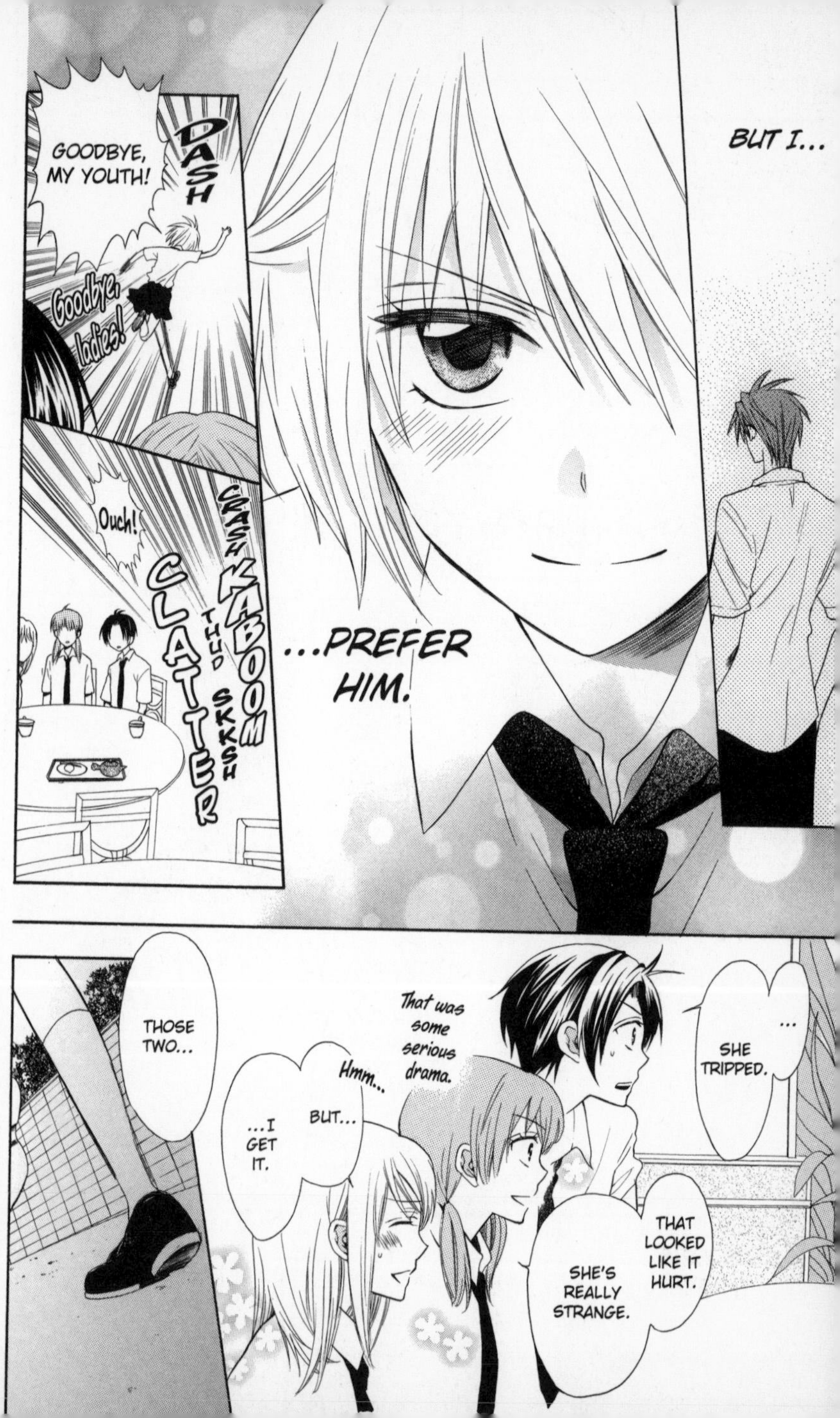
BUT I...
...PREFER HIM.
GOODBYE, MY YOUTH!
DASH
Goodbye, ladies!
Ouch!
CRASH
KABOOM
THUD
SKKSH
CLATTER
...
SHE TRIPPED.
THAT LOOKED LIKE IT HURT.
SHE'S REALLY STRANGE.
That was some serious drama.
Hmm...
BUT...
...I GET IT.
THOSE TWO...

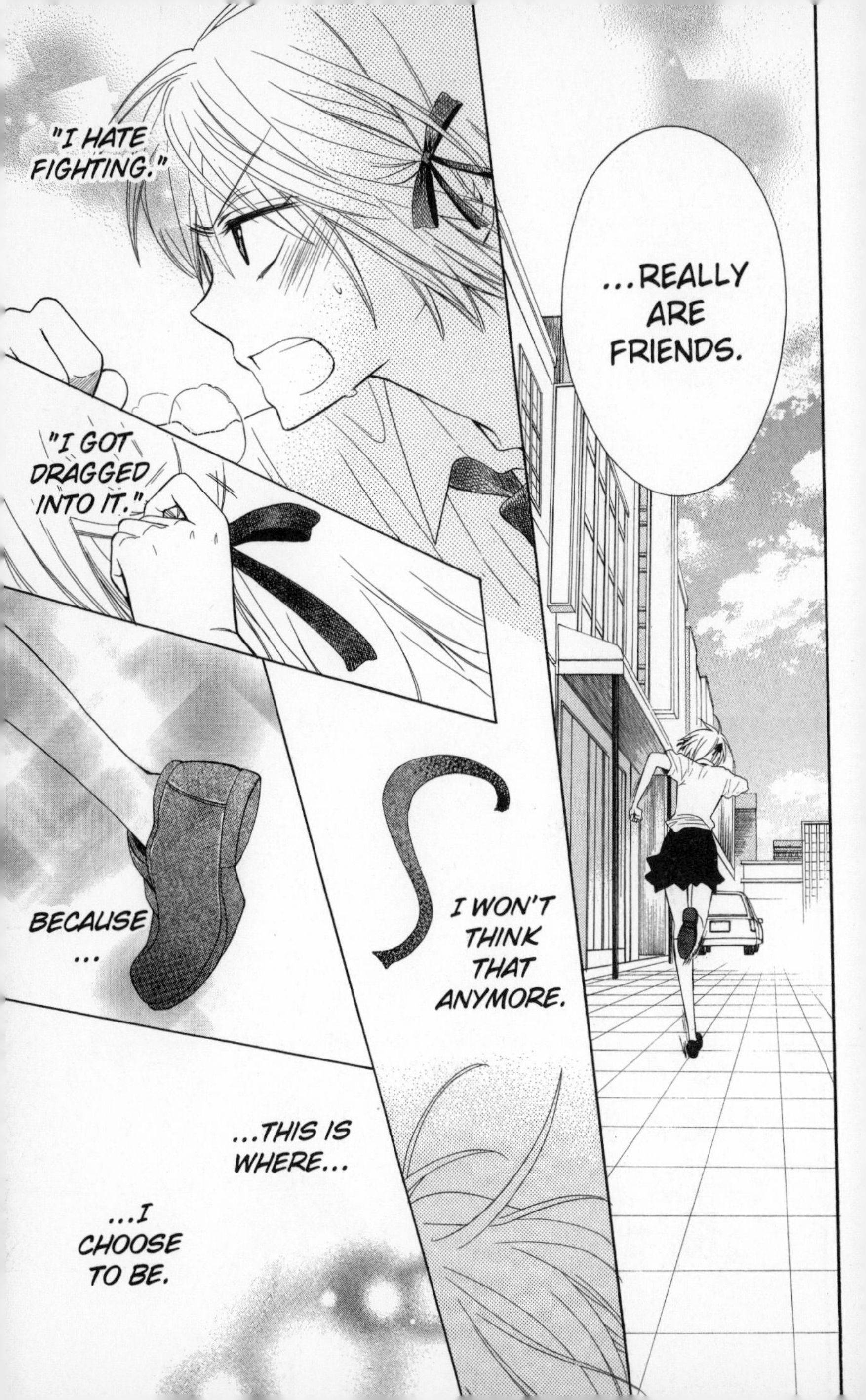
...REALLY ARE FRIENDS.
"I HATE FIGHTING."
"I GOT DRAGGED INTO IT."
I WON'T THINK THAT ANYMORE.
BECAUSE...
...THIS IS WHERE...
...I CHOOSE TO BE.

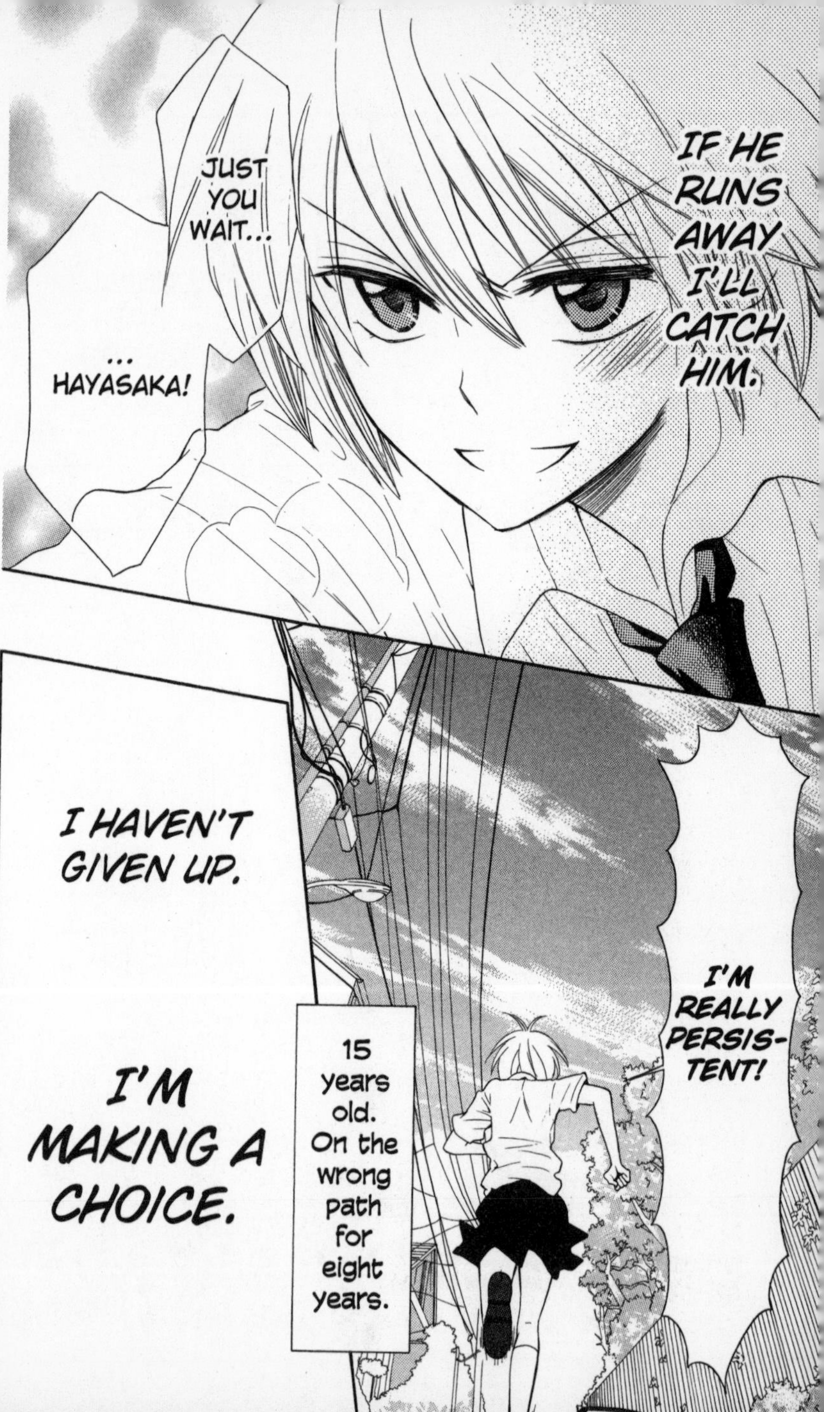
IF HE RUNS AWAY I'LL CATCH HIM.
JUST YOU WAIT...
...HAYASAKA!
I'M REALLY PERSIS-TENT!
15 years old. On the wrong path for eight years.
I HAVEN'T GIVEN UP.
I'M MAKING A CHOICE.

Chapter 33

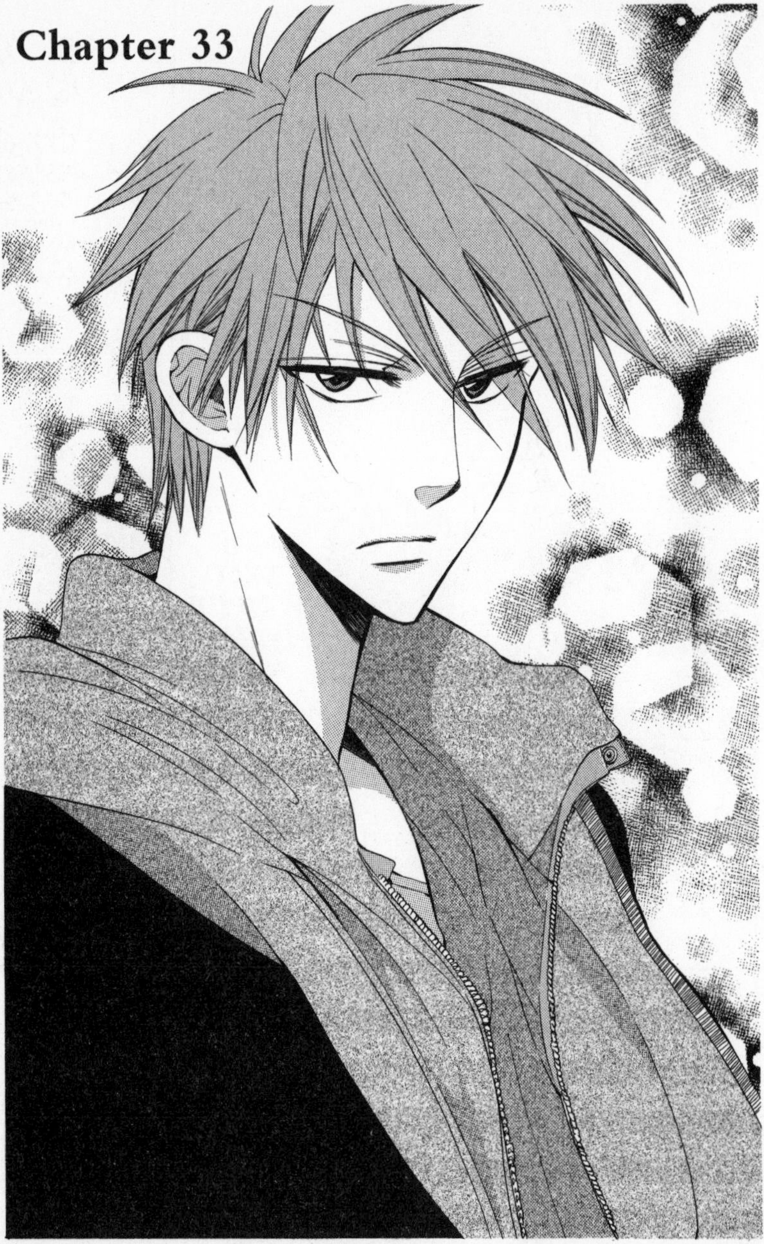

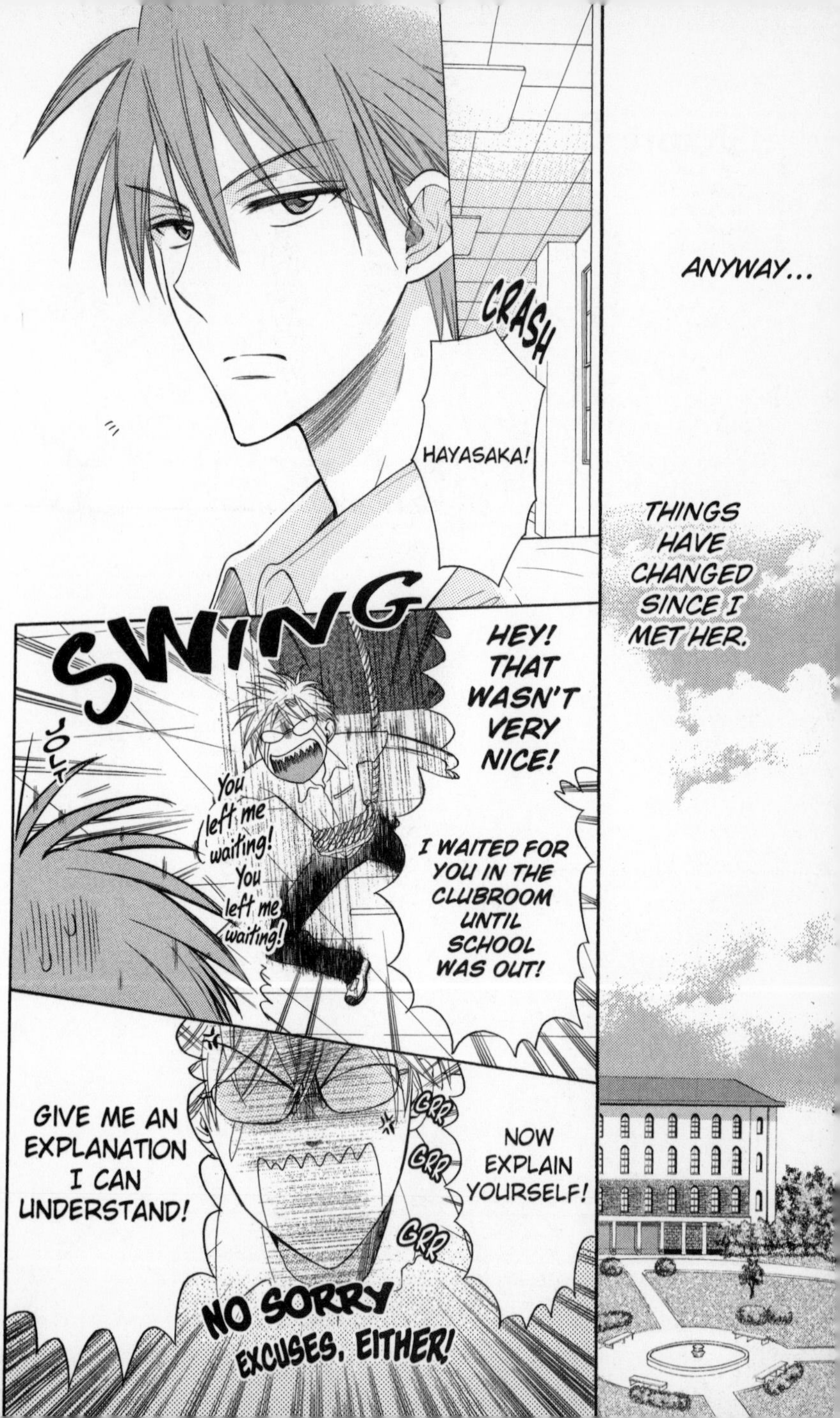
ANYWAY...
THINGS HAVE CHANGED SINCE I MET HER.
CRASH
HAYASAKA!
SWING
HEY! THAT WASN'T VERY NICE!
JOLT
I WAITED FOR YOU IN THE CLUBROOM UNTIL SCHOOL WAS OUT!
You left me waiting! You left me waiting!
NOW EXPLAIN YOURSELF!
GRR
GRR
GRR
GIVE ME AN EXPLANATION I CAN UNDERSTAND!
NO SORRY EXCUSES, EITHER!

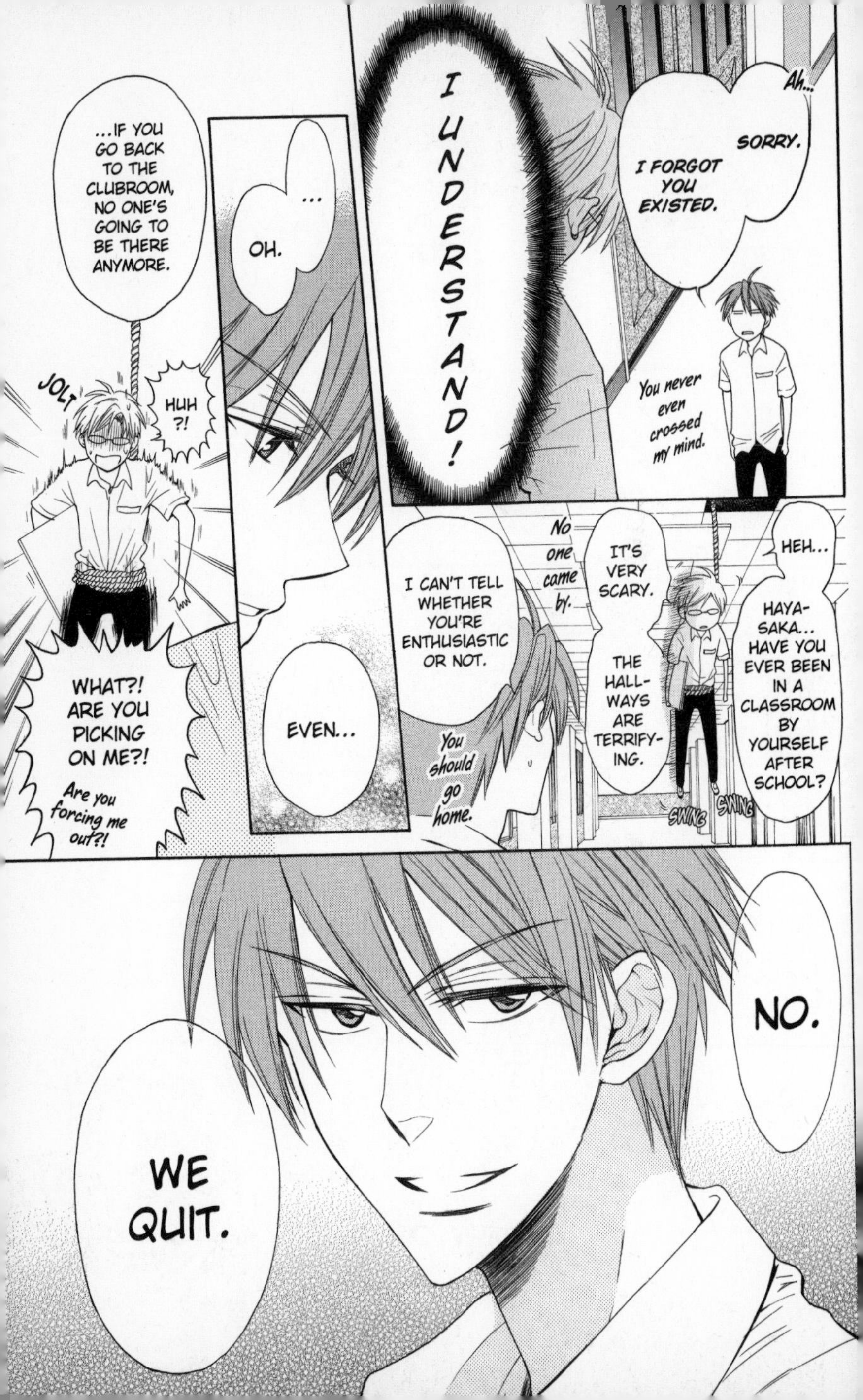
Ah... SORRY. I FORGOT YOU EXISTED.
You never even crossed my mind.
I UNDERSTAND!
HEH... HAYA-SAKA... HAVE YOU EVER BEEN IN A CLASSROOM BY YOURSELF AFTER SCHOOL?
IT'S VERY SCARY. THE HALL-WAYS ARE TERRIFY-ING.
No one came by.
SWING SWING
I CAN'T TELL WHETHER YOU'RE ENTHUSIASTIC OR NOT.
You should go home.
... OH.
EVEN...
...IF YOU GO BACK TO THE CLUBROOM, NO ONE'S GOING TO BE THERE ANYMORE.
HUH ?!
JOLT
WHAT?! ARE YOU PICKING ON ME?!
Are you forcing me out?!
NO.
WE QUIT.

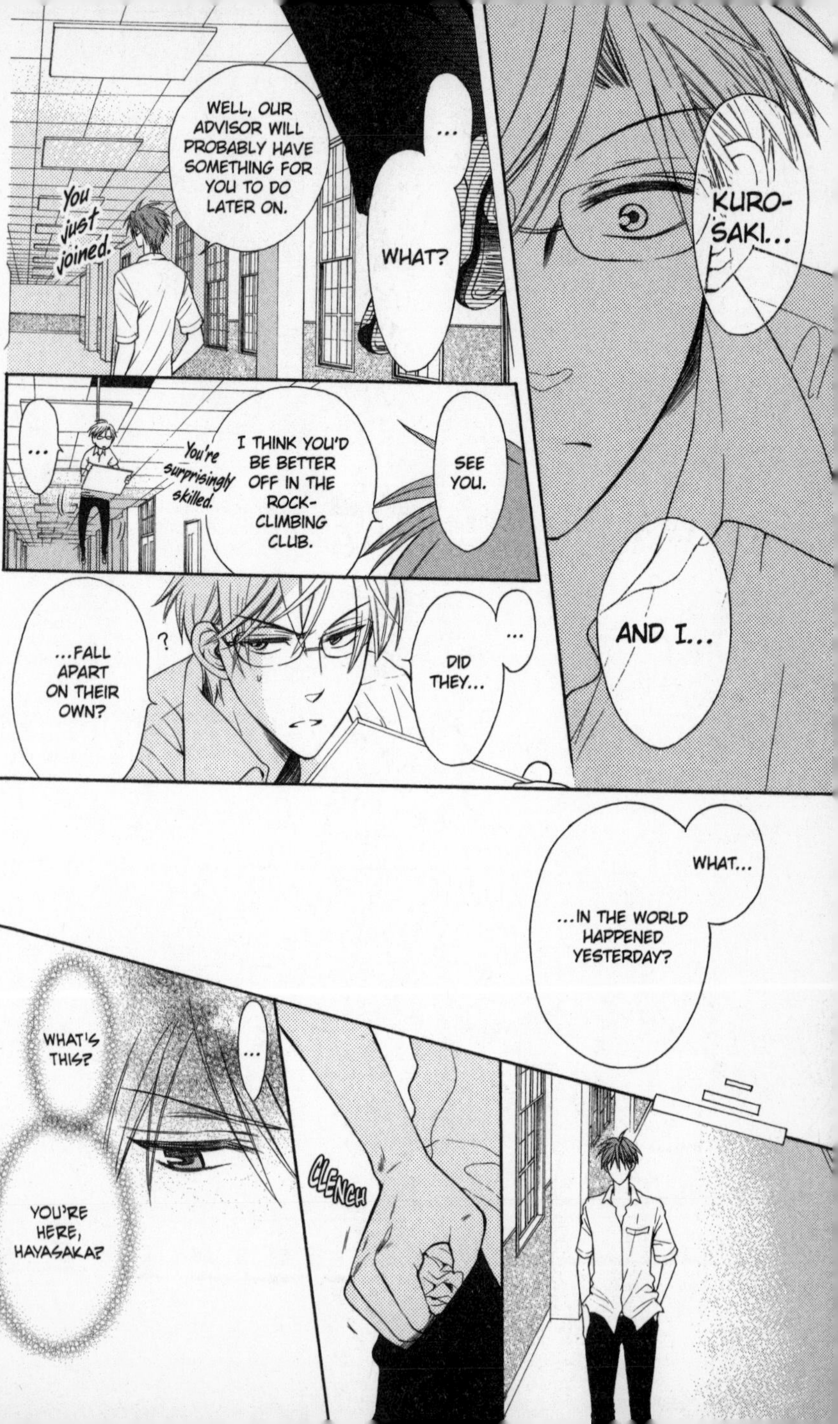
KURO-SAKI...
AND I...
...
WHAT?
WELL, OUR ADVISOR WILL PROBABLY HAVE SOMETHING FOR YOU TO DO LATER ON.
You just joined.
SEE YOU.
I THINK YOU'D BE BETTER OFF IN THE ROCK-CLIMBING CLUB.
You're surprisingly skilled.
...
...
DID THEY...
?
...FALL APART ON THEIR OWN?
WHAT...
...IN THE WORLD HAPPENED YESTERDAY?
...
CLENCH
WHAT'S THIS?
YOU'RE HERE, HAYASAKA?

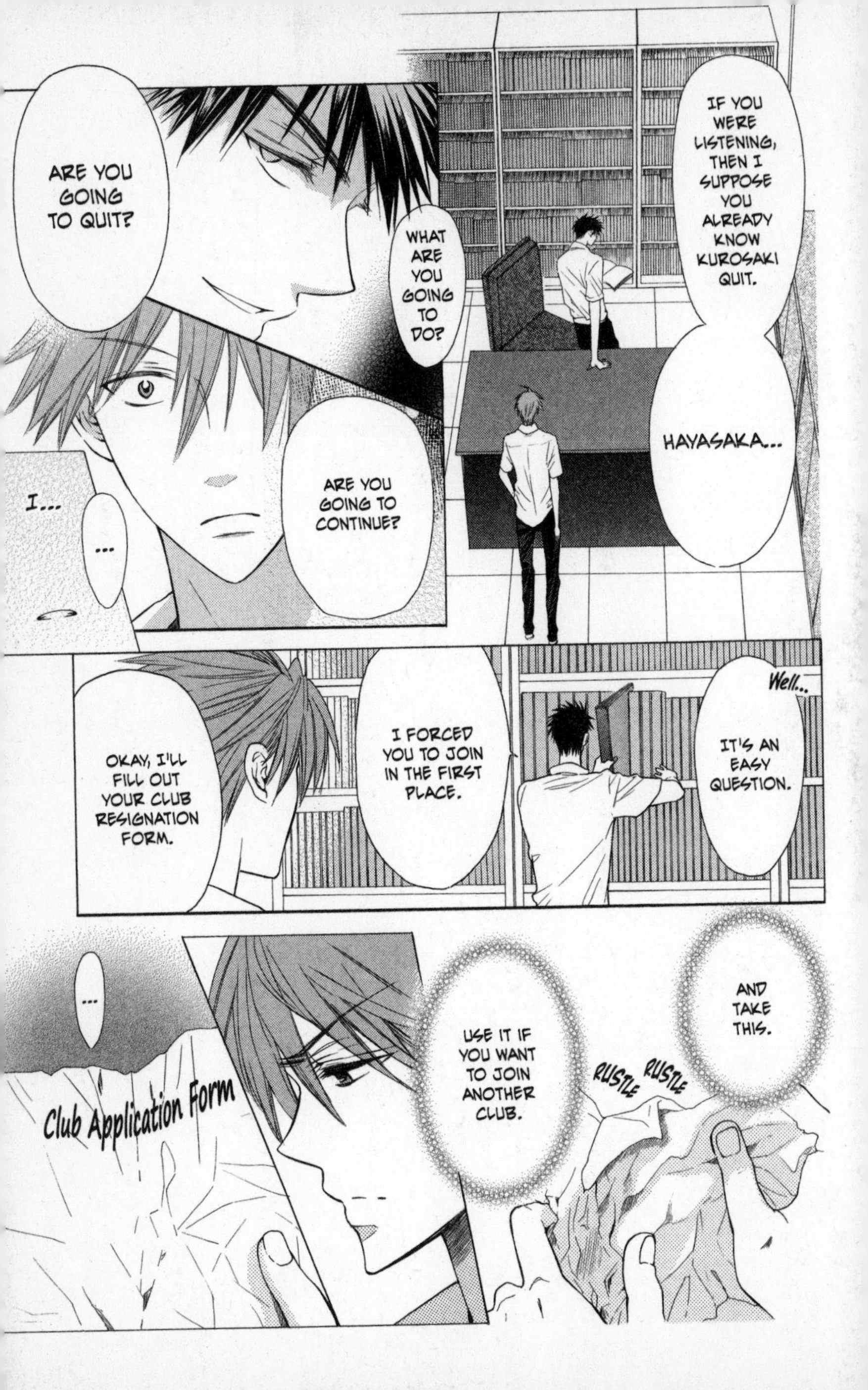
IF YOU WERE LISTENING, THEN I SUPPOSE YOU ALREADY KNOW KUROSAKI QUIT.
HAYASAKA...
WHAT ARE YOU GOING TO DO?
ARE YOU GOING TO QUIT?
ARE YOU GOING TO CONTINUE?
I...
...
Well...
IT'S AN EASY QUESTION.
I FORCED YOU TO JOIN IN THE FIRST PLACE.
OKAY, I'LL FILL OUT YOUR CLUB RESIGNATION FORM.
AND TAKE THIS.
RUSTLE
RUSTLE
USE IT IF YOU WANT TO JOIN ANOTHER CLUB.
...
Club Application Form

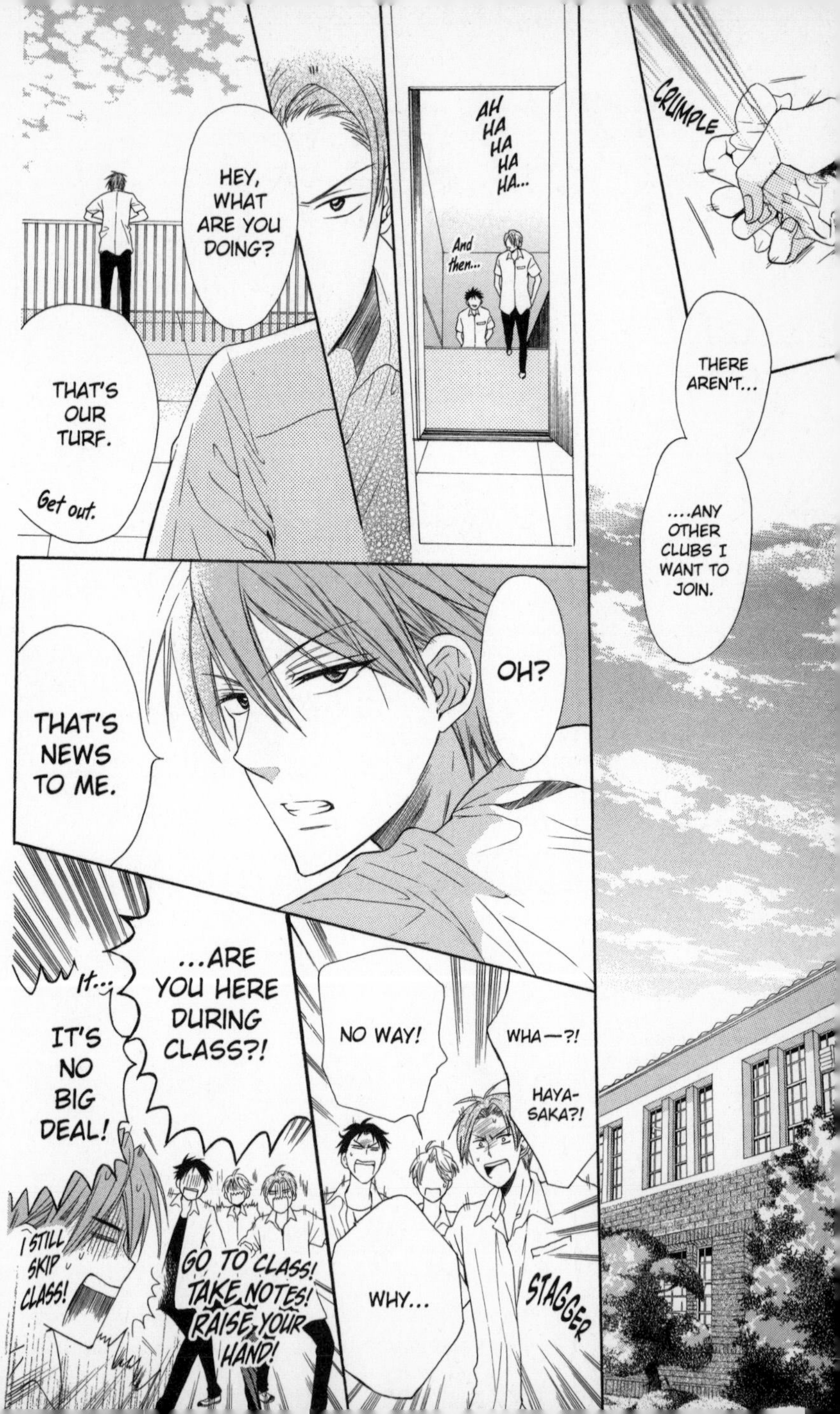

CRUMPLE
THERE AREN'T...
....ANY OTHER CLUBS I WANT TO JOIN.
AH HA HA HA HA...
And then...
HEY, WHAT ARE YOU DOING?
THAT'S OUR TURF.
Get out.
OH?
THAT'S NEWS TO ME.
WHA—?!
HAYA-SAKA?!
NO WAY!
WHY...
STAGGER
...ARE YOU HERE DURING CLASS?!
It...
IT'S NO BIG DEAL!
I STILL SKIP CLASS!
GO TO CLASS! TAKE NOTES! RAISE YOUR HAND!

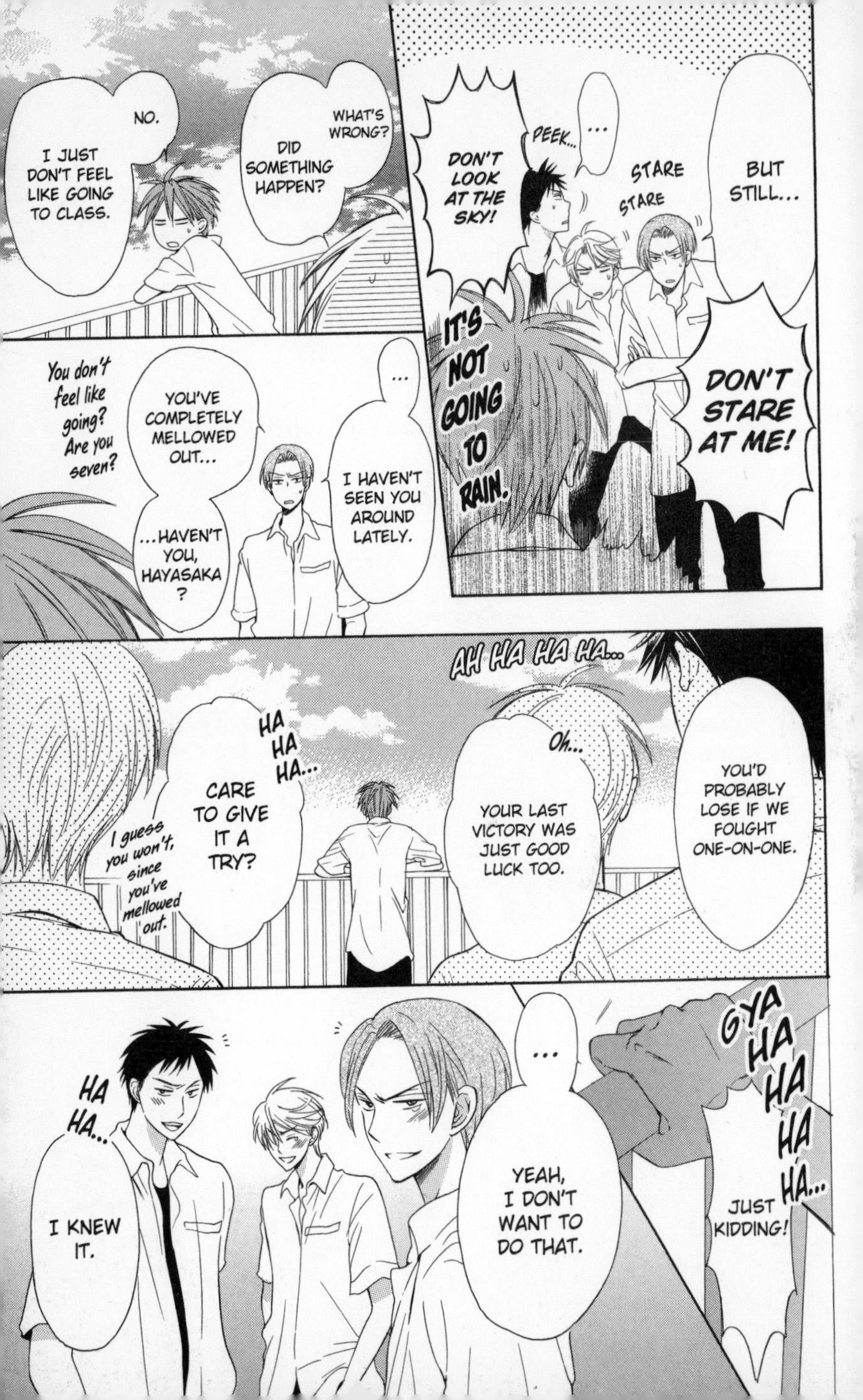
BUT STILL...
STARE
STARE
...
PEEK...
DON'T LOOK AT THE SKY!
DON'T STARE AT ME!
IT'S NOT GOING TO RAIN.
WHAT'S WRONG?
DID SOMETHING HAPPEN?
NO.
I JUST DON'T FEEL LIKE GOING TO CLASS.
...
I HAVEN'T SEEN YOU AROUND LATELY.
YOU'VE COMPLETELY MELLOWED OUT...
...HAVEN'T YOU, HAYASAKA?
You don't feel like going? Are you seven?
AH HA HA HA...
YOU'D PROBABLY LOSE IF WE FOUGHT ONE-ON-ONE.
Oh...
YOUR LAST VICTORY WAS JUST GOOD LUCK TOO.
HA HA HA...
CARE TO GIVE IT A TRY?
I guess you won't, since you've mellowed out.
GYA HA HA HA HA HA...
JUST KIDDING!
...
YEAH, I DON'T WANT TO DO THAT.
HA HA...
I KNEW IT.

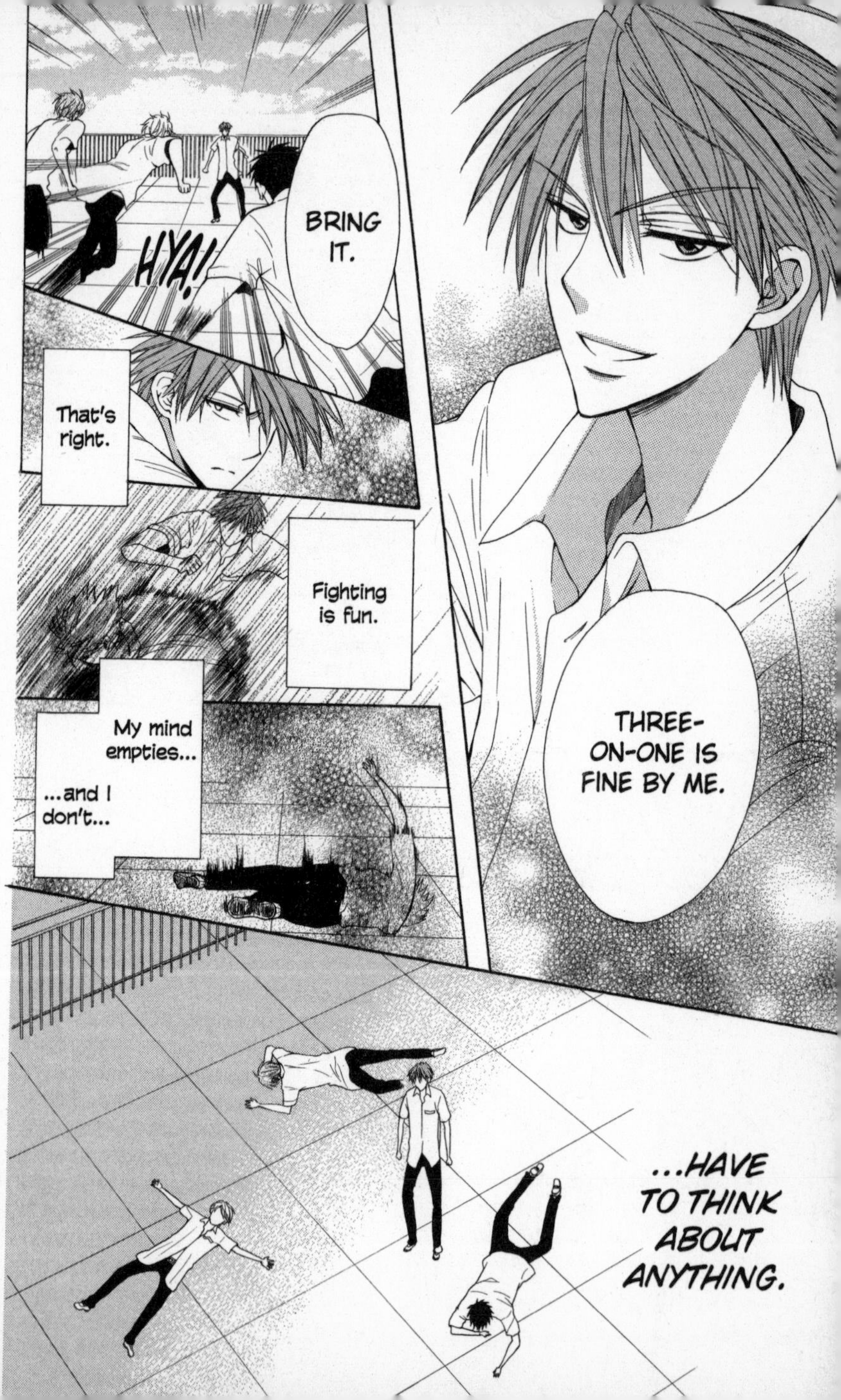
THREE-ON-ONE IS FINE BY ME.
BRING IT.
HYA!
That's right.
Fighting is fun.
My mind empties...
...and I don't...
...HAVE TO THINK ABOUT ANYTHING.

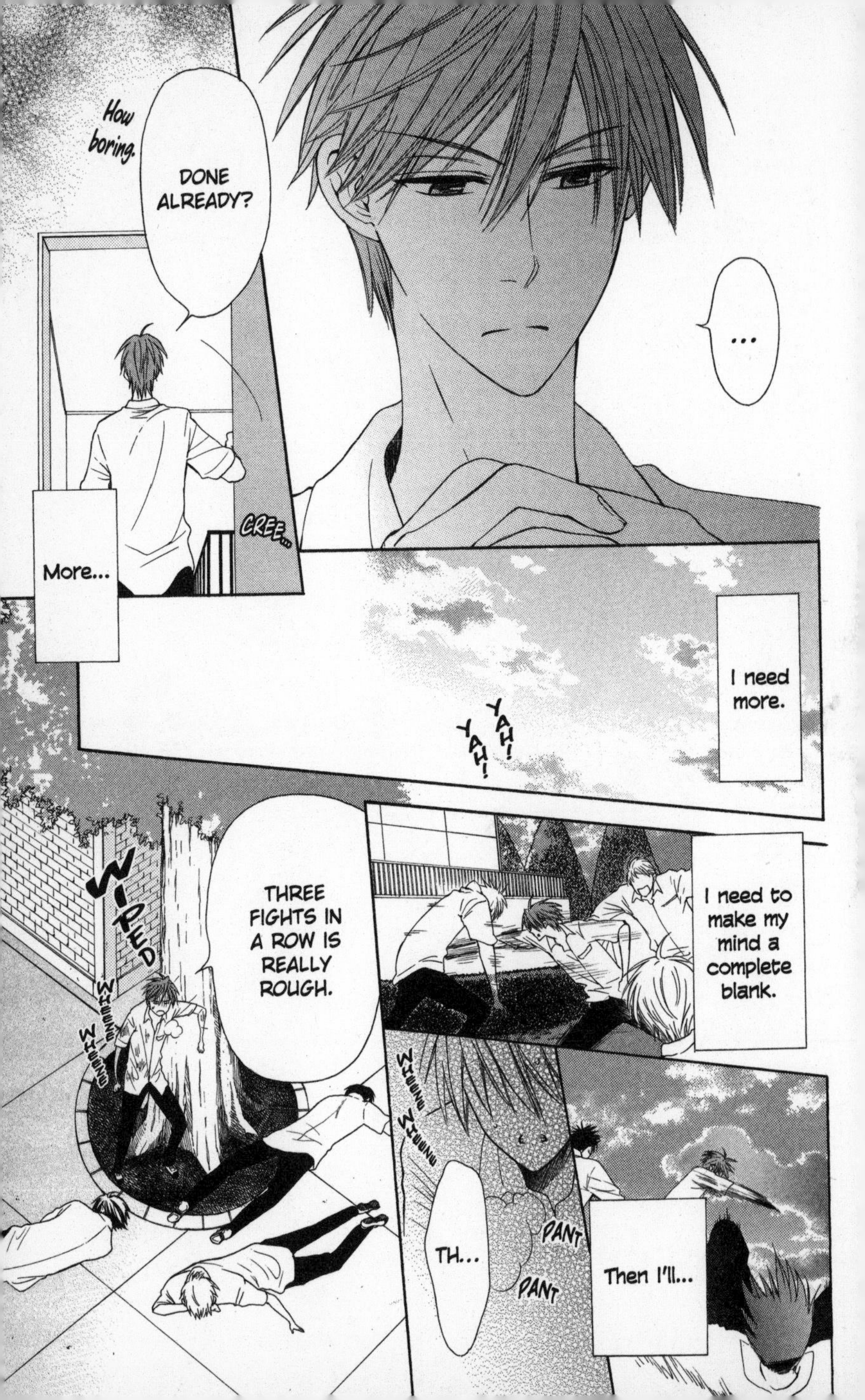
...
DONE ALREADY?
How boring.
CREE...
More...
I need more.
YAH! YAH!
I need to make my mind a complete blank.
Then I'll...
WHEEZE WHEEZE
PANT PANT
TH...
THREE FIGHTS IN A ROW IS REALLY ROUGH.
WIPED
WHEEZE WHEEZE

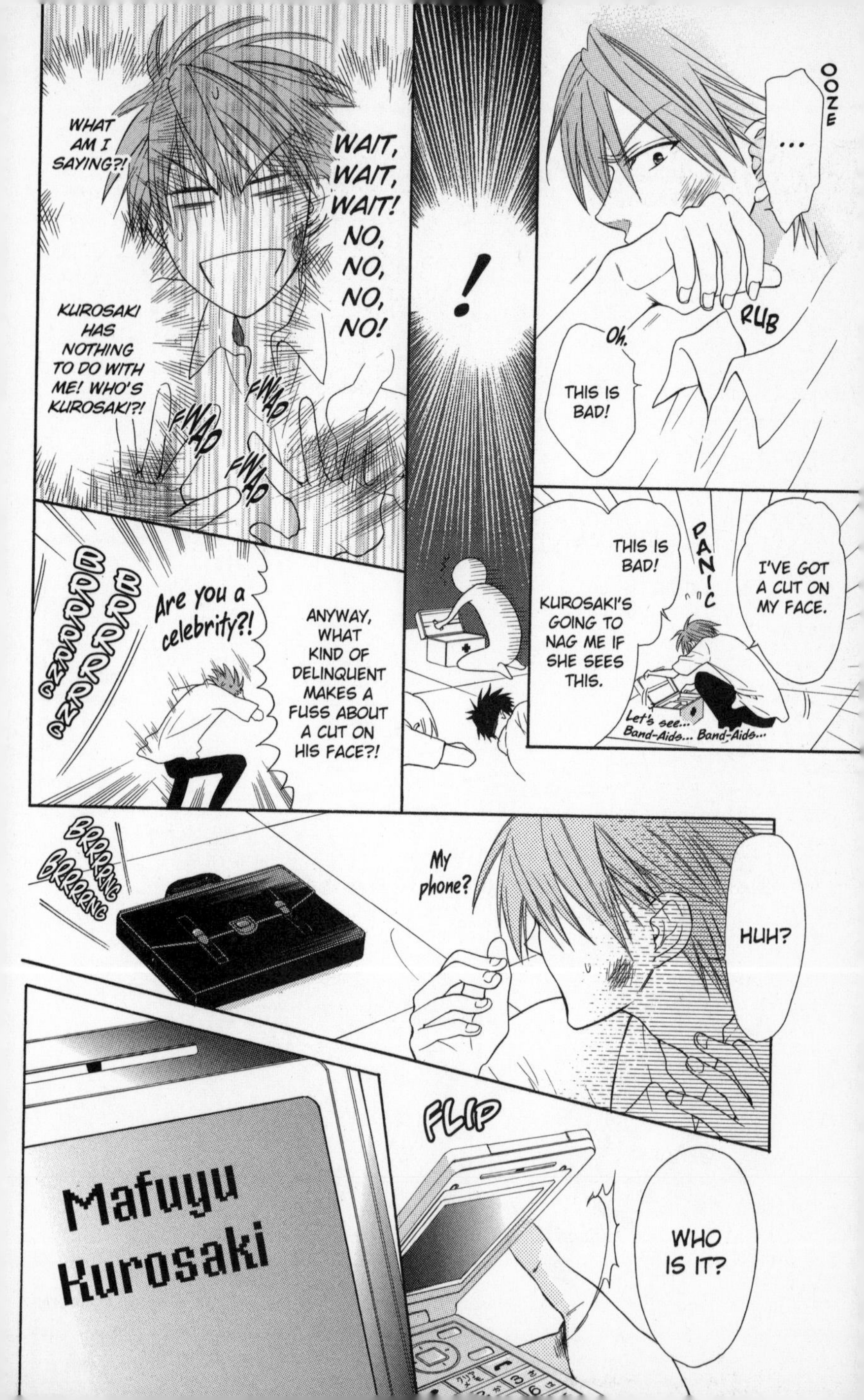
OOZE
...
RUB
Oh.
THIS IS BAD!
I'VE GOT A CUT ON MY FACE.
PANIC
THIS IS BAD!
KUROSAKI'S GOING TO NAG ME IF SHE SEES THIS.
Let's see... Band-Aids... Band-Aids...
!
WAIT, WAIT, WAIT! NO, NO, NO, NO!
WHAT AM I SAYING?!
KUROSAKI HAS NOTHING TO DO WITH ME! WHO'S KUROSAKI?!
FWAP FWAP FWAP
ANYWAY, WHAT KIND OF DELINQUENT MAKES A FUSS ABOUT A CUT ON HIS FACE?!
Are you a celebrity?!
BRRRRRR
HUH?
My phone?
BRRRRNG BRRRRNG
FLIP
WHO IS IT?
Mafuyu Kurosaki

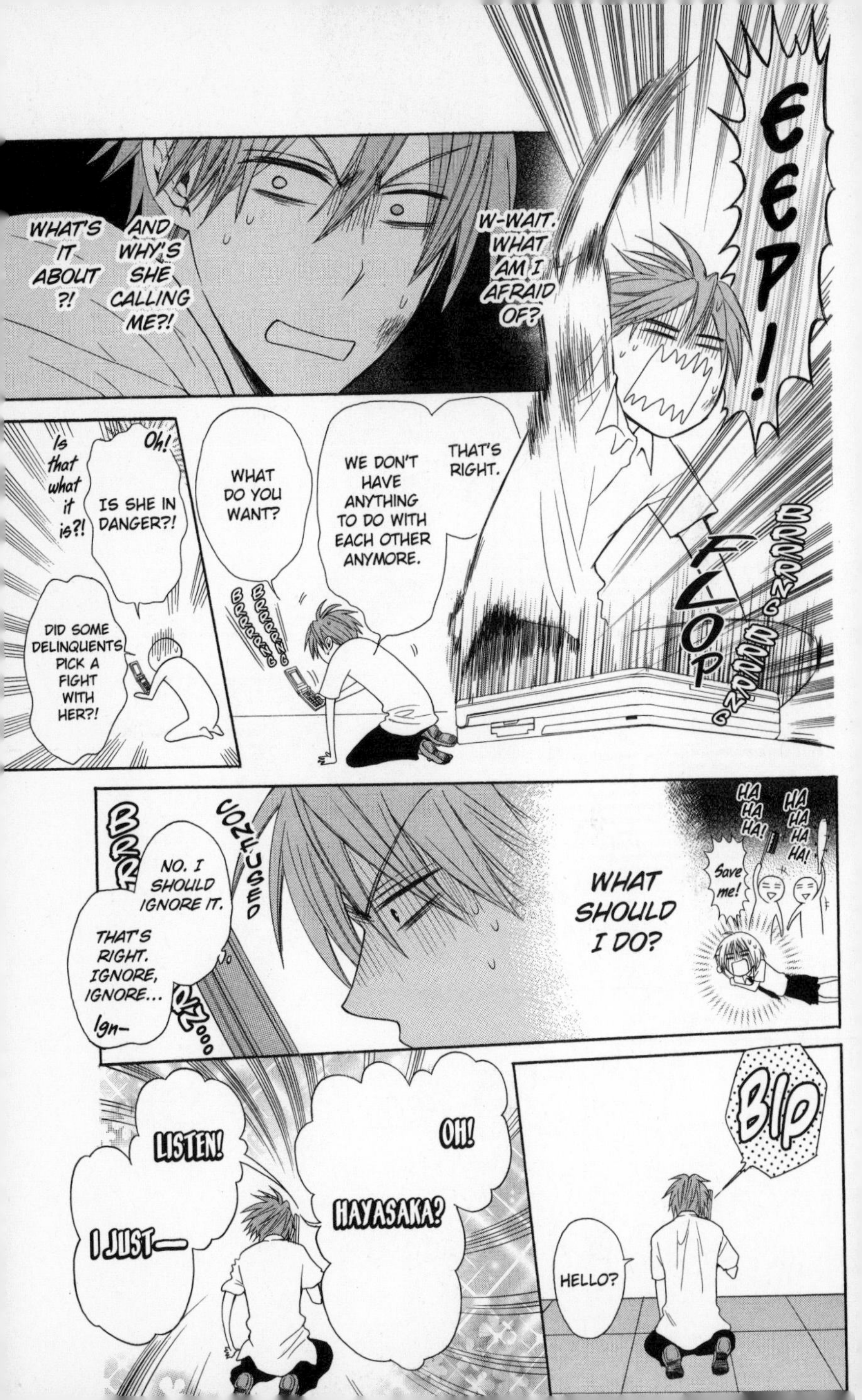
EEP!
W-WAIT. WHAT AM I AFRAID OF?
FLOP
BRRRNG BRRRNG
AND WHY'S SHE CALLING ME?!
WHAT'S IT ABOUT?!
THAT'S RIGHT.
WE DON'T HAVE ANYTHING TO DO WITH EACH OTHER ANYMORE.
WHAT DO YOU WANT?
Oh!
IS SHE IN DANGER?!
Is that what it is?!
DID SOME DELINQUENTS PICK A FIGHT WITH HER?!
WHAT SHOULD I DO?
HA HA HA!
HA HA HA HA!
Save me!
NO. I SHOULD IGNORE IT.
THAT'S RIGHT. IGNORE, IGNORE...
Ign-
BIP
HELLO?
OH!
HAYASAKA?
LISTEN!
I JUST—

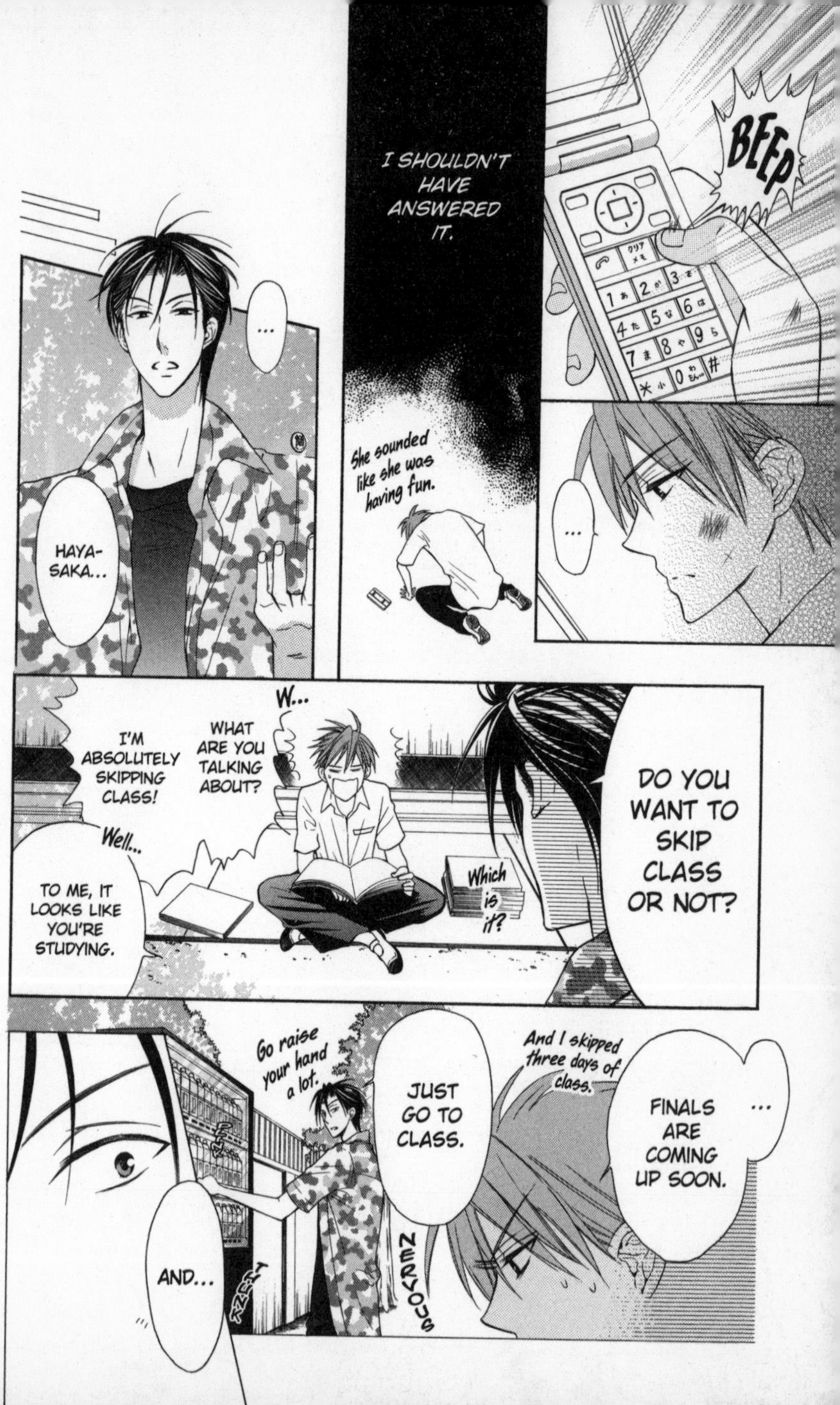
BEEP
...
I SHOULDN'T HAVE ANSWERED IT.
She sounded like she was having fun.
...
HAYA-SAKA...
DO YOU WANT TO SKIP CLASS OR NOT?
Which is it?
W...
WHAT ARE YOU TALKING ABOUT?
I'M ABSOLUTELY SKIPPING CLASS!
Well...
TO ME, IT LOOKS LIKE YOU'RE STUDYING.
...
FINALS ARE COMING UP SOON.
And I skipped three days of class.
NERVOUS
JUST GO TO CLASS.
Go raise your hand a lot.
AND...

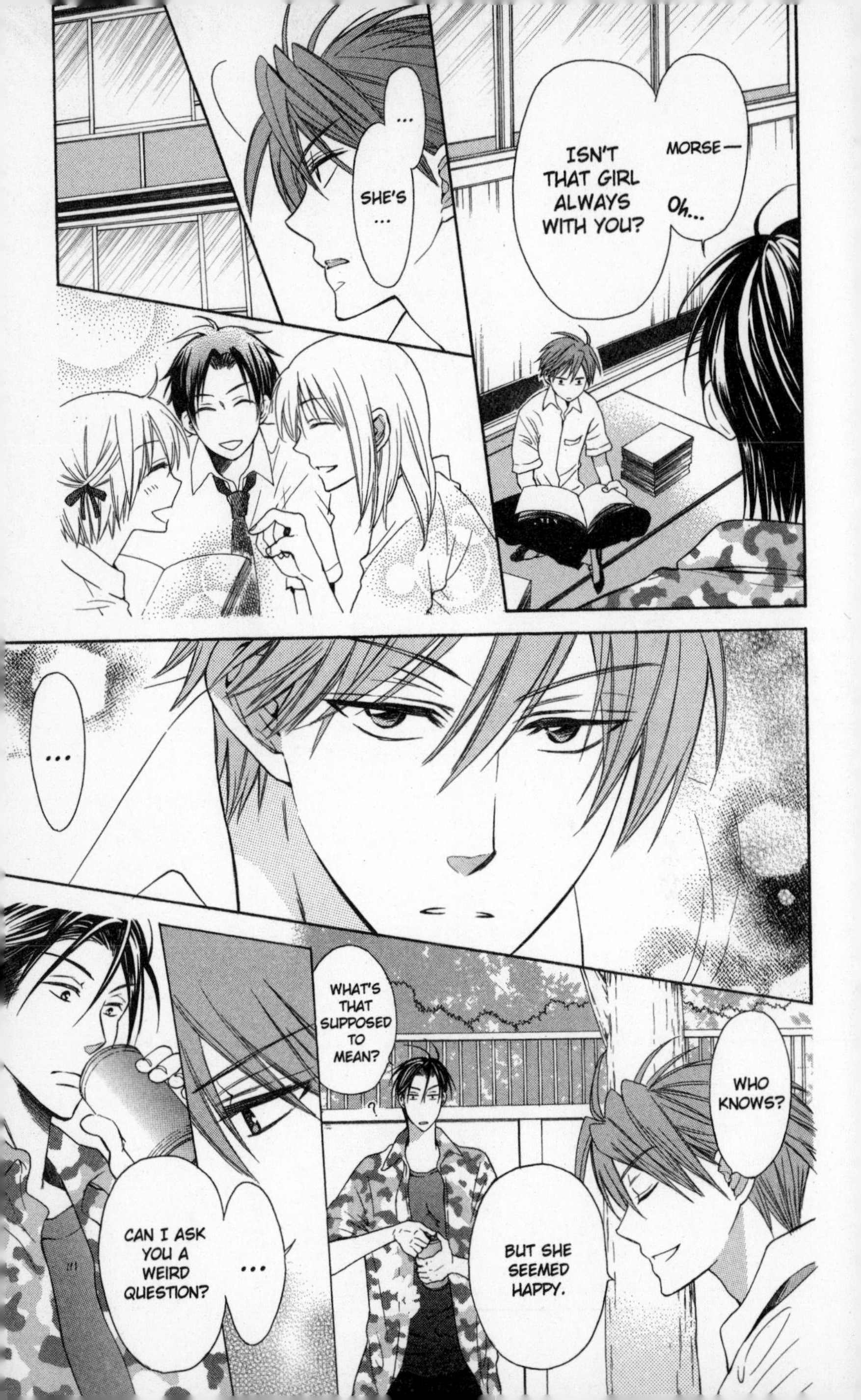
MORSE— Oh...
ISN'T THAT GIRL ALWAYS WITH YOU?
...
SHE'S ...
...
WHO KNOWS?
BUT SHE SEEMED HAPPY.
WHAT'S THAT SUPPOSED TO MEAN?
...
CAN I ASK YOU A WEIRD QUESTION?

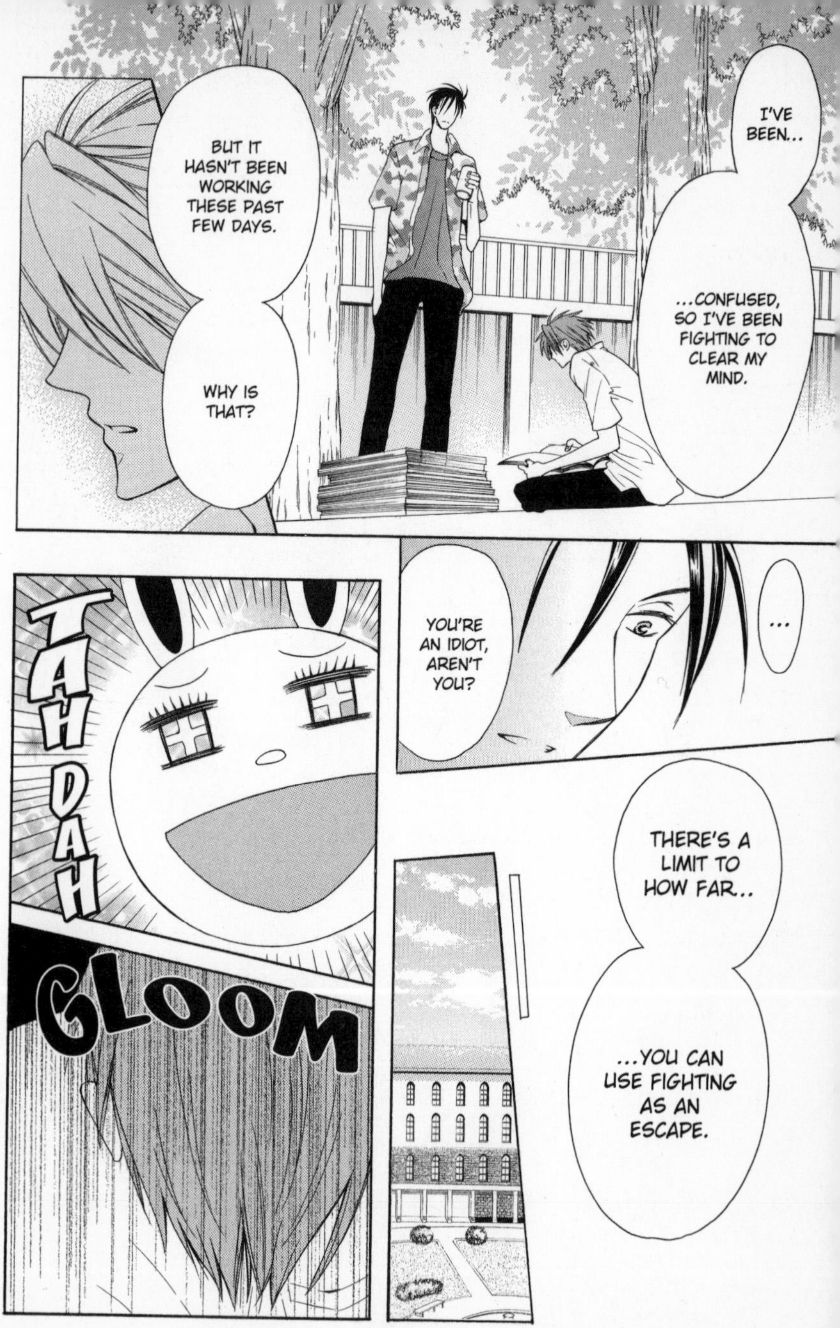
I'VE BEEN...
...CONFUSED, SO I'VE BEEN FIGHTING TO CLEAR MY MIND.
BUT IT HASN'T BEEN WORKING THESE PAST FEW DAYS.
WHY IS THAT?
...
YOU'RE AN IDIOT, AREN'T YOU?
TAH DAH
THERE'S A LIMIT TO HOW FAR...
...YOU CAN USE FIGHTING AS AN ESCAPE.
GLOOM

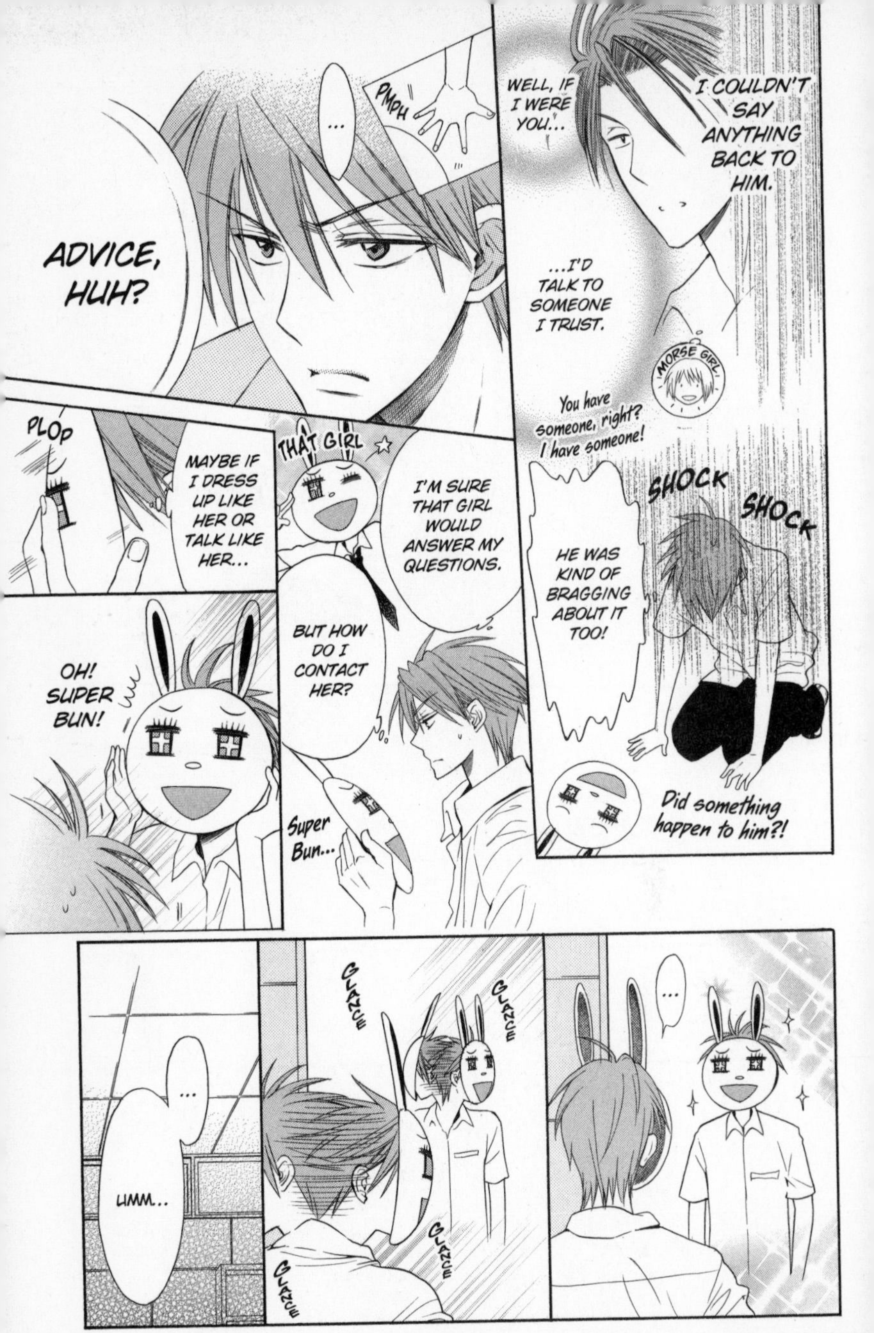

WELL, IF I WERE YOU...
I COULDN'T SAY ANYTHING BACK TO HIM.
...I'D TALK TO SOMEONE I TRUST.
MORSE GIRL
You have someone, right? I have someone!
SHOCK
SHOCK
HE WAS KIND OF BRAGGING ABOUT IT TOO!
Did something happen to him?!
PMPH
...
ADVICE, HUH?
THAT GIRL
I'M SURE THAT GIRL WOULD ANSWER MY QUESTIONS.
BUT HOW DO I CONTACT HER?
Super Bun...
PLOP
MAYBE IF I DRESS UP LIKE HER OR TALK LIKE HER...
OH! SUPER BUN!
...
GLANCE
GLANCE
GLANCE
GLANCE
...
UMM...

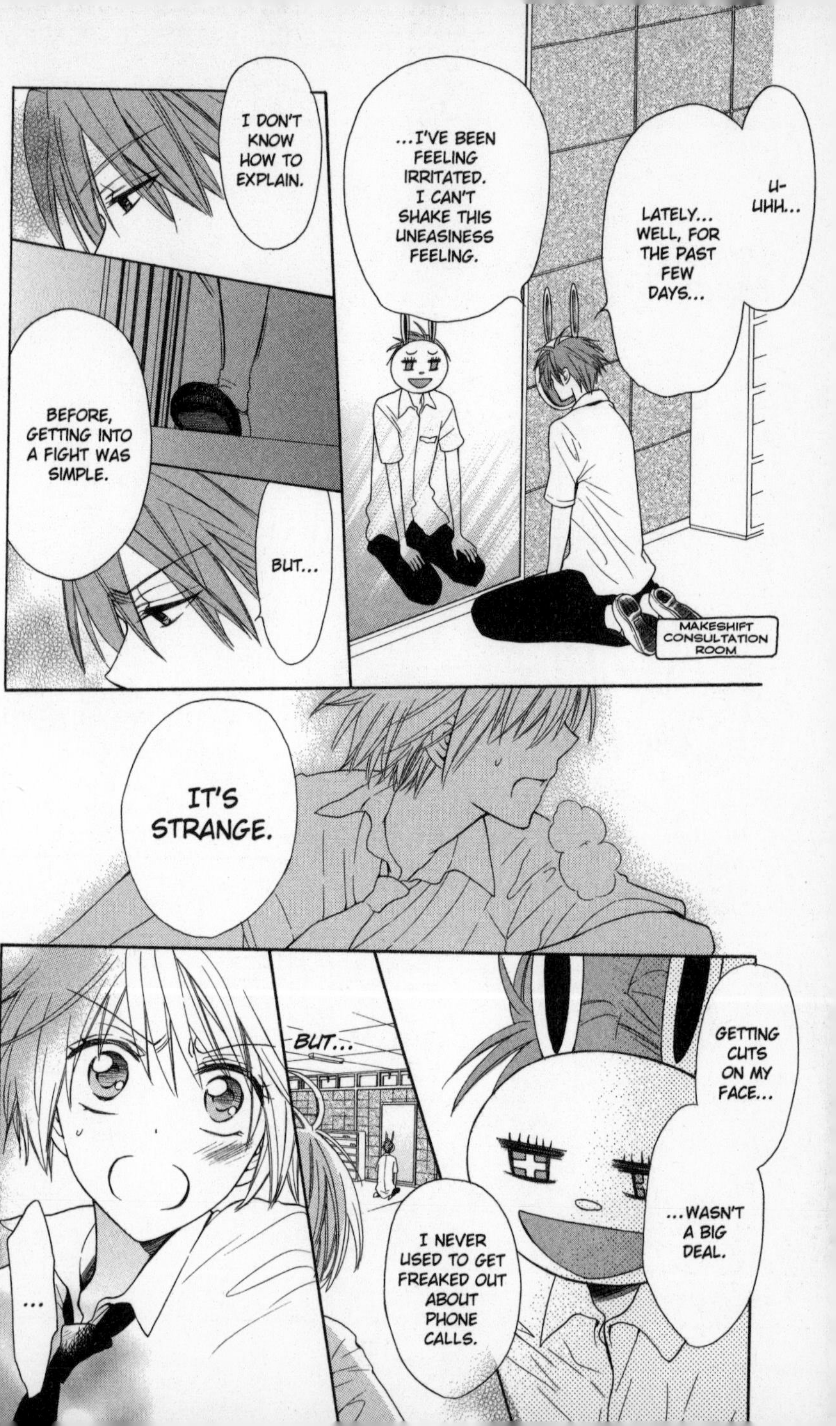
U-UHH...
LATELY... WELL, FOR THE PAST FEW DAYS...
...I'VE BEEN FEELING IRRITATED. I CAN'T SHAKE THIS UNEASINESS FEELING.
MAKESHIFT CONSULTATION ROOM
I DON'T KNOW HOW TO EXPLAIN.
BEFORE, GETTING INTO A FIGHT WAS SIMPLE.
BUT...
IT'S STRANGE.
GETTING CUTS ON MY FACE...
...WASN'T A BIG DEAL.
I NEVER USED TO GET FREAKED OUT ABOUT PHONE CALLS.
BUT...
...

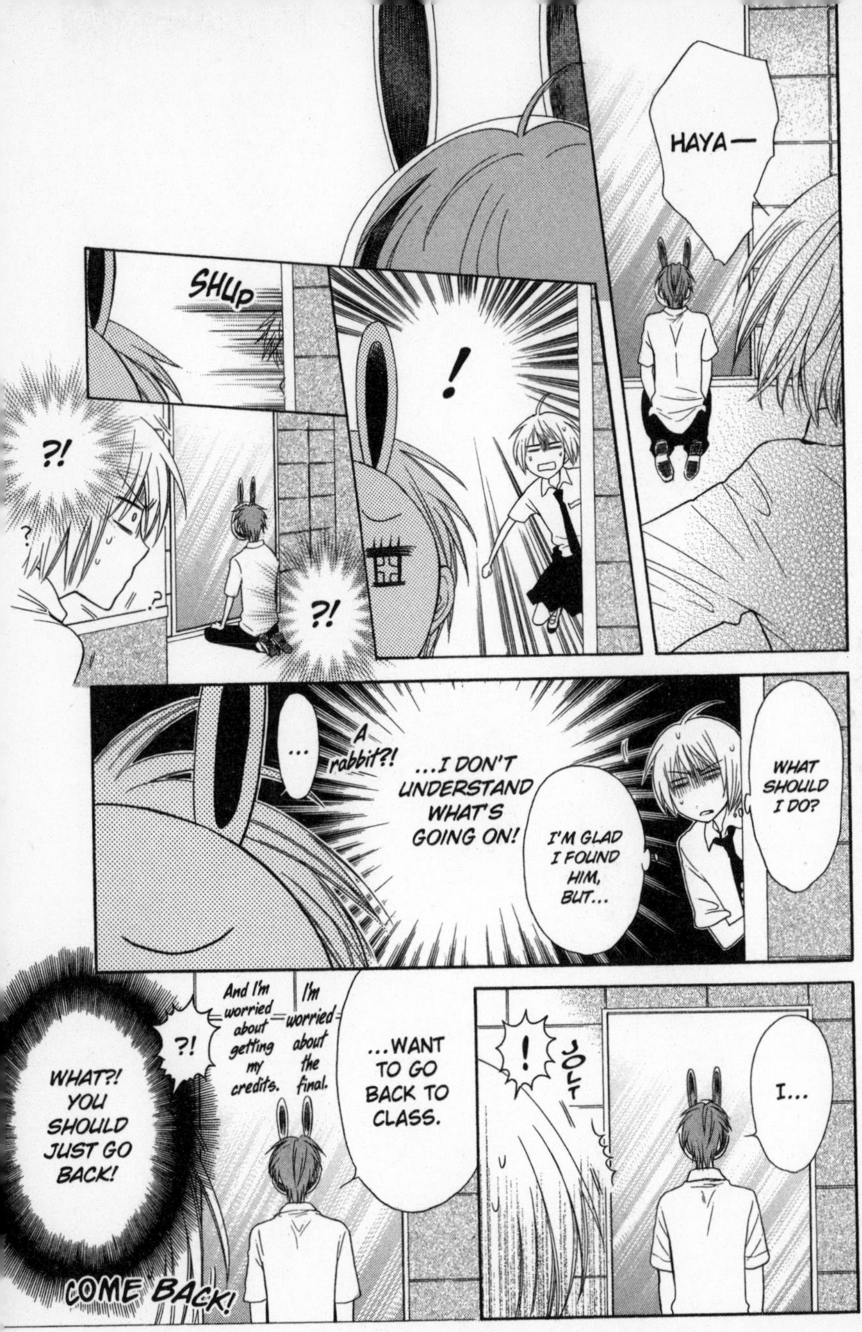
HAYA—
!
SHUp
?!
?!
?
?
WHAT SHOULD I DO?
I'M GLAD I FOUND HIM, BUT...
...I DON'T UNDERSTAND WHAT'S GOING ON!
A rabbit?!
...
I...
JOLT
!
...WANT TO GO BACK TO CLASS.
I'm worried about the final.
And I'm worried about getting my credits.
?!
WHAT?! YOU SHOULD JUST GO BACK!
COME BACK!

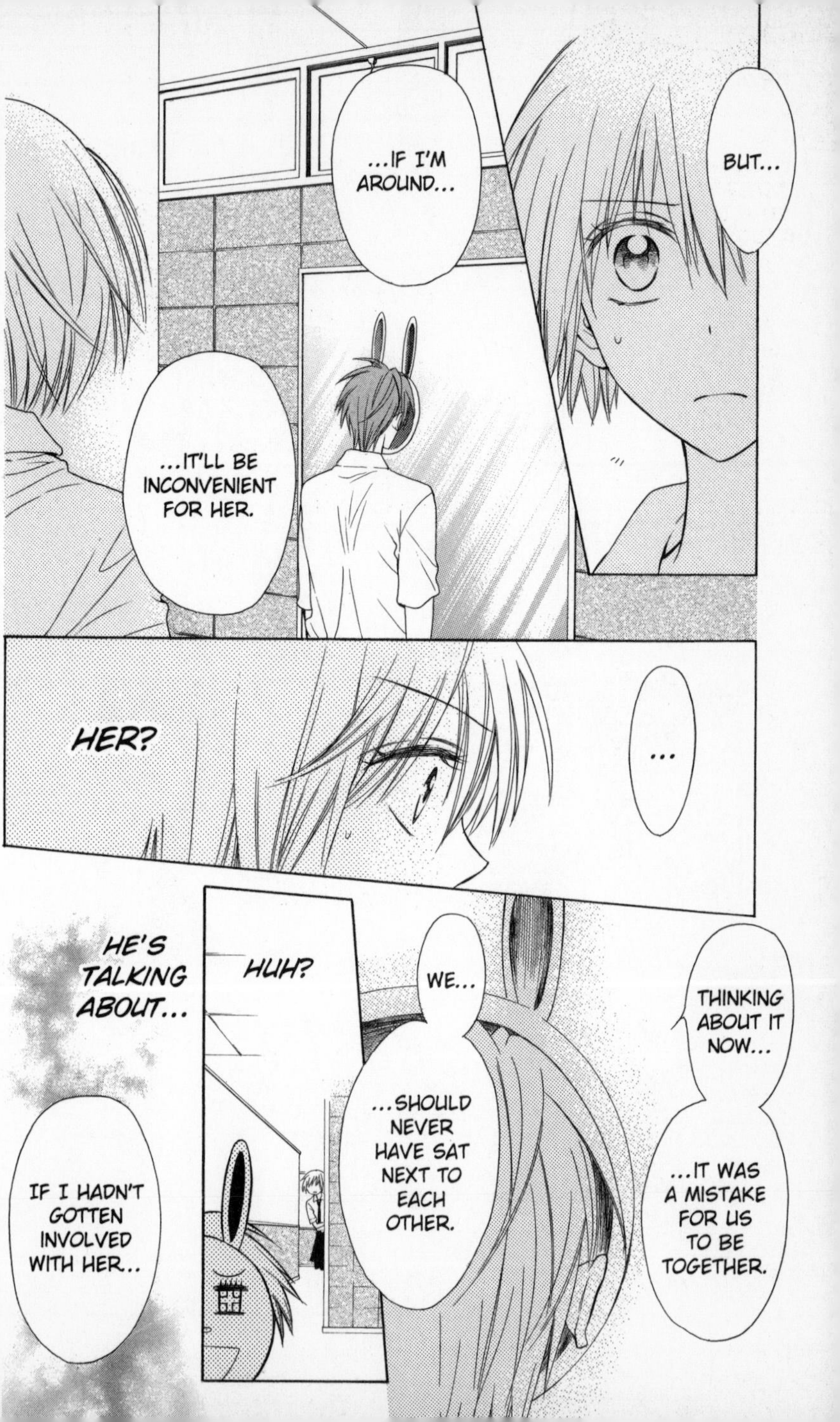

BUT...
...IF I'M AROUND...
...IT'LL BE INCONVENIENT FOR HER.
...
HER?
THINKING ABOUT IT NOW...
...IT WAS A MISTAKE FOR US TO BE TOGETHER.
WE...
...SHOULD NEVER HAVE SAT NEXT TO EACH OTHER.
HUH?
HE'S TALKING ABOUT...
IF I HADN'T GOTTEN INVOLVED WITH HER...

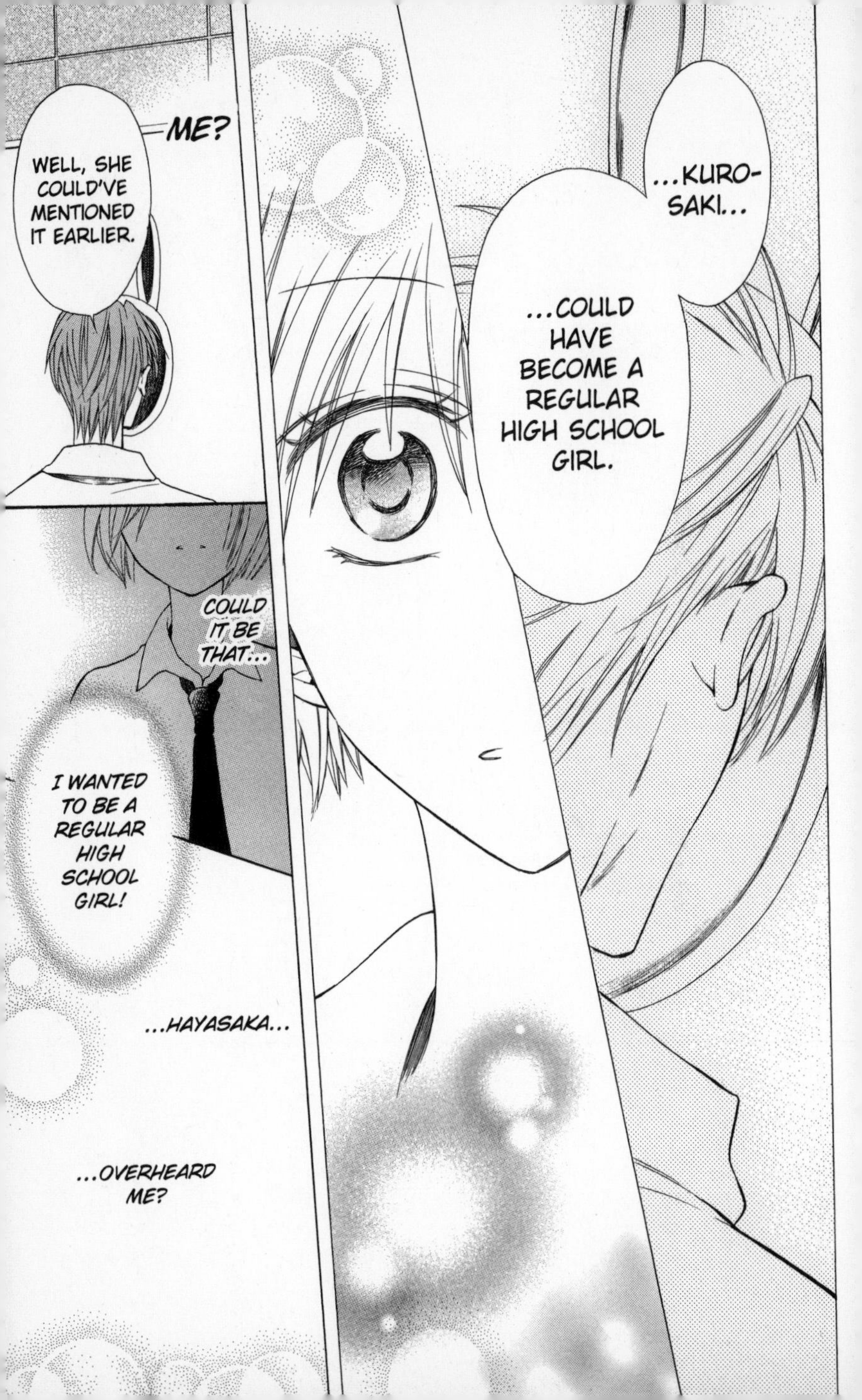
...KURO-SAKI...
...COULD HAVE BECOME A REGULAR HIGH SCHOOL GIRL.
WELL, SHE COULD'VE MENTIONED IT EARLIER.
—ME?
COULD IT BE THAT...
I WANTED TO BE A REGULAR HIGH SCHOOL GIRL!
...HAYASAKA...
...OVERHEARD ME?

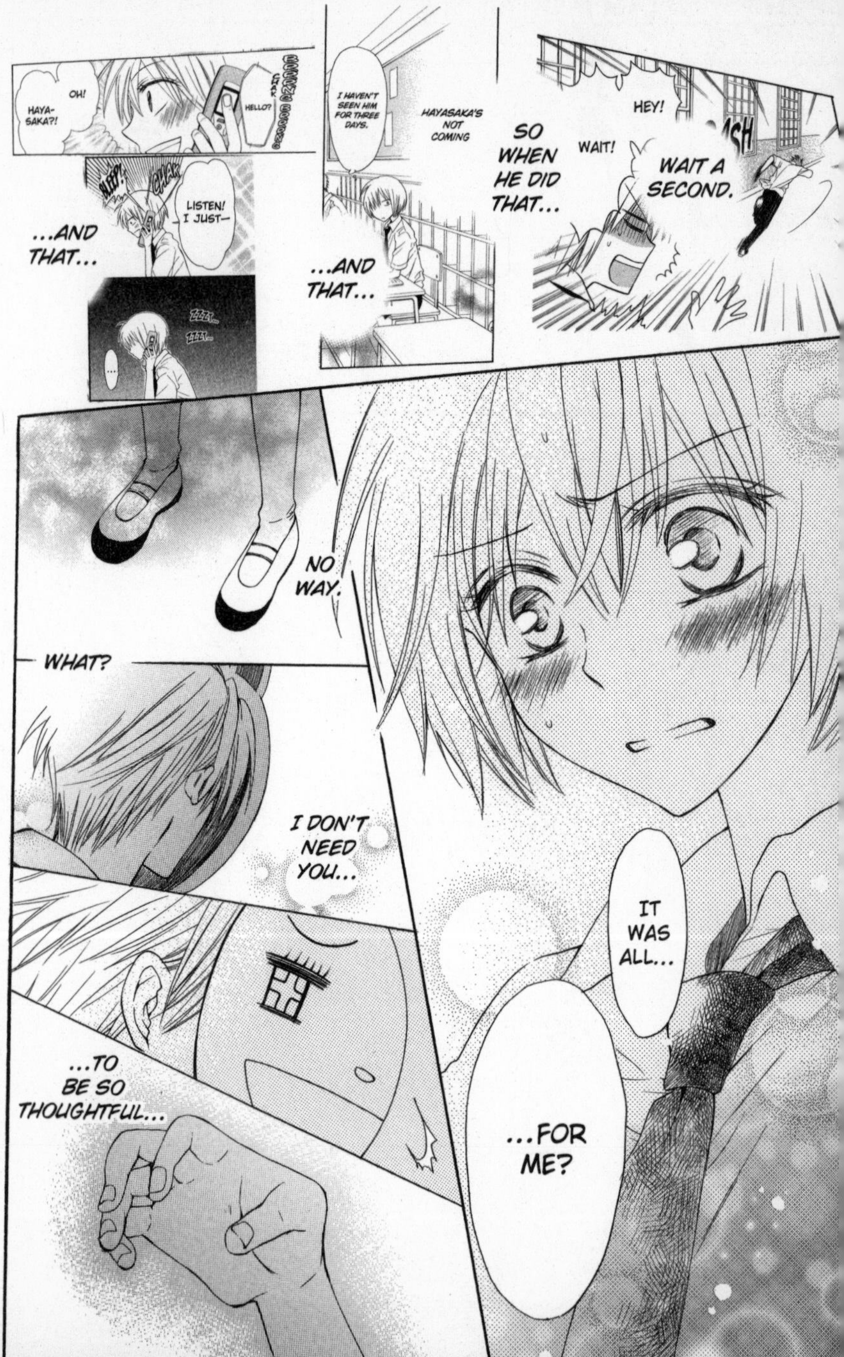
HEY!
WAIT!
WAIT A SECOND.
SO WHEN HE DID THAT...
HAYASAKA'S NOT COMING
I HAVEN'T SEEN HIM FOR THREE DAYS.
...AND THAT...
OH!
HAYASAKA?!
CHAK
HELLO?
BLEEP!
CHAK
LISTEN! I JUST—
...AND THAT...
ZZZT...
ZZZT...
...
IT WAS ALL...
...FOR ME?
NO WAY.
WHAT?
I DON'T NEED YOU...
...TO BE SO THOUGHTFUL...

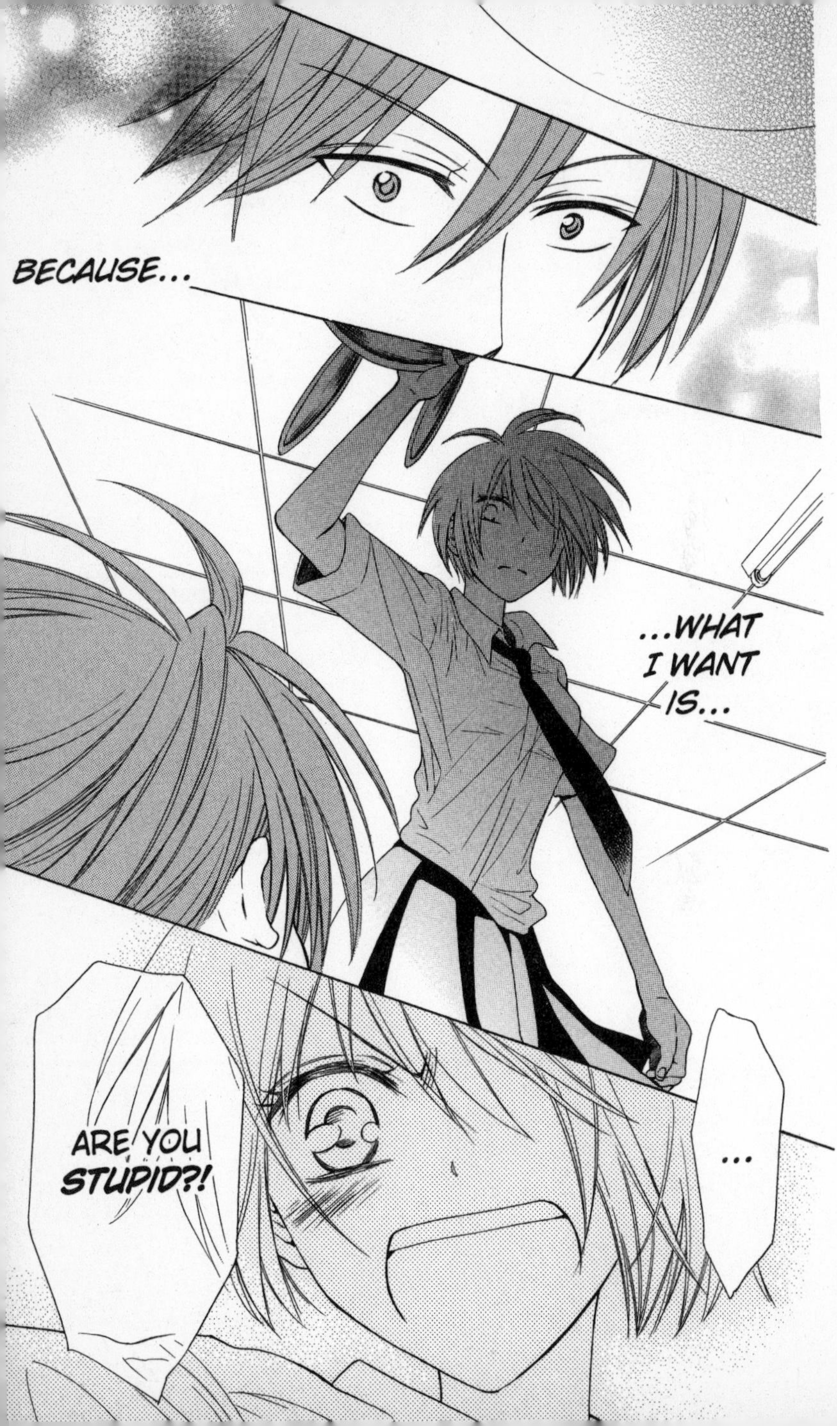
BECAUSE...
...WHAT I WANT IS...
...
ARE YOU STUPID?!

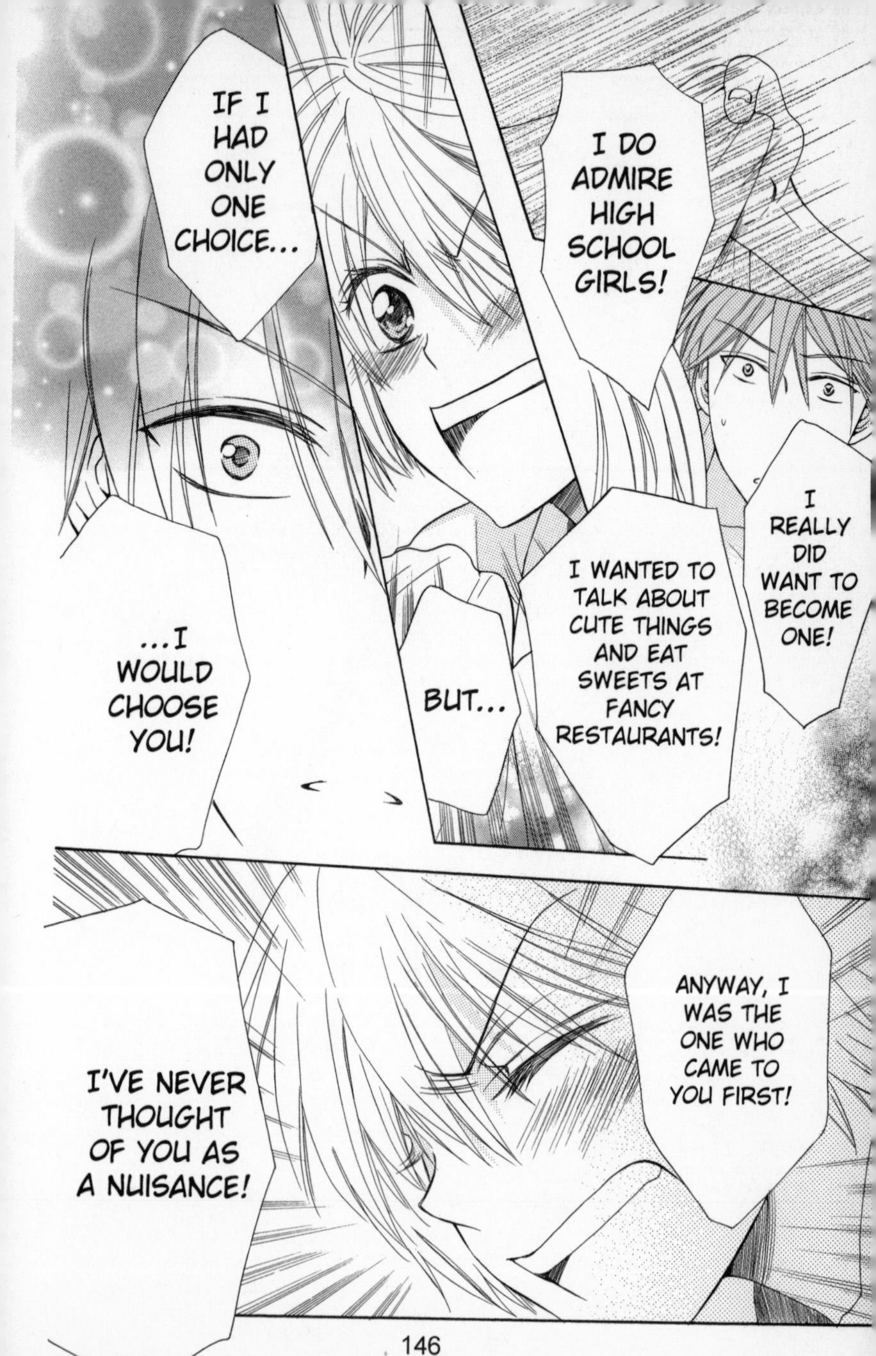
I DO ADMIRE HIGH SCHOOL GIRLS!
I REALLY DID WANT TO BECOME ONE!
I WANTED TO TALK ABOUT CUTE THINGS AND EAT SWEETS AT FANCY RESTAURANTS!
BUT...
IF I HAD ONLY ONE CHOICE...
...I WOULD CHOOSE YOU!
ANYWAY, I WAS THE ONE WHO CAME TO YOU FIRST!
I'VE NEVER THOUGHT OF YOU AS A NUISANCE!

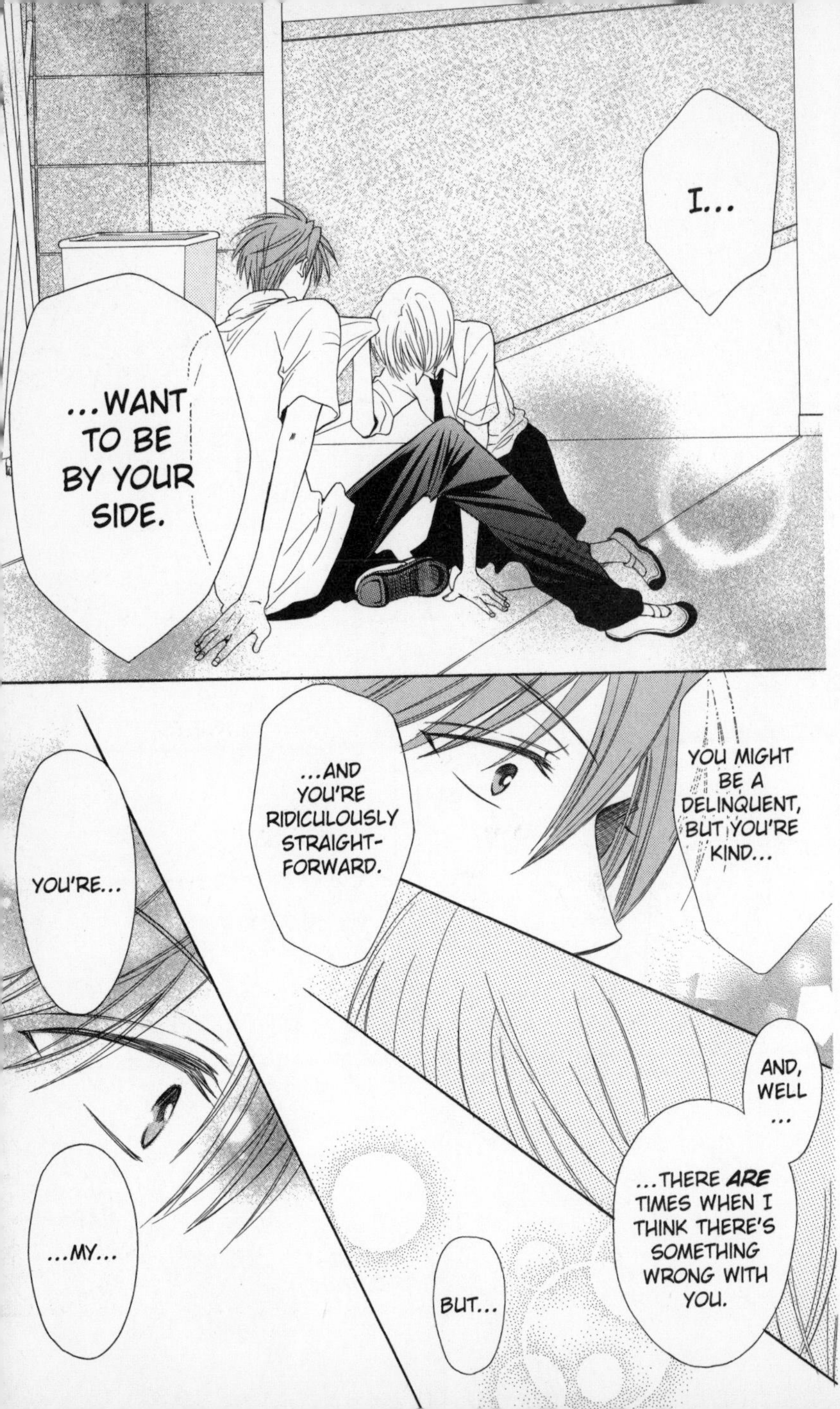
I...
...WANT TO BE BY YOUR SIDE.
YOU MIGHT BE A DELINQUENT, BUT YOU'RE KIND...
...AND YOU'RE RIDICULOUSLY STRAIGHT-FORWARD.
AND, WELL ...
...THERE *ARE* TIMES WHEN I THINK THERE'S SOMETHING WRONG WITH YOU.
BUT...
YOU'RE...
...MY...

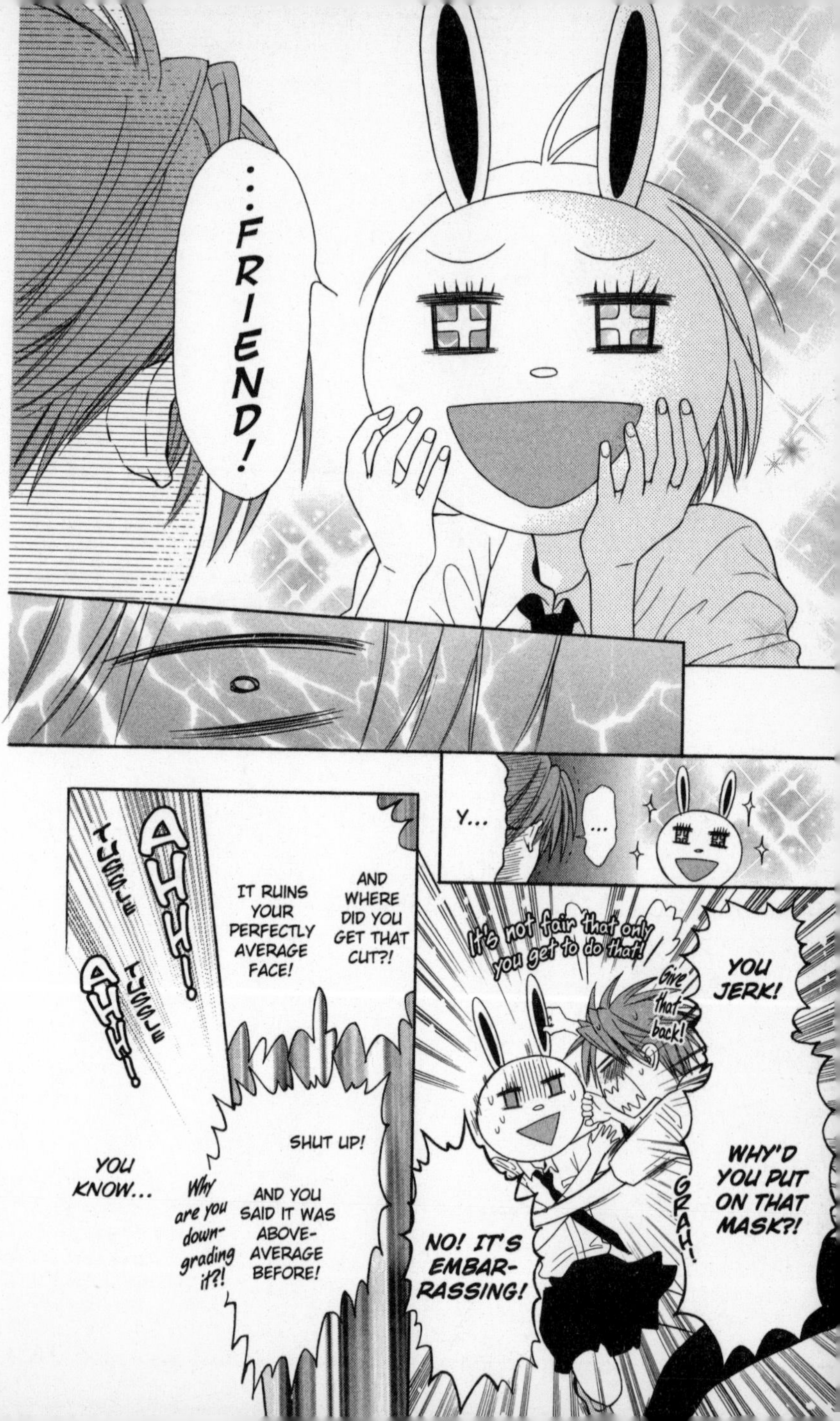
...FRIEND!
Y...
...
It's not fair that only you get to do that!
YOU JERK!
Give that back!
WHY'D YOU PUT ON THAT MASK?!
GRAH!
NO! IT'S EMBARRASSING!
AHH!
TUSSLE
TUSSLE
AHH!
AND WHERE DID YOU GET THAT CUT?!
IT RUINS YOUR PERFECTLY AVERAGE FACE!
SHUT UP!
AND YOU SAID IT WAS ABOVE-AVERAGE BEFORE!
Why are you downgrading it?!
YOU KNOW...

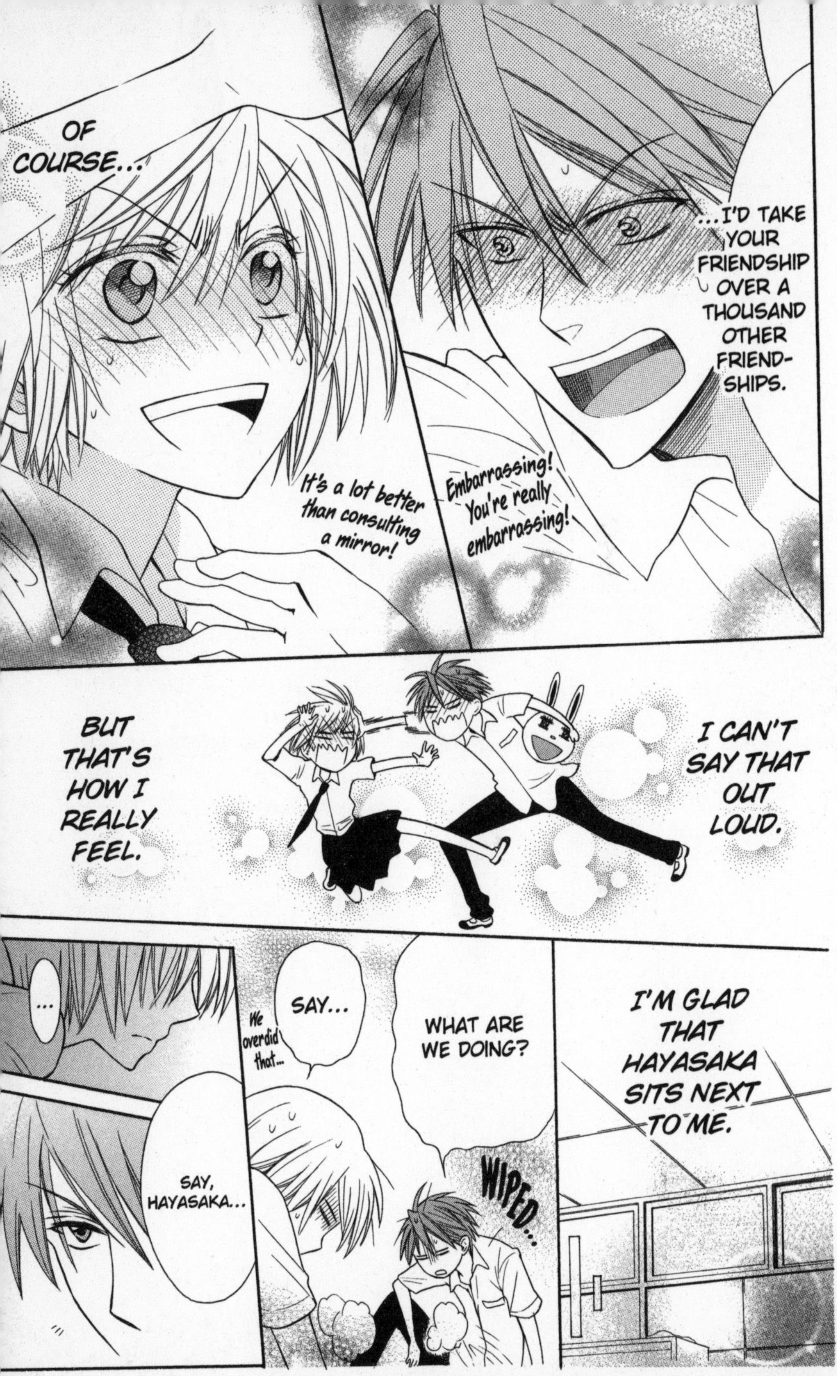
OF COURSE...
It's a lot better than consulting a mirror!
...I'D TAKE YOUR FRIENDSHIP OVER A THOUSAND OTHER FRIENDSHIPS.
Embarrassing! You're really embarrassing!
I CAN'T SAY THAT OUT LOUD.
BUT THAT'S HOW I REALLY FEEL.
I'M GLAD THAT HAYASAKA SITS NEXT TO ME.
WHAT ARE WE DOING?
WIPED...
SAY...
We overdid that...
...
SAY, HAYASAKA...

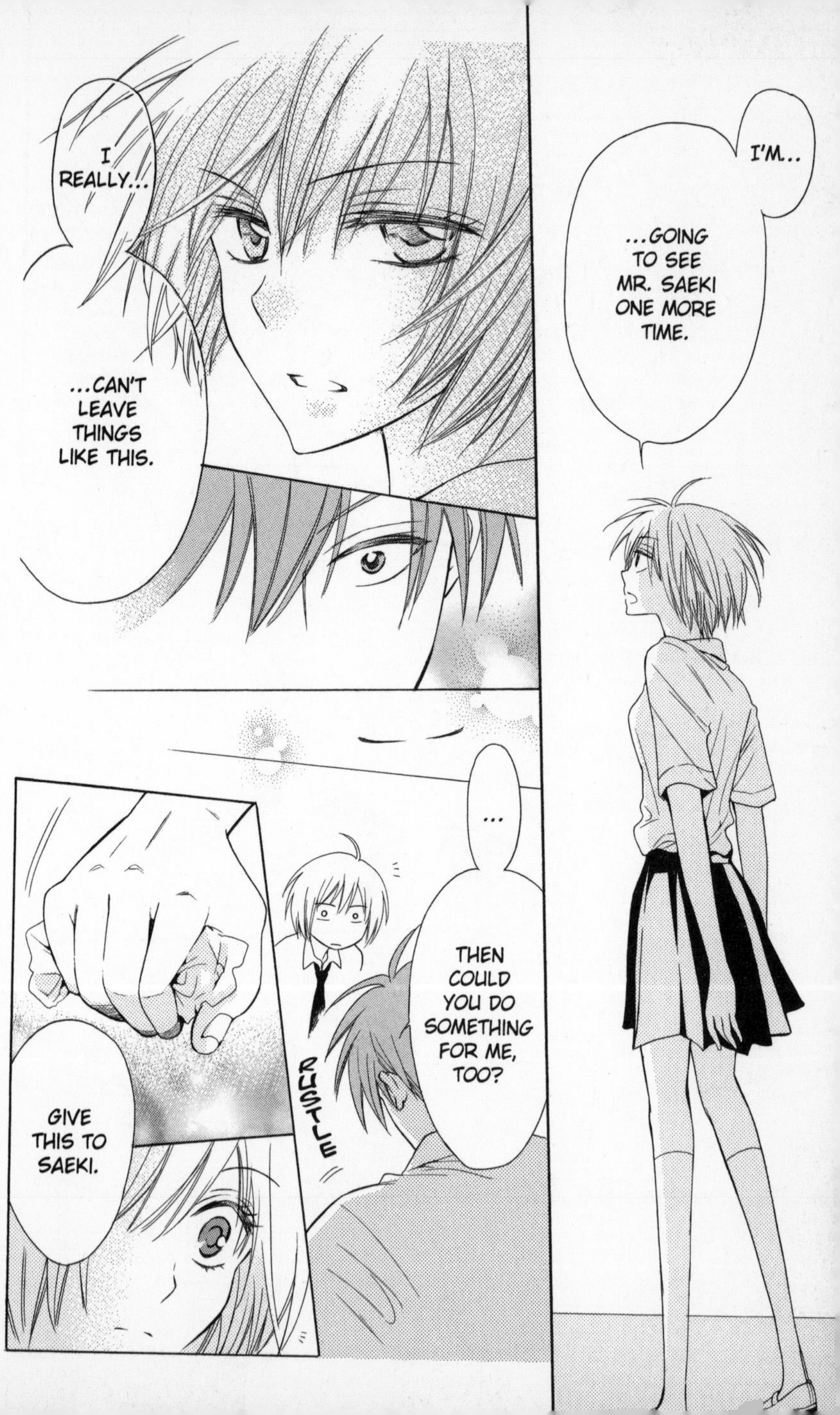
I'M...
...GOING TO SEE MR. SAEKI ONE MORE TIME.
I REALLY...
...CAN'T LEAVE THINGS LIKE THIS.
...
THEN COULD YOU DO SOMETHING FOR ME, TOO?
RUSTLE
GIVE THIS TO SAEKI.

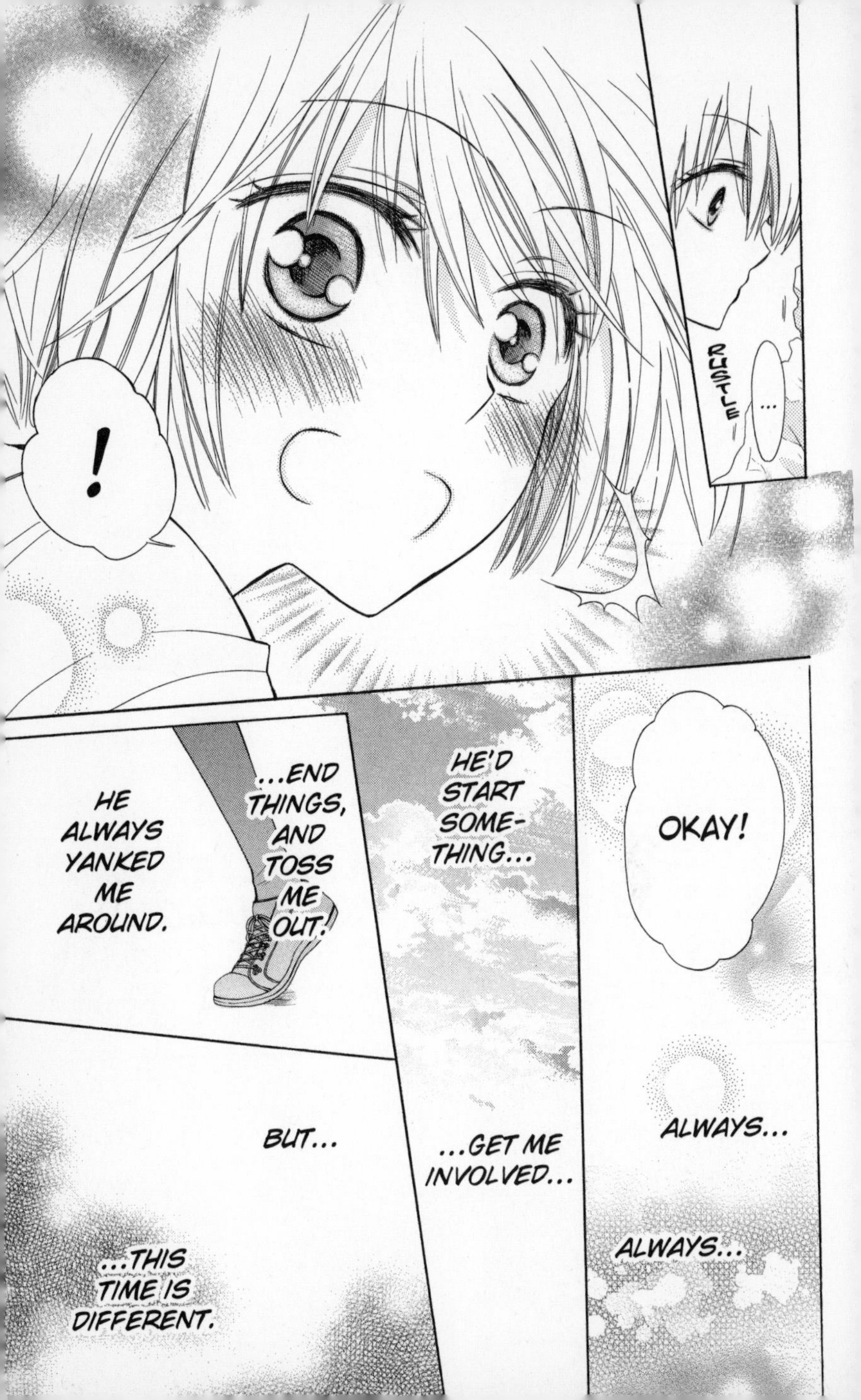
RUSTLE
...
!
OKAY!
ALWAYS...
ALWAYS...
HE'D START SOME-THING...
...GET ME INVOLVED...
...END THINGS, AND TOSS ME OUT.
HE ALWAYS YANKED ME AROUND.
BUT...
...THIS TIME IS DIFFERENT.

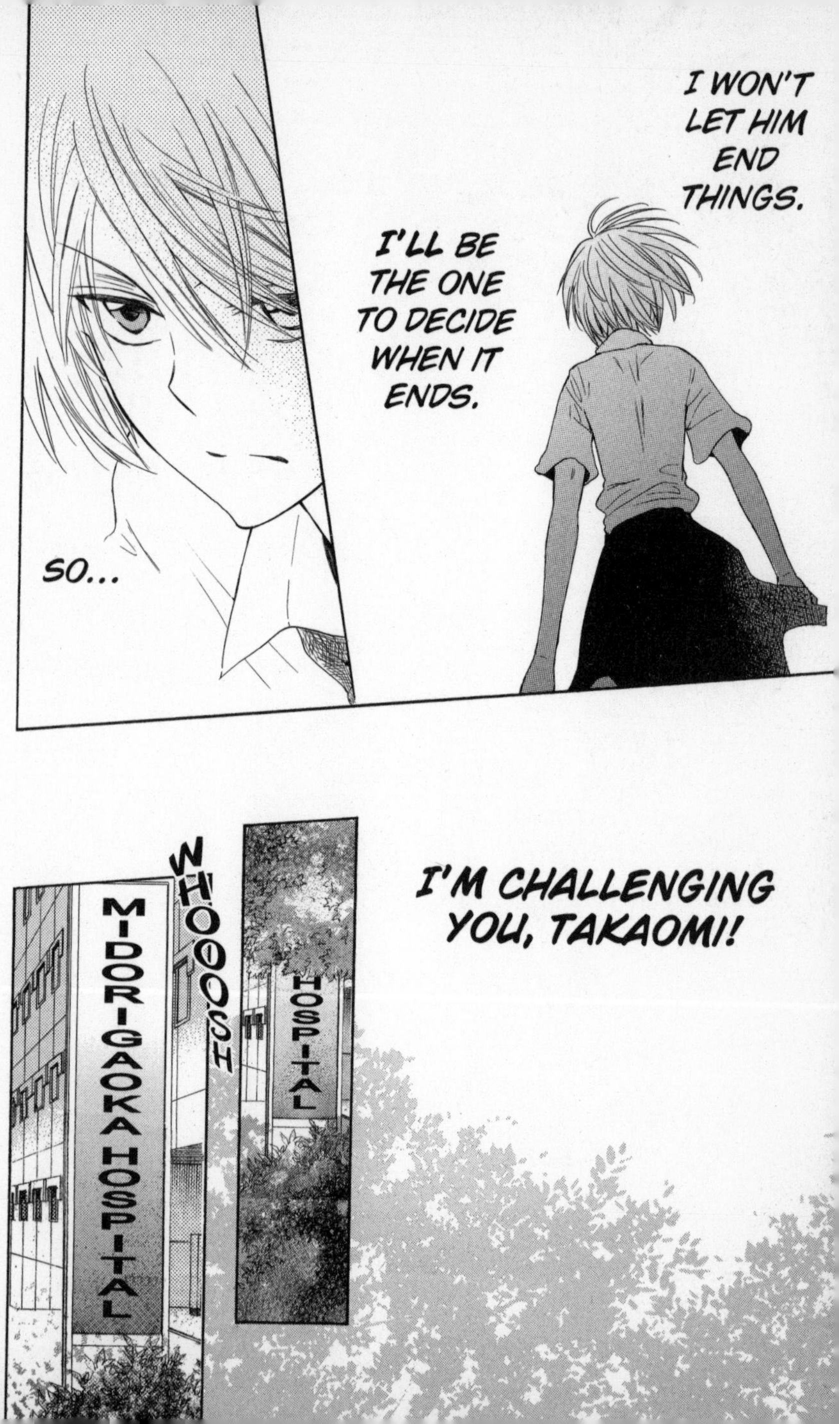
I WON'T LET HIM END THINGS.
I'LL BE THE ONE TO DECIDE WHEN IT ENDS.
SO...
I'M CHALLENGING YOU, TAKAOMI!
HOSPITAL
WHOOOOSH
MIDORIGAOKA HOSPITAL

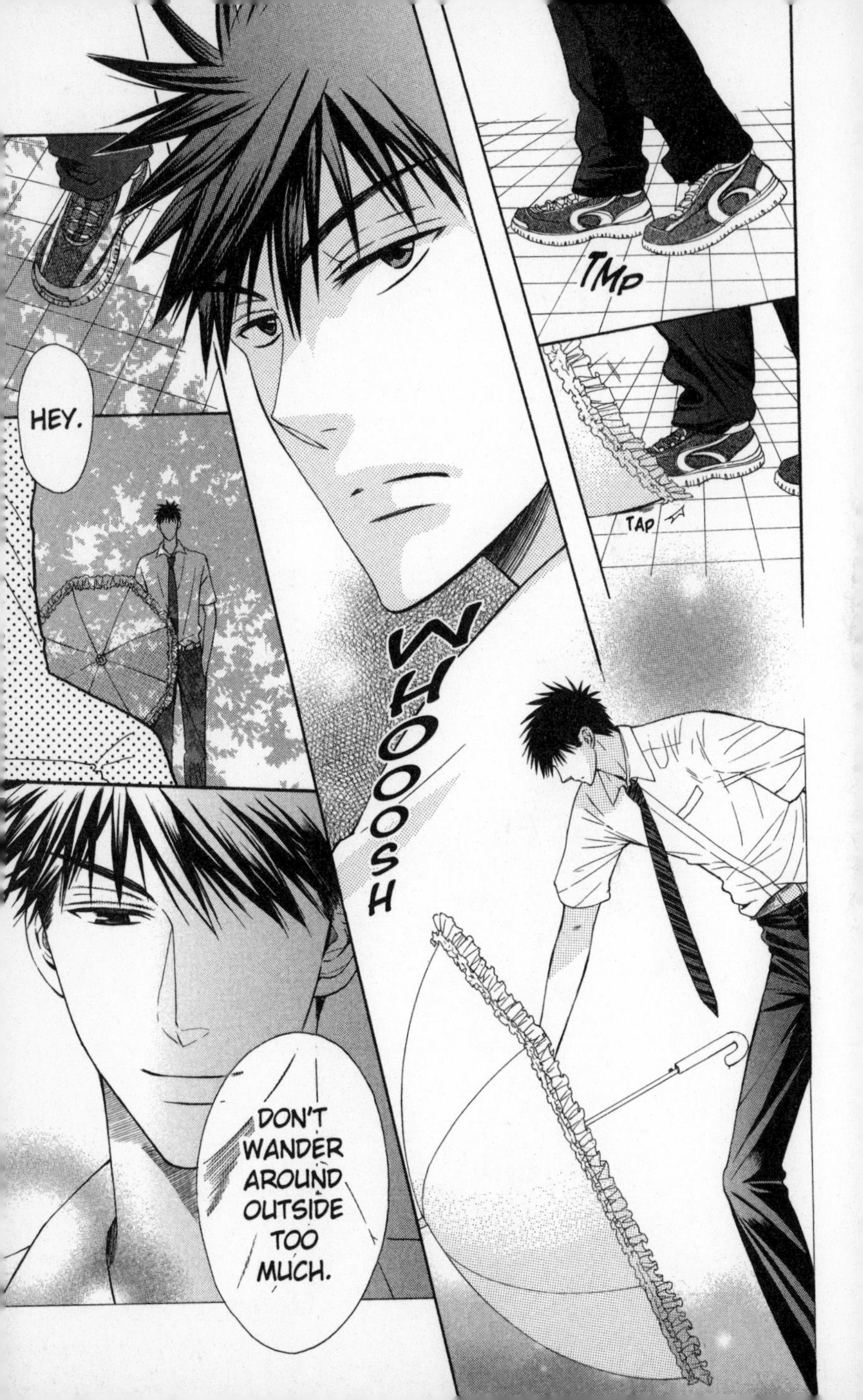
TMP
TAP
WHOOOOSH
HEY.
DON'T WANDER AROUND OUTSIDE TOO MUCH.

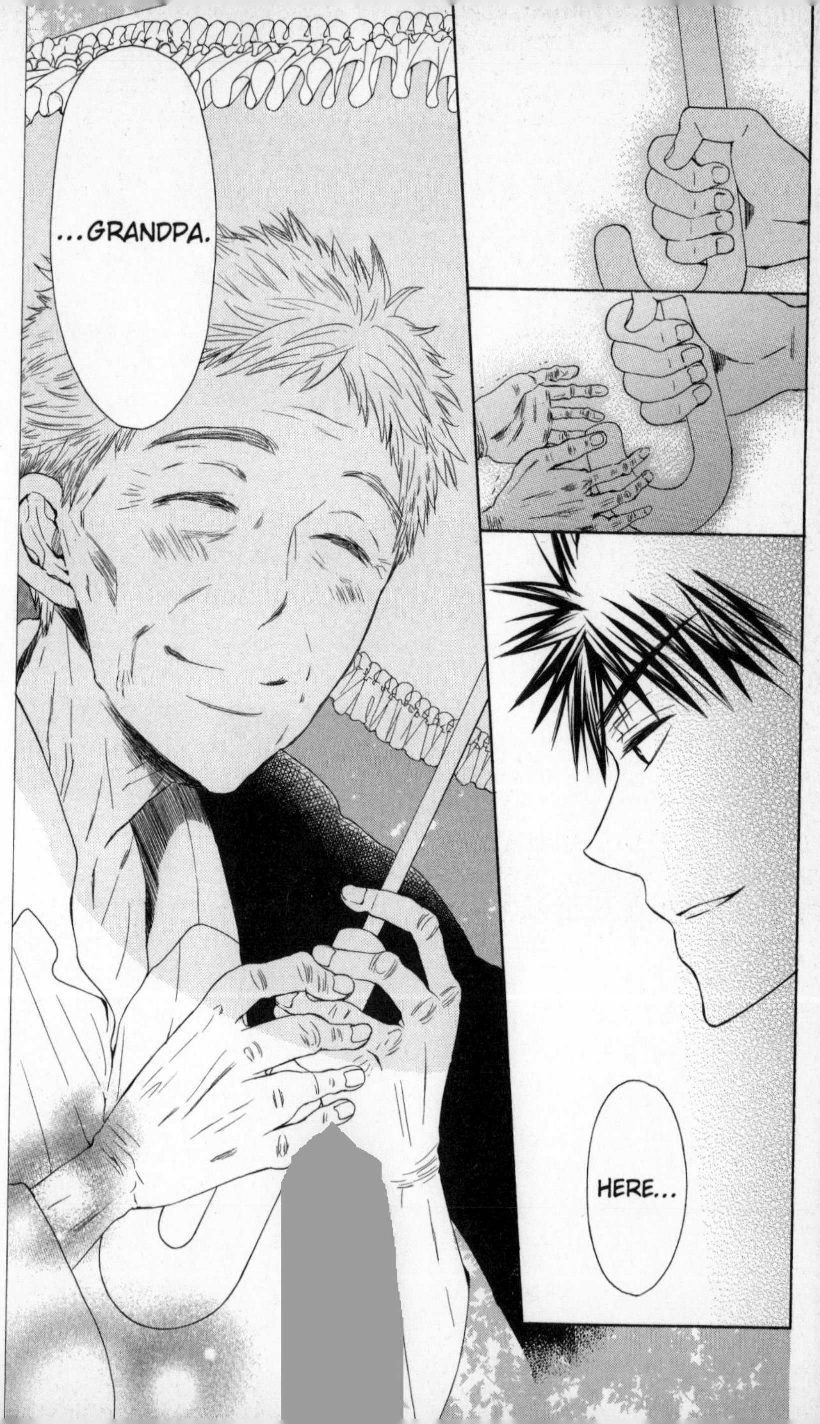
HERE...
...GRANDPA.

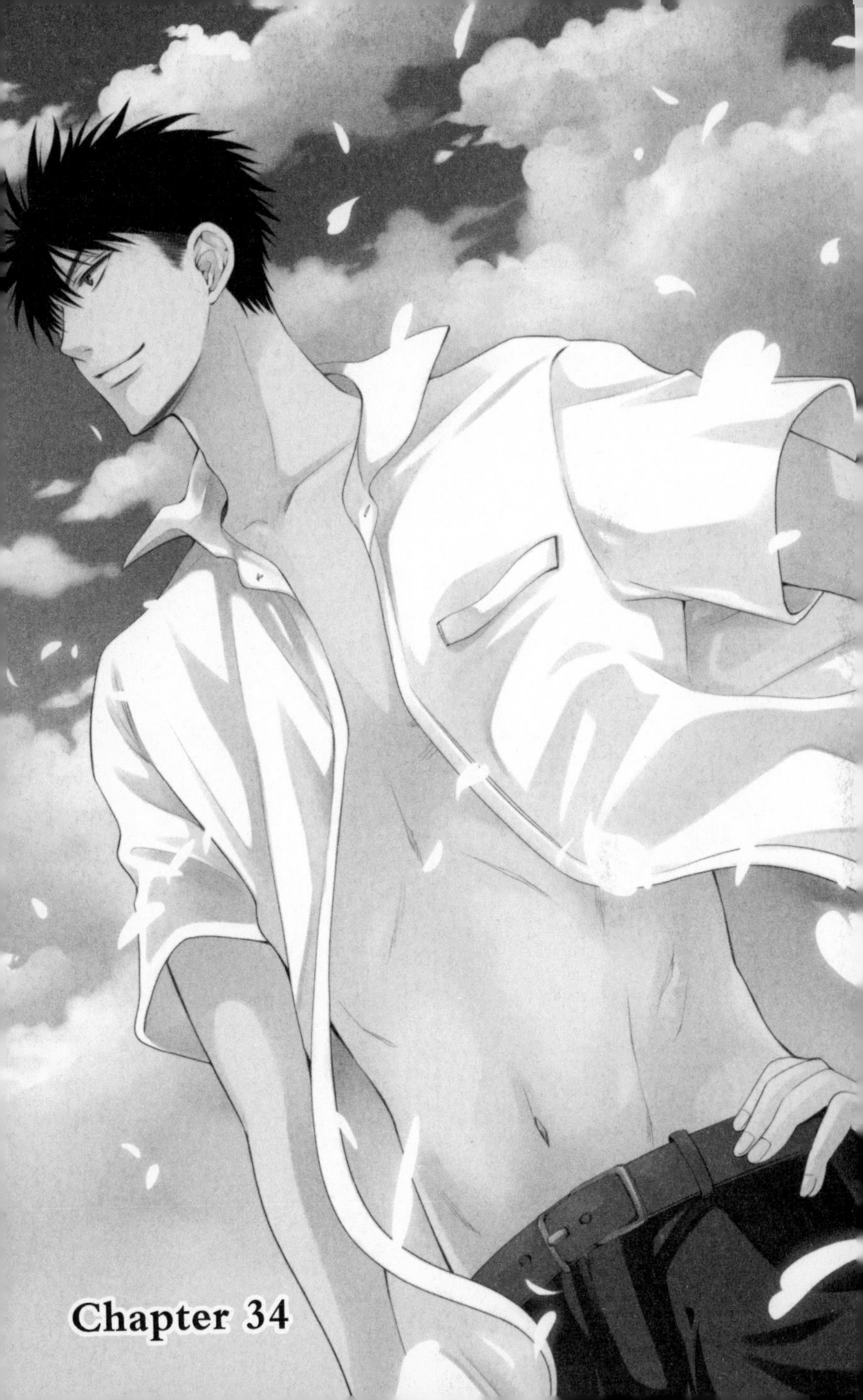

Chapter 34

I MADE A FRIEND, PART 1

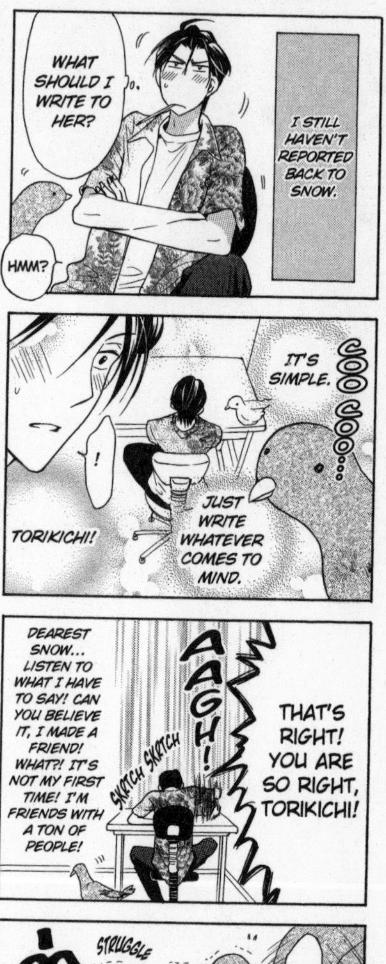
I STILL HAVEN'T REPORTED BACK TO SNOW.
WHAT SHOULD I WRITE TO HER?
HMM?
COO COO...
IT'S SIMPLE.
JUST WRITE WHATEVER COMES TO MIND.
!
TORIKICHI!
THAT'S RIGHT! YOU ARE SO RIGHT, TORIKICHI!
AAGH!
DEAREST SNOW... LISTEN TO WHAT I HAVE TO SAY! CAN YOU BELIEVE IT, I MADE A FRIEND! WHAT?! IT'S NOT MY FIRST TIME! I'M FRIENDS WITH A TON OF PEOPLE!
SKRTCH SKRTCH
...
IMPOSSIBLE.
STRUGGLE
STRUGGLE
FLAP
FLAP
FLAP

I MADE A FRIEND, PART 2

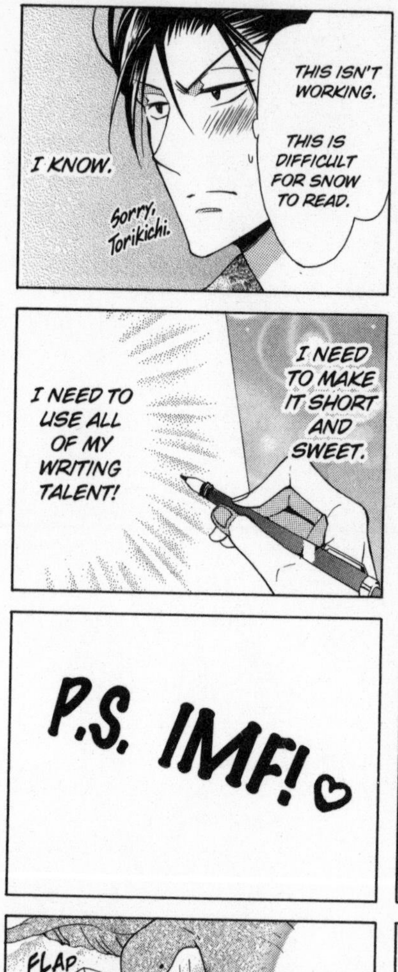
THIS ISN'T WORKING.
THIS IS DIFFICULT FOR SNOW TO READ.
I KNOW.
Sorry, Torikichi.
I NEED TO MAKE IT SHORT AND SWEET.
I NEED TO USE ALL OF MY WRITING TALENT!
P.S. IMF! ♡
FLAP
I MADE A FRIEND! ♡
SHE DIDN'T UNDERSTAND HIS LETTER.

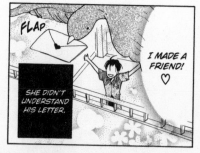

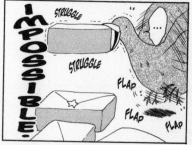

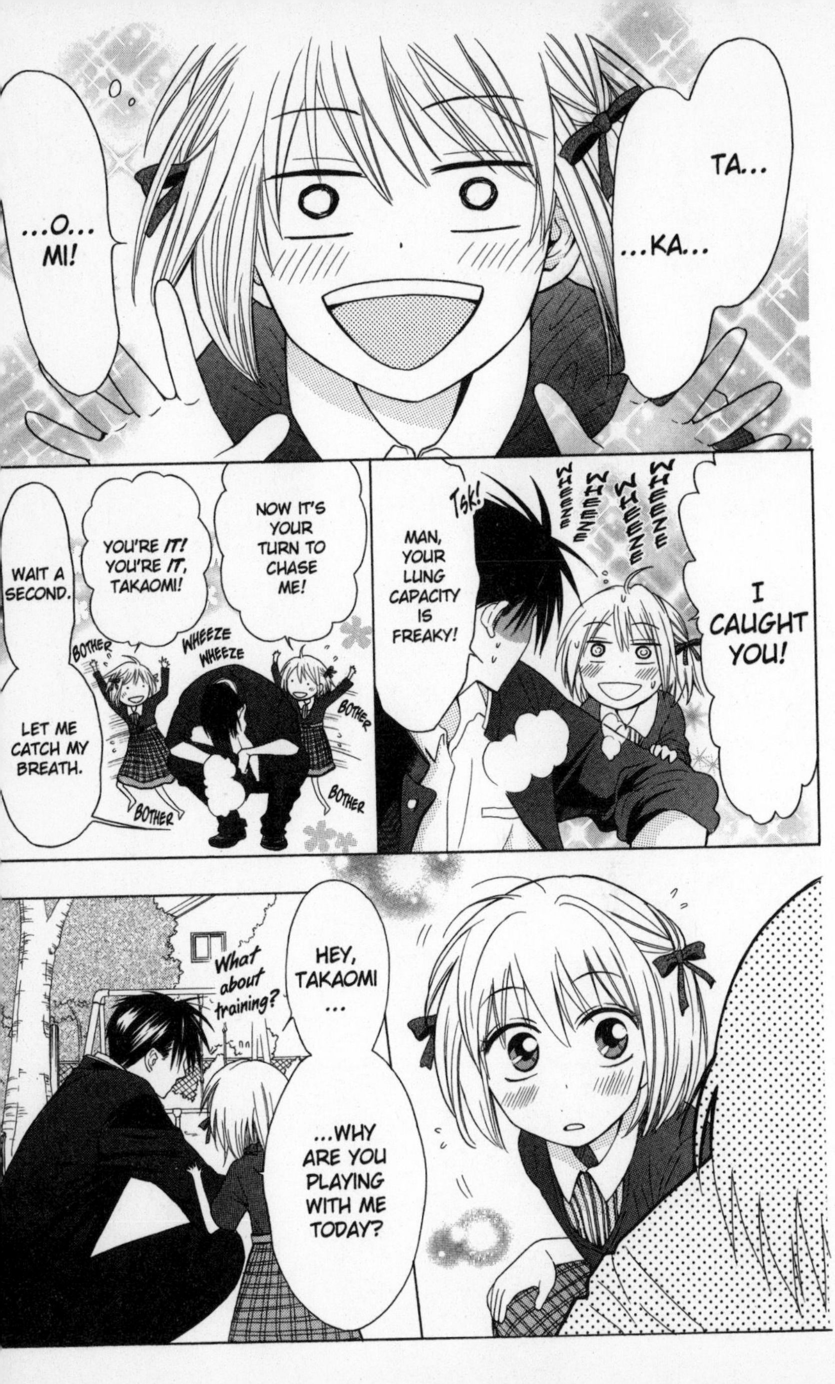
TA...
...KA...
...O... MI!
I CAUGHT YOU!
WHEEZE WHEEZE WHEEZE WHEEZE
Tsk!
MAN, YOUR LUNG CAPACITY IS FREAKY!
NOW IT'S YOUR TURN TO CHASE ME!
BOTHER BOTHER
WHEEZE WHEEZE
YOU'RE *IT*! YOU'RE *IT*, TAKAOMI!
BOTHER BOTHER
WAIT A SECOND.
LET ME CATCH MY BREATH.
HEY, TAKAOMI ...
...WHY ARE YOU PLAYING WITH ME TODAY?
What about training?

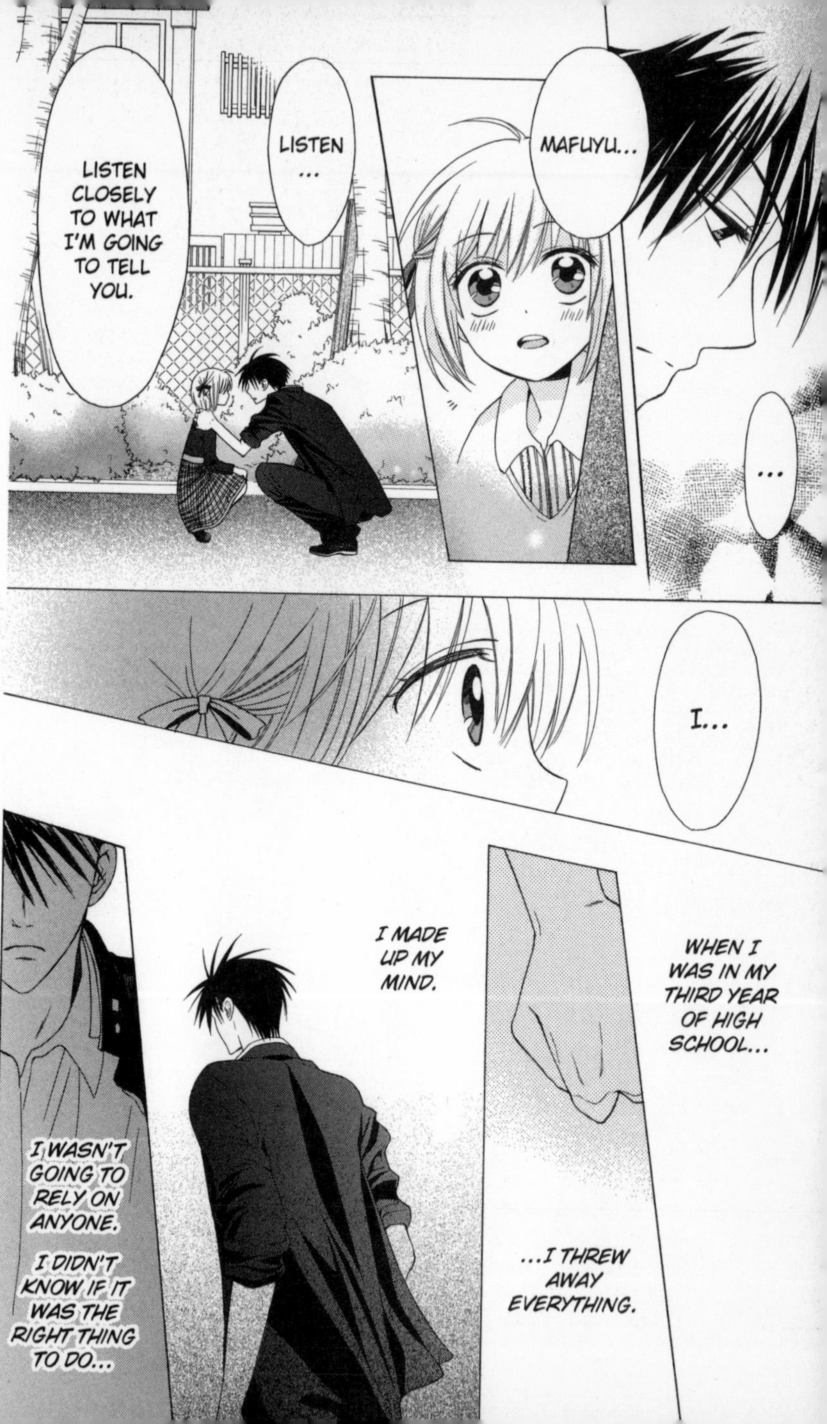
MAFUYU...
...
LISTEN...
LISTEN CLOSELY TO WHAT I'M GOING TO TELL YOU.
I...
WHEN I WAS IN MY THIRD YEAR OF HIGH SCHOOL...
...I THREW AWAY EVERYTHING.
I MADE UP MY MIND.
I WASN'T GOING TO RELY ON ANYONE.
I DIDN'T KNOW IF IT WAS THE RIGHT THING TO DO...

...I WANTED...

...TO GET IT ALL BACK...

...FOR YOU.

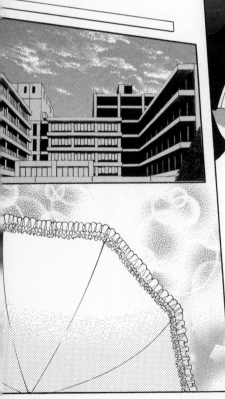

...BUT...

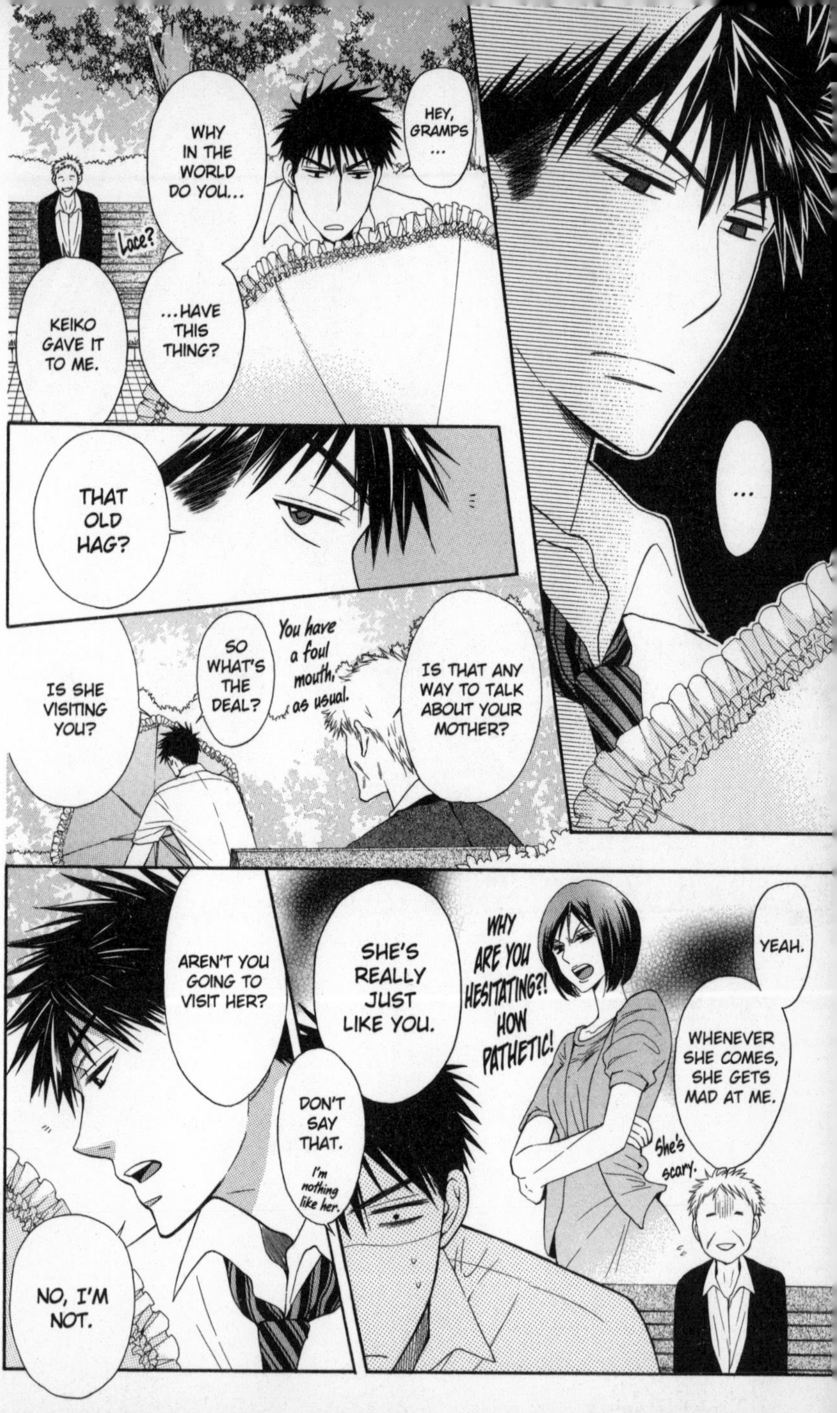
...
HEY, GRAMPS...
WHY IN THE WORLD DO YOU...
Lace?
...HAVE THIS THING?
KEIKO GAVE IT TO ME.
THAT OLD HAG?
IS THAT ANY WAY TO TALK ABOUT YOUR MOTHER?
You have a foul mouth, as usual.
SO WHAT'S THE DEAL?
IS SHE VISITING YOU?
YEAH.
WHENEVER SHE COMES, SHE GETS MAD AT ME.
She's scary.
WHY ARE YOU HESITATING?! HOW PATHETIC!
SHE'S REALLY JUST LIKE YOU.
DON'T SAY THAT.
I'm nothing like her.
AREN'T YOU GOING TO VISIT HER?
NO, I'M NOT.

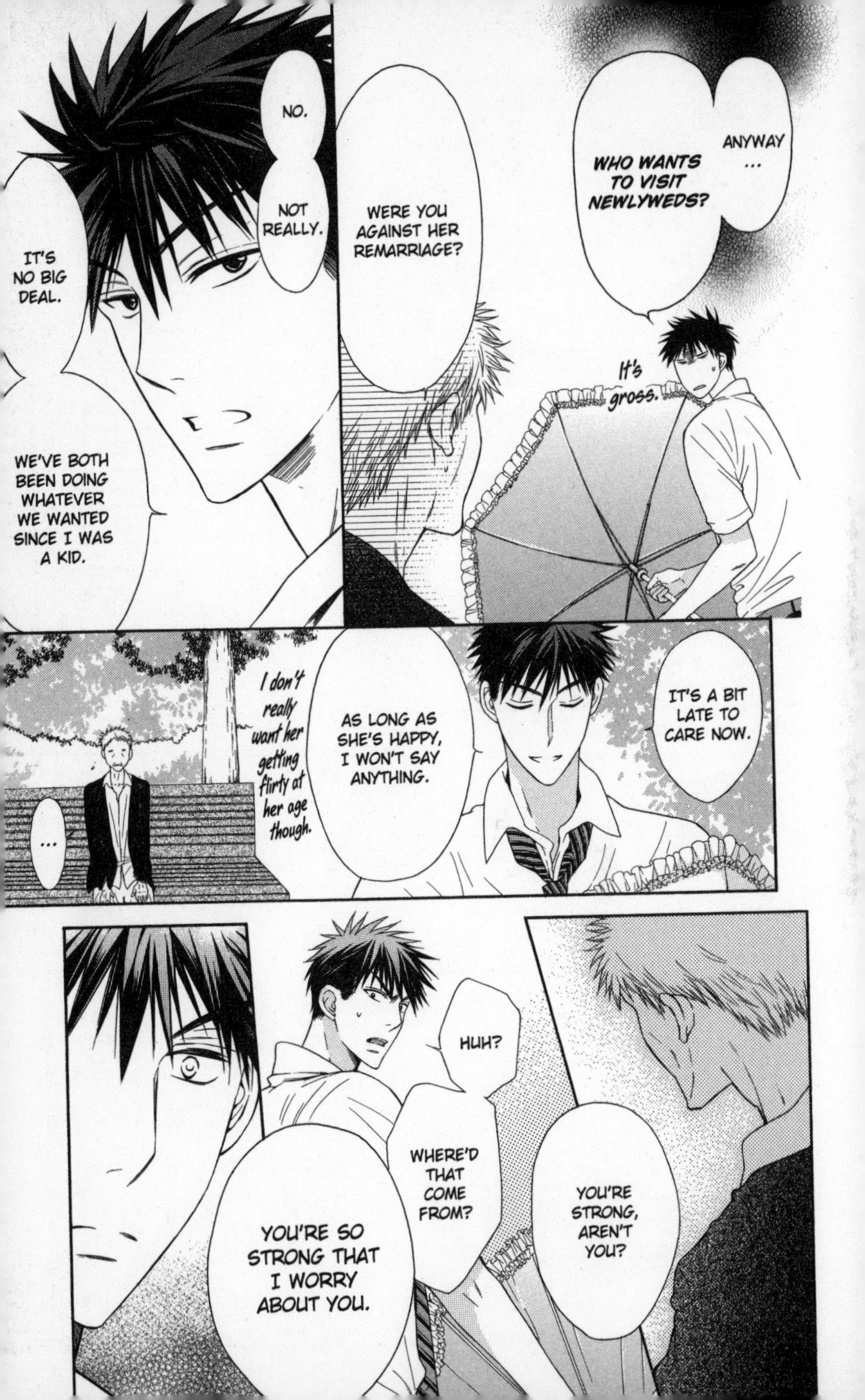
ANYWAY ...
WHO WANTS TO VISIT NEWLYWEDS?
It's gross.
WERE YOU AGAINST HER REMARRIAGE?
NO.
NOT REALLY.
IT'S NO BIG DEAL.
WE'VE BOTH BEEN DOING WHATEVER WE WANTED SINCE I WAS A KID.
IT'S A BIT LATE TO CARE NOW.
AS LONG AS SHE'S HAPPY, I WON'T SAY ANYTHING.
I don't really want her getting flirty at her age though.
...
YOU'RE STRONG, AREN'T YOU?
HUH?
WHERE'D THAT COME FROM?
YOU'RE SO STRONG THAT I WORRY ABOUT YOU.

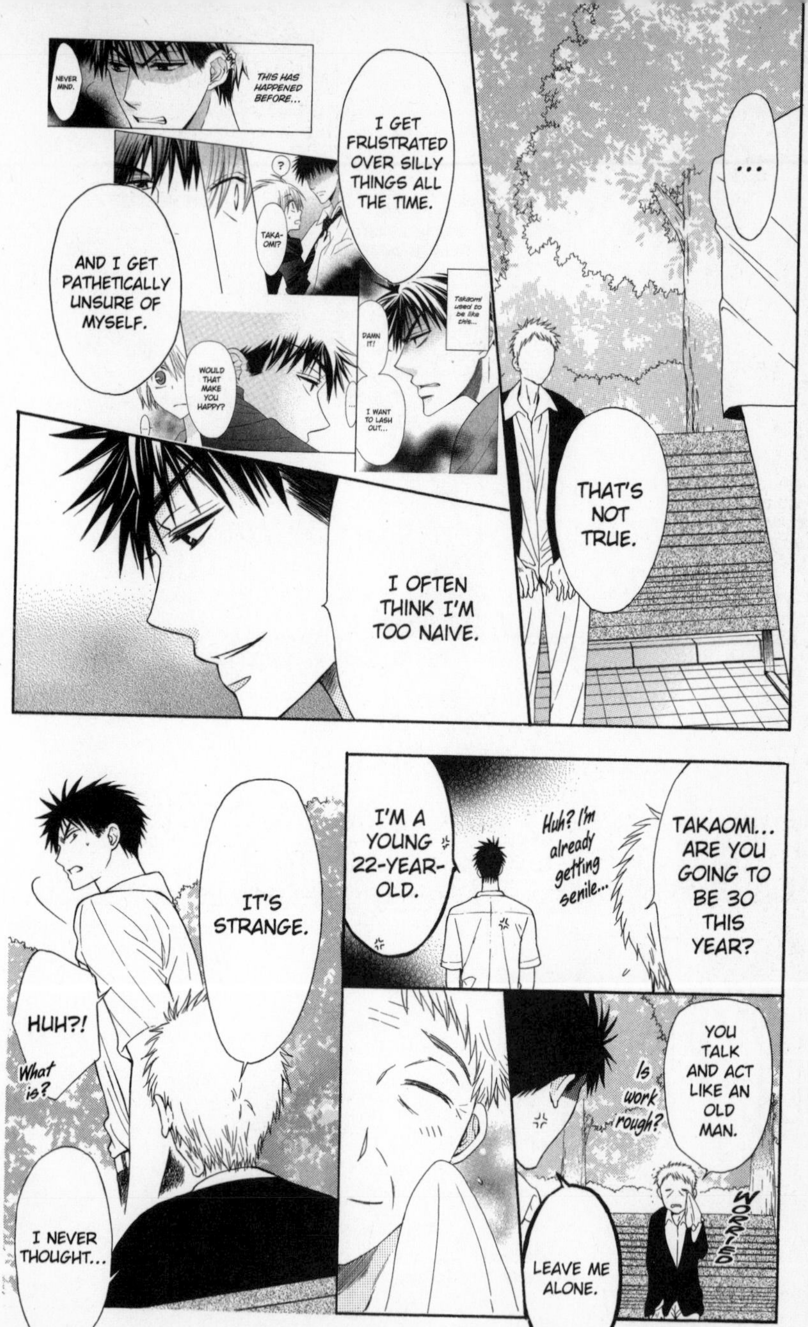
...
THAT'S NOT TRUE.
THIS HAS HAPPENED BEFORE...
NEVER MIND.
I GET FRUSTRATED OVER SILLY THINGS ALL THE TIME.
?
TAKA-OMI?
AND I GET PATHETICALLY UNSURE OF MYSELF.
Takaomi used to be like this...
DAMN IT!
I WANT TO LASH OUT...
...
WOULD THAT MAKE YOU HAPPY?
...
I OFTEN THINK I'M TOO NAIVE.
TAKAOMI... ARE YOU GOING TO BE 30 THIS YEAR?
Huh? I'm already getting senile...
I'M A YOUNG 22-YEAR-OLD.
YOU TALK AND ACT LIKE AN OLD MAN.
Is work rough?
WORRIED
LEAVE ME ALONE.
IT'S STRANGE.
HUH?!
What is?
I NEVER THOUGHT...

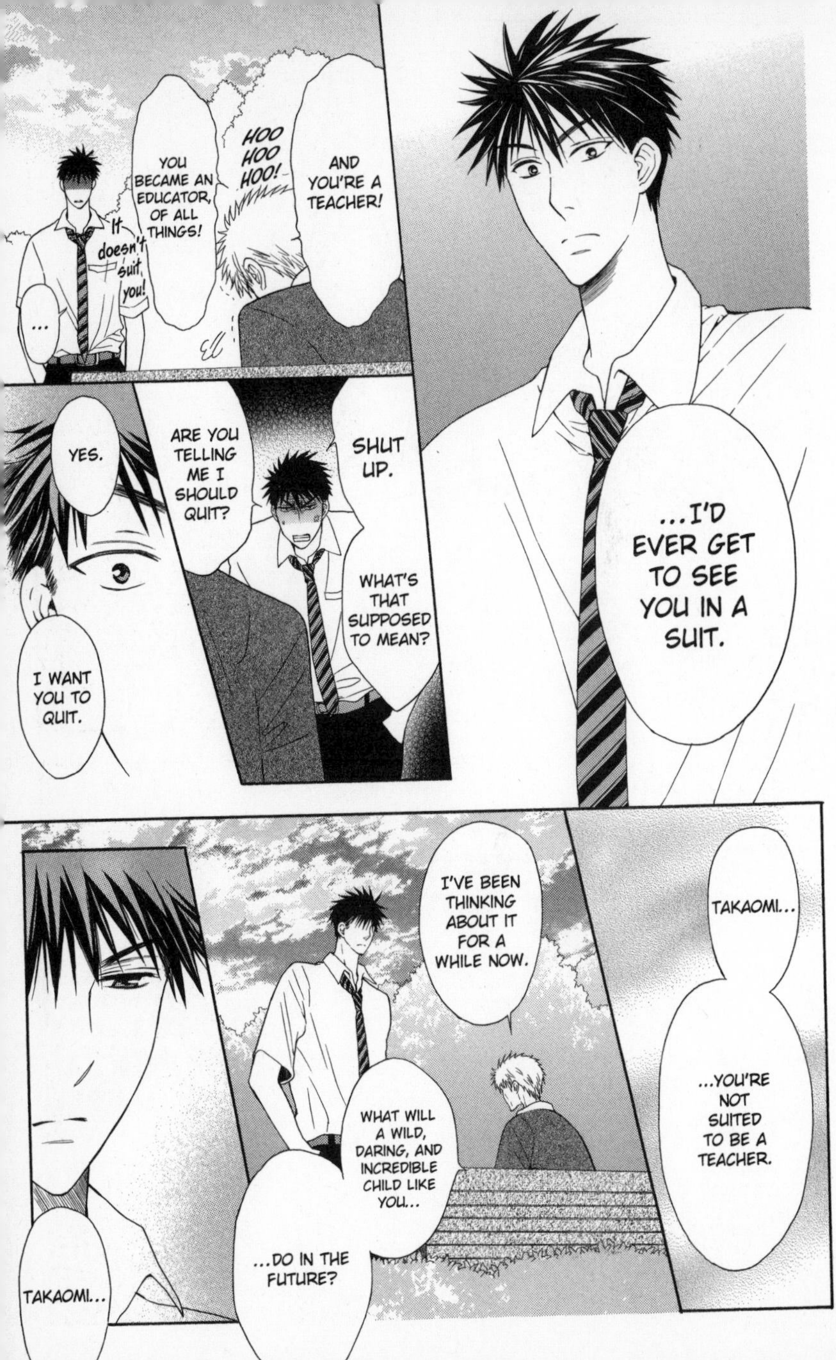
...I'D EVER GET TO SEE YOU IN A SUIT.
AND YOU'RE A TEACHER!
HOO HOO HOO!
YOU BECAME AN EDUCATOR, OF ALL THINGS!
It doesn't suit you!
...
SHUT UP.
WHAT'S THAT SUPPOSED TO MEAN?
ARE YOU TELLING ME I SHOULD QUIT?
YES.
I WANT YOU TO QUIT.
TAKAOMI...
...YOU'RE NOT SUITED TO BE A TEACHER.
I'VE BEEN THINKING ABOUT IT FOR A WHILE NOW.
WHAT WILL A WILD, DARING, AND INCREDIBLE CHILD LIKE YOU...
...DO IN THE FUTURE?
TAKAOMI...

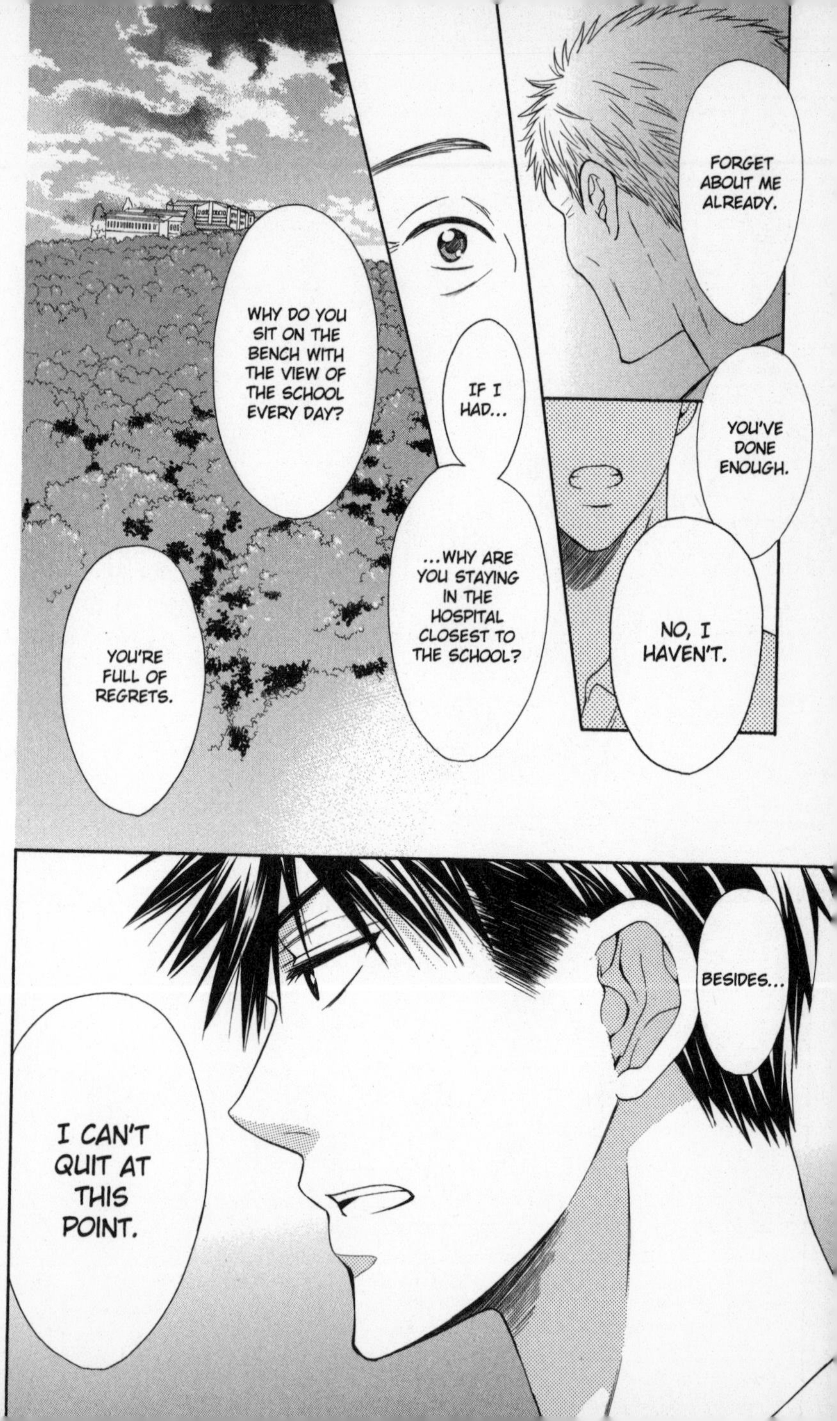
FORGET ABOUT ME ALREADY.
YOU'VE DONE ENOUGH.
NO, I HAVEN'T.
IF I HAD...
...WHY ARE YOU STAYING IN THE HOSPITAL CLOSEST TO THE SCHOOL?
WHY DO YOU SIT ON THE BENCH WITH THE VIEW OF THE SCHOOL EVERY DAY?
YOU'RE FULL OF REGRETS.
BESIDES...
I CAN'T QUIT AT THIS POINT.

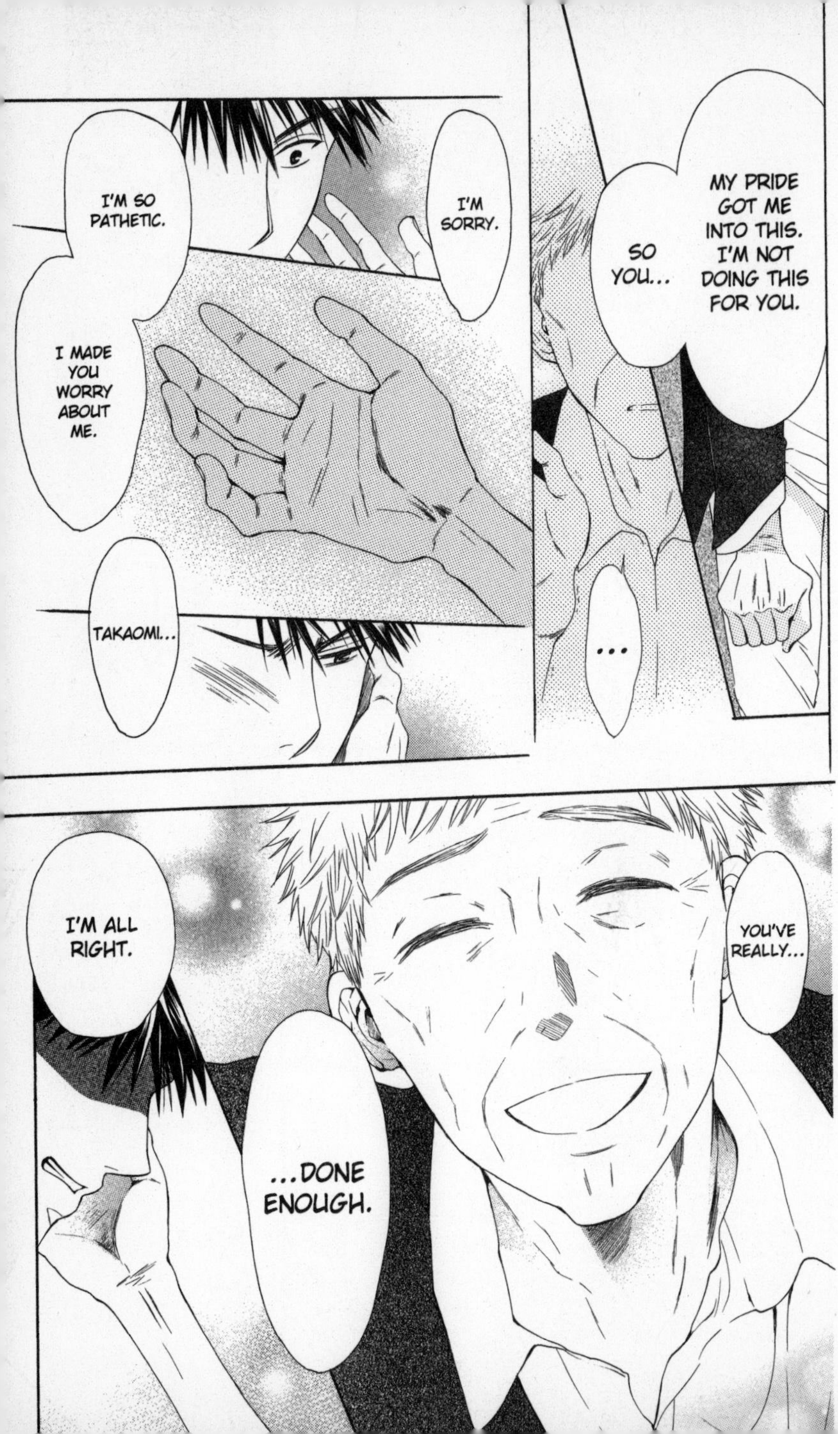
MY PRIDE GOT ME INTO THIS. I'M NOT DOING THIS FOR YOU.
SO YOU...
...
I'M SORRY.
I'M SO PATHETIC.
I MADE YOU WORRY ABOUT ME.
TAKAOMI...
YOU'VE REALLY...
...DONE ENOUGH.
I'M ALL RIGHT.

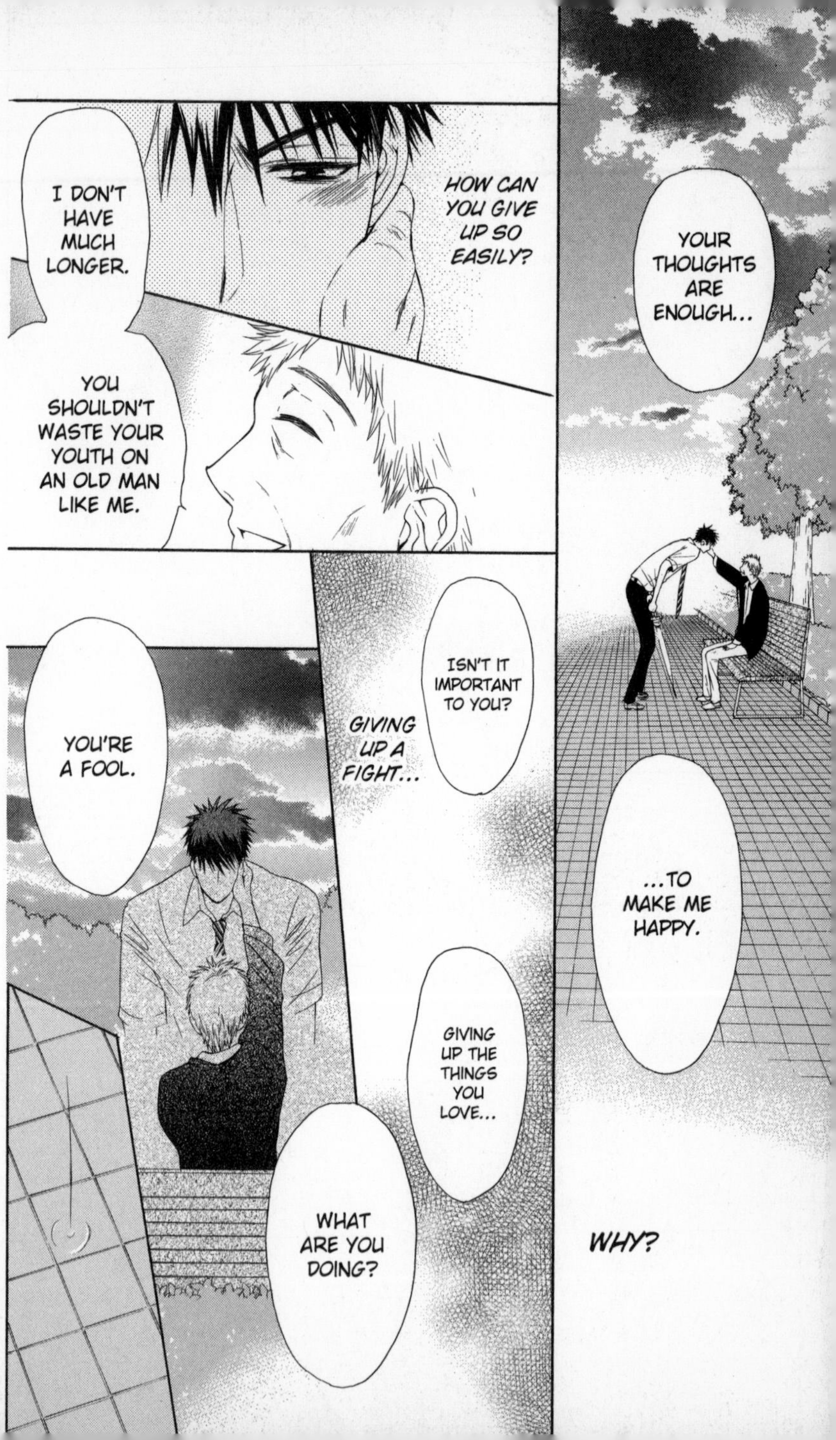
YOUR THOUGHTS ARE ENOUGH...
...TO MAKE ME HAPPY.
WHY?
HOW CAN YOU GIVE UP SO EASILY?
I DON'T HAVE MUCH LONGER.
YOU SHOULDN'T WASTE YOUR YOUTH ON AN OLD MAN LIKE ME.
ISN'T IT IMPORTANT TO YOU?
GIVING UP A FIGHT...
GIVING UP THE THINGS YOU LOVE...
WHAT ARE YOU DOING?
YOU'RE A FOOL.

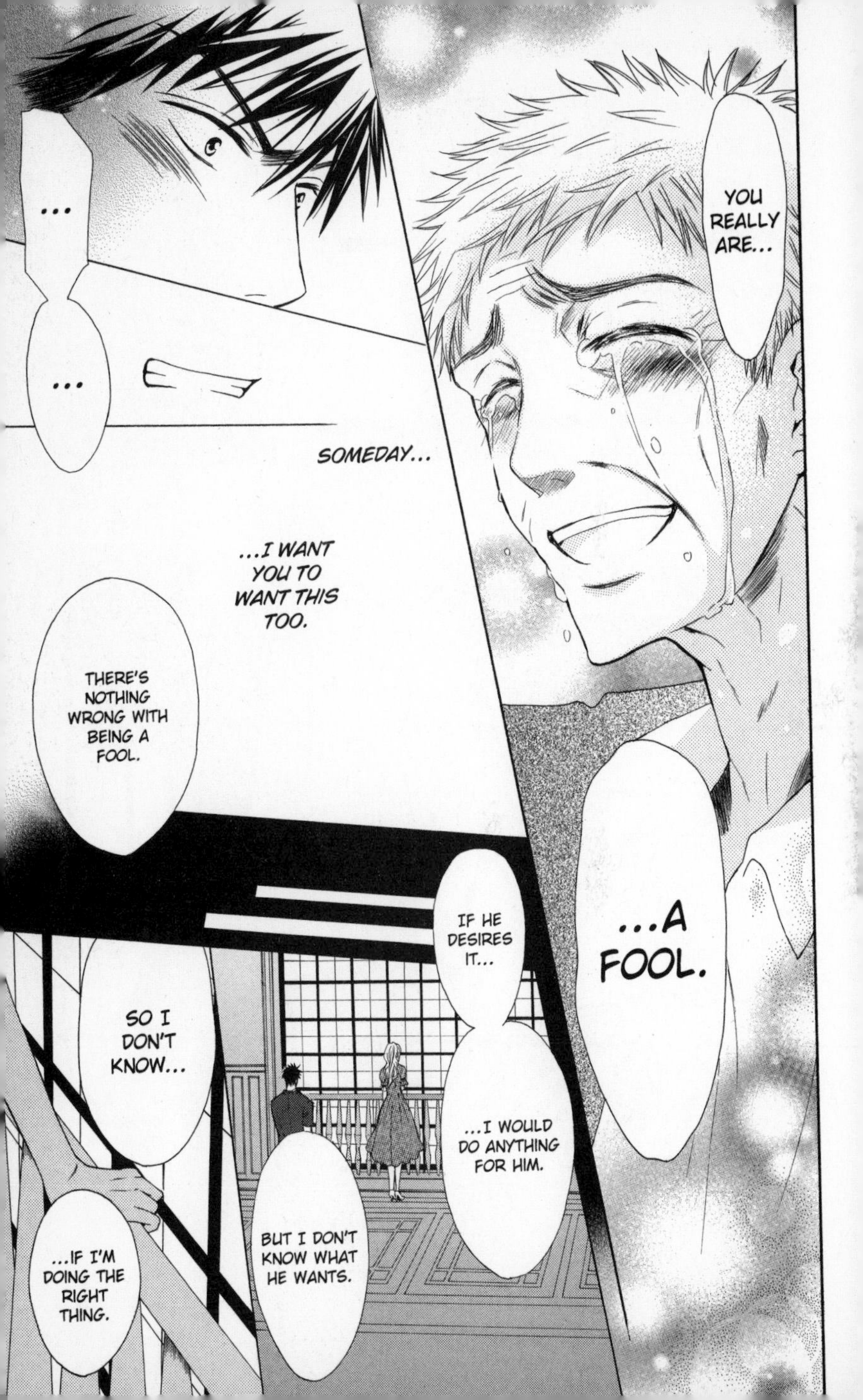
YOU REALLY ARE...
...A FOOL.
...
...
SOMEDAY...
...I WANT YOU TO WANT THIS TOO.
THERE'S NOTHING WRONG WITH BEING A FOOL.
IF HE DESIRES IT...
...I WOULD DO ANYTHING FOR HIM.
BUT I DON'T KNOW WHAT HE WANTS.
SO I DON'T KNOW...
...IF I'M DOING THE RIGHT THING.

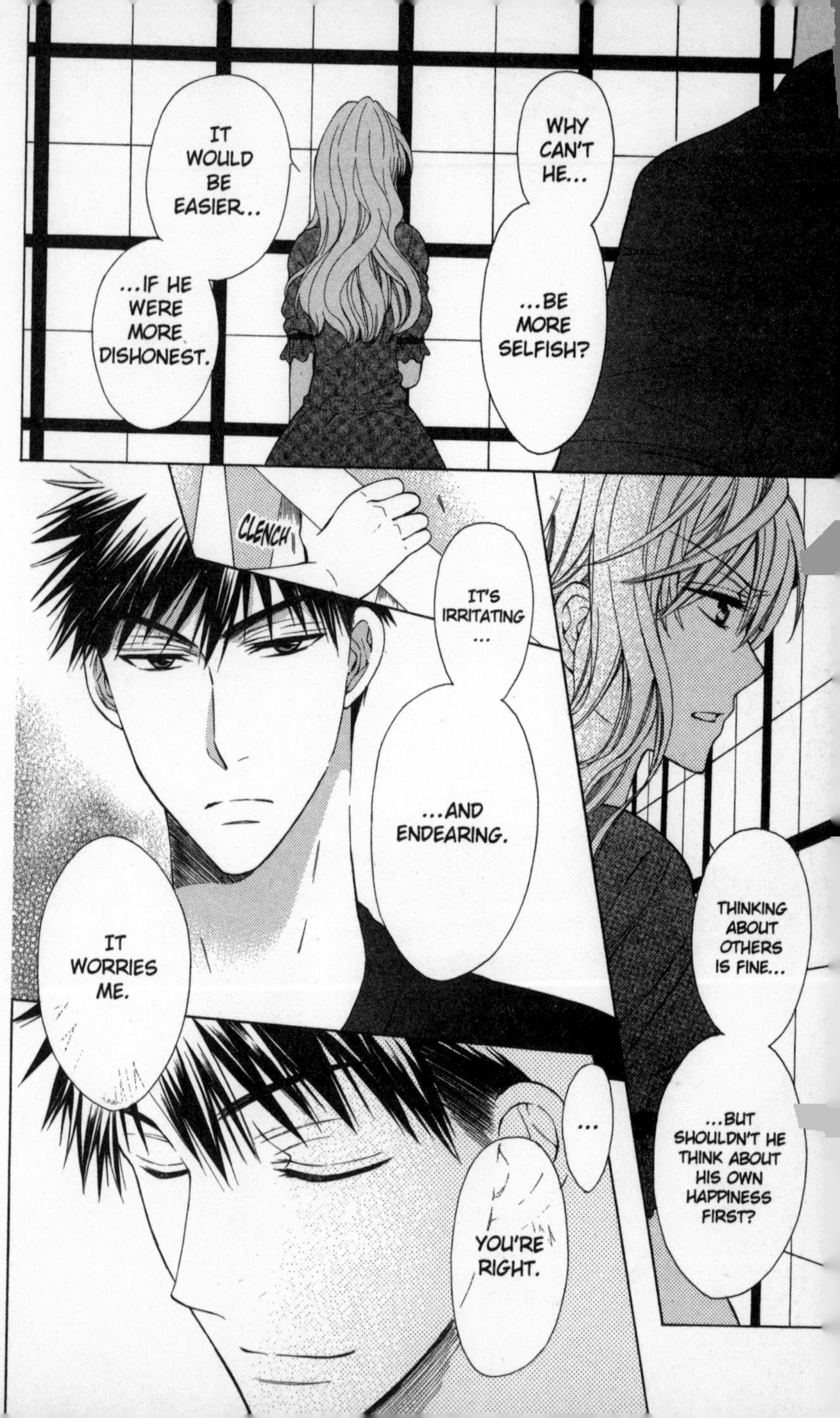
WHY CAN'T HE...
...BE MORE SELFISH?
IT WOULD BE EASIER...
...IF HE WERE MORE DISHONEST.
THINKING ABOUT OTHERS IS FINE...
...BUT SHOULDN'T HE THINK ABOUT HIS OWN HAPPINESS FIRST?
CLENCH
IT'S IRRITATING...
...AND ENDEARING.
IT WORRIES ME.
...
YOU'RE RIGHT.

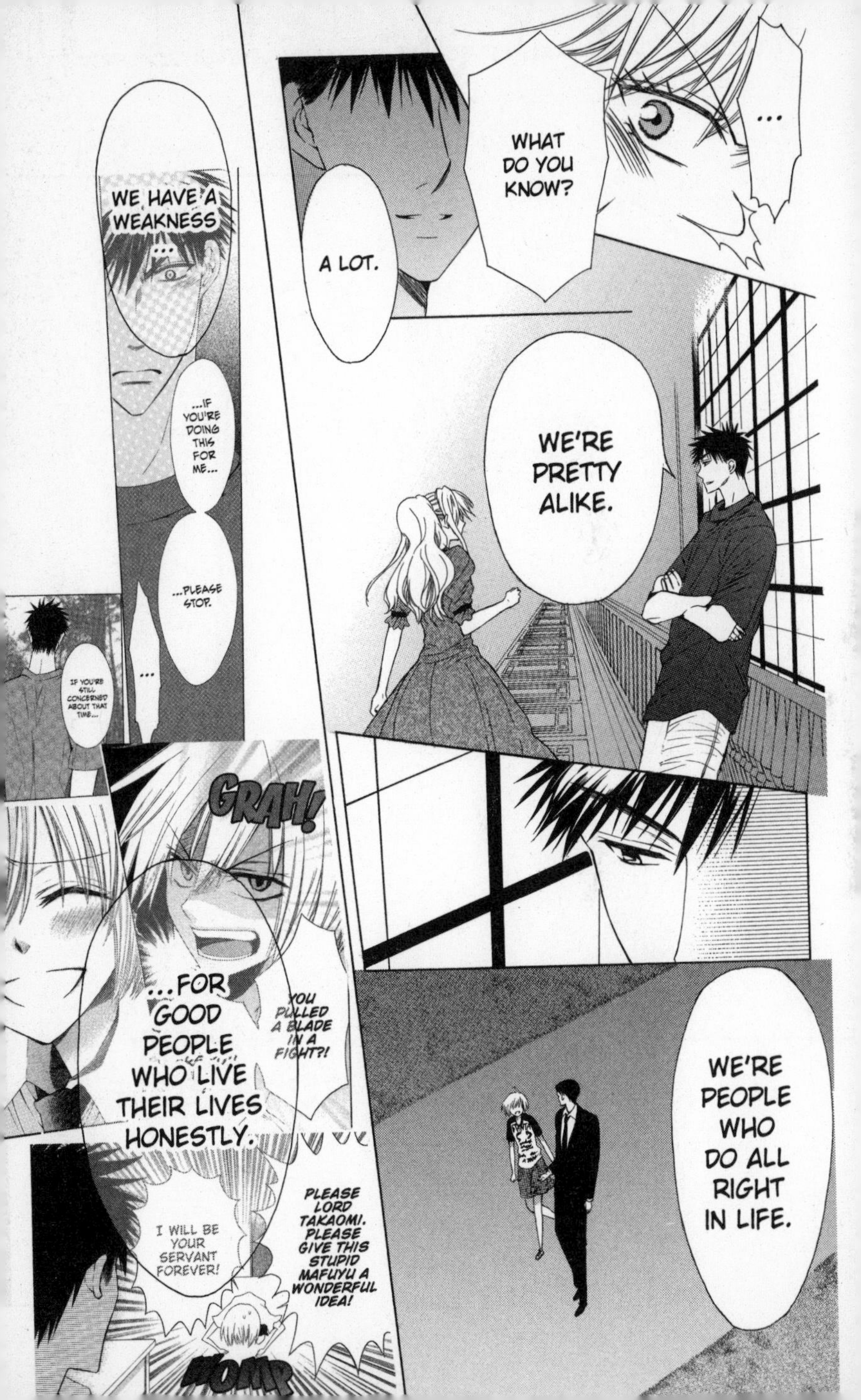
...
WHAT DO YOU KNOW?
A LOT.
WE'RE PRETTY ALIKE.
WE'RE PEOPLE WHO DO ALL RIGHT IN LIFE.
...FOR GOOD PEOPLE WHO LIVE THEIR LIVES HONESTLY.
GRAH!
YOU PULLED A BLADE IN A FIGHT?!
PLEASE LORD TAKAOMI. PLEASE GIVE THIS STUPID MAFUYU A WONDERFUL IDEA!
I WILL BE YOUR SERVANT FOREVER!
WOMP
WE HAVE A WEAKNESS ...
...IF YOU'RE DOING THIS FOR ME...
...PLEASE STOP.
...
IF YOU'RE STILL CONCERNED ABOUT THAT TIME...

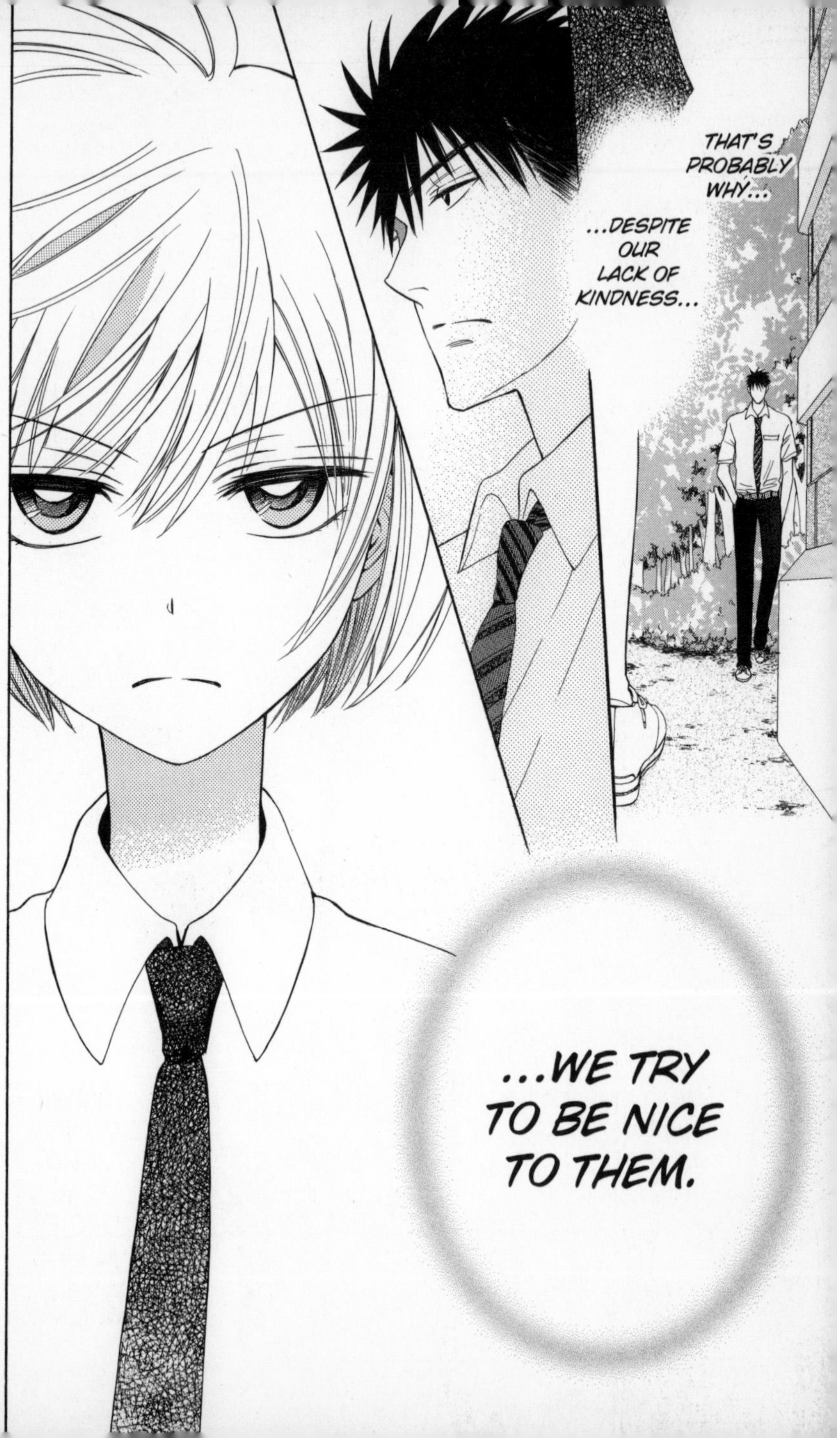
THAT'S PROBABLY WHY...
...DESPITE OUR LACK OF KINDNESS...
...WE TRY TO BE NICE TO THEM.

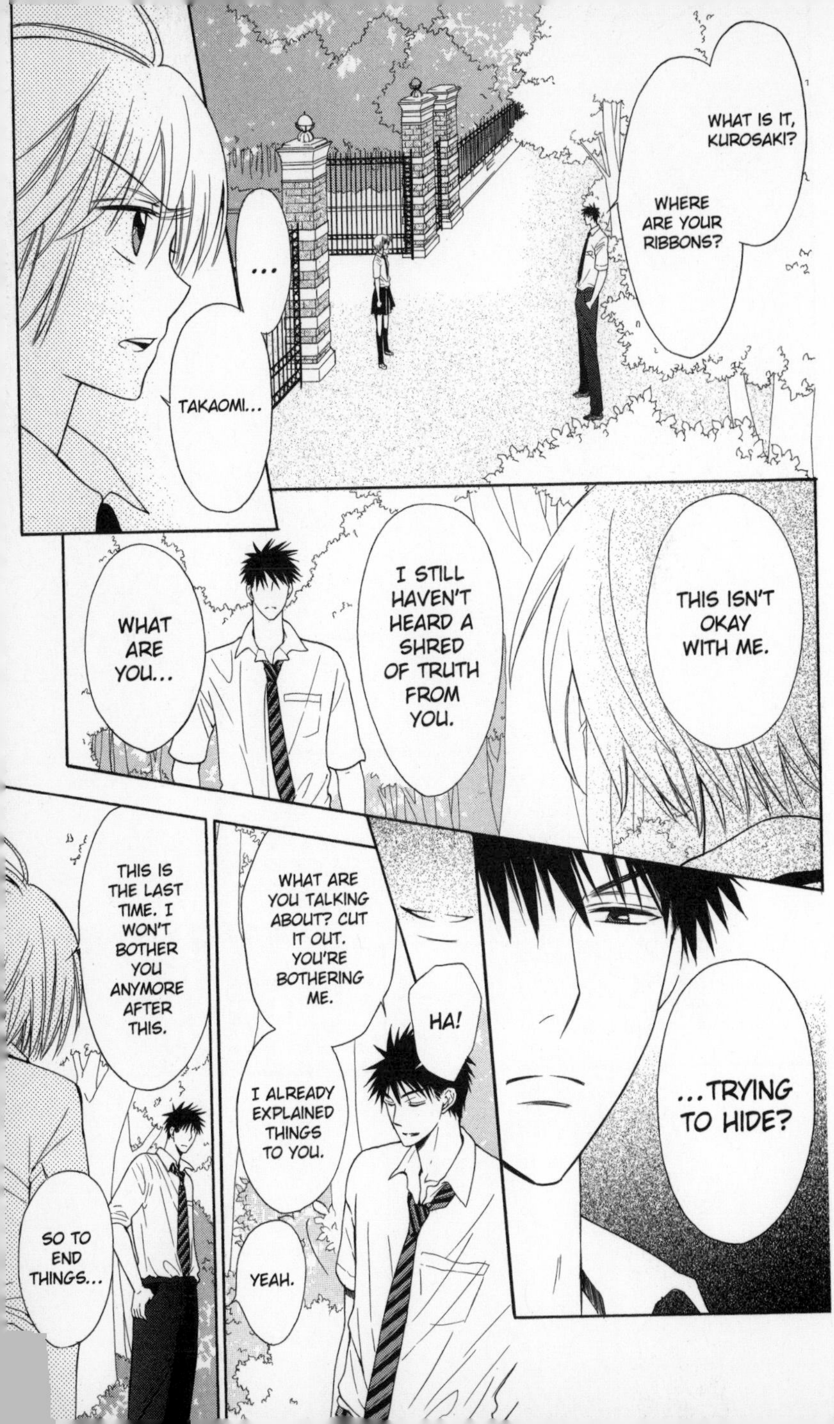
WHAT IS IT, KUROSAKI?
WHERE ARE YOUR RIBBONS?
...
TAKAOMI...
THIS ISN'T OKAY WITH ME.
I STILL HAVEN'T HEARD A SHRED OF TRUTH FROM YOU.
WHAT ARE YOU...
...TRYING TO HIDE?
WHAT ARE YOU TALKING ABOUT? CUT IT OUT. YOU'RE BOTHERING ME.
HA!
I ALREADY EXPLAINED THINGS TO YOU.
YEAH.
THIS IS THE LAST TIME. I WON'T BOTHER YOU ANYMORE AFTER THIS.
SO TO END THINGS...

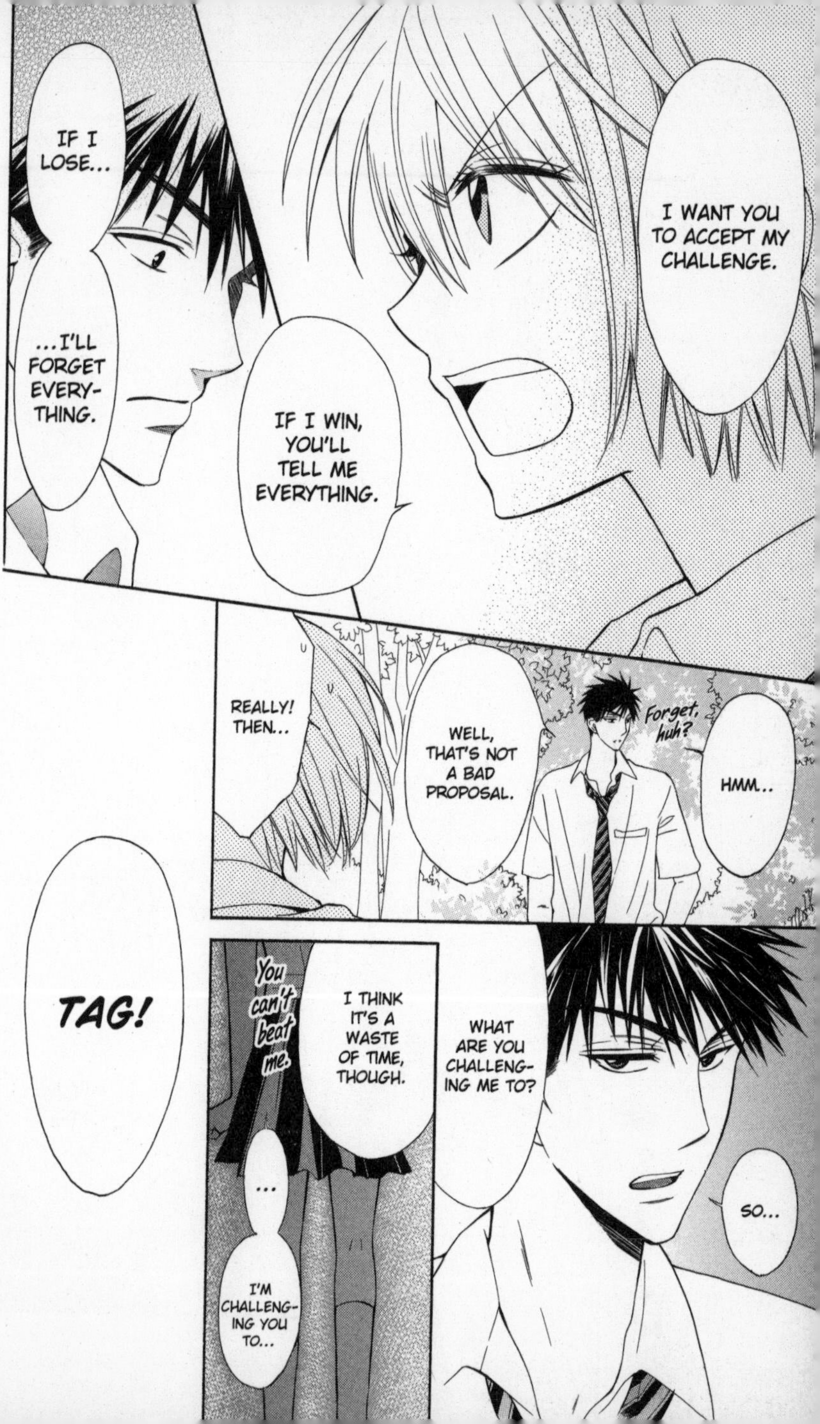
I WANT YOU TO ACCEPT MY CHALLENGE.
IF I WIN, YOU'LL TELL ME EVERYTHING.
IF I LOSE...
...I'LL FORGET EVERYTHING.
HMM...
Forget, huh?
WELL, THAT'S NOT A BAD PROPOSAL.
REALLY! THEN...
SO...
WHAT ARE YOU CHALLENGING ME TO?
I THINK IT'S A WASTE OF TIME, THOUGH.
You can't beat me.
...
I'M CHALLENGING YOU TO...
TAG!

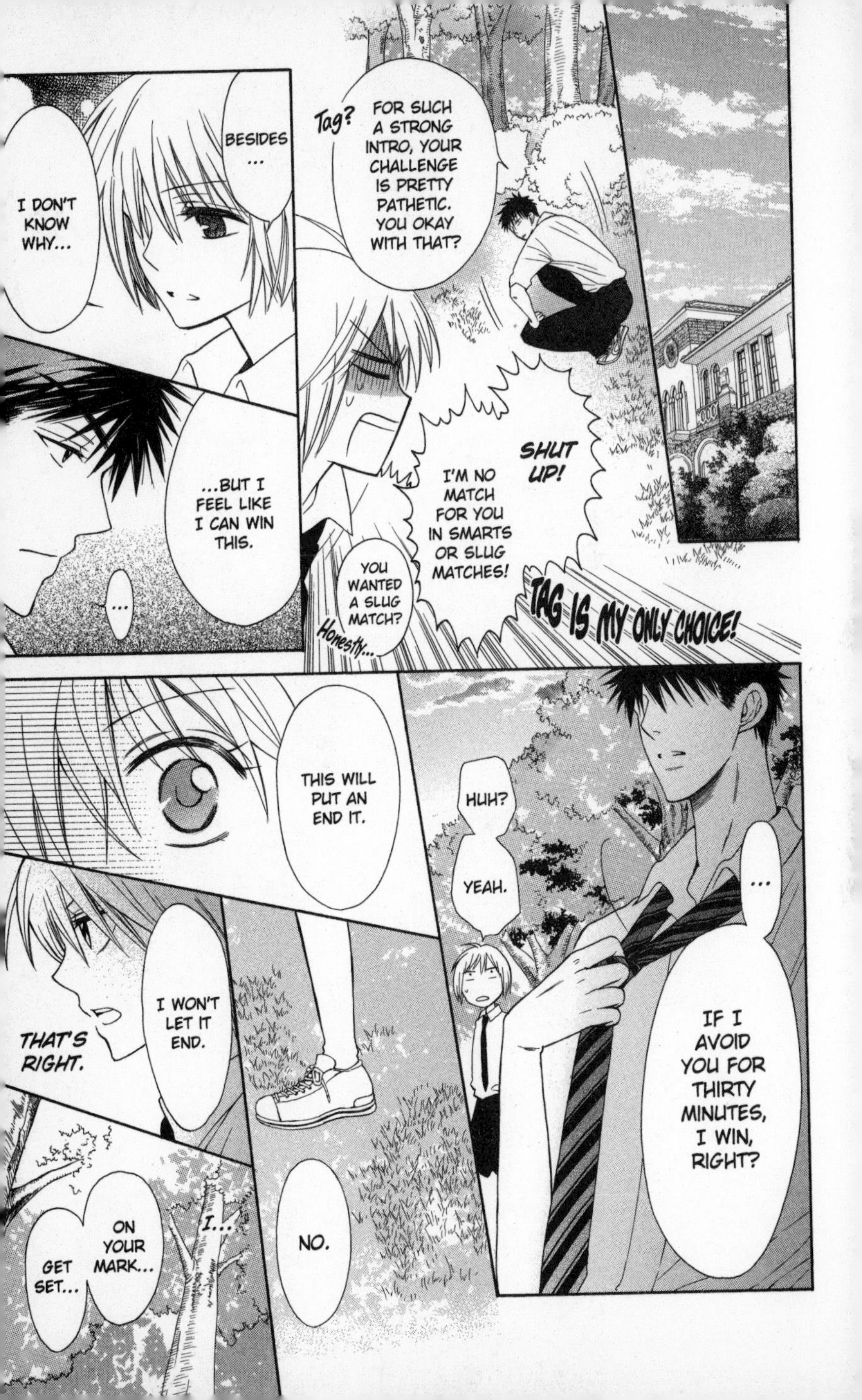
Tag?
FOR SUCH A STRONG INTRO, YOUR CHALLENGE IS PRETTY PATHETIC. YOU OKAY WITH THAT?
SHUT UP!
I'M NO MATCH FOR YOU IN SMARTS OR SLUG MATCHES!
TAG IS MY ONLY CHOICE!
YOU WANTED A SLUG MATCH?
Honestly...
BESIDES...
I DON'T KNOW WHY...
...BUT I FEEL LIKE I CAN WIN THIS.
...
...
IF I AVOID YOU FOR THIRTY MINUTES, I WIN, RIGHT?
HUH?
YEAH.
THIS WILL PUT AN END IT.
I WON'T LET IT END.
THAT'S RIGHT.
NO.
I...
ON YOUR MARK...
GET SET...

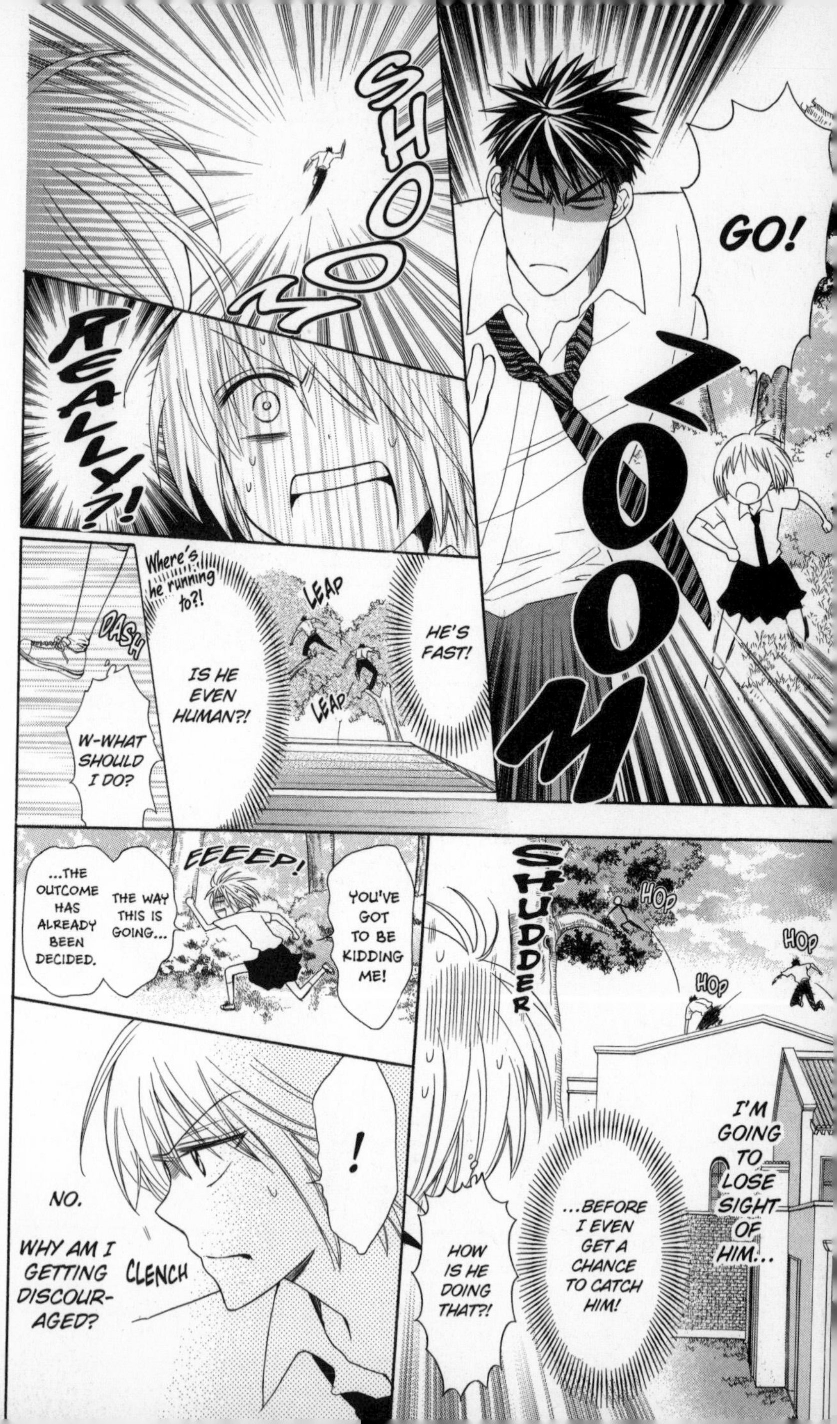
GO!
ZOOM
SHOOM
REALLY?!
HE'S FAST!
LEAP
LEAP
Where's he running to?!
IS HE EVEN HUMAN?!
DASH
W-WHAT SHOULD I DO?
SHUDDER
HOP
HOP
HOP
I'M GOING TO LOSE SIGHT OF HIM...
...BEFORE I EVEN GET A CHANCE TO CATCH HIM!
HOW IS HE DOING THAT?!
YOU'VE GOT TO BE KIDDING ME!
EEEEP!
THE WAY THIS IS GOING...
...THE OUTCOME HAS ALREADY BEEN DECIDED.
!
NO.
CLENCH
WHY AM I GETTING DISCOURAGED?

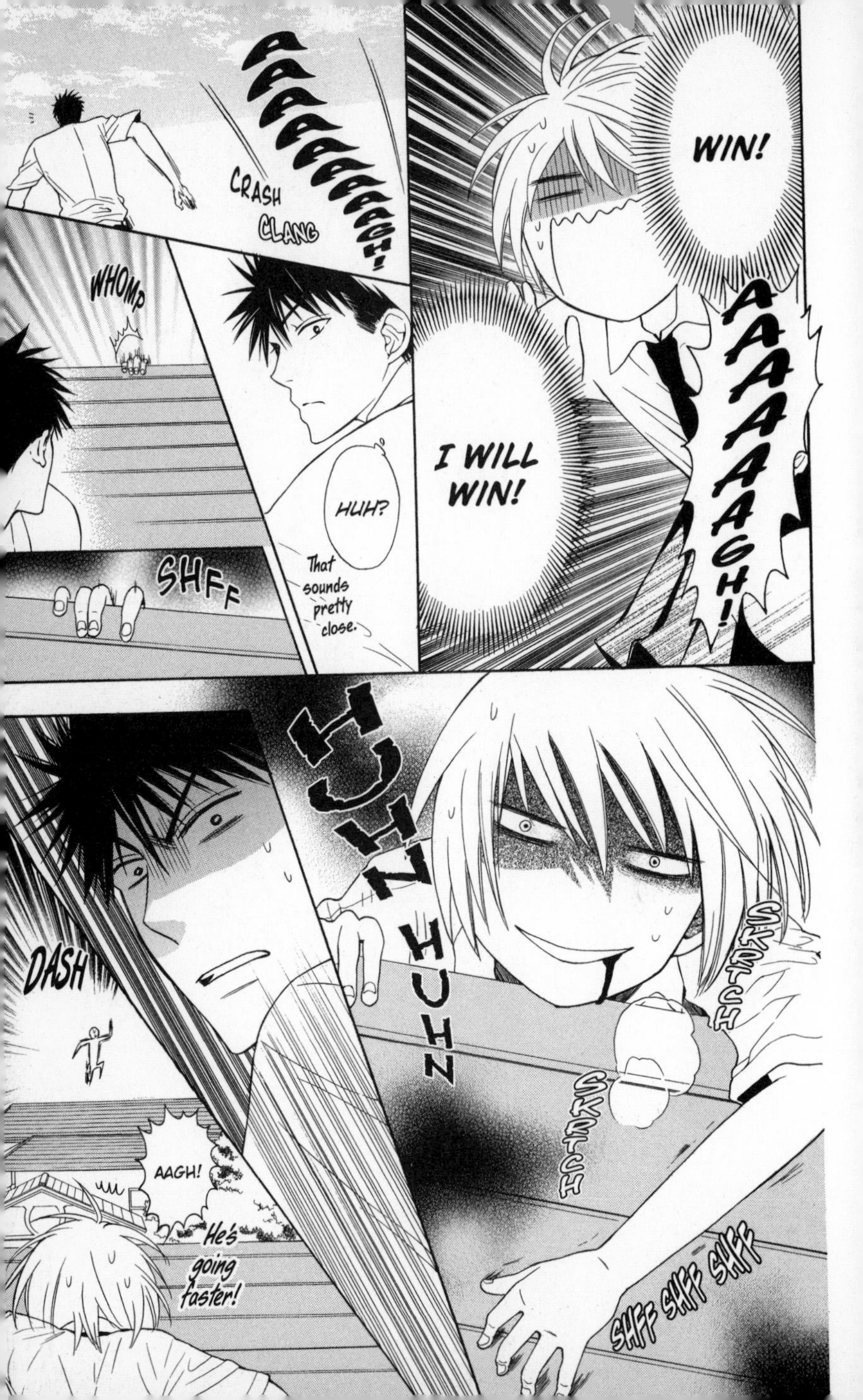
WIN!
I WILL WIN!
AAAAAAAAGH!
AAAAAAAAAGH!
CRASH
CLANG
HUH?
That sounds pretty close.
WHOMP
SHFF
HUHN
HUHN
SKRTCH
SKRTCH
SHFF SHFF SHFF
DASH
AAGH!
He's going faster!

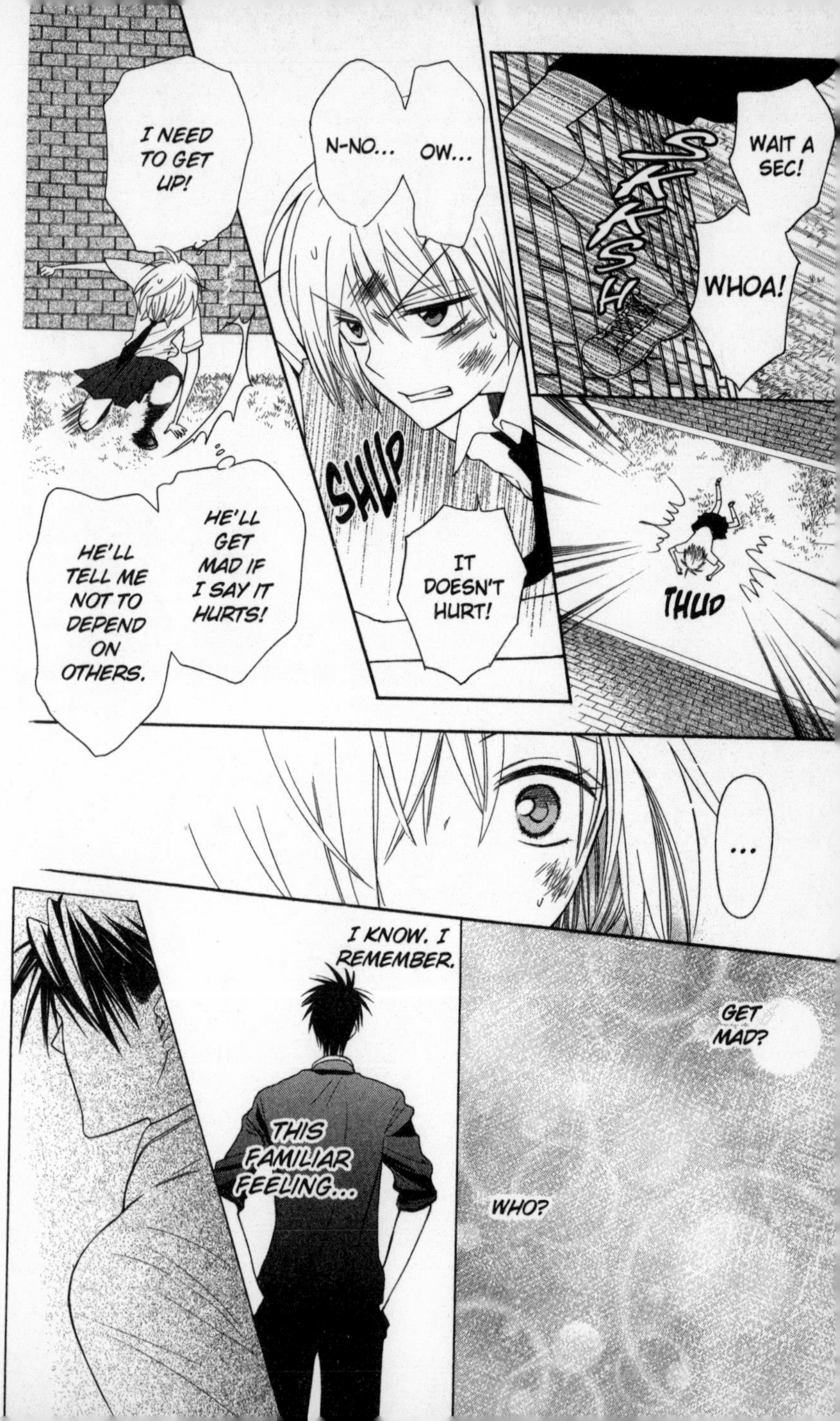
WAIT A SEC!
SKKSH
WHOA!
THUD
N-NO... OW...
SHUP
IT DOESN'T HURT!
I NEED TO GET UP!
HE'LL GET MAD IF I SAY IT HURTS!
HE'LL TELL ME NOT TO DEPEND ON OTHERS.
...
GET MAD?
WHO?
I KNOW. I REMEMBER.
THIS FAMILIAR FEELING...

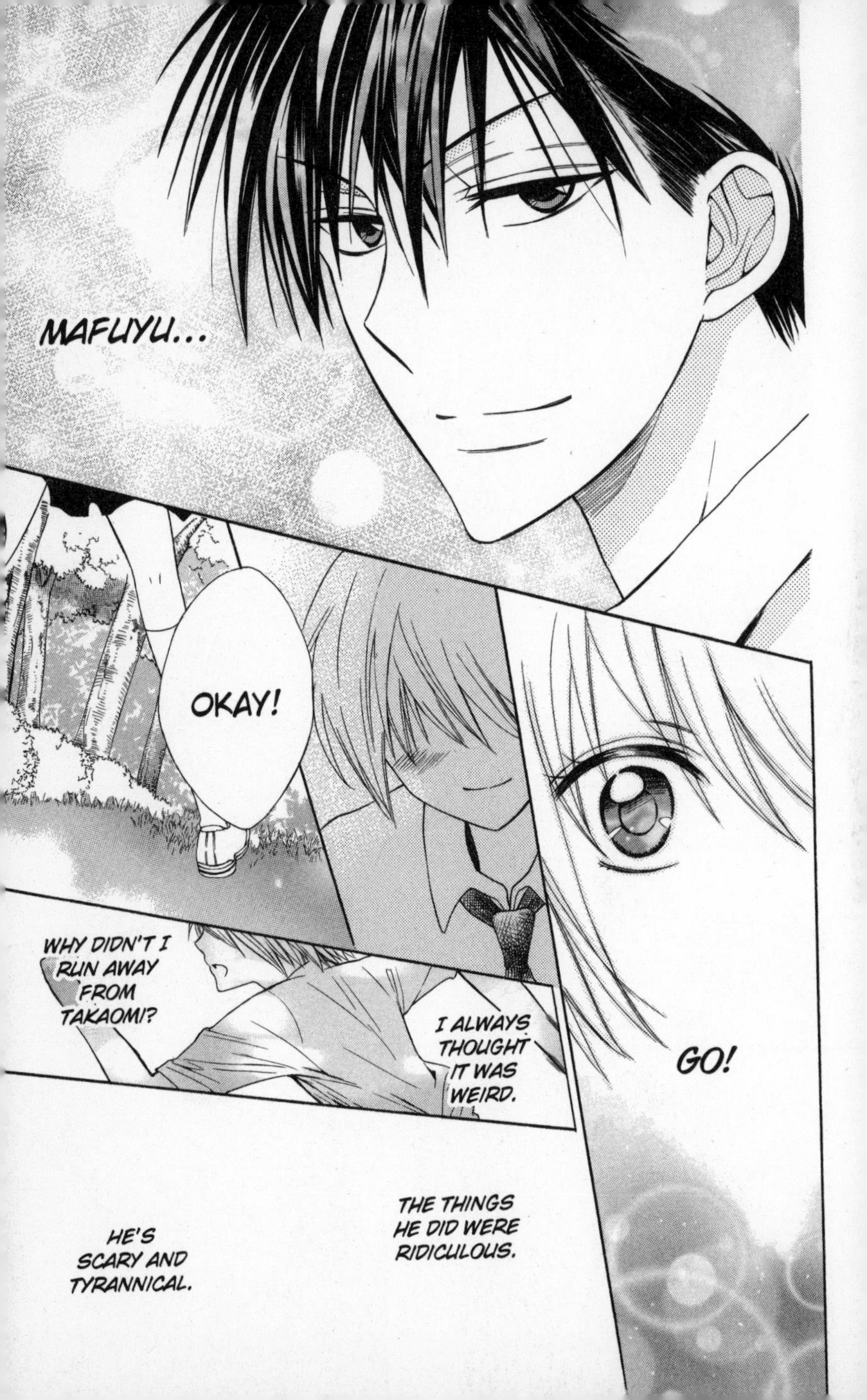
MAFUYU...
GO!
OKAY!
I ALWAYS THOUGHT IT WAS WEIRD.
WHY DIDN'T I RUN AWAY FROM TAKAOMI?
THE THINGS HE DID WERE RIDICULOUS.
HE'S SCARY AND TYRANNICAL.

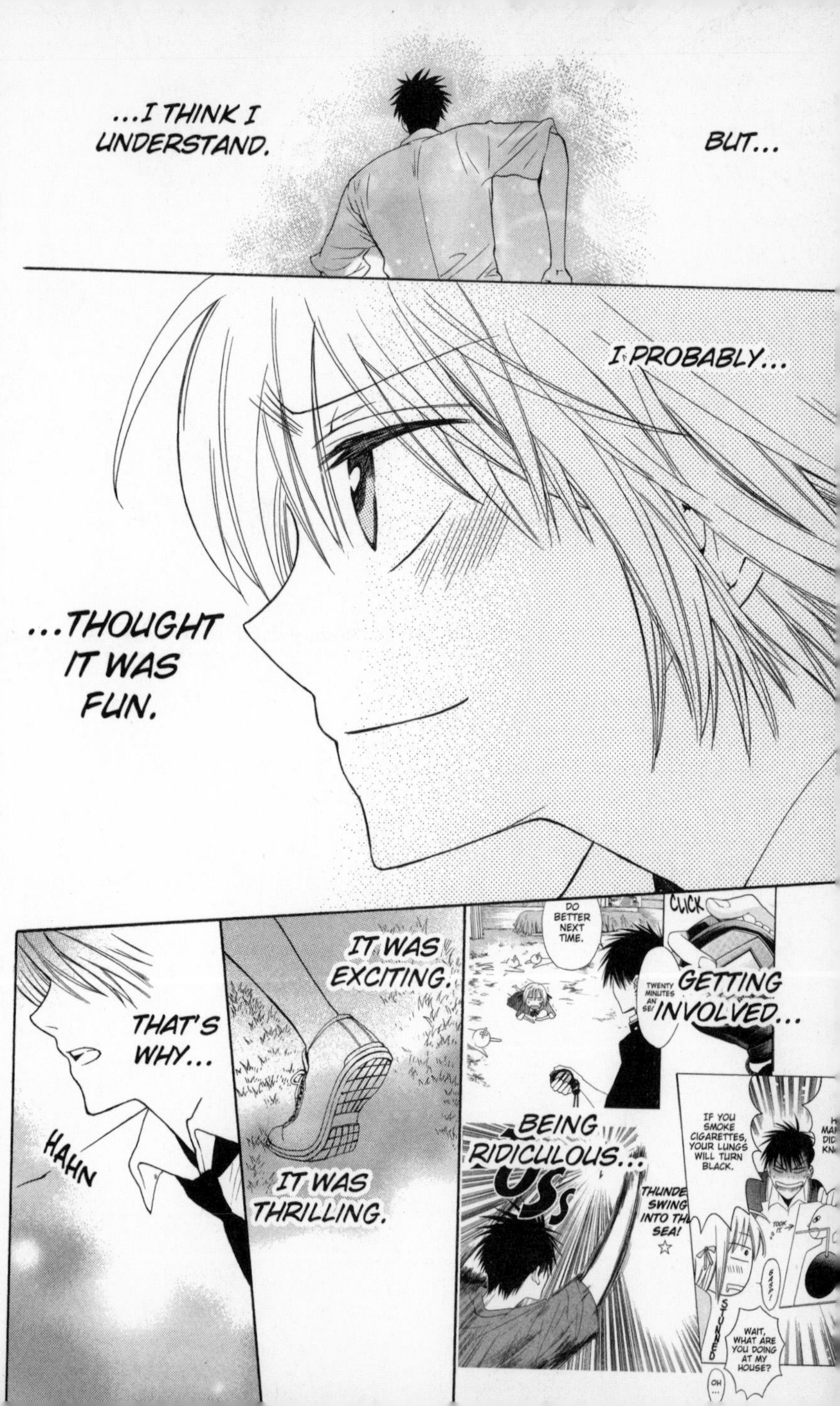
BUT...
...I THINK I UNDERSTAND.
I PROBABLY...
...THOUGHT IT WAS FUN.
CLICK
GETTING INVOLVED...
DO BETTER NEXT TIME.
IF YOU SMOKE CIGARETTES, YOUR LUNGS WILL TURN BLACK.
GASP!
STUNNED
WAIT, WHAT ARE YOU DOING AT MY HOUSE?
OH...
BEING RIDICULOUS...
US
IT WAS EXCITING.
IT WAS THRILLING.
THAT'S WHY...
HAHN

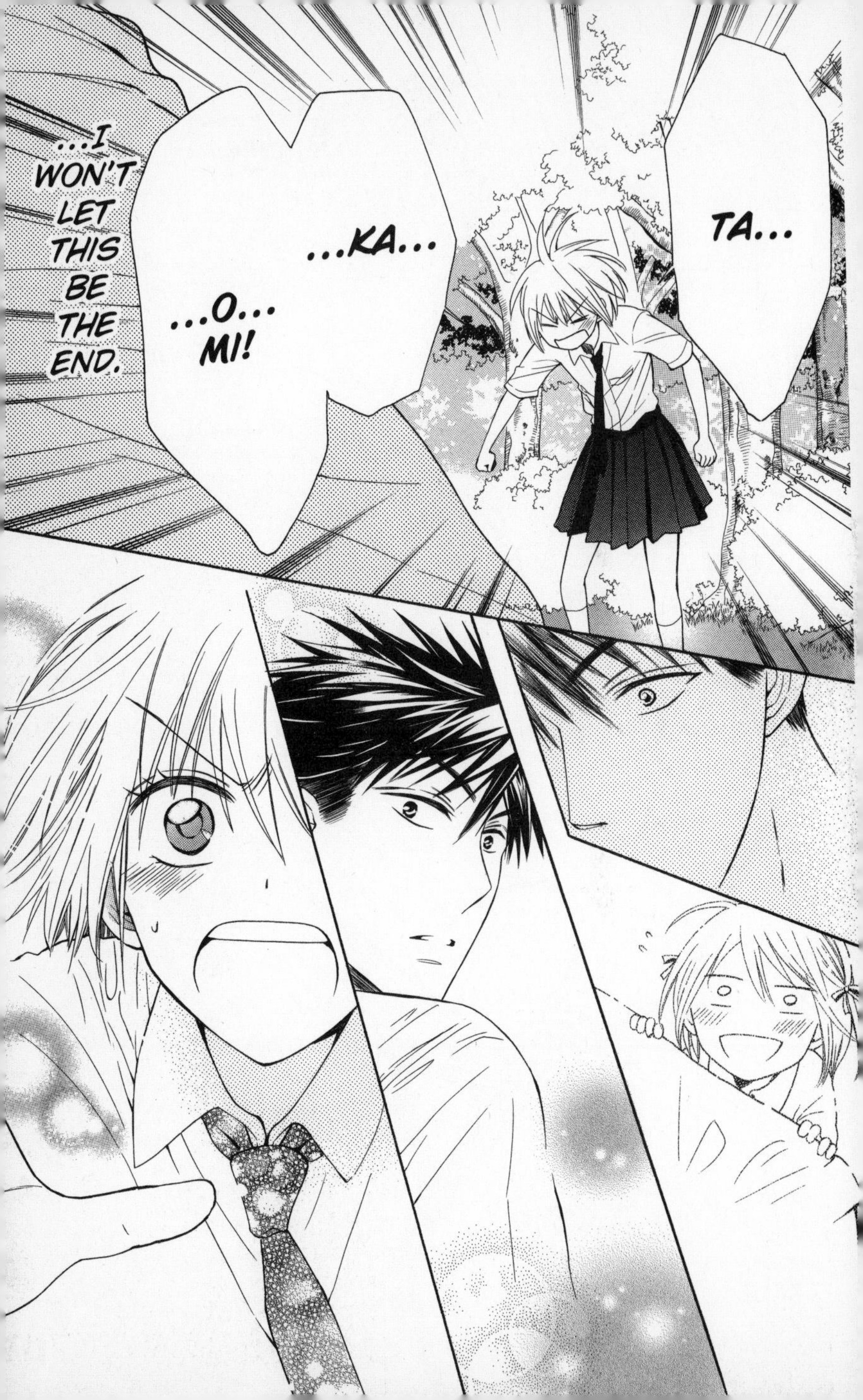
TA...
...KA...
...O... MI!
...I WON'T LET THIS BE THE END.

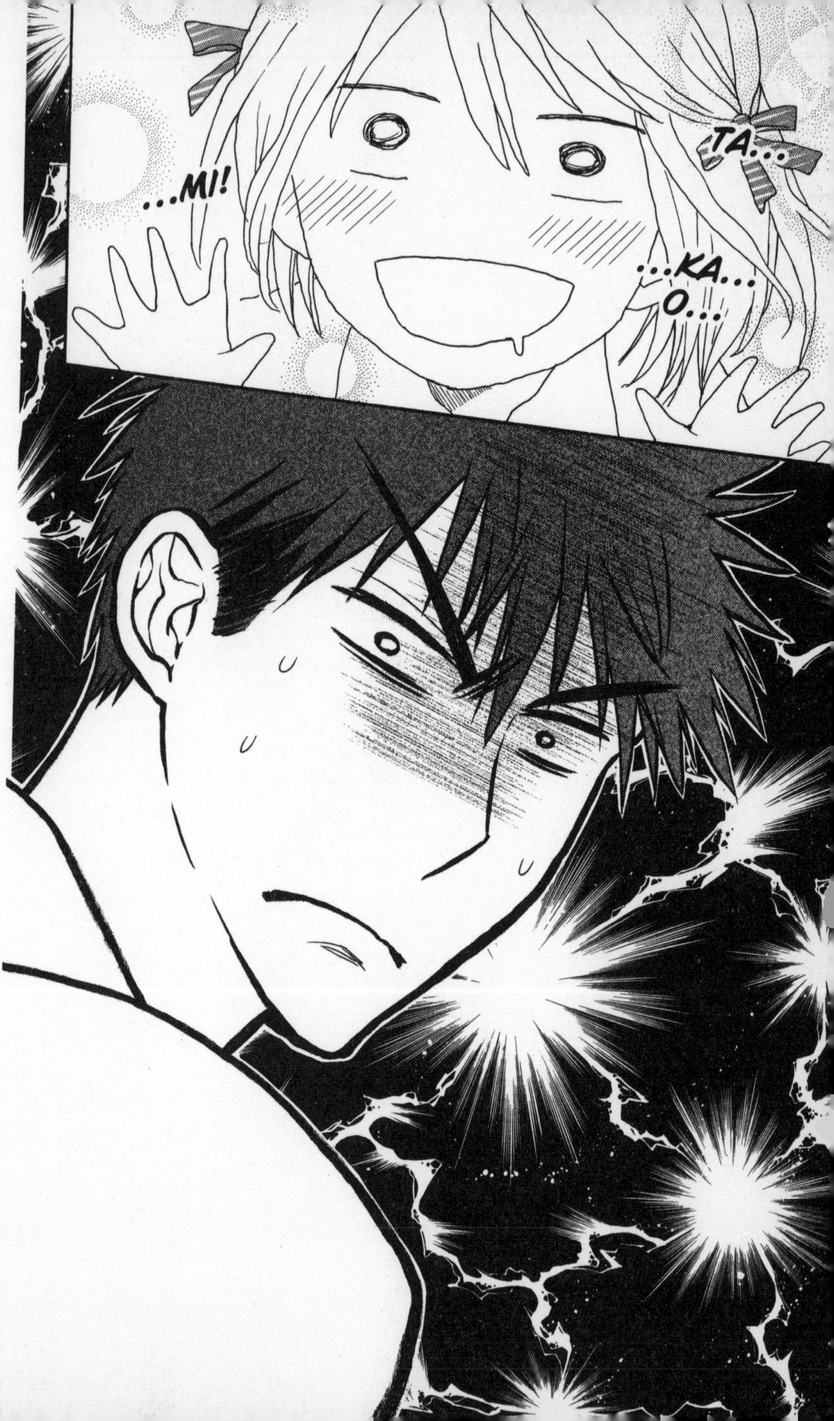
TA...
...KA...
O...
...MI!

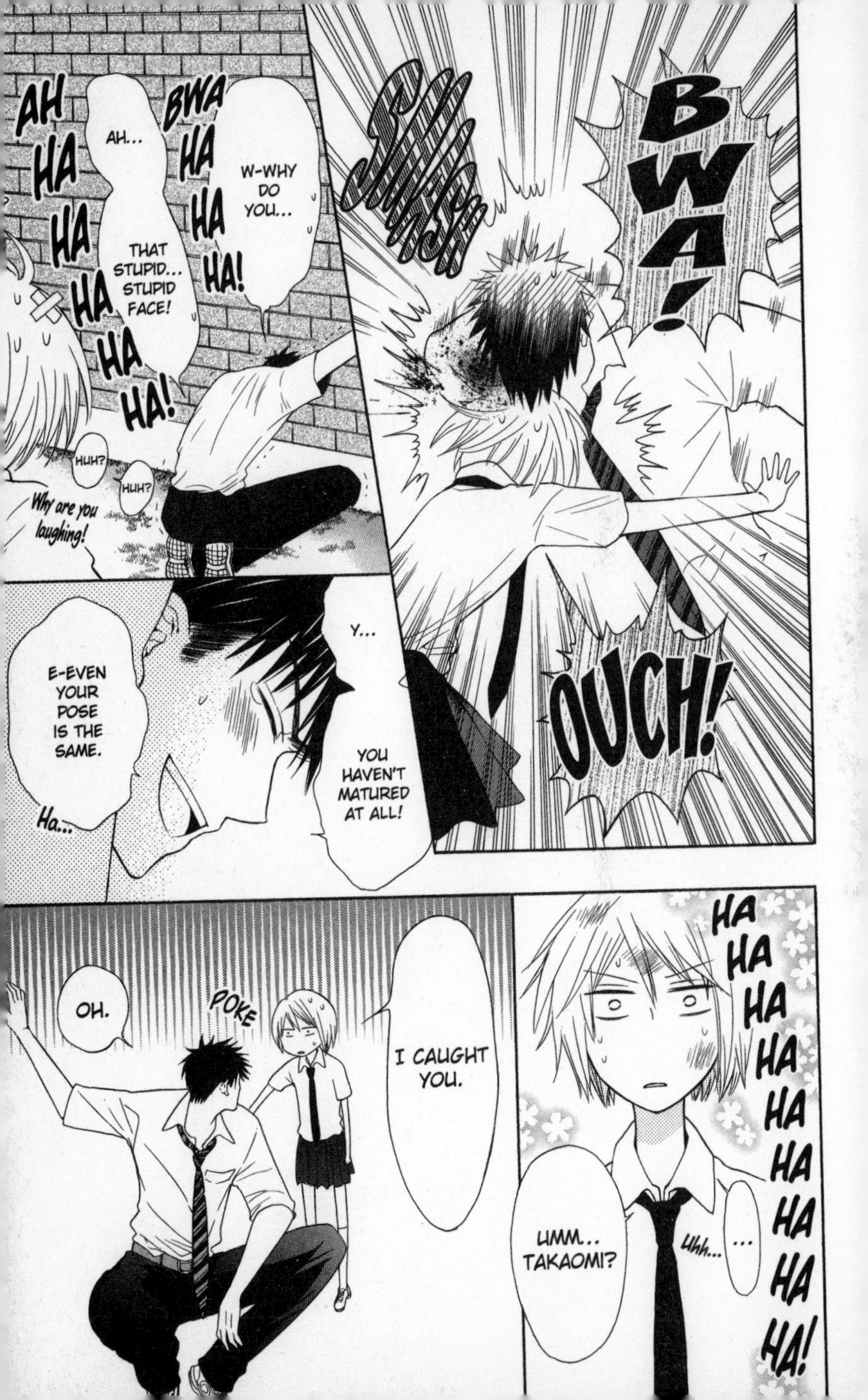
BWA!
OUCH!
W-WHY DO YOU...
BWA HA HA HA HA!
AH...
THAT STUPID... STUPID FACE!
AH HA HA HA HA HA HA!
HUH?
HUH?
Why are you laughing!
Y...
YOU HAVEN'T MATURED AT ALL!
E-EVEN YOUR POSE IS THE SAME.
Ha...
HA HA HA HA HA HA HA HA HA HA!
...
Uhh...
UMM.. TAKAOMI?
I CAUGHT YOU.
POKE
OH.

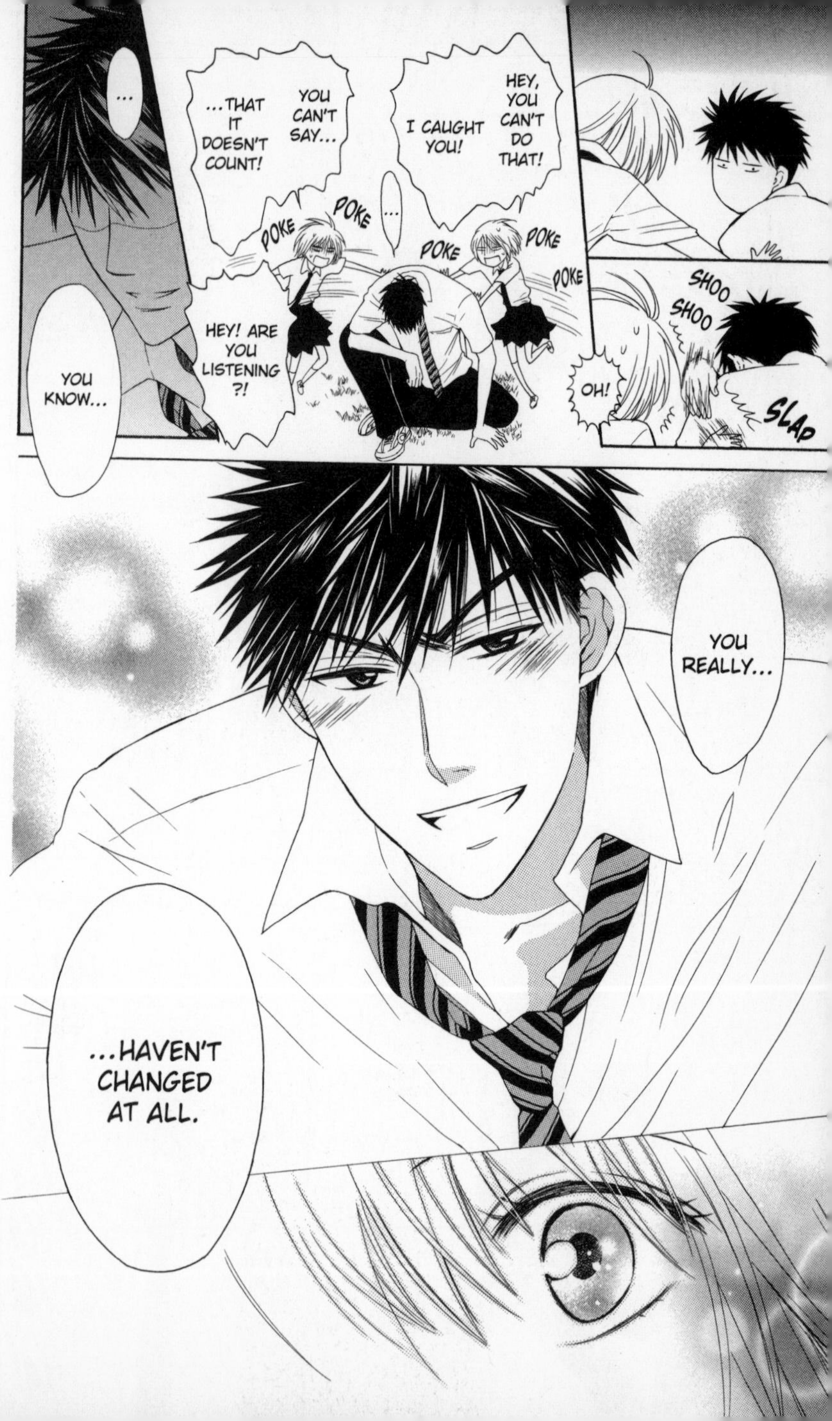
SHOO
SHOO
OH!
SLAP
HEY, YOU CAN'T DO THAT!
I CAUGHT YOU!
...
YOU CAN'T SAY...
...THAT IT DOESN'T COUNT!
POKE
POKE
POKE
POKE
POKE
HEY! ARE YOU LISTENING ?!
...
YOU KNOW...
YOU REALLY...
...HAVEN'T CHANGED AT ALL.

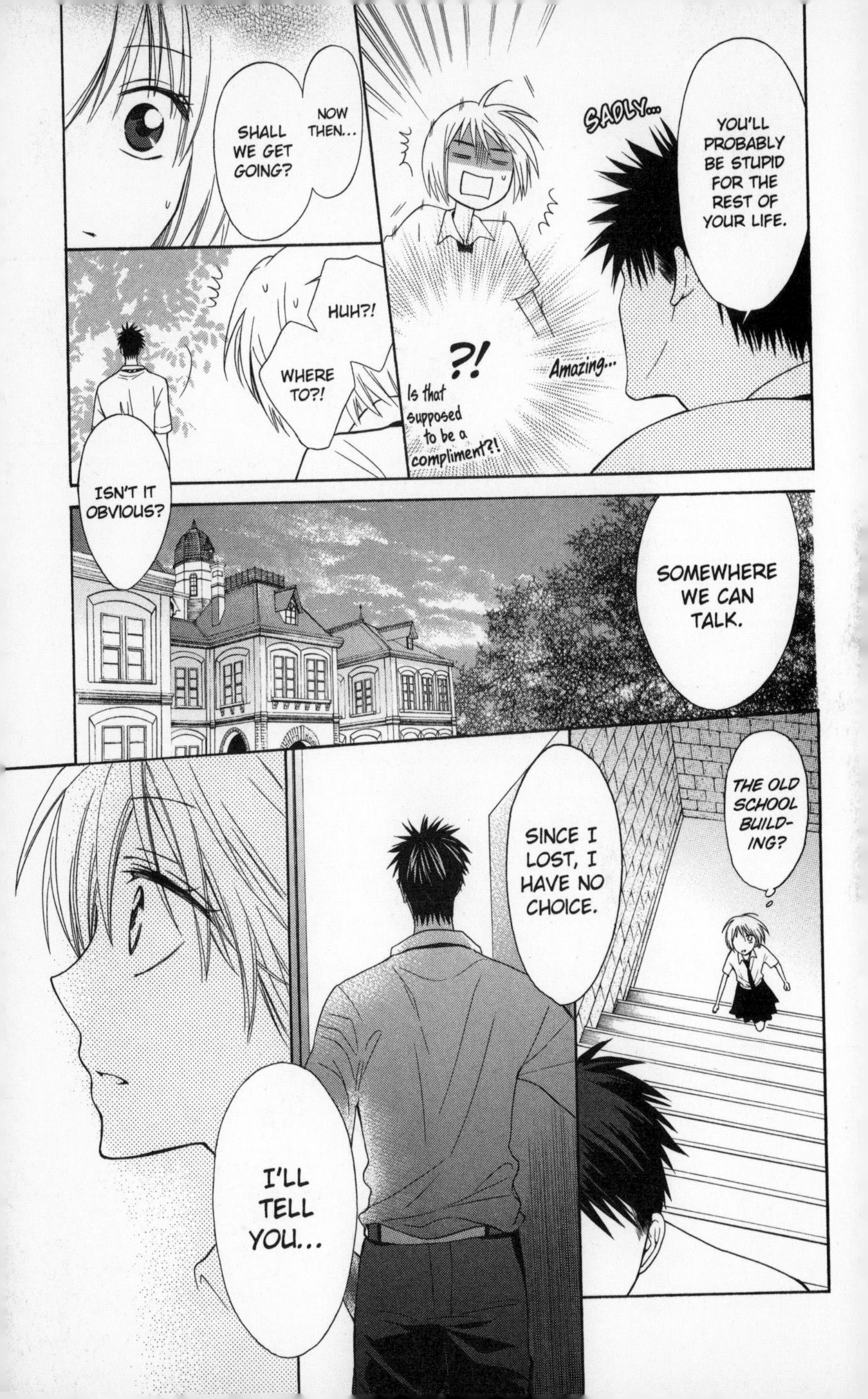
SADLY...
YOU'LL PROBABLY BE STUPID FOR THE REST OF YOUR LIFE.
Amazing...
?!
Is that supposed to be a compliment?!
NOW THEN...
SHALL WE GET GOING?
HUH?!
WHERE TO?!
ISN'T IT OBVIOUS?
SOMEWHERE WE CAN TALK.
THE OLD SCHOOL BUILD-ING?
SINCE I LOST, I HAVE NO CHOICE.
I'LL TELL YOU...

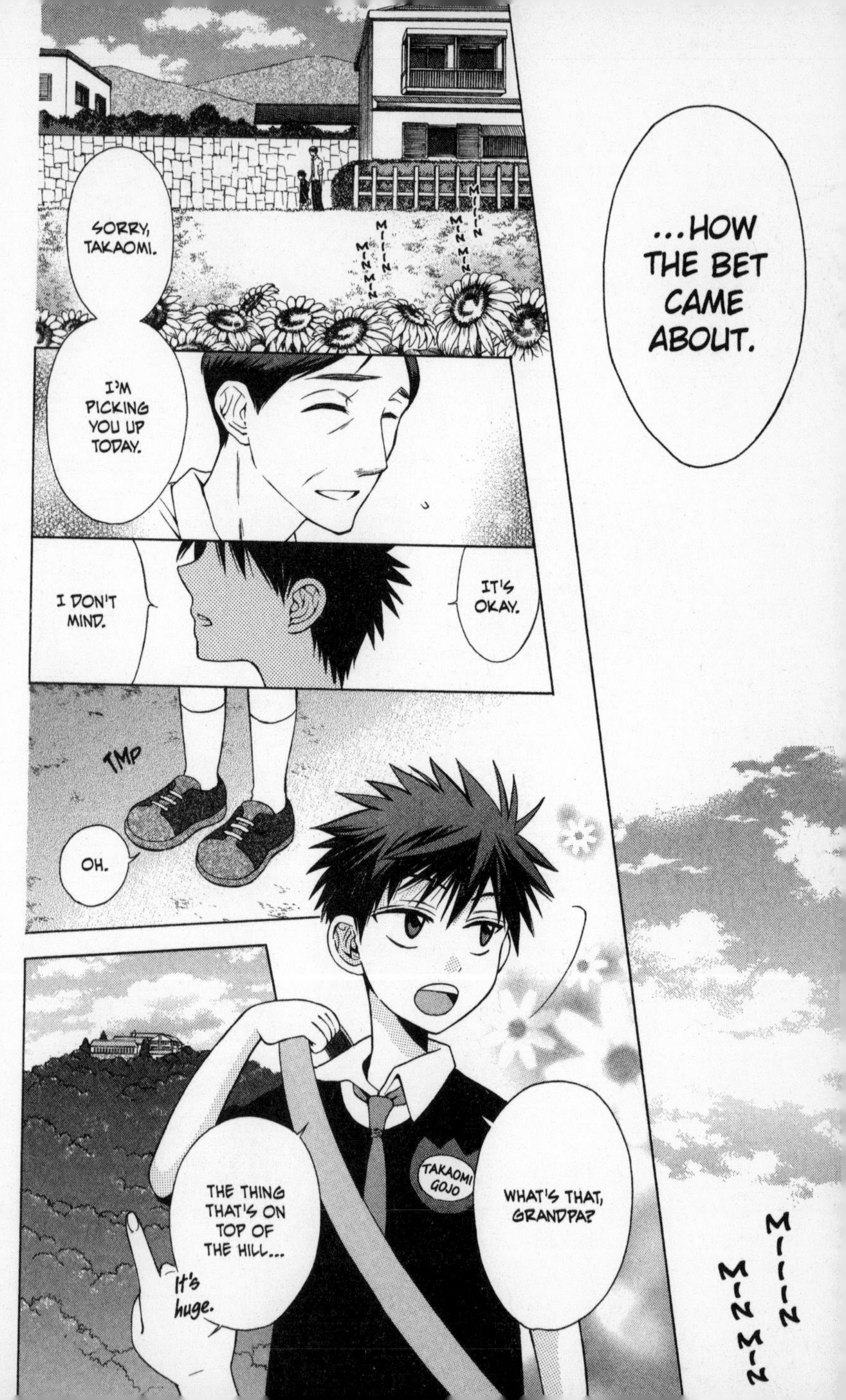
...HOW THE BET CAME ABOUT.
MIIIN MIN MIN
MIIIN MIN MIN
SORRY, TAKAOMI.
I'M PICKING YOU UP TODAY.
IT'S OKAY.
I DON'T MIND.
TMP
OH.
MIIIN MIN MIN
WHAT'S THAT, GRANDPA?
TAKAOMI GOJO
THE THING THAT'S ON TOP OF THE HILL...
It's huge.

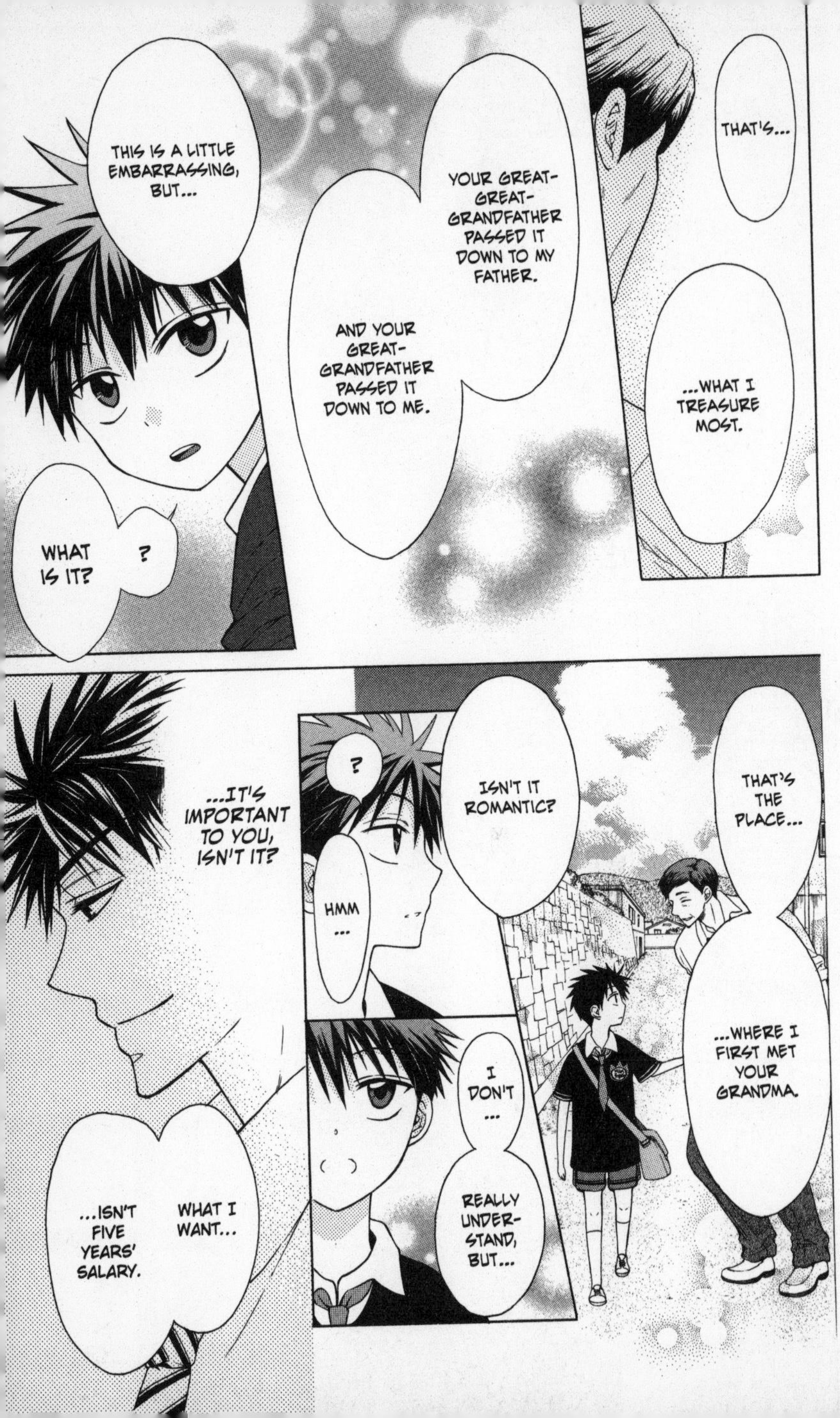
THAT'S...
...WHAT I TREASURE MOST.
THIS IS A LITTLE EMBARRASSING, BUT...
YOUR GREAT-GREAT-GRANDFATHER PASSED IT DOWN TO MY FATHER.
AND YOUR GREAT-GRANDFATHER PASSED IT DOWN TO ME.
WHAT IS IT?
?
THAT'S THE PLACE...
...WHERE I FIRST MET YOUR GRANDMA.
ISN'T IT ROMANTIC?
?
HMM...
I DON'T...
REALLY UNDERSTAND, BUT...
...IT'S IMPORTANT TO YOU, ISN'T IT?
WHAT I WANT...
...ISN'T FIVE YEARS' SALARY.

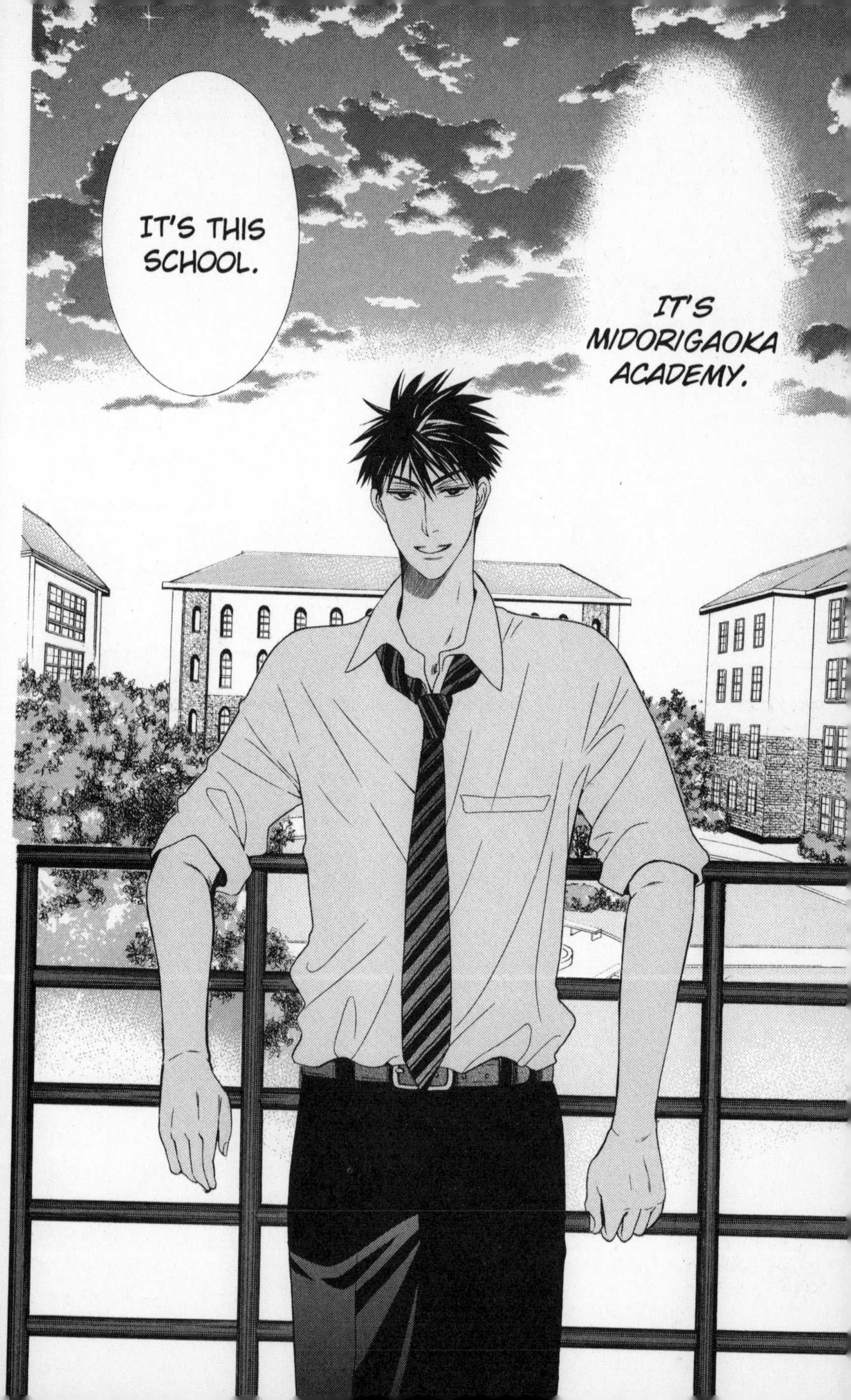
IT'S THIS SCHOOL.
IT'S MIDORIGAOKA ACADEMY.

IT'S VOLUME 6

Thank you for purchasing this comic! Oresama Teacher has quickly reached volume 6! Amazingly, they're still in the first semester! How slow!

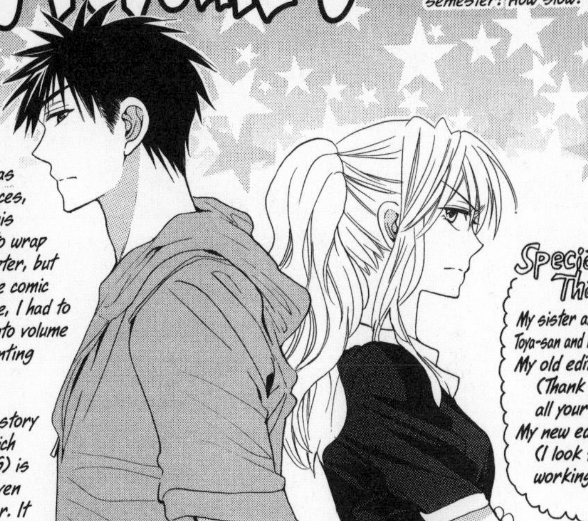

Takaomi's story, which has appeared in bits and pieces, takes center stage in this volume. I was planning to wrap it up with one more chapter, but because I inserted those comic strips in the last volume, I had to move the last chapter into volume 7. Stupid Sakurada! (venting my anger)

Oh, on a side note, the story in volume 5 about the rich girl (chapter 25 and 26) is totally about Takaomi. Even the monologue is similar. It would please me if you read it again.

Takaomi is a character without monologues, so Marika's words and thoughts are stand-ins for Takaomi.

But it's really gross to imagine Takaomi saying, "Don't say that you're satisfied! That'll make me sad! Stupid stupid grandpa! I don't know you anymore!" ⇨

⇨ "People who don't desire things are annoying. And yet, I love them!" That's what her story was about.

Special Thanks
My sister and my family
Toya-san and my assistants
My old editor
(Thank you for all your help)
My new editor
(I look forward to working with you)

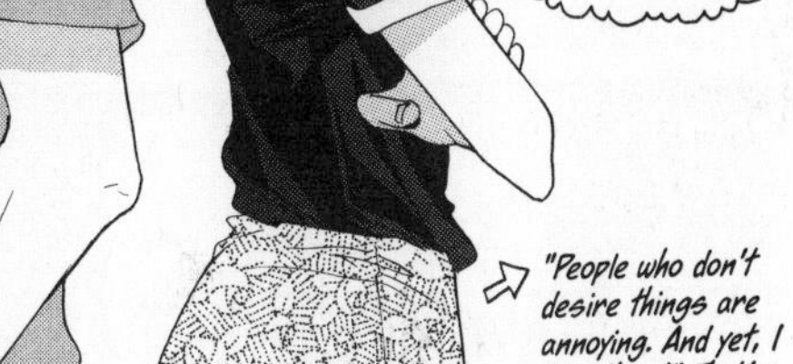
TRUE STORY COMIC
(TAKAOMI ARC) RIFT BETWEEN GIRLS
I want to make Takaomi a bit kinder.
That'll make him a failure as an arrogant bastard.
Sister
Tsubaki
Terrible! I feel sorry for Mafuyu! Takaomi's despicable! You demon!
WHAT?!
Letters
Letters

I was shocked.

Recently, someone asked me whether this comic has love in it.

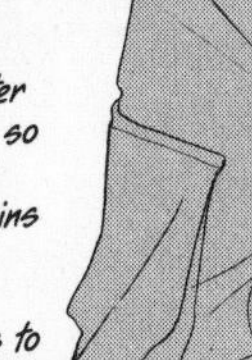
It has love!

The next pages are about Shinobu, who has been completely forgotten for the past few days.

Volume 6 is filled with Shinobu, isn't it?!

THE GUY AFTER SCHOOL

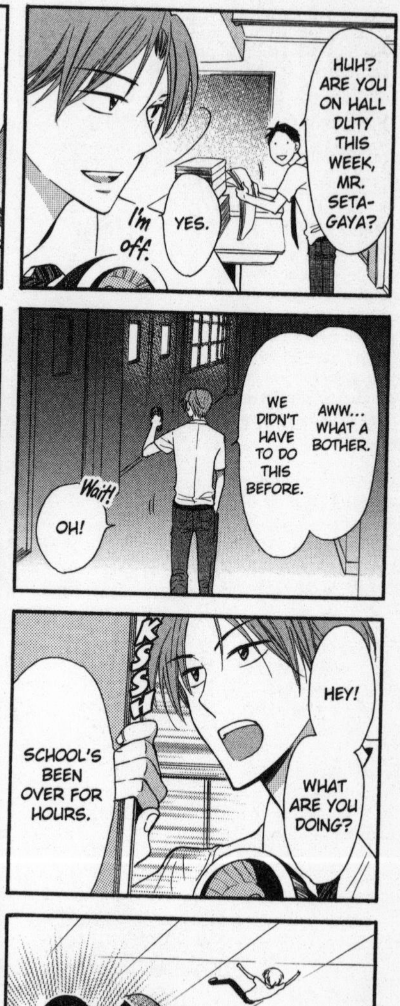
HUH? ARE YOU ON HALL DUTY THIS WEEK, MR. SETAGAYA?
YES.
I'm off.
AWW... WHAT A BOTHER.
WE DIDN'T HAVE TO DO THIS BEFORE.
Wait!
OH!
KSSH
HEY!
WHAT ARE YOU DOING?
SCHOOL'S BEEN OVER FOR HOURS.
?!

SEARCHLIGHT

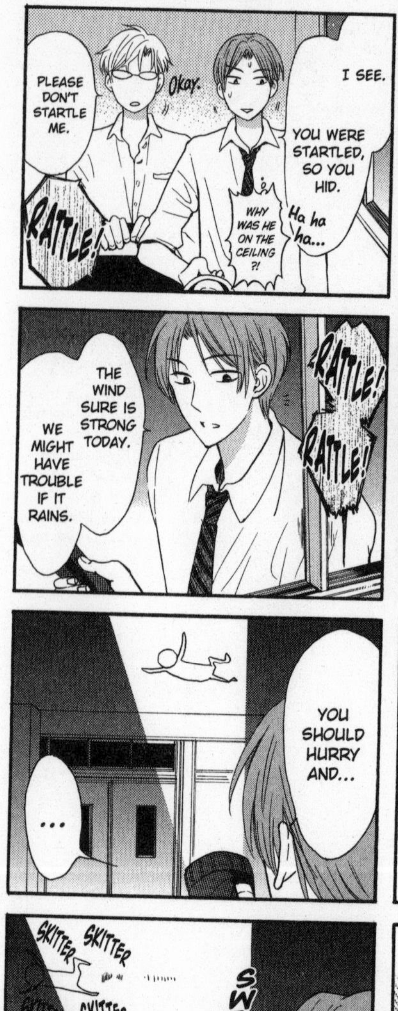
I SEE.
YOU WERE STARTLED, SO YOU HID.
Ha ha ha...
WHY WAS HE ON THE CEILING?!
Okay.
PLEASE DON'T STARTLE ME.
RATTLE!
RATTLE!
RATTLE!
THE WIND SURE IS STRONG TODAY.
WE MIGHT HAVE TROUBLE IF IT RAINS.
YOU SHOULD HURRY AND...
...
SWEEP SWEEP
SKITTER SKITTER
SKITTER SKITTER

WAVERING FEELINGS

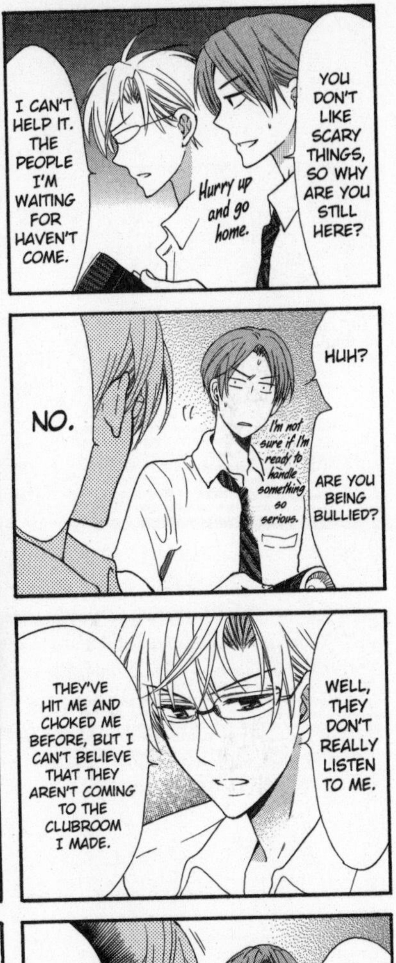
YOU DON'T LIKE SCARY THINGS, SO WHY ARE YOU STILL HERE?
Hurry up and go home.
I CAN'T HELP IT. THE PEOPLE I'M WAITING FOR HAVEN'T COME.
HUH?
ARE YOU BEING BULLIED?
I'm not sure if I'm ready to handle something so serious.
NO.
WELL, THEY DON'T REALLY LISTEN TO ME.
THEY'VE HIT ME AND CHOKED ME BEFORE, BUT I CAN'T BELIEVE THAT THEY AREN'T COMING TO THE CLUBROOM I MADE.
ISN'T THAT BULLYING?
HUH? IS THAT BULLYING?!

I'm not sure anymore!

IF YOU INSIST

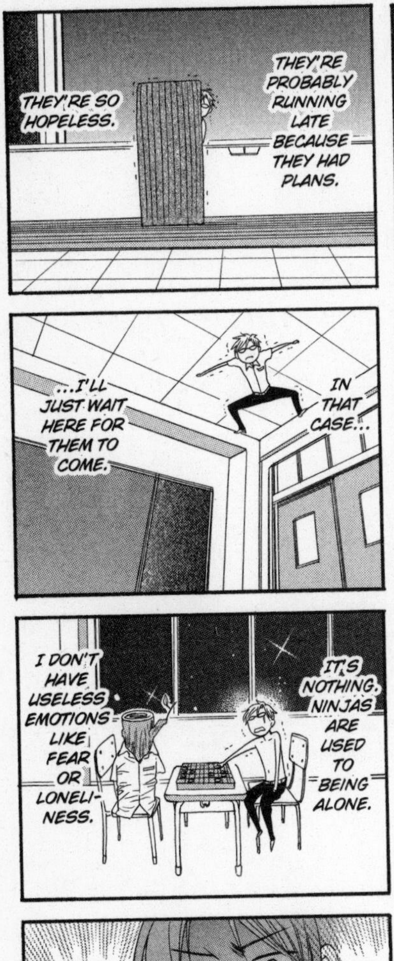
THEY'RE PROBABLY RUNNING LATE BECAUSE THEY HAD PLANS.
THEY'RE SO HOPELESS.
IN THAT CASE...
...I'LL JUST WAIT HERE FOR THEM TO COME.
IT'S NOTHING. NINJAS ARE USED TO BEING ALONE.
I DON'T HAVE USELESS EMOTIONS LIKE FEAR OR LONELINESS.
I DON'T KNOW WHO HE'S WAITING FOR...
...BUT PLEASE COME QUICKLY!

To be continued in chapter 33

BONUS MANGA / THE END

Izumi Tsubaki began drawing manga in her first year of high school. She was soon selected to be in the top ten of *Hana to Yume*'s HMC (*Hana to Yume* Mangaka Course), and subsequently won *Hana to Yume*'s Big Challenge contest. Her debut title, *Chijimete Distance* (Shrink the Distance), ran in 2002 in *Hana to Yume* magazine, issue 17. Her other works include *The Magic Touch* (*Oyayubi kara Romance*) and *Oresama Teacher*, which she is currently working on.